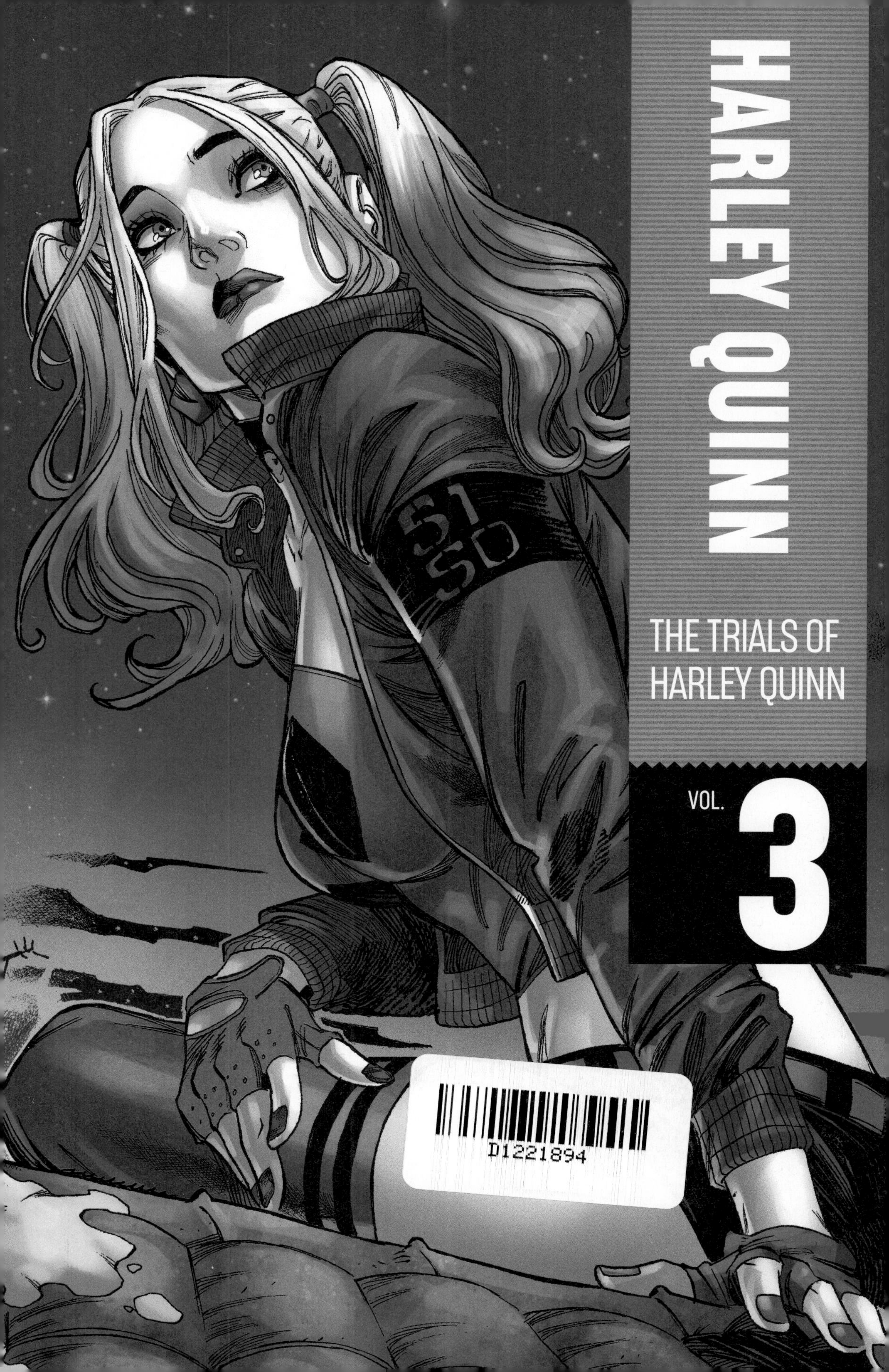
HARLEY QUINN
THE TRIALS OF HARLEY QUINN
VOL. 3
51 SD

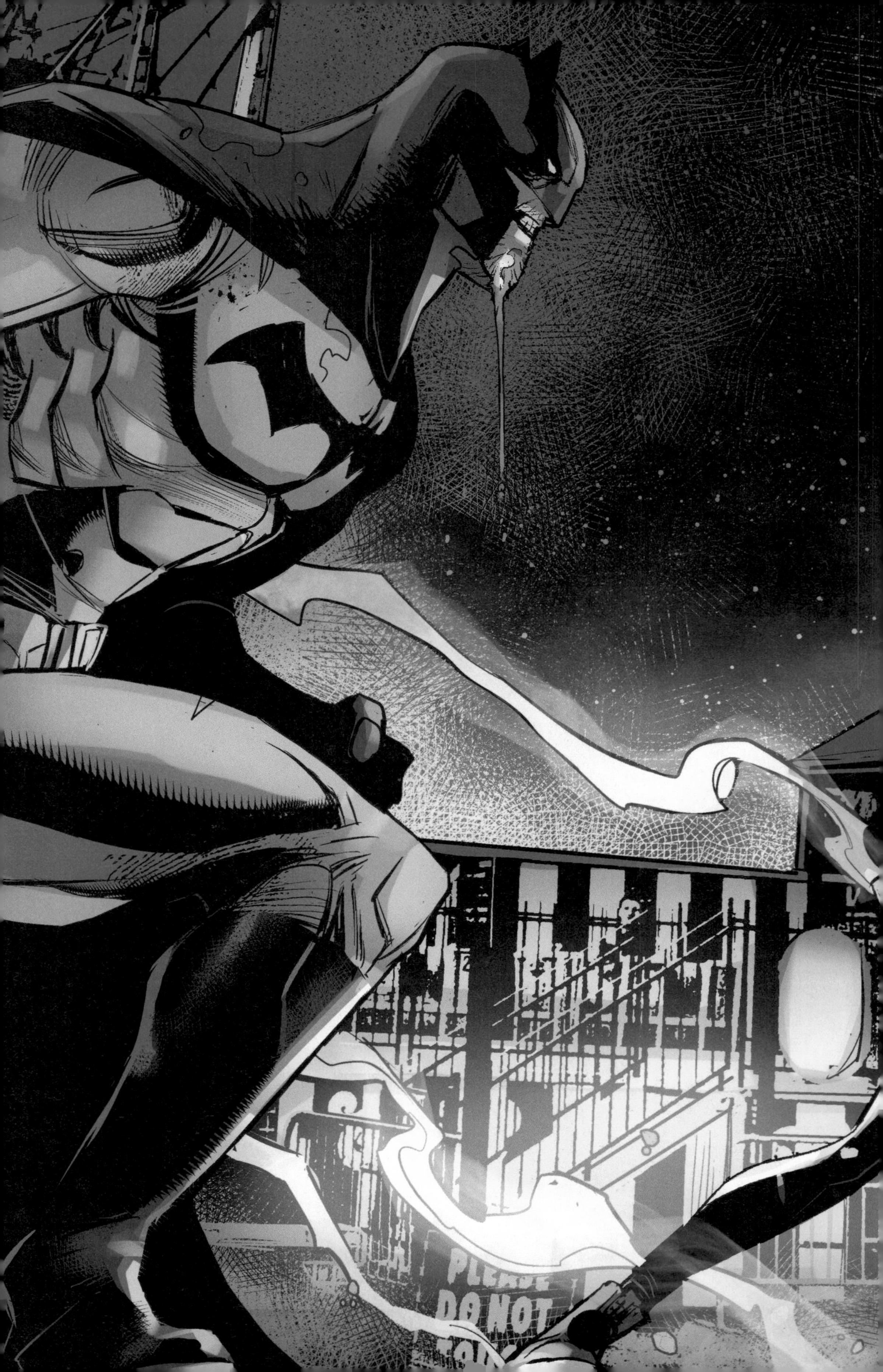
DO NOT

HARLEY QUINN
THE TRIALS OF HARLEY QUINN

writer

SAM HUMPHRIES

artists

JOHN TIMMS
OTTO SCHMIDT
SAMI BASRI

colorists

ALEX SINCLAIR
OTTO SCHMIDT

letterer

DAVE SHARPE

collection cover artists

GUILLEM MARCH and **ARIF PRIANTO**

HARLEY QUINN created by **PAUL DINI** and **BRUCE TIMM**

VOL.

3

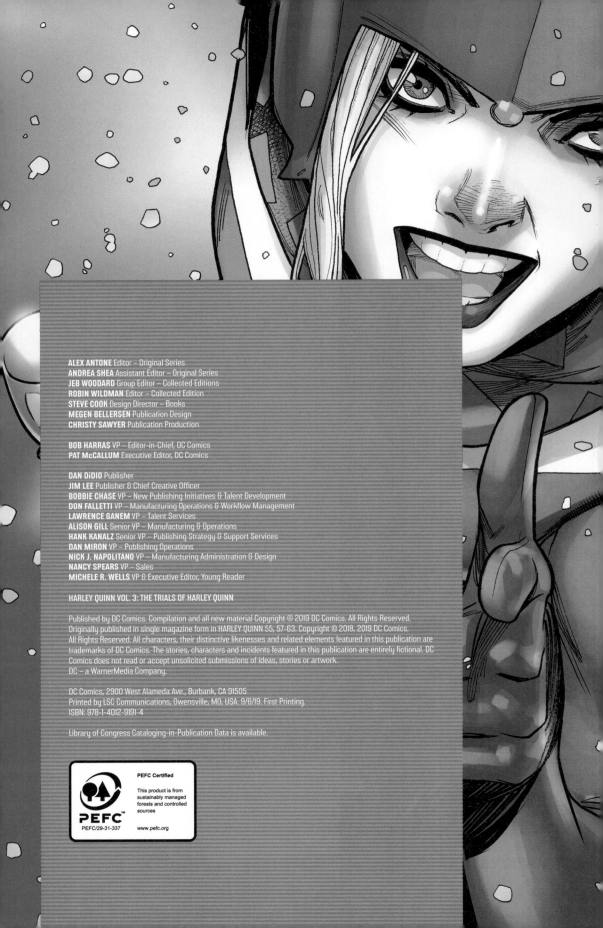

ALEX ANTONE Editor – Original Series
ANDREA SHEA Assistant Editor – Original Series
JEB WOODARD Group Editor – Collected Editions
ROBIN WILDMAN Editor – Collected Edition
STEVE COOK Design Director – Books
MEGEN BELLERSEN Publication Design
CHRISTY SAWYER Publication Production

BOB HARRAS VP – Editor-in-Chief, DC Comics
PAT McCALLUM Executive Editor, DC Comics

DAN DiDIO Publisher
JIM LEE Publisher & Chief Creative Officer
BOBBIE CHASE VP – New Publishing Initiatives & Talent Development
DON FALLETTI VP – Manufacturing Operations & Workflow Management
LAWRENCE GANEM VP – Talent Services
ALISON GILL Senior VP – Manufacturing & Operations
HANK KANALZ Senior VP – Publishing Strategy & Support Services
DAN MIRON VP – Publishing Operations
NICK J. NAPOLITANO VP – Manufacturing Administration & Design
NANCY SPEARS VP – Sales
MICHELE R. WELLS VP & Executive Editor, Young Reader

HARLEY QUINN VOL. 3: THE TRIALS OF HARLEY QUINN

DC Comics, 2900 West Alameda Ave., Burbank, CA 91505
Printed by LSC Communications, Owensville, MO, USA. 9/6/19. First Printing.
ISBN: 978-1-4012-9191-4

Library of Congress Cataloging-in-Publication Data is available.

PEFC Certified
This product is from sustainably managed forests and controlled sources
www.pefc.org
PEFC/29-31-337

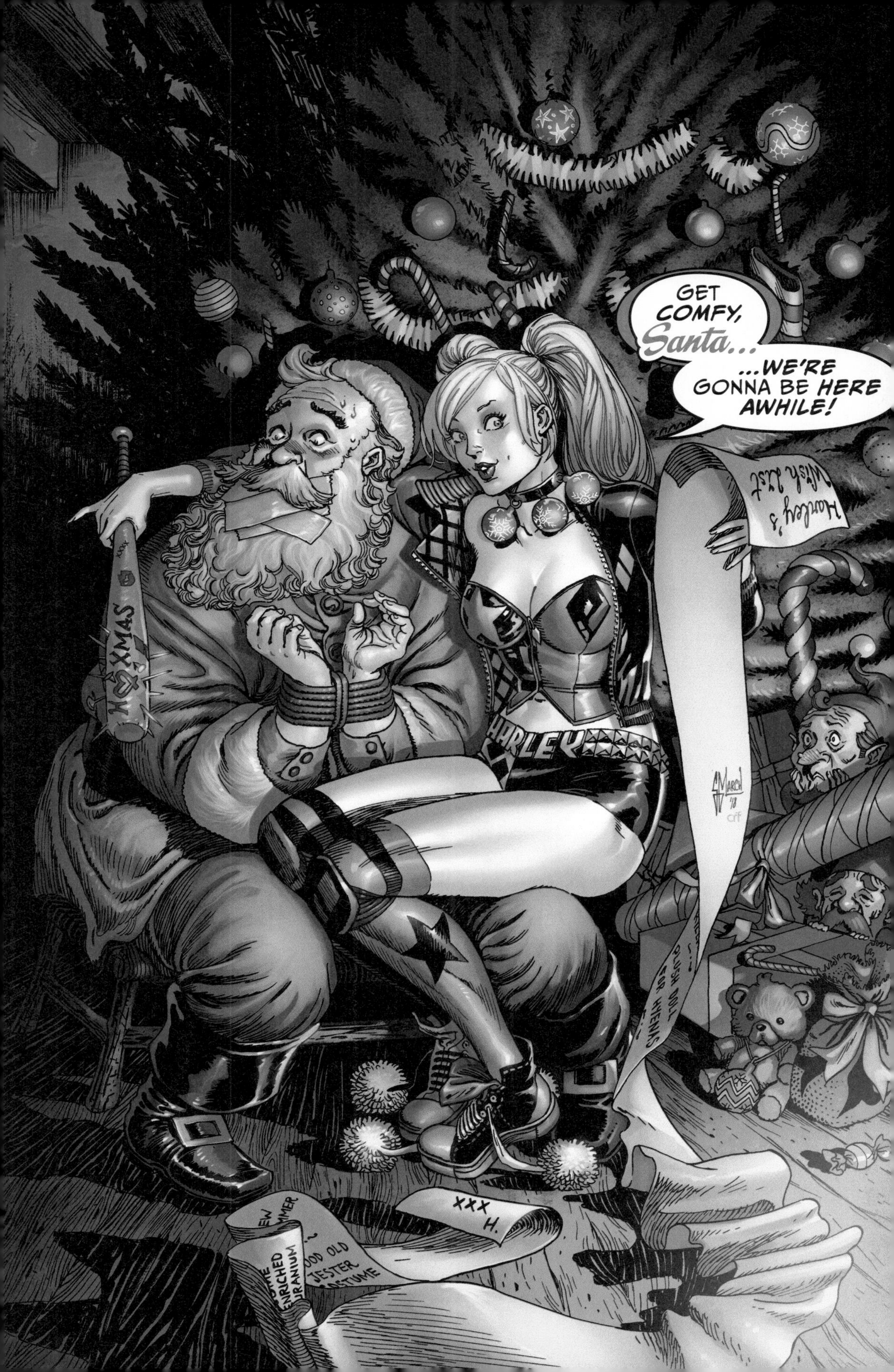
GET COMFY, Santa...
...WE'RE GONNA BE HERE AWHILE!
Harley's Wish List
XMAS
HARLEY
PLUSH DOLL FOR HYENAS
XXX H.
ENRICHED URANIUM
JESTER

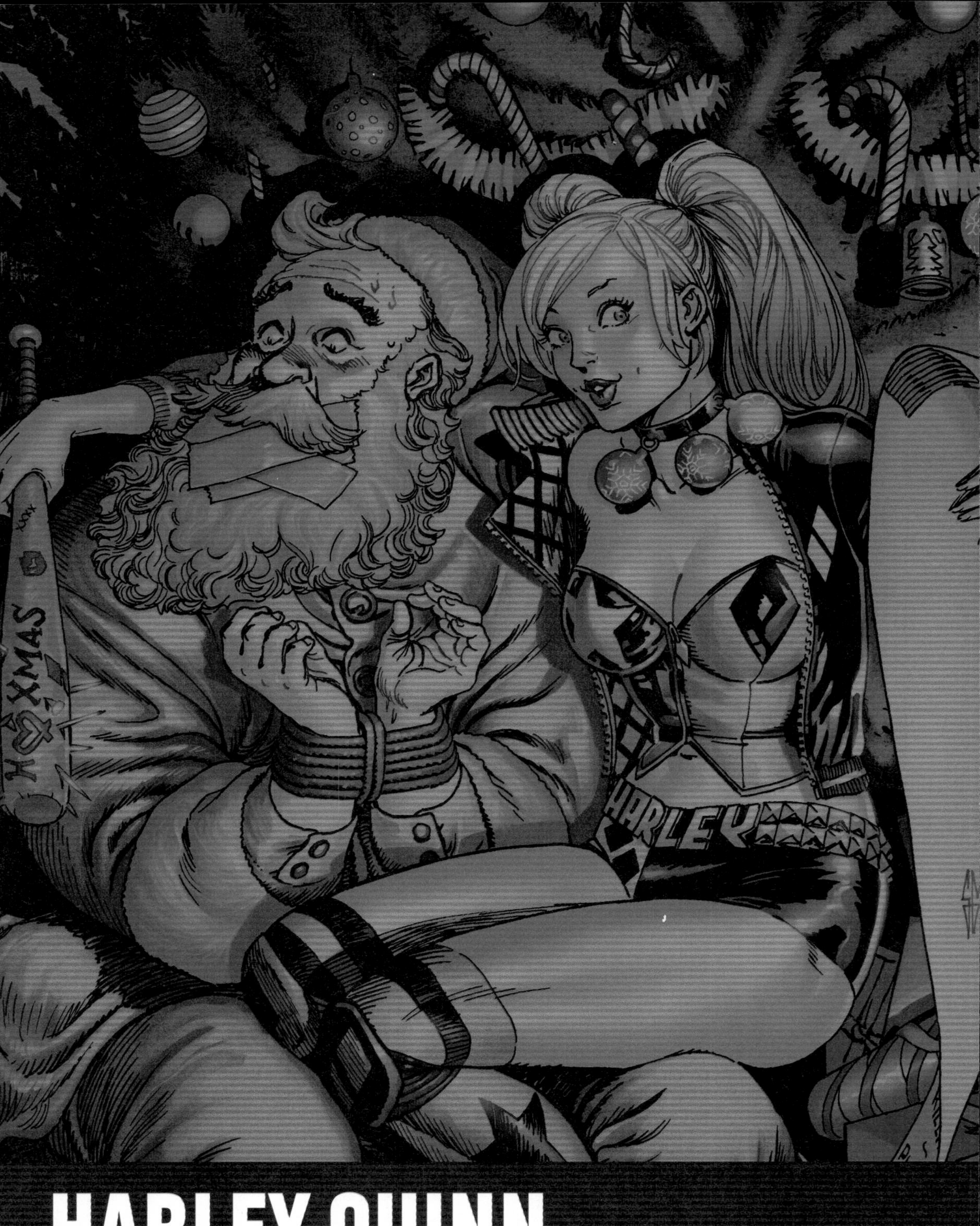
XMAS
HARLEY

HARLEY QUINN

#55

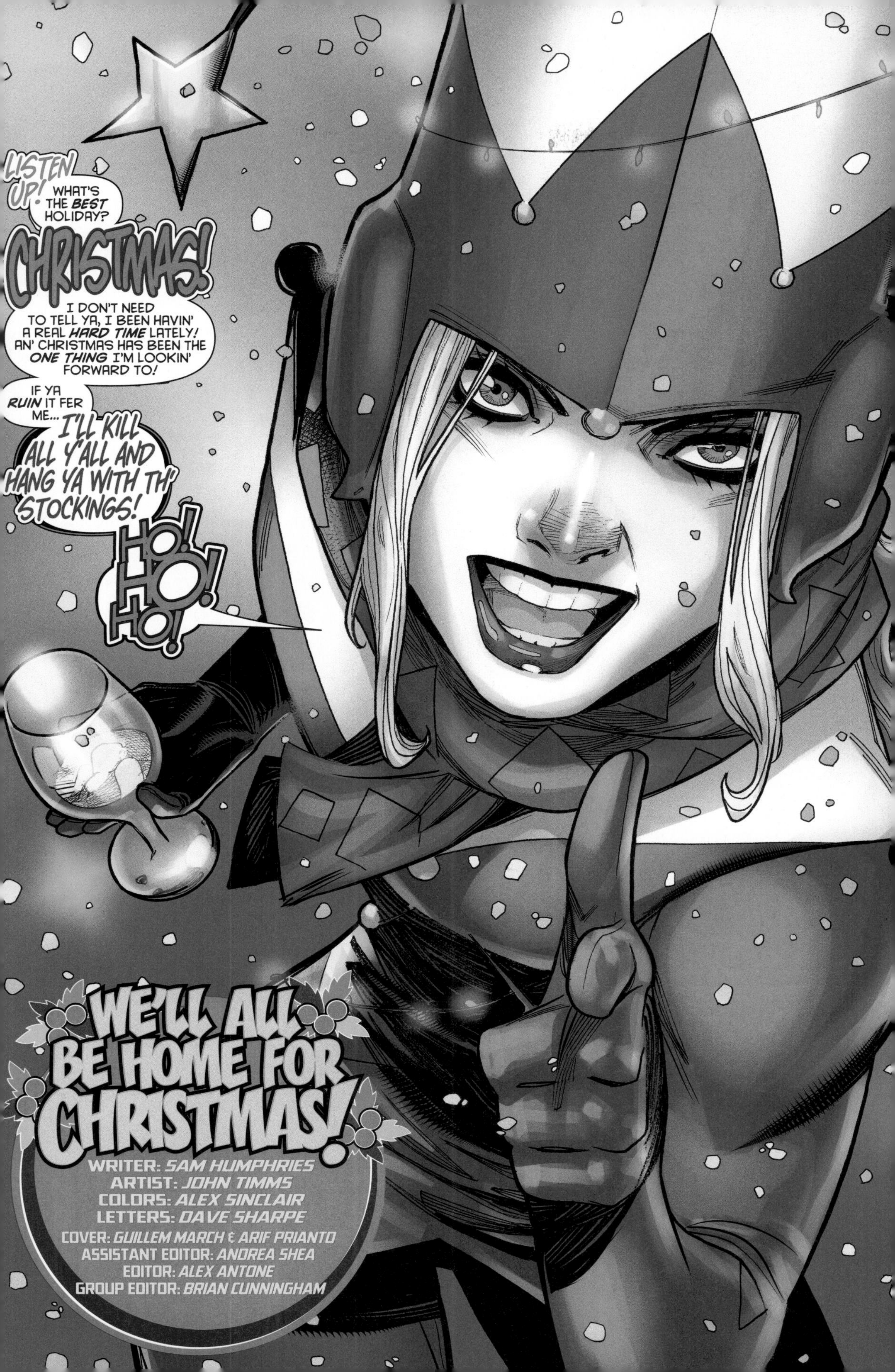

LISTEN UP!
WHAT'S THE BEST HOLIDAY?
CHRISTMAS!
I DON'T NEED TO TELL YA, I BEEN HAVIN' A REAL HARD TIME LATELY! AN' CHRISTMAS HAS BEEN THE ONE THING I'M LOOKIN' FORWARD TO!
IF YA RUIN IT FER ME...
I'LL KILL ALL Y'ALL AND HANG YA WITH TH' STOCKINGS!
HO! HO! HO!
WE'LL ALL BE HOME FOR CHRISTMAS!
WRITER: SAM HUMPHRIES
ARTIST: JOHN TIMMS
COLORS: ALEX SINCLAIR
LETTERS: DAVE SHARPE
COVER: GUILLEM MARCH & ARIF PRIANTO
ASSISTANT EDITOR: ANDREA SHEA
EDITOR: ALEX ANTONE
GROUP EDITOR: BRIAN CUNNINGHAM

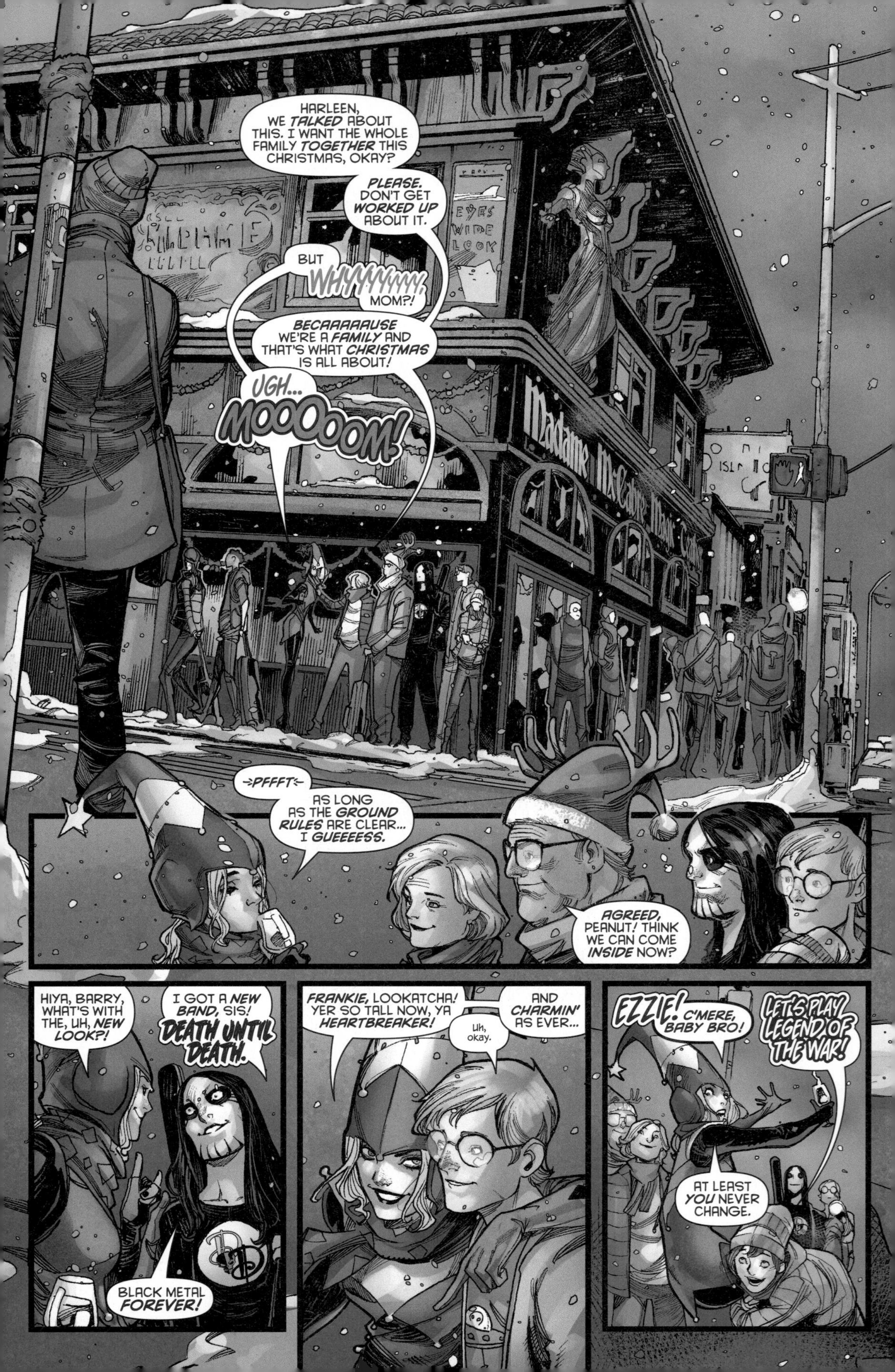
HARLEEN, WE TALKED ABOUT THIS. I WANT THE WHOLE FAMILY TOGETHER THIS CHRISTMAS, OKAY?
PLEASE. DON'T GET WORKED UP ABOUT IT.
BUT WHYYYYYYY, MOM?!
BECAAAAAUSE WE'RE A FAMILY AND THAT'S WHAT CHRISTMAS IS ALL ABOUT!
UGH... MOOOOOM!
EYES WIDE LOOK
PFFFT
AS LONG AS THE GROUND RULES ARE CLEAR... I GUEEEESS.
AGREED, PEANUT! THINK WE CAN COME INSIDE NOW?
HIYA, BARRY, WHAT'S WITH THE, UH, NEW LOOK?!
I GOT A NEW BAND, SIS! DEATH UNTIL DEATH.
BLACK METAL FOREVER!
FRANKIE, LOOKATCHA! YER SO TALL NOW, YA HEARTBREAKER!
uh, okay.
AND CHARMIN' AS EVER...
EZZIE! C'MERE, BABY BRO!
LET'S PLAY LEGEND OF THE WAR!
AT LEAST YOU NEVER CHANGE.

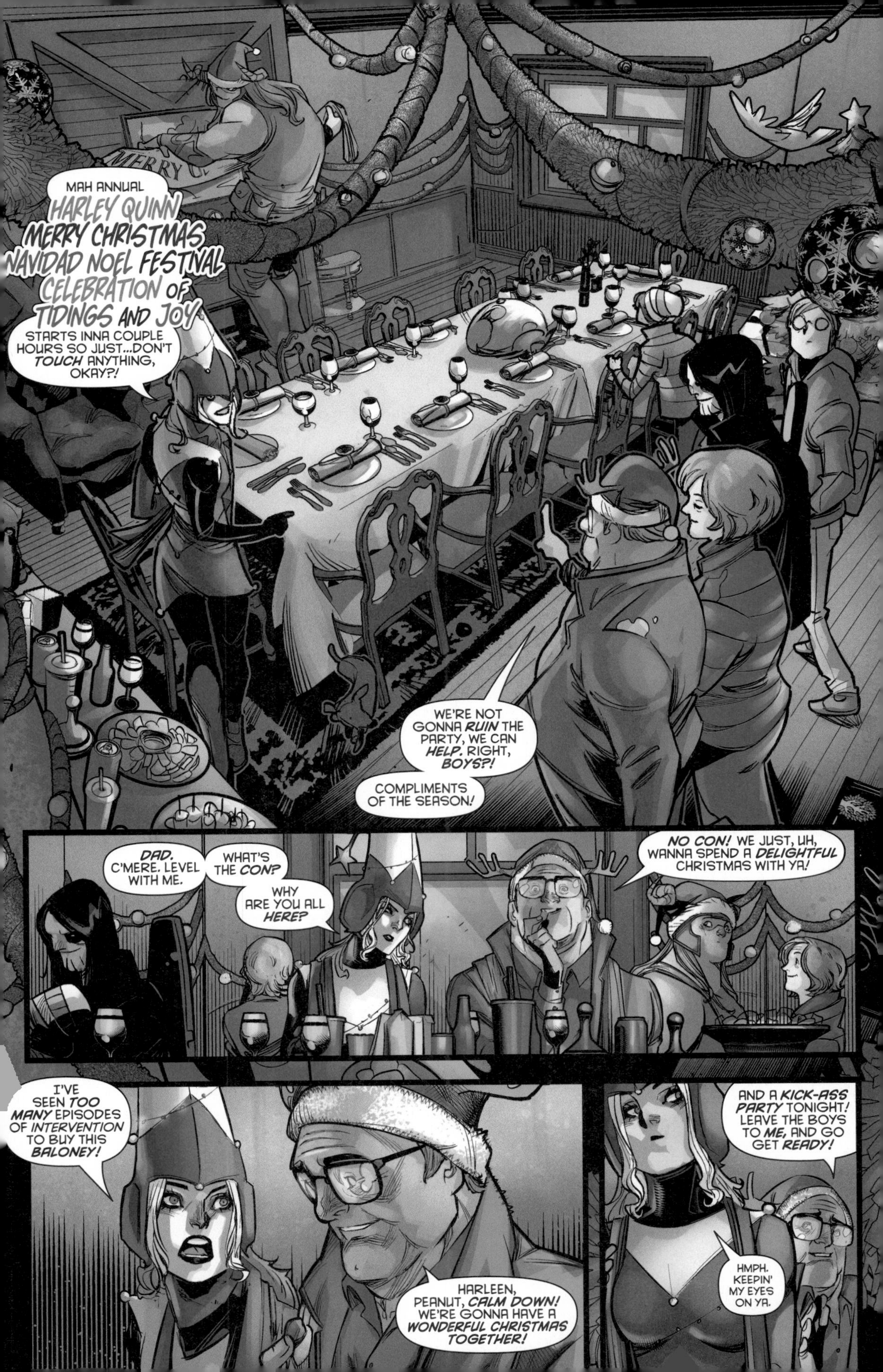
MAH ANNUAL HARLEY QUINN MERRY CHRISTMAS NAVIDAD NOEL FESTIVAL CELEBRATION OF TIDINGS AND JOY STARTS INNA COUPLE HOURS SO JUST...DON'T TOUCH ANYTHING, OKAY?!
WE'RE NOT GONNA RUIN THE PARTY, WE CAN HELP. RIGHT, BOYS?!
COMPLIMENTS OF THE SEASON!
DAD. C'MERE. LEVEL WITH ME.
WHAT'S THE CON?
WHY ARE YOU ALL HERE?
NO CON! WE JUST, UH, WANNA SPEND A DELIGHTFUL CHRISTMAS WITH YA!
I'VE SEEN TOO MANY EPISODES OF INTERVENTION TO BUY THIS BALONEY!
HARLEEN, PEANUT, CALM DOWN! WE'RE GONNA HAVE A WONDERFUL CHRISTMAS TOGETHER!
AND A KICK-ASS PARTY TONIGHT! LEAVE THE BOYS TO ME, AND GO GET READY!
HMPH. KEEPIN' MY EYES ON YA.

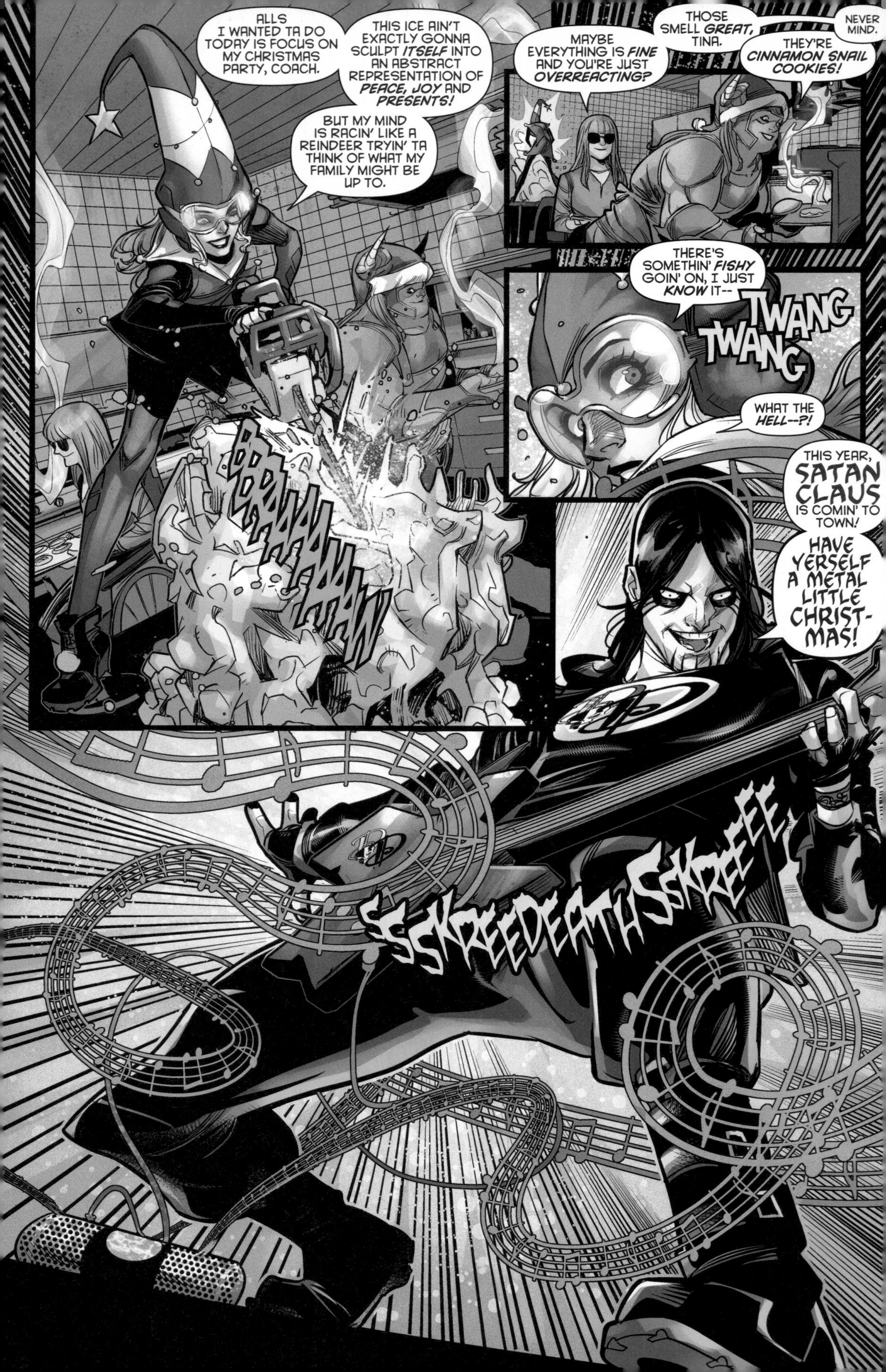

ALLS I WANTED TA DO TODAY IS FOCUS ON MY CHRISTMAS PARTY, COACH.
THIS ICE AIN'T EXACTLY GONNA SCULPT ITSELF INTO AN ABSTRACT REPRESENTATION OF PEACE, JOY AND PRESENTS!
BUT MY MIND IS RACIN' LIKE A REINDEER TRYIN' TA THINK OF WHAT MY FAMILY MIGHT BE UP TO.
BRRAAAAAAAAAAN
MAYBE EVERYTHING IS FINE AND YOU'RE JUST OVERREACTING?
THOSE SMELL GREAT, TINA.
NEVER MIND.
THEY'RE CINNAMON SNAIL COOKIES!
THERE'S SOMETHIN' FISHY GOIN' ON, I JUST KNOW IT--
TWANG
TWANG
WHAT THE HELL--?!
THIS YEAR, SATAN CLAUS IS COMIN' TO TOWN!
HAVE YERSELF A METAL LITTLE CHRIST-MAS!
SSKREEEE
SSKREEDEATHSSKREE

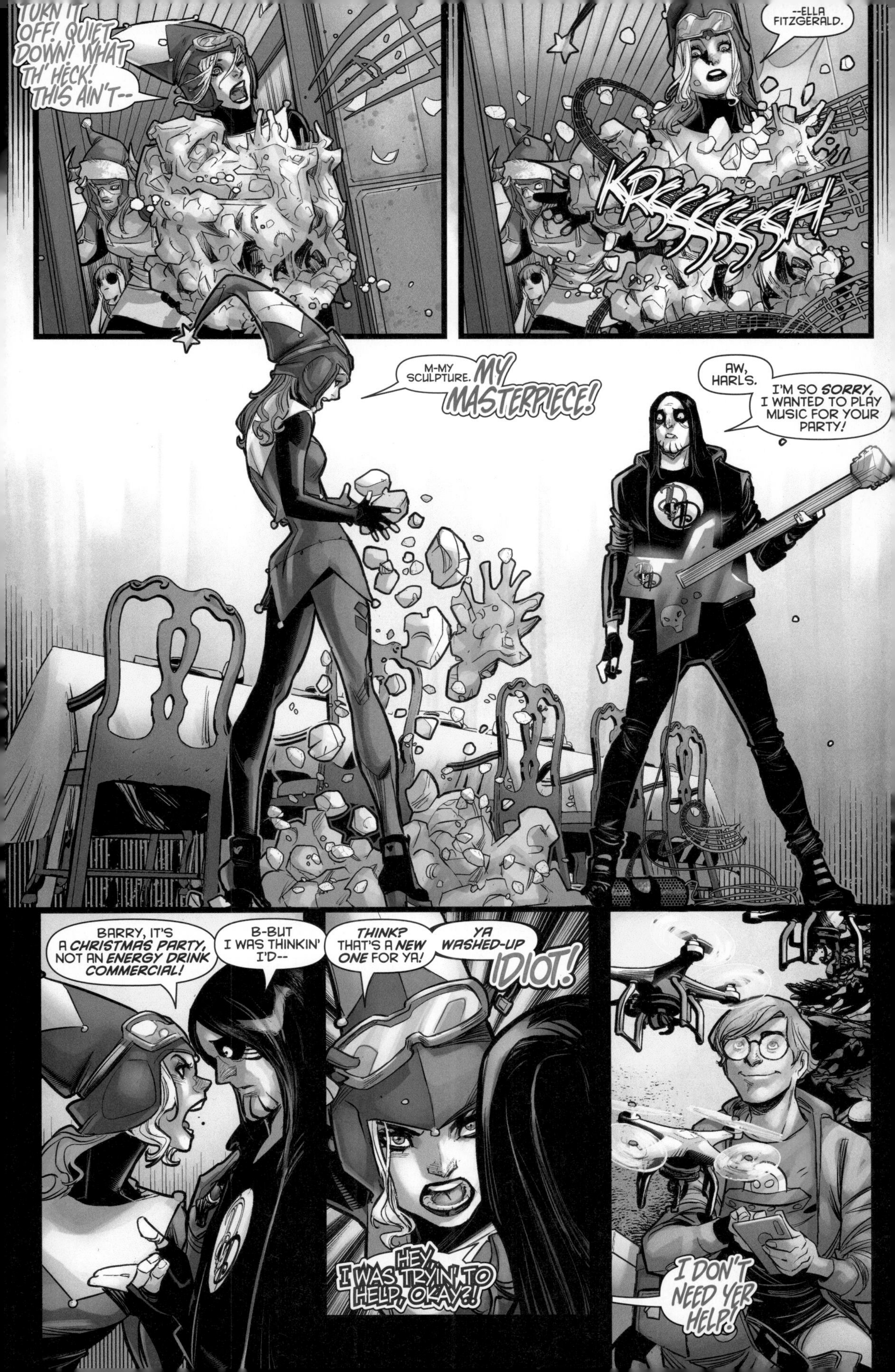
TURN IT OFF! QUIET DOWN! WHAT TH' HECK! THIS AIN'T--
--ELLA FITZGERALD.
KRSSSSSSH
M-MY SCULPTURE. MY MASTERPIECE!
AW, HARL'S.
I'M SO SORRY, I WANTED TO PLAY MUSIC FOR YOUR PARTY!
BARRY, IT'S A CHRISTMAS PARTY, NOT AN ENERGY DRINK COMMERCIAL!
B-BUT I WAS THINKIN' I'D--
THINK? THAT'S A NEW ONE FOR YA!
YA WASHED-UP IDIOT!
HEY, I WAS TRYIN' TO HELP, OKAY?!
I DON'T NEED YER HELP!

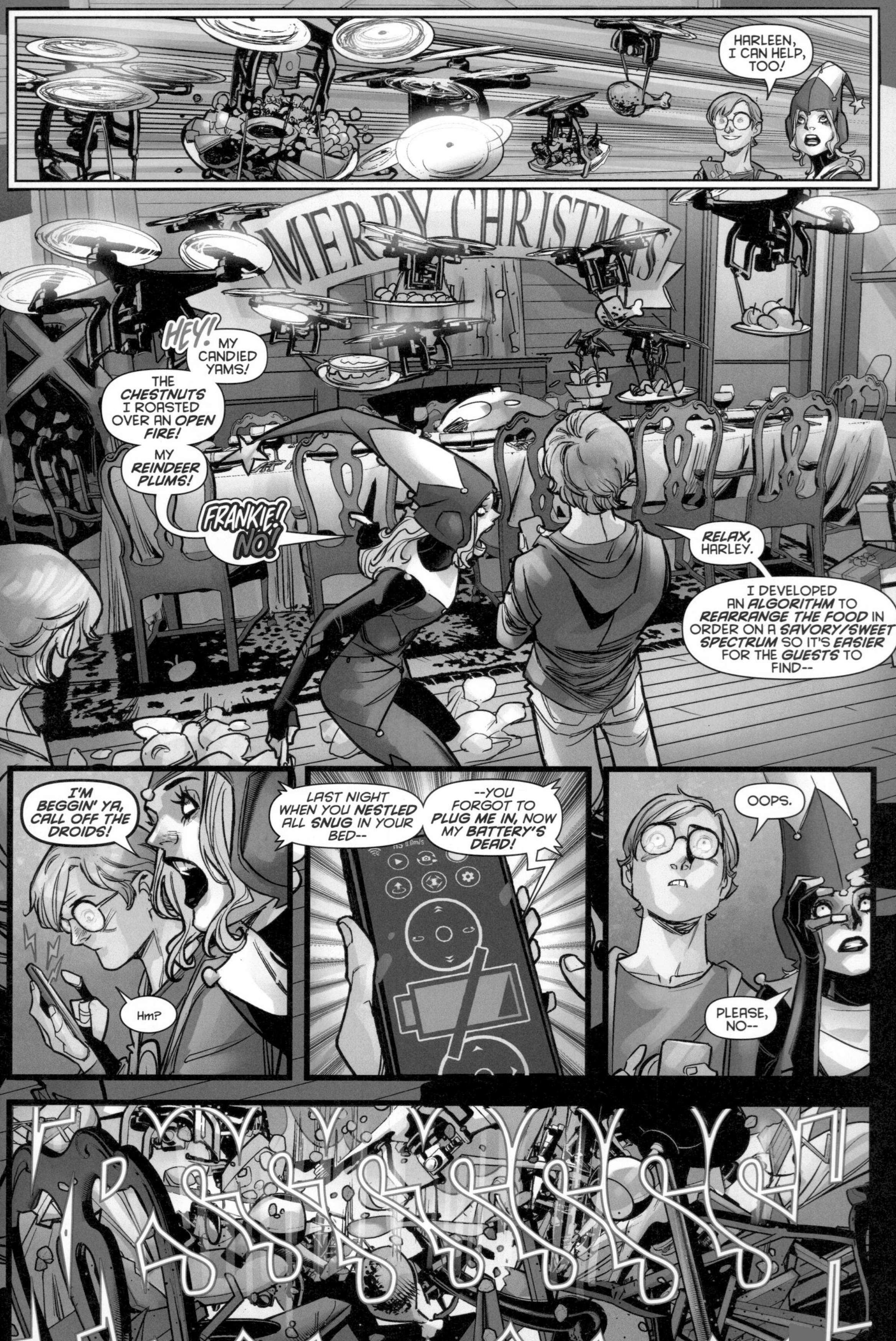
HARLEEN, I CAN HELP, TOO!
HEY! MY CANDIED YAMS!
THE CHESTNUTS I ROASTED OVER AN OPEN FIRE!
MY REINDEER PLUMS!
FRANKIE! NO!
RELAX, HARLEY.
I DEVELOPED AN ALGORITHM TO REARRANGE THE FOOD IN ORDER ON A SAVORY/SWEET SPECTRUM SO IT'S EASIER FOR THE GUESTS TO FIND--
I'M BEGGIN' YA, CALL OFF THE DROIDS!
Hm?
LAST NIGHT WHEN YOU NESTLED ALL SNUG IN YOUR BED--
--YOU FORGOT TO PLUG ME IN, NOW MY BATTERY'S DEAD!
OOPS.
PLEASE, NO--

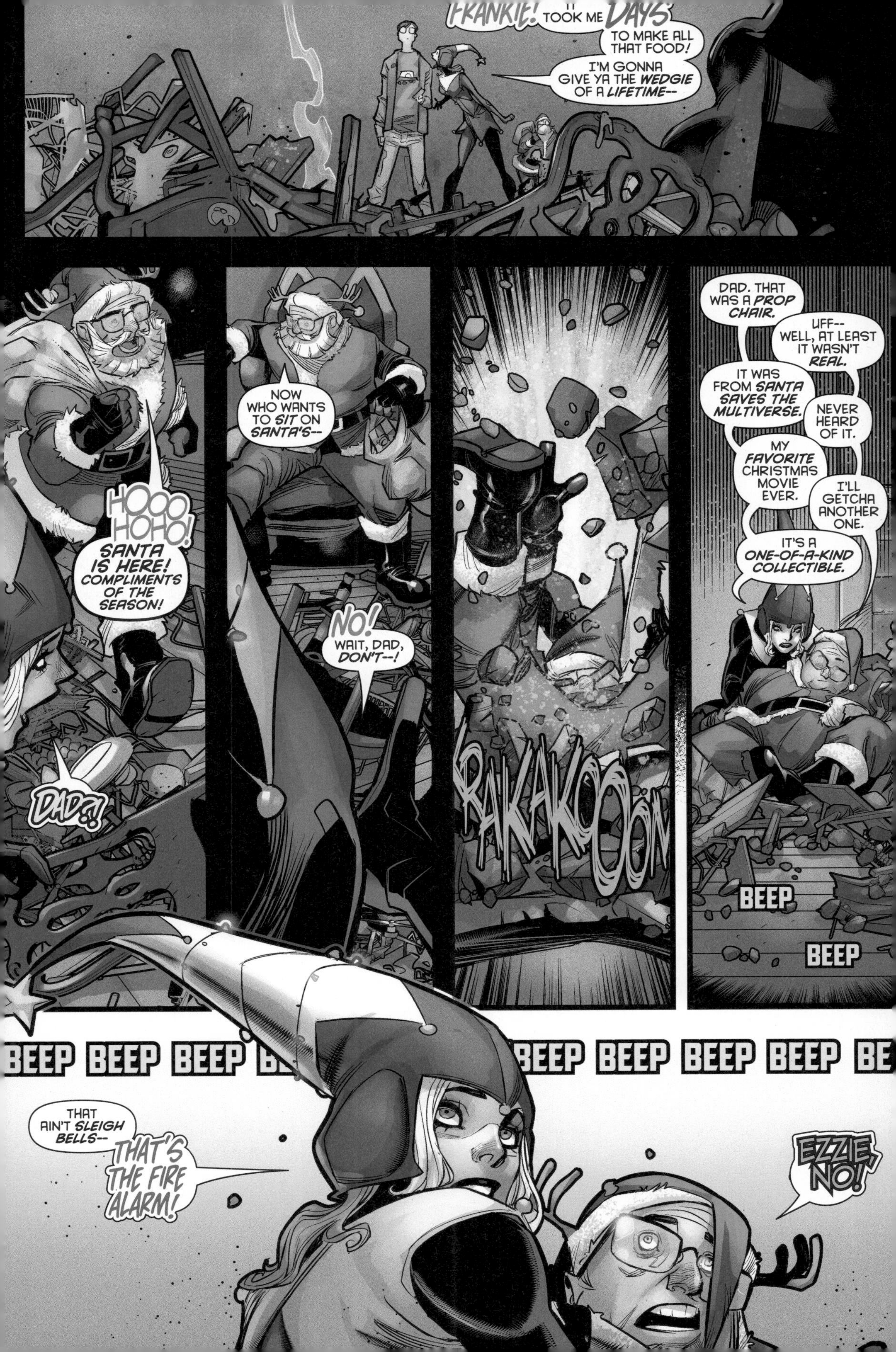
FRANKIE! IT TOOK ME DAYS TO MAKE ALL THAT FOOD!
I'M GONNA GIVE YA THE WEDGIE OF A LIFETIME--
HOOO HOHO! SANTA IS HERE! COMPLIMENTS OF THE SEASON!
DAD?!
NOW WHO WANTS TO SIT ON SANTA'S--
NO! WAIT, DAD, DON'T--!
KRAKAKOOOOM
DAD. THAT WAS A PROP CHAIR.
UFF-- WELL, AT LEAST IT WASN'T REAL.
IT WAS FROM SANTA SAVES THE MULTIVERSE.
NEVER HEARD OF IT.
MY FAVORITE CHRISTMAS MOVIE EVER.
I'LL GETCHA ANOTHER ONE.
IT'S A ONE-OF-A-KIND COLLECTIBLE.
BEEP
BEEP
BEEP BEEP BEEP BEEP BEEP BEEP BEEP BEEP
THAT AIN'T SLEIGH BELLS-- THAT'S THE FIRE ALARM!
EZZIE, NO!

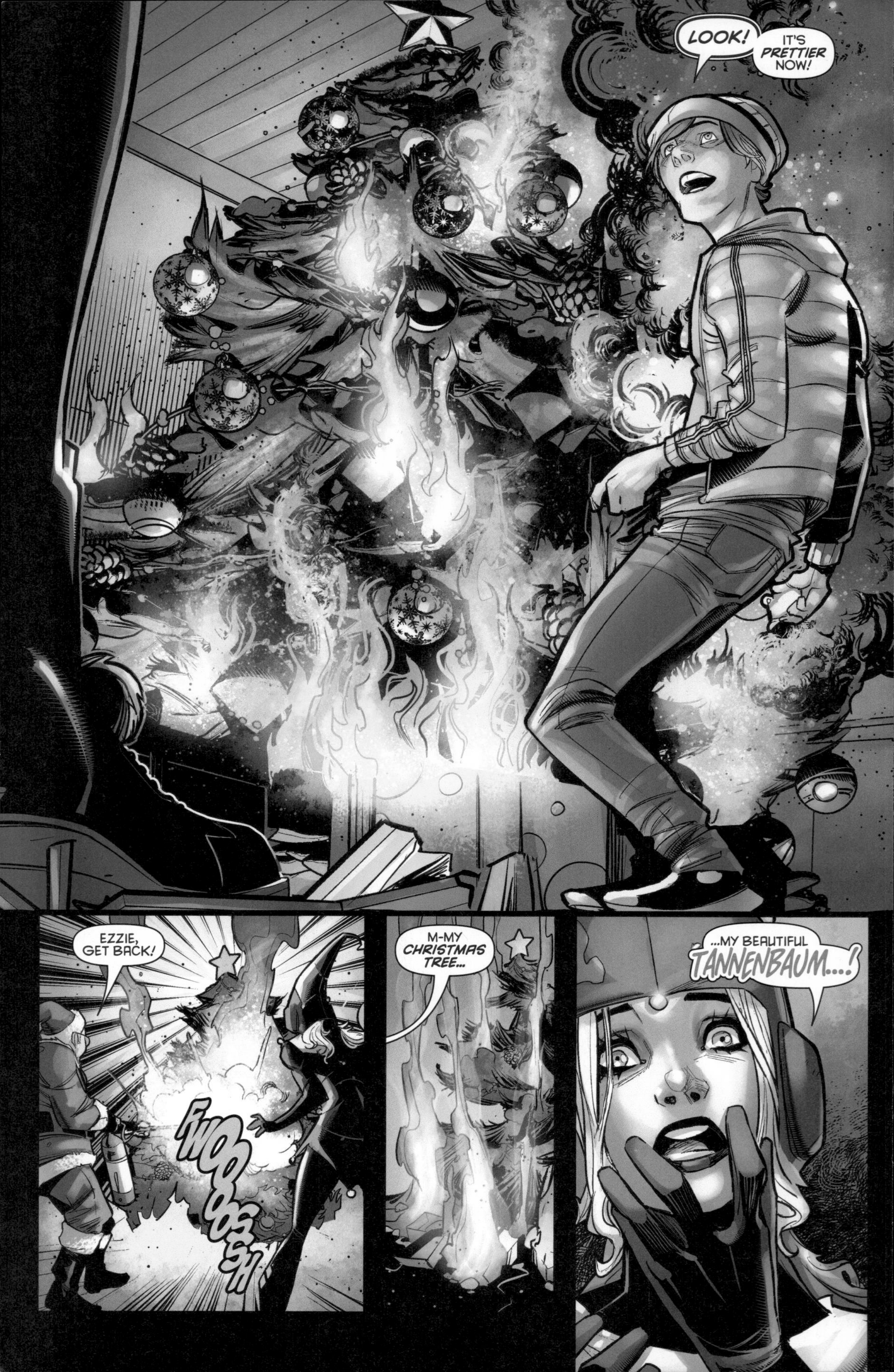
LOOK!
IT'S PRETTIER NOW!
EZZIE, GET BACK!
FWOOOOSH
M-MY CHRISTMAS TREE...
...MY BEAUTIFUL TANNENBAUM...!

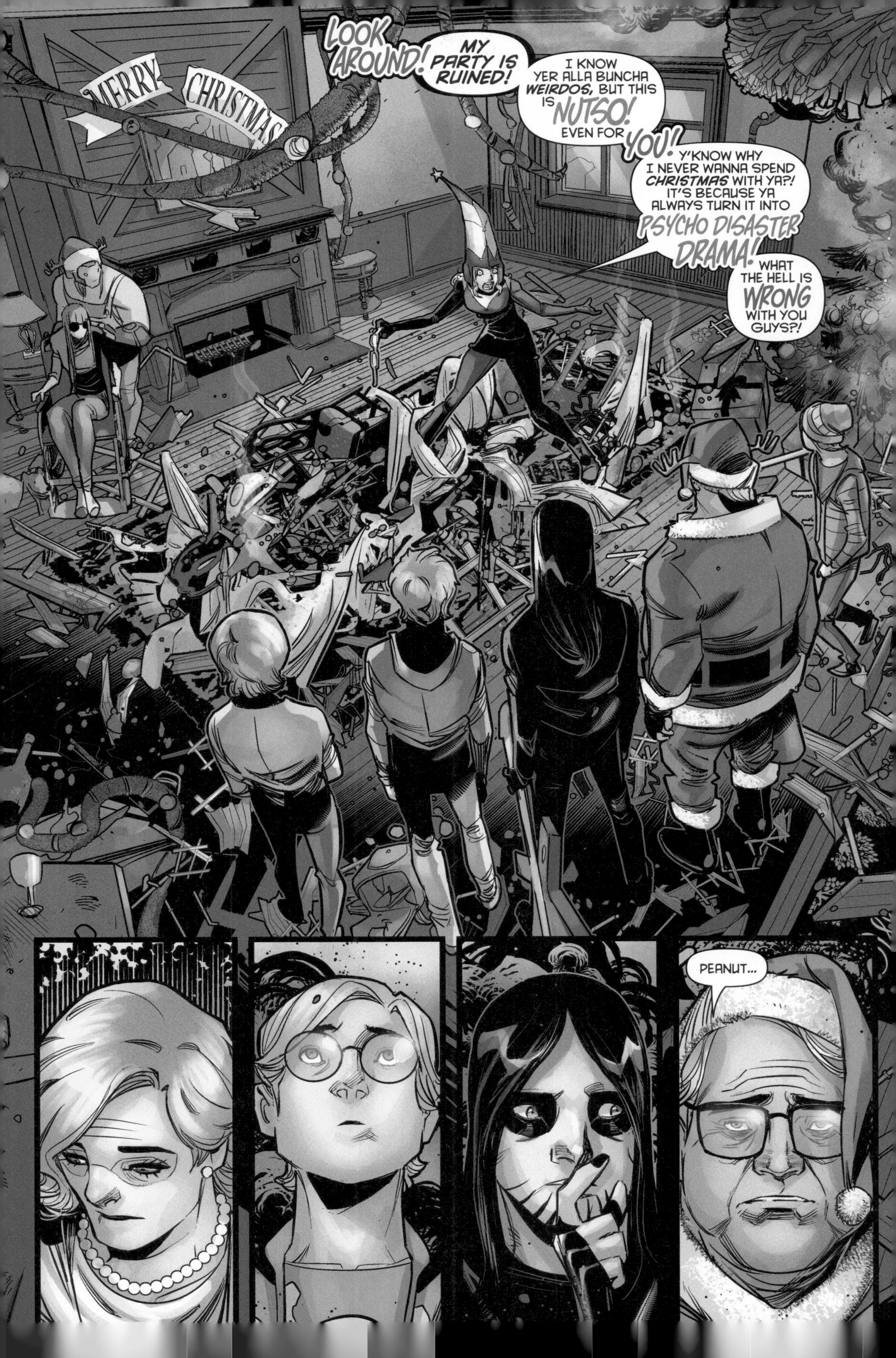
MERRY CHRISTMAS
LOOK AROUND!
MY PARTY IS RUINED!
I KNOW YER ALLA BUNCHA WEIRDOS, BUT THIS IS NUTSO! EVEN FOR YOU!
Y'KNOW WHY I NEVER WANNA SPEND CHRISTMAS WITH YA?! IT'S BECAUSE YA ALWAYS TURN IT INTO PSYCHO DISASTER DRAMA!
WHAT THE HELL IS WRONG WITH YOU GUYS?!
PEANUT...

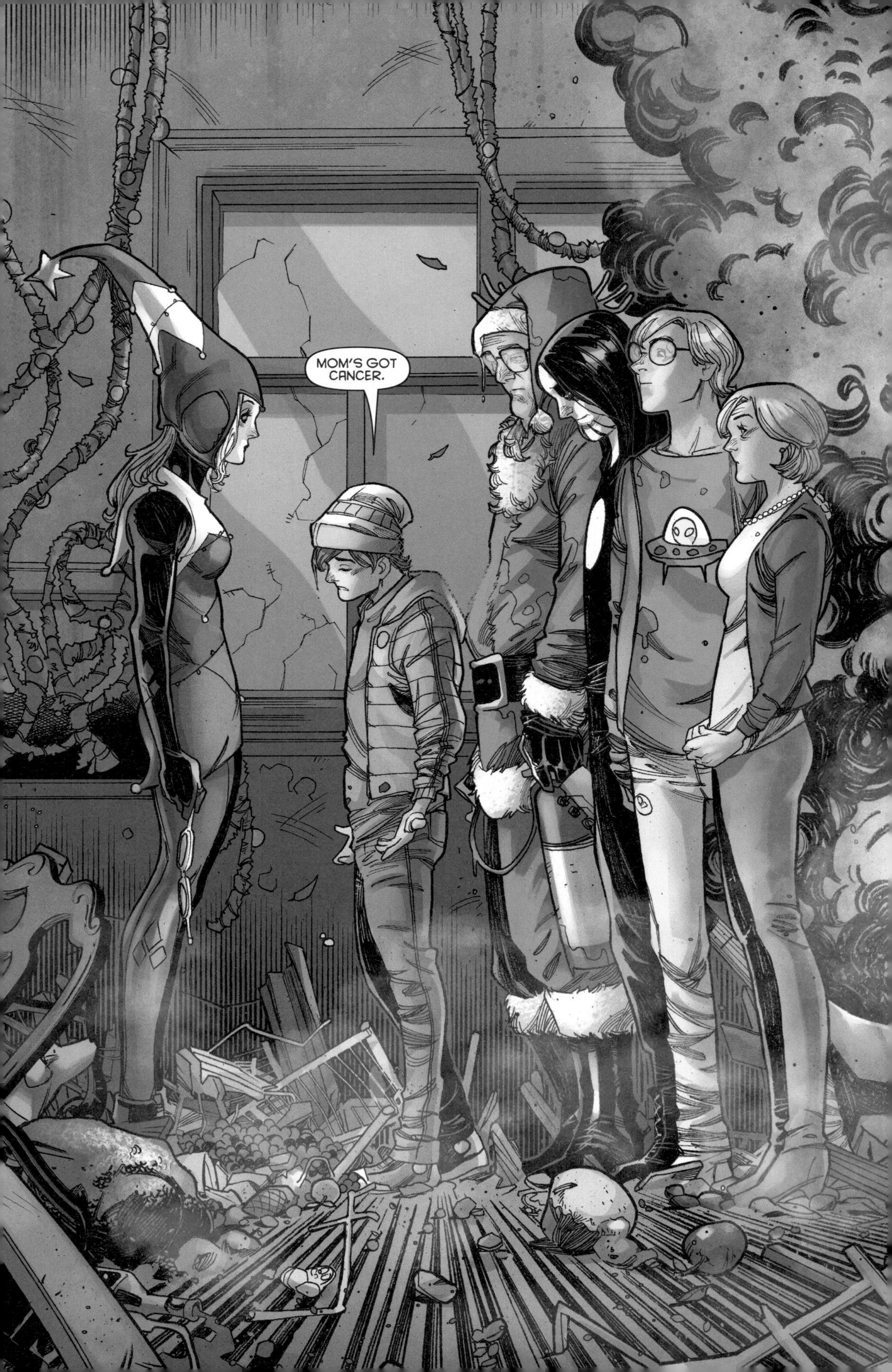
MOM'S GOT CANCER.

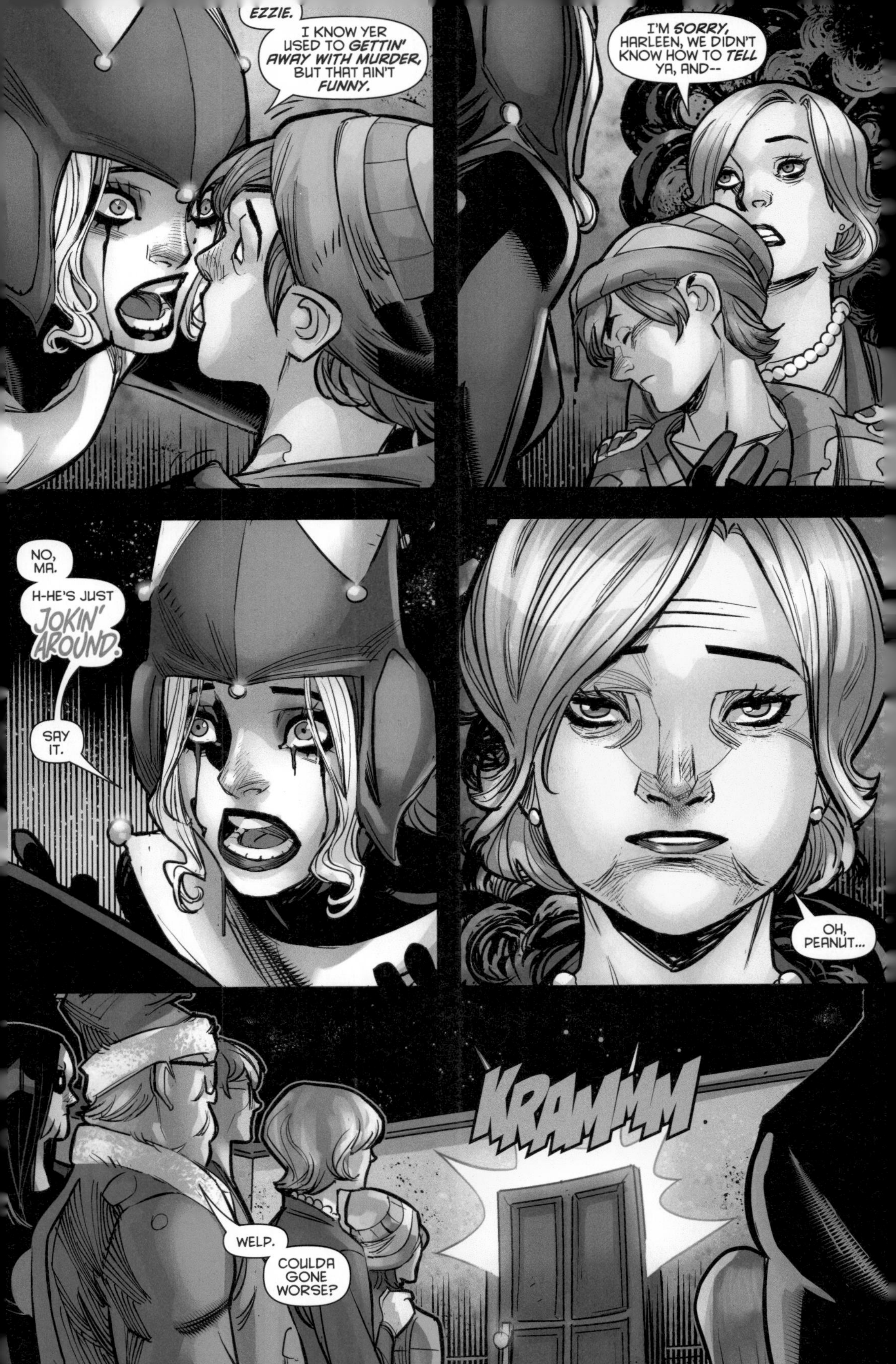
EZZIE.
I KNOW YER USED TO GETTIN' AWAY WITH MURDER, BUT THAT AIN'T FUNNY.
I'M SORRY, HARLEEN, WE DIDN'T KNOW HOW TO TELL YA, AND--
NO, MA.
H-HE'S JUST JOKIN' AROUND.
SAY IT.
OH, PEANUT...
KRAMMM
WELP.
COULDA GONE WORSE?

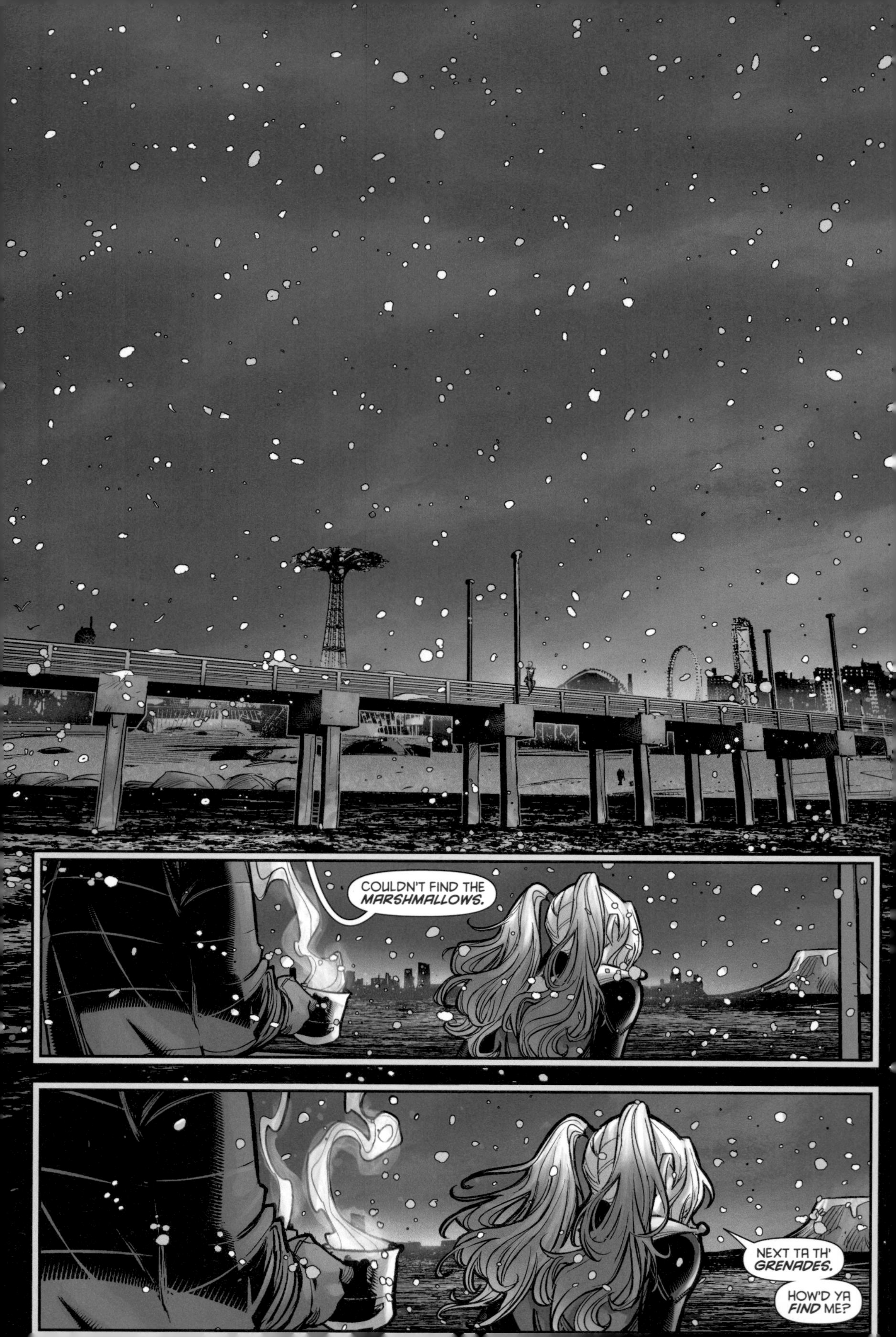
COULDN'T FIND THE *MARSHMALLOWS.*
NEXT TA TH' *GRENADES.*
HOW'D YA *FIND* ME?

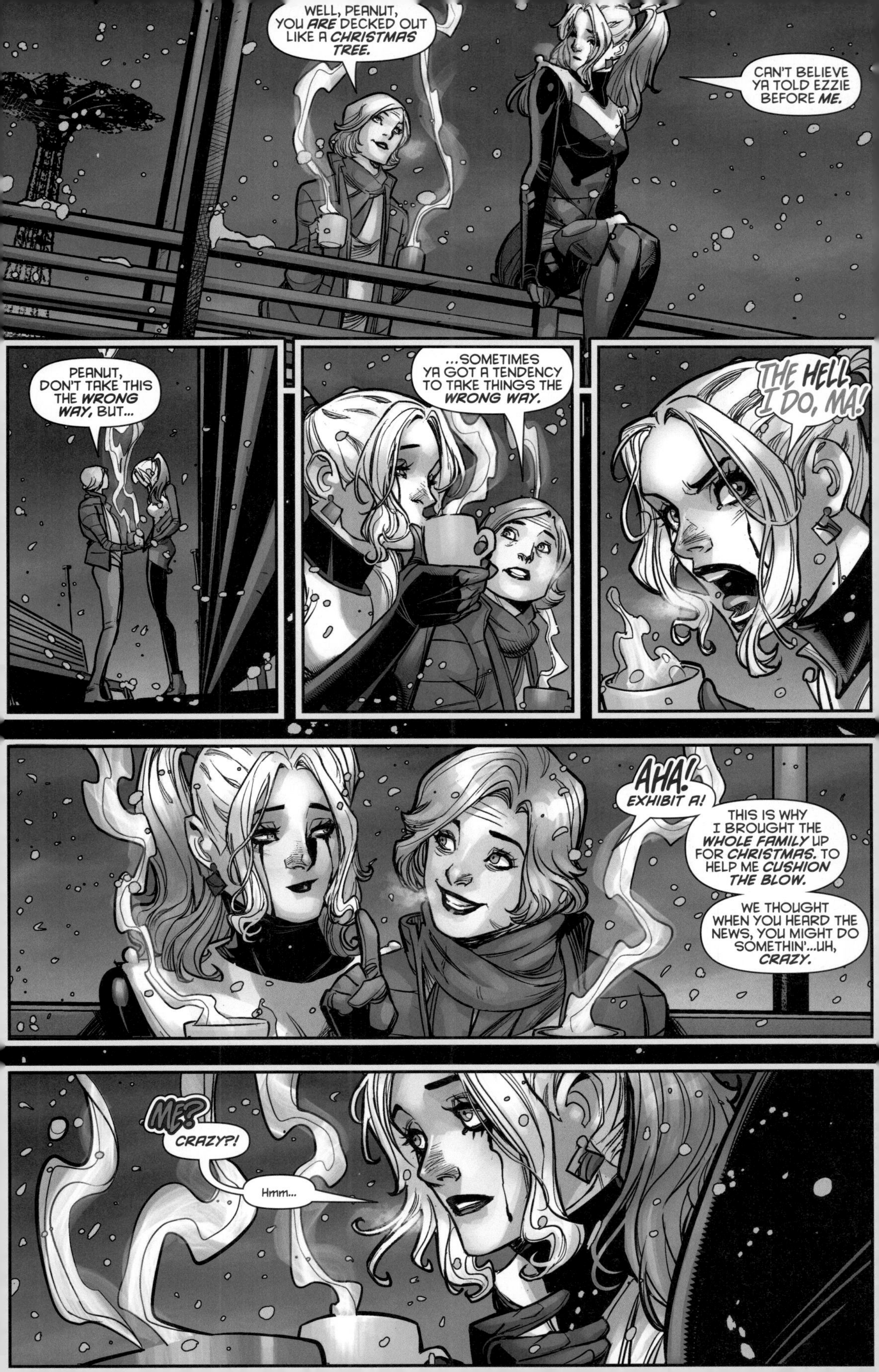
WELL, PEANUT, YOU ARE DECKED OUT LIKE A CHRISTMAS TREE.
CAN'T BELIEVE YA TOLD EZZIE BEFORE ME.
PEANUT, DON'T TAKE THIS THE WRONG WAY, BUT...
...SOMETIMES YA GOT A TENDENCY TO TAKE THINGS THE WRONG WAY.
THE HELL I DO, MA!
AHA! EXHIBIT A!
THIS IS WHY I BROUGHT THE WHOLE FAMILY UP FOR CHRISTMAS. TO HELP ME CUSHION THE BLOW.
WE THOUGHT WHEN YOU HEARD THE NEWS, YOU MIGHT DO SOMETHIN'...UH, CRAZY.
ME? CRAZY?!
Hmm...

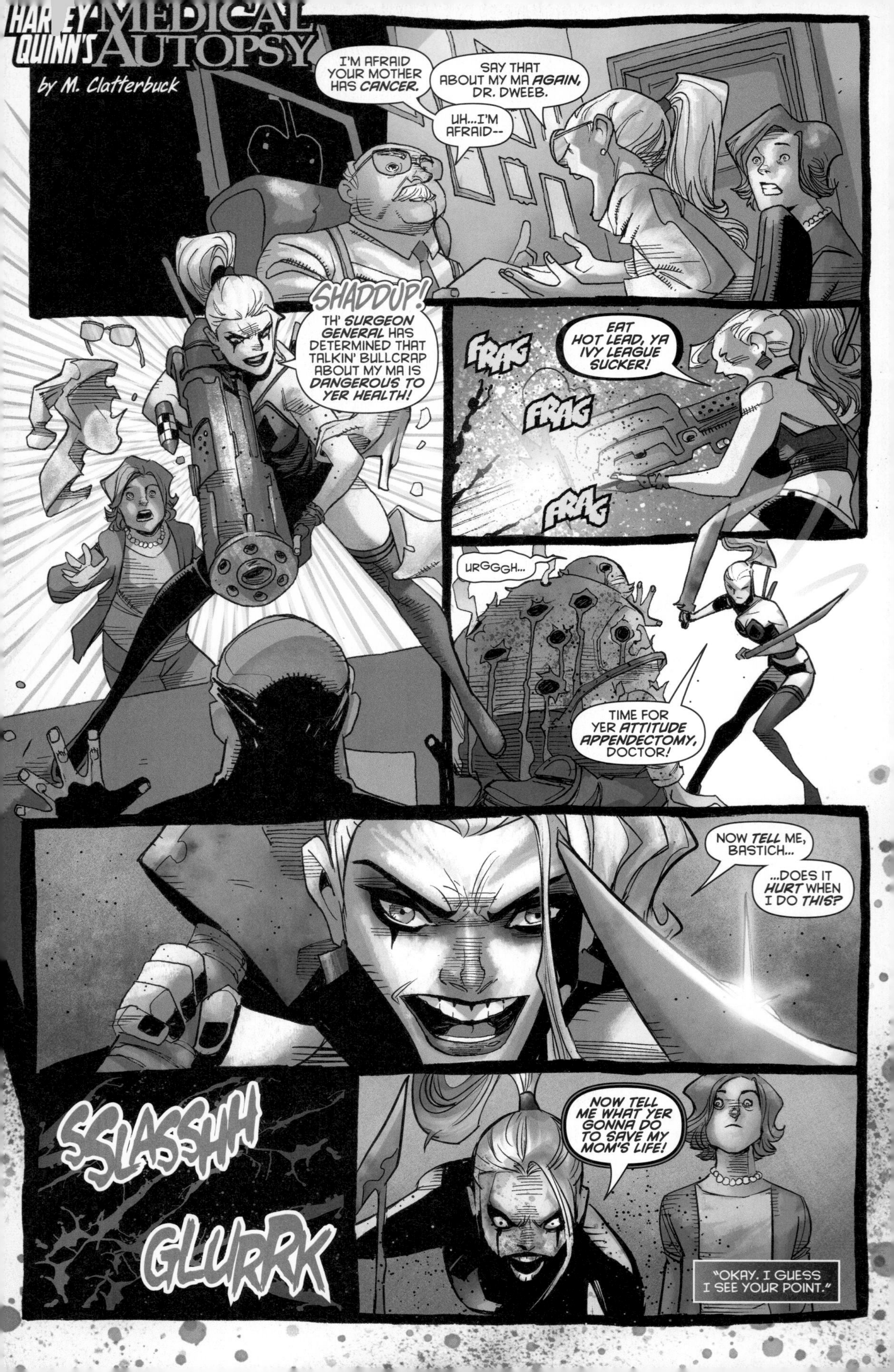
HARLEY QUINN'S MEDICAL AUTOPSY
by M. Clatterbuck
I'M AFRAID YOUR MOTHER HAS CANCER.
SAY THAT ABOUT MY MA AGAIN, DR. DWEEB.
UH...I'M AFRAID--
SHADDUP!
TH' SURGEON GENERAL HAS DETERMINED THAT TALKIN' BULLCRAP ABOUT MY MA IS DANGEROUS TO YER HEALTH!
FRAG
EAT HOT LEAD, YA IVY LEAGUE SUCKER!
FRAG
FRAG
URGGGH...
TIME FOR YER ATTITUDE APPENDECTOMY, DOCTOR!
NOW TELL ME, BASTICH...
...DOES IT HURT WHEN I DO THIS?
SSLASSHH
GLURRK
NOW TELL ME WHAT YER GONNA DO TO SAVE MY MOM'S LIFE!
"OKAY. I GUESS I SEE YOUR POINT."

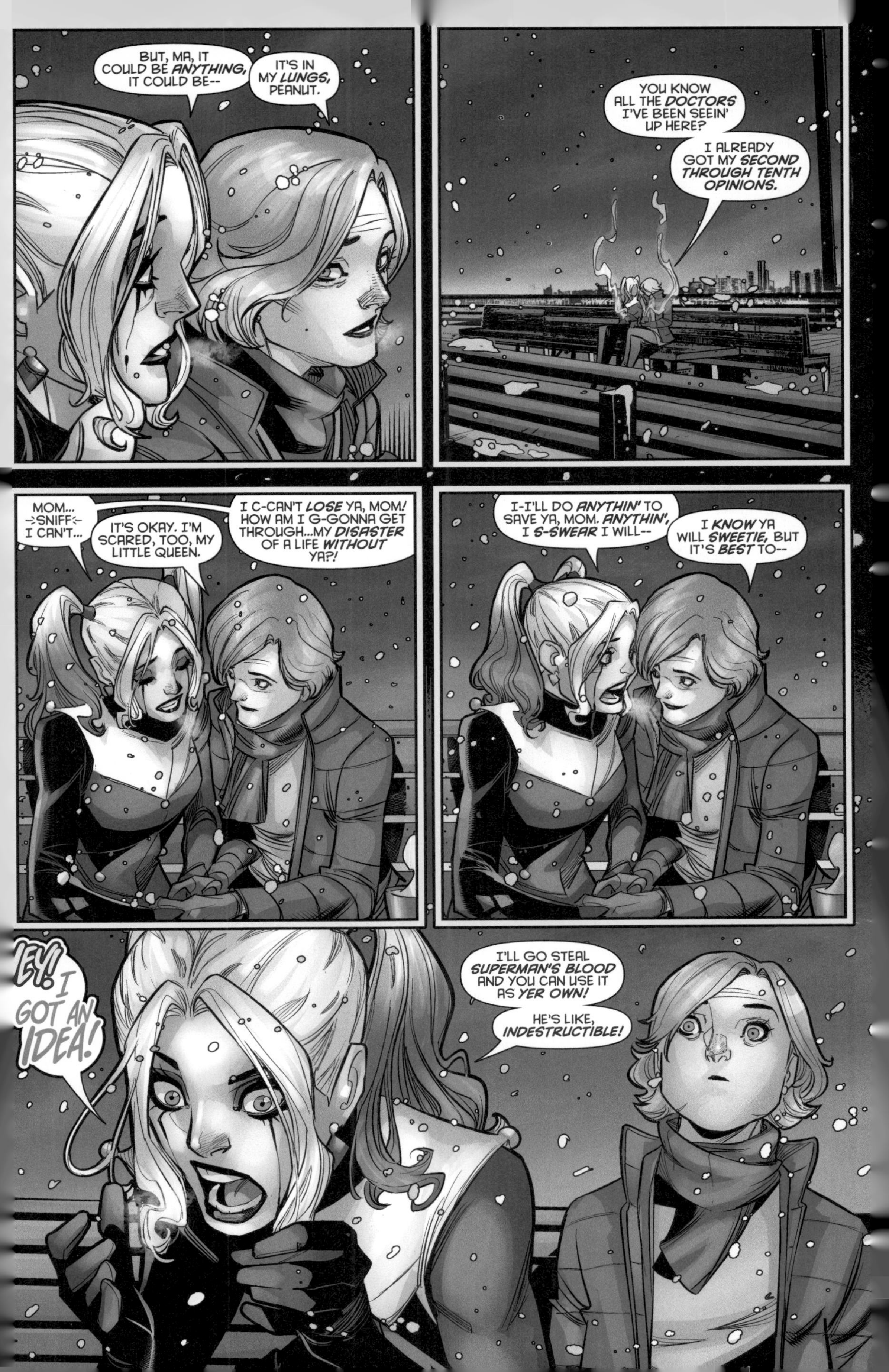

BUT, MA, IT COULD BE ANYTHING, IT COULD BE--
IT'S IN MY LUNGS, PEANUT.
YOU KNOW ALL THE DOCTORS I'VE BEEN SEEIN' UP HERE?
I ALREADY GOT MY SECOND THROUGH TENTH OPINIONS.
MOM... -SNIFF- I CAN'T...
IT'S OKAY. I'M SCARED, TOO, MY LITTLE QUEEN.
I C-CAN'T LOSE YA, MOM! HOW AM I G-GONNA GET THROUGH...MY DISASTER OF A LIFE WITHOUT YA?!
I-I'LL DO ANYTHIN' TO SAVE YA, MOM. ANYTHIN', I S-SWEAR I WILL--
I KNOW YA WILL SWEETIE, BUT IT'S BEST TO--
I GOT AN IDEA!
I'LL GO STEAL SUPERMAN'S BLOOD AND YOU CAN USE IT AS YER OWN!
HE'S LIKE, INDESTRUCTIBLE!

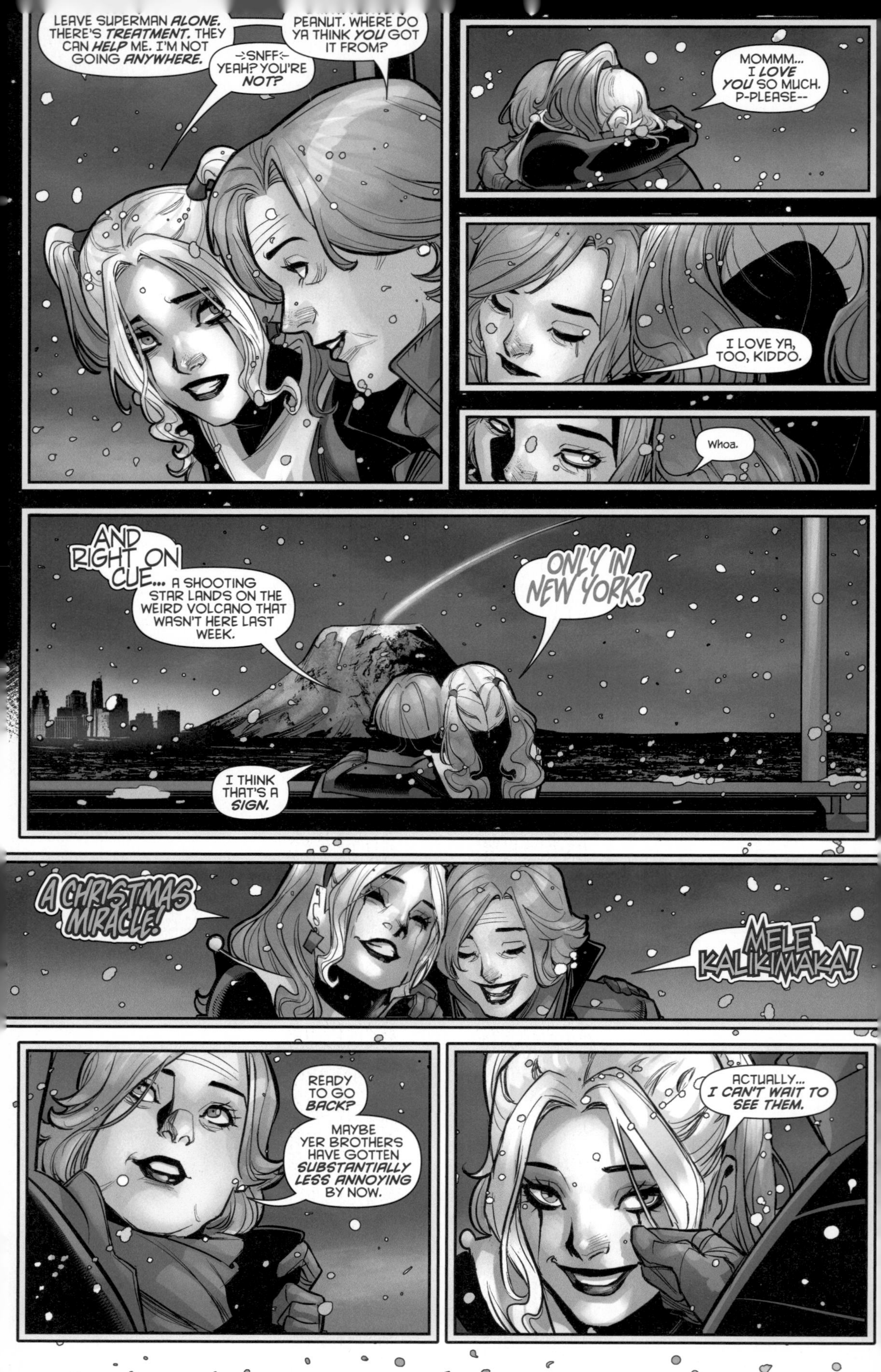

LEAVE SUPERMAN ALONE. THERE'S TREATMENT. THEY CAN HELP ME. I'M NOT GOING ANYWHERE.
-SNFF- YEAH? YOU'RE NOT?
PEANUT. WHERE DO YA THINK YOU GOT IT FROM?
MOMMM... I LOVE YOU SO MUCH. P-PLEASE--
I LOVE YA, TOO, KIDDO.
Whoa.
AND RIGHT ON CUE... A SHOOTING STAR LANDS ON THE WEIRD VOLCANO THAT WASN'T HERE LAST WEEK.
ONLY IN NEW YORK!
I THINK THAT'S A SIGN.
A CHRISTMAS MIRACLE!
MELE KALIKIMAKA!
READY TO GO BACK?
MAYBE YER BROTHERS HAVE GOTTEN SUBSTANTIALLY LESS ANNOYING BY NOW.
ACTUALLY... I CAN'T WAIT TO SEE THEM.

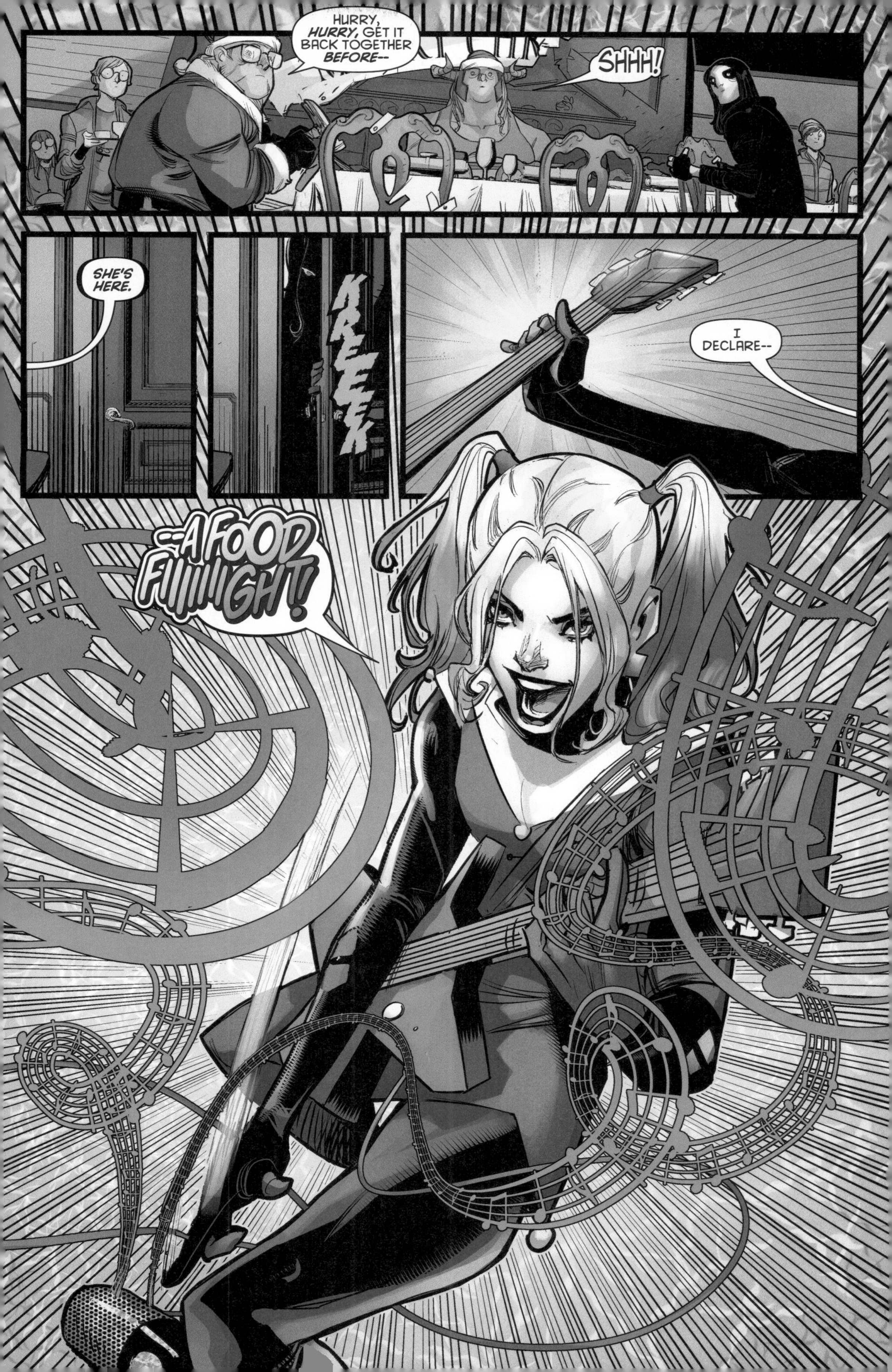
HURRY, *HURRY,* GET IT BACK TOGETHER *BEFORE--*
SHHH!
SHE'S HERE.
KREEEK
I DECLARE--
--A FOOD FIIIIIIGHT!

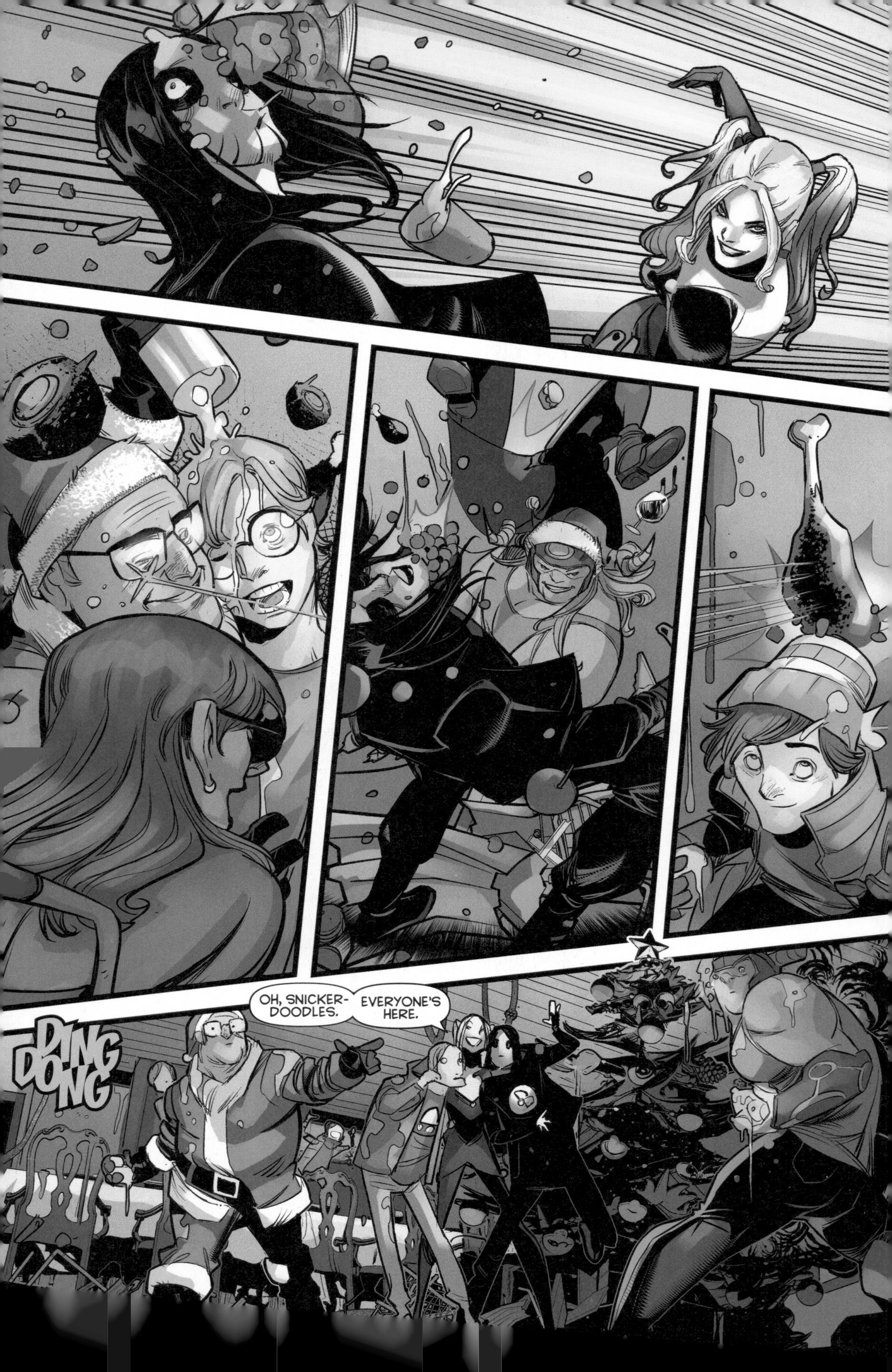
DING DONG
OH, SNICKER-DOODLES.
EVERYONE'S HERE.

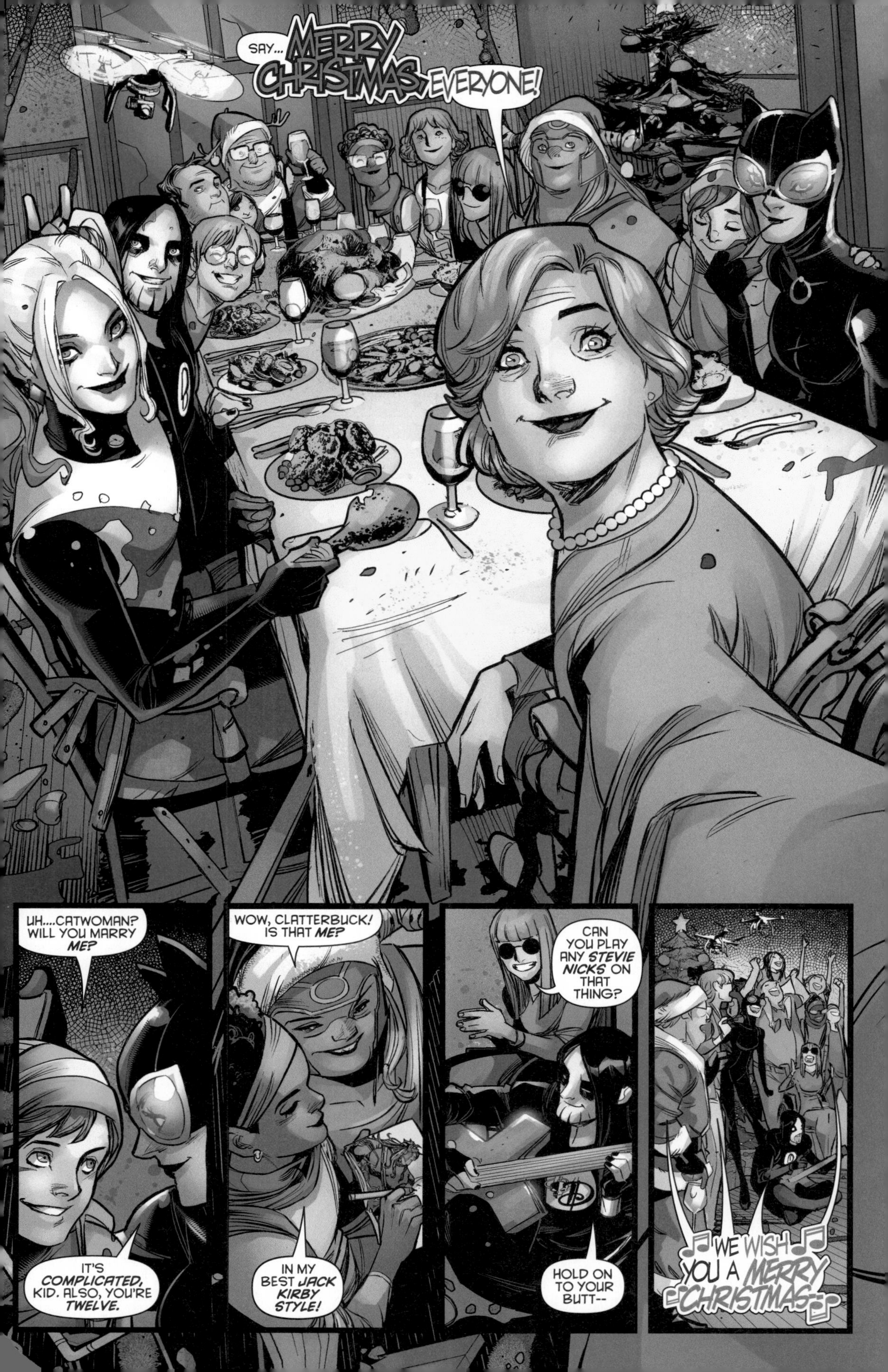
SAY... MERRY CHRISTMAS, EVERYONE!
UH....CATWOMAN? WILL YOU MARRY ME?
IT'S COMPLICATED, KID. ALSO, YOU'RE TWELVE.
WOW, CLATTERBUCK! IS THAT ME?
IN MY BEST JACK KIRBY STYLE!
CAN YOU PLAY ANY STEVIE NICKS ON THAT THING?
HOLD ON TO YOUR BUTT--
WE WISH YOU A MERRY CHRISTMAS

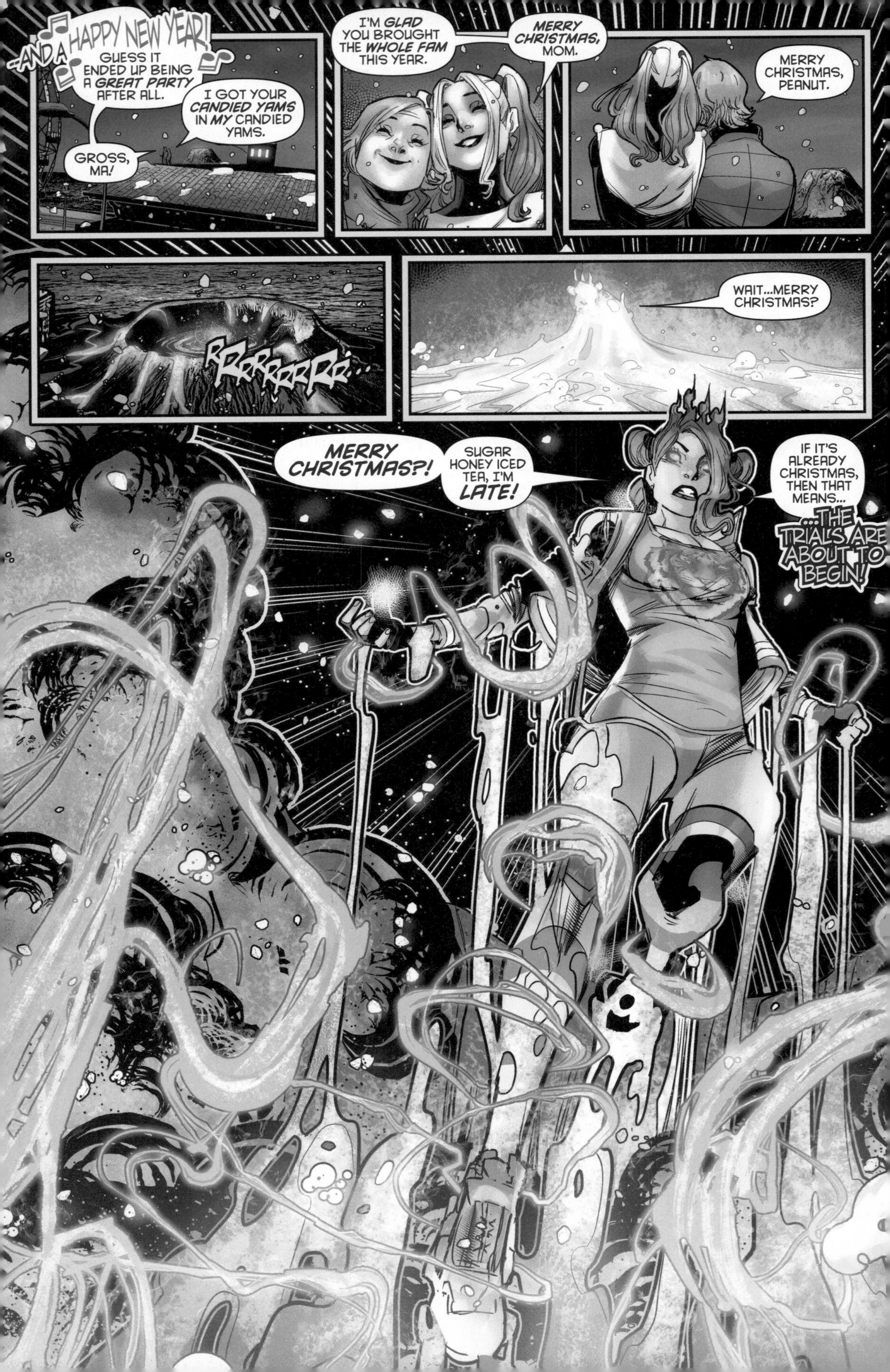
-AND A HAPPY NEW YEAR!
GUESS IT ENDED UP BEING A GREAT PARTY AFTER ALL.
I GOT YOUR CANDIED YAMS IN MY CANDIED YAMS.
GROSS, MA!
I'M GLAD YOU BROUGHT THE WHOLE FAM THIS YEAR.
MERRY CHRISTMAS, MOM.
MERRY CHRISTMAS, PEANUT.
RRRRRRRRR
WAIT...MERRY CHRISTMAS?
MERRY CHRISTMAS?!
SUGAR HONEY ICED TEA, I'M LATE!
IF IT'S ALREADY CHRISTMAS, THEN THAT MEANS...
...THE TRIALS ARE ABOUT TO BEGIN!

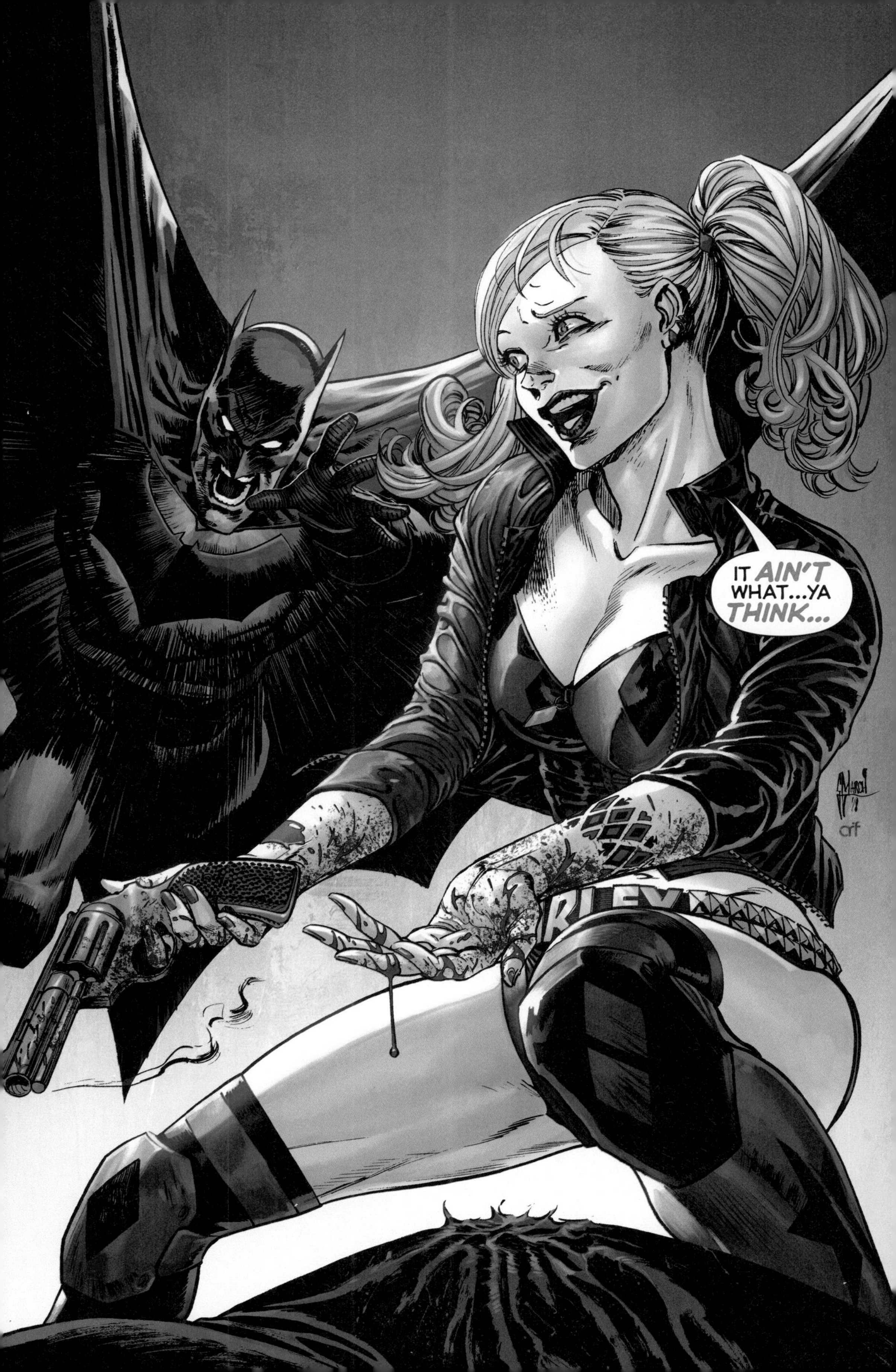
IT AIN'T WHAT...YA THINK...

HARLEY QUINN

#57

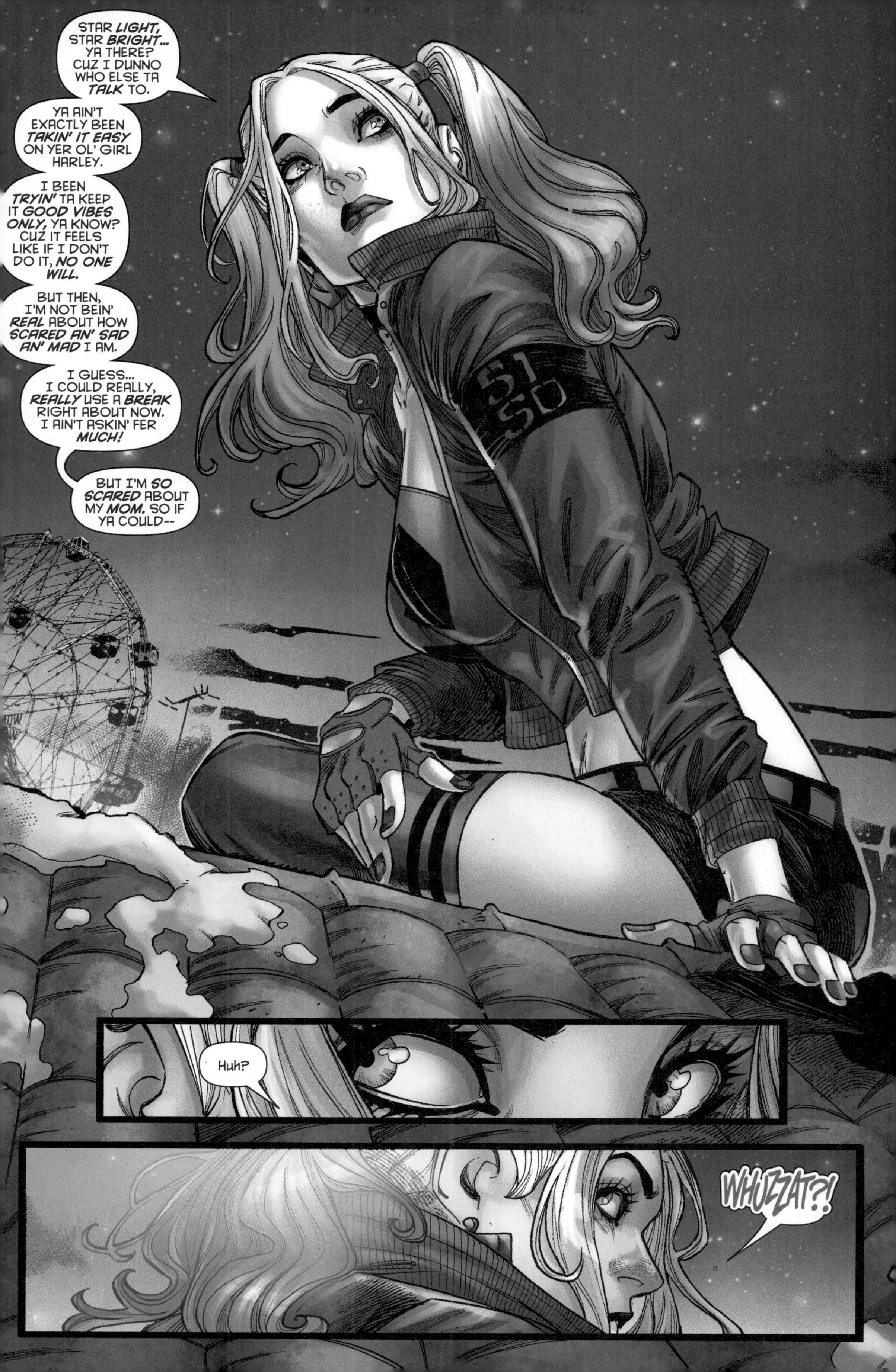
STAR LIGHT, STAR BRIGHT... YA THERE? CUZ I DUNNO WHO ELSE TA TALK TO.
YA AIN'T EXACTLY BEEN TAKIN' IT EASY ON YER OL' GIRL HARLEY.
I BEEN TRYIN' TA KEEP IT GOOD VIBES ONLY, YA KNOW? CUZ IT FEELS LIKE IF I DON'T DO IT, NO ONE WILL.
BUT THEN, I'M NOT BEIN' REAL ABOUT HOW SCARED AN' SAD AN' MAD I AM.
I GUESS... I COULD REALLY, REALLY USE A BREAK RIGHT ABOUT NOW. I AIN'T ASKIN' FER MUCH!
BUT I'M SO SCARED ABOUT MY MOM. SO IF YA COULD--
Huh?
WHUZZAT?!

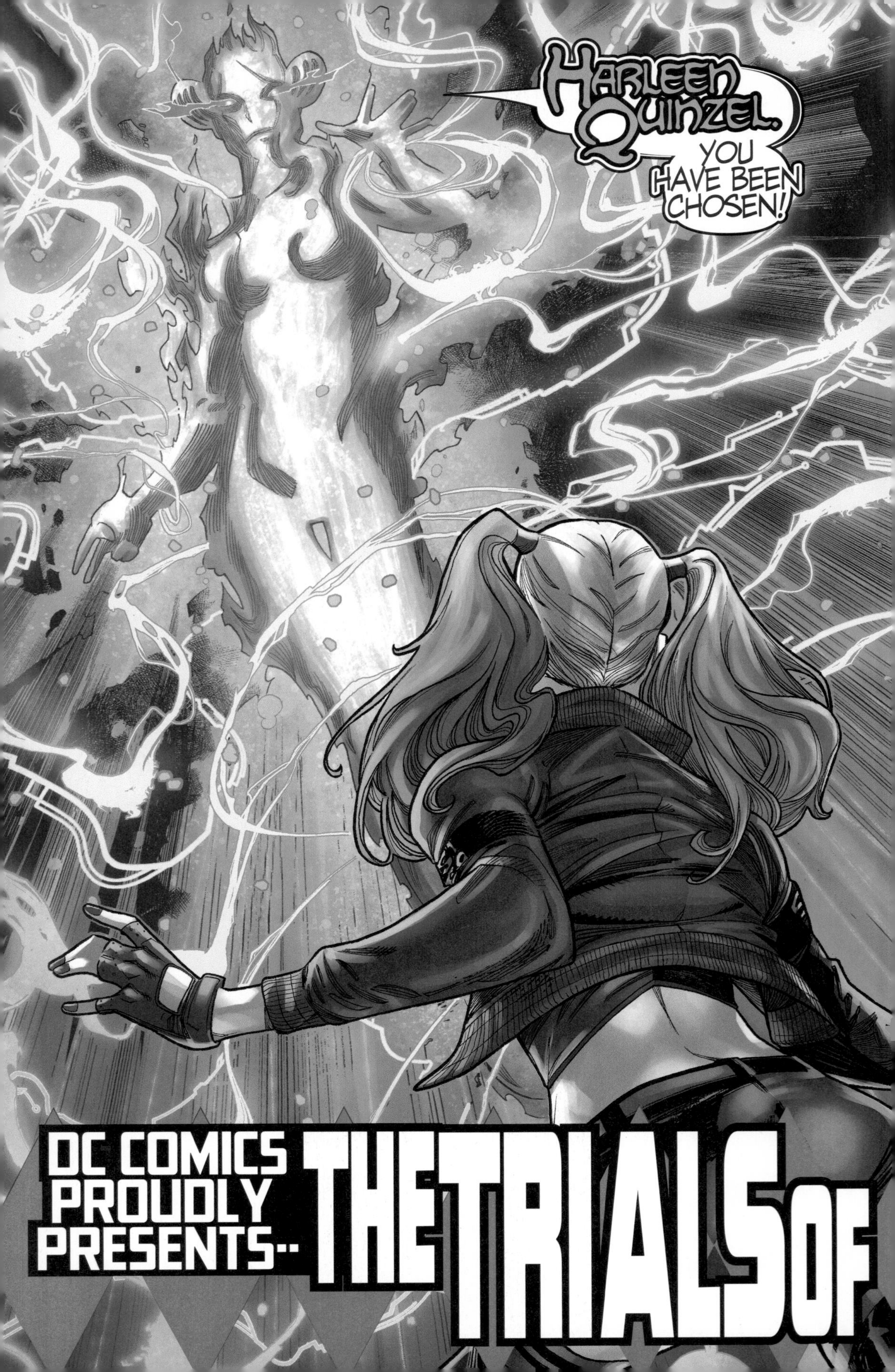
HARLEEN QUINZEL.
YOU HAVE BEEN CHOSEN!
DC COMICS PROUDLY PRESENTS--
THE TRIALS OF

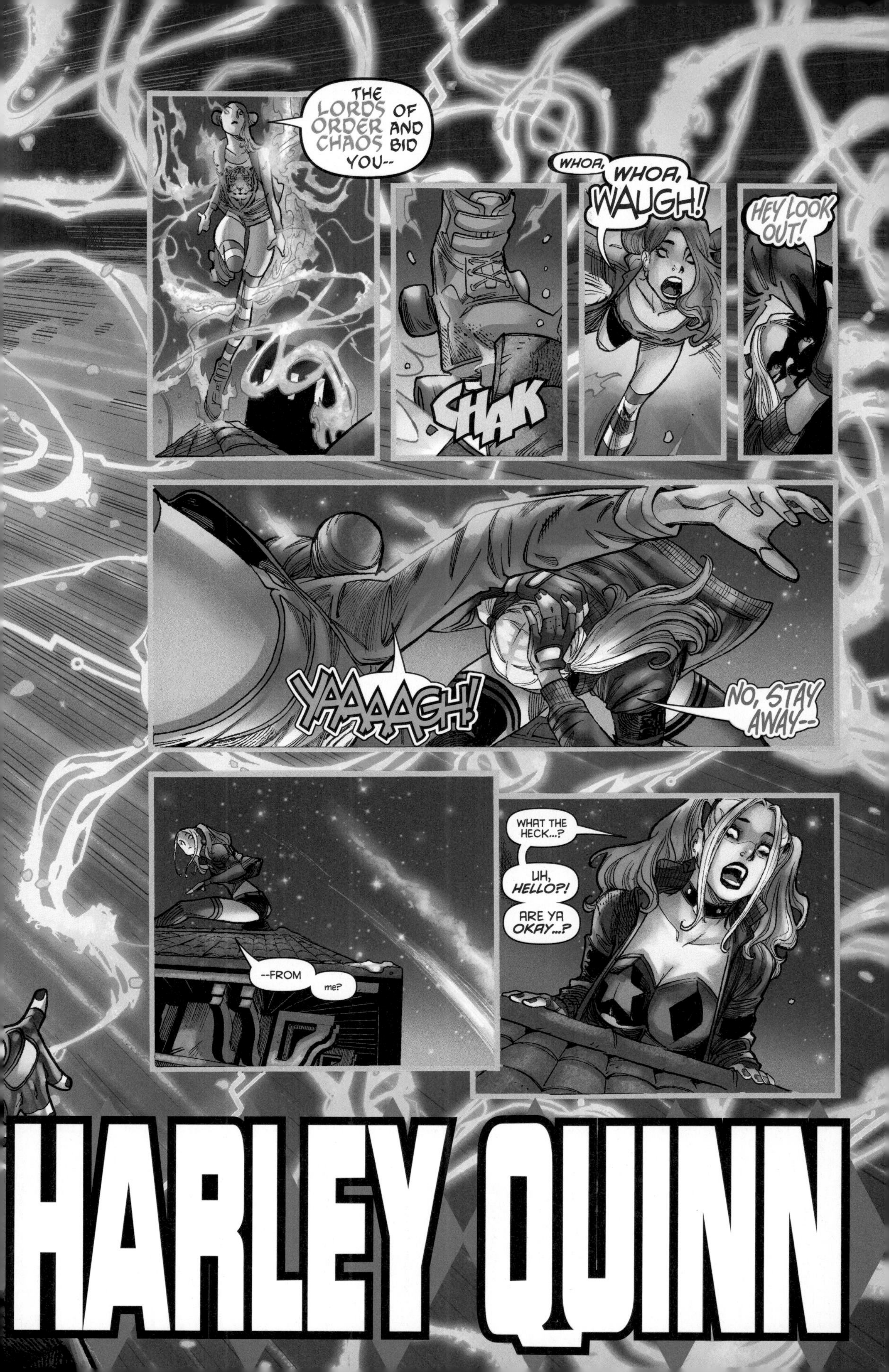
THE LORDS OF ORDER AND CHAOS BID YOU--
CHAK
WHOA, WHOA, WAUGH!
HEY LOOK OUT!
YAAAAGH!
NO, STAY AWAY--
--FROM me?
WHAT THE HECK...?
UH, HELLO?!
ARE YA OKAY...?
HARLEY QUINN

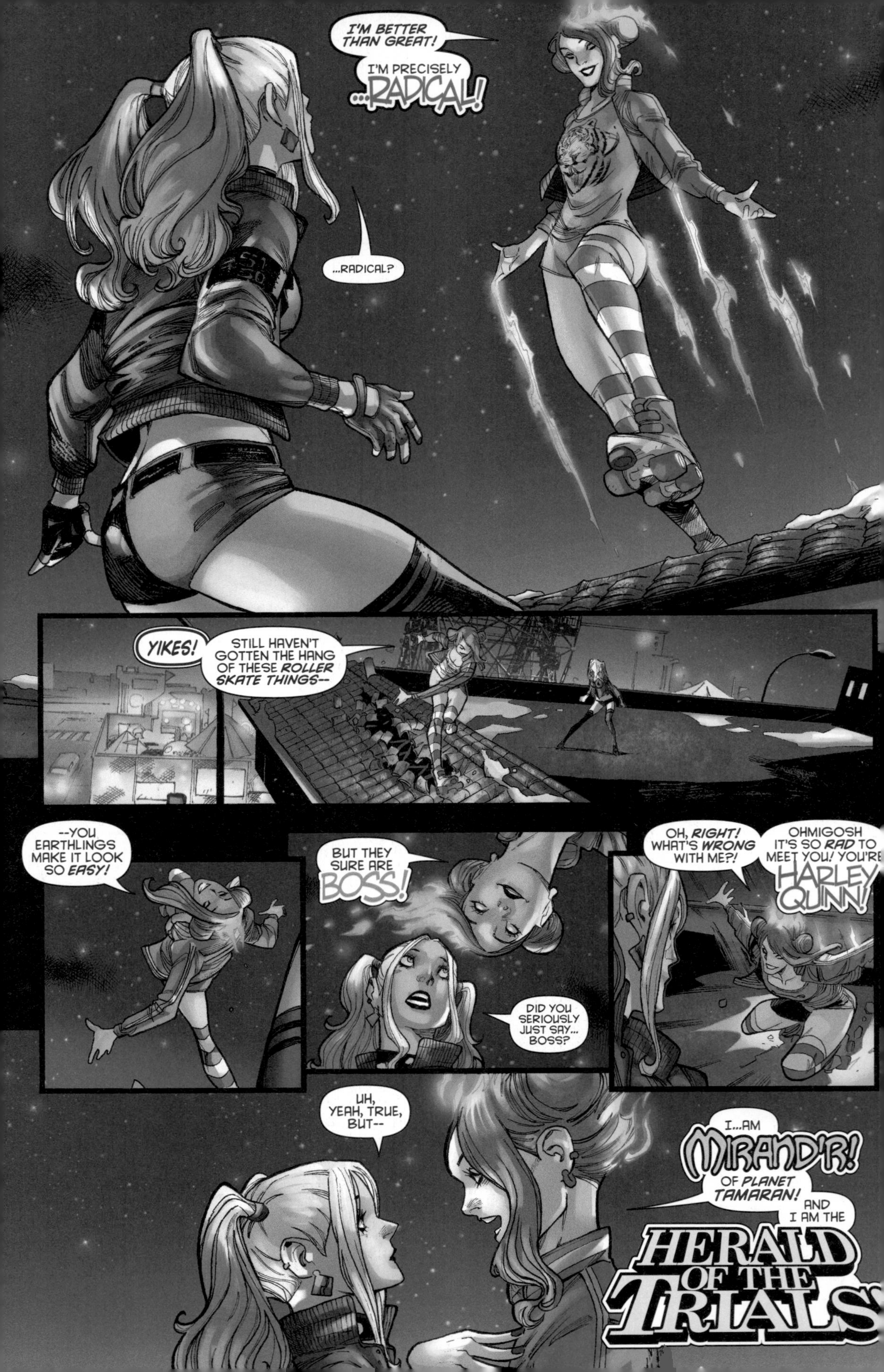
I'M BETTER THAN GREAT!
I'M PRECISELY ...RADICAL!
...RADICAL?
YIKES!
STILL HAVEN'T GOTTEN THE HANG OF THESE ROLLER SKATE THINGS--
--YOU EARTHLINGS MAKE IT LOOK SO EASY!
BUT THEY SURE ARE BOSS!
DID YOU SERIOUSLY JUST SAY... BOSS?
OH, RIGHT! WHAT'S WRONG WITH ME?!
OHMIGOSH IT'S SO RAD TO MEET YOU! YOU'RE HARLEY QUINN!
UH, YEAH, TRUE, BUT--
I...AM MIRAND'R! OF PLANET TAMARAN!
AND I AM THE HERALD OF THE TRIALS!

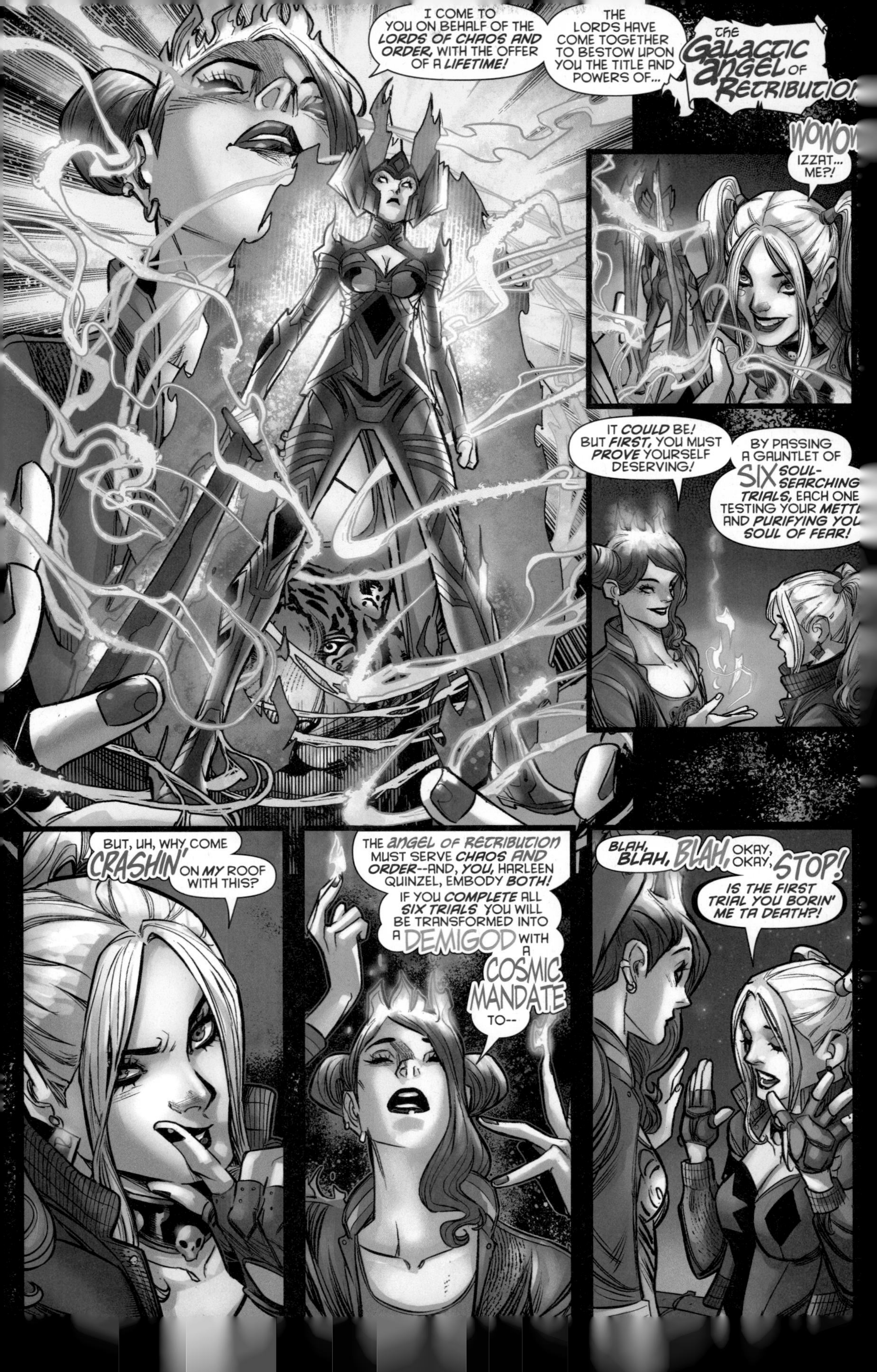
I COME TO YOU ON BEHALF OF THE LORDS OF CHAOS AND ORDER, WITH THE OFFER OF A LIFETIME!
THE LORDS HAVE COME TOGETHER TO BESTOW UPON YOU THE TITLE AND POWERS OF...
THE GALACTIC ANGEL OF RETRIBUTION
WOWOW
IZZAT... ME?!
IT COULD BE! BUT FIRST, YOU MUST PROVE YOURSELF DESERVING!
BY PASSING A GAUNTLET OF SIX SOUL-SEARCHING TRIALS, EACH ONE TESTING YOUR METTLE AND PURIFYING YOUR SOUL OF FEAR!
BUT, UH, WHY COME CRASHIN' ON MY ROOF WITH THIS?
THE ANGEL OF RETRIBUTION MUST SERVE CHAOS AND ORDER--AND, YOU, HARLEEN QUINZEL, EMBODY BOTH!
IF YOU COMPLETE ALL SIX TRIALS YOU WILL BE TRANSFORMED INTO A DEMIGOD WITH A COSMIC MANDATE TO--
BLAH, BLAH, BLAH, OKAY, OKAY, STOP!
IS THE FIRST TRIAL YOU BORIN' ME TA DEATH?!

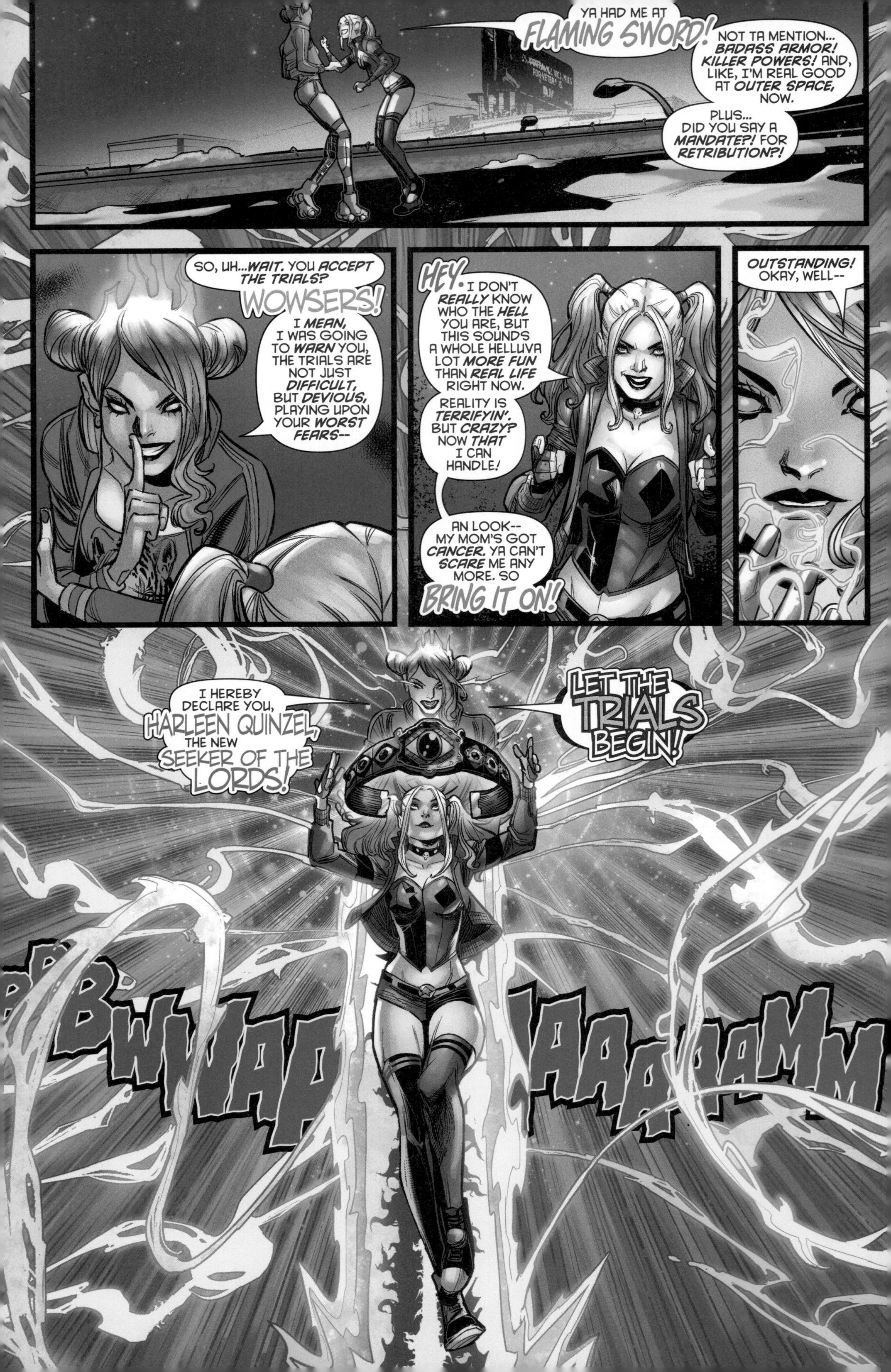
YA HAD ME AT FLAMING SWORD!
NOT TA MENTION... BADASS ARMOR! KILLER POWERS! AND, LIKE, I'M REAL GOOD AT OUTER SPACE, NOW.
PLUS... DID YOU SAY A MANDATE?! FOR RETRIBUTION?!
SO, UH...WAIT. YOU ACCEPT THE TRIALS?
WOWSERS!
I MEAN, I WAS GOING TO WARN YOU, THE TRIALS ARE NOT JUST DIFFICULT, BUT DEVIOUS, PLAYING UPON YOUR WORST FEARS--
HEY. I DON'T REALLY KNOW WHO THE HELL YOU ARE, BUT THIS SOUNDS A WHOLE HELLUVA LOT MORE FUN THAN REAL LIFE RIGHT NOW.
REALITY IS TERRIFYIN'. BUT CRAZY? NOW THAT I CAN HANDLE!
AN LOOK-- MY MOM'S GOT CANCER. YA CAN'T SCARE ME ANY MORE. SO
BRING IT ON!
OUTSTANDING! OKAY, WELL--
I HEREBY DECLARE YOU, HARLEEN QUINZEL, THE NEW SEEKER OF THE LORDS!
LET THE TRIALS BEGIN!
BWWAA
AAAAAMM

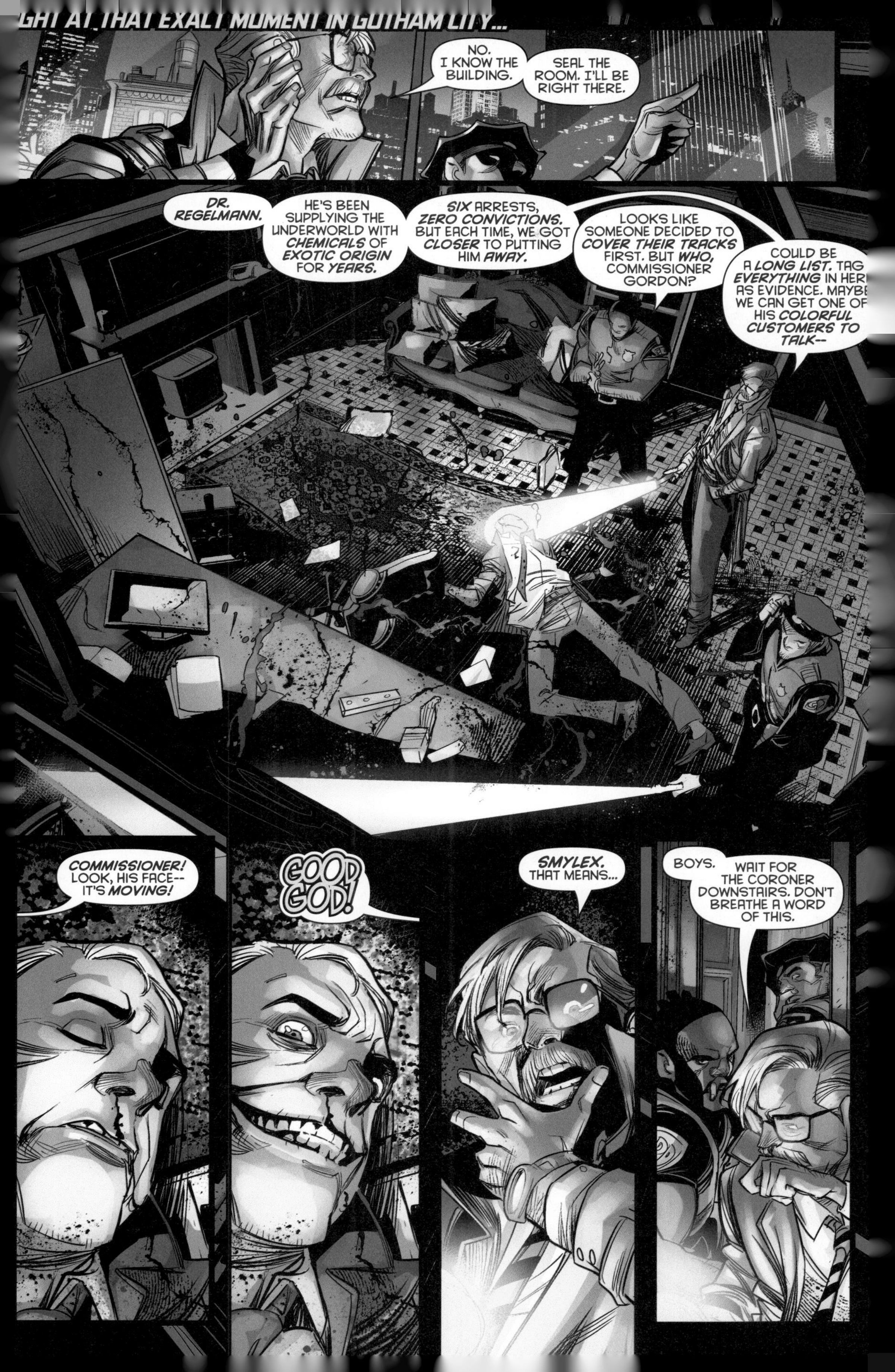

GHT AT THAT EXACT MOMENT IN GOTHAM CITY...
NO. I KNOW THE BUILDING.
SEAL THE ROOM. I'LL BE RIGHT THERE.
DR. REGELMANN.
HE'S BEEN SUPPLYING THE UNDERWORLD WITH CHEMICALS OF EXOTIC ORIGIN FOR YEARS.
SIX ARRESTS, ZERO CONVICTIONS. BUT EACH TIME, WE GOT CLOSER TO PUTTING HIM AWAY.
LOOKS LIKE SOMEONE DECIDED TO COVER THEIR TRACKS FIRST. BUT WHO, COMMISSIONER GORDON?
COULD BE A LONG LIST. TAG EVERYTHING IN HER AS EVIDENCE. MAYBE WE CAN GET ONE OF HIS COLORFUL CUSTOMERS TO TALK--
COMMISSIONER! LOOK, HIS FACE-- IT'S MOVING!
GOOD GOD!
SMYLEX. THAT MEANS...
BOYS.
WAIT FOR THE CORONER DOWNSTAIRS. DON'T BREATHE A WORD OF THIS.

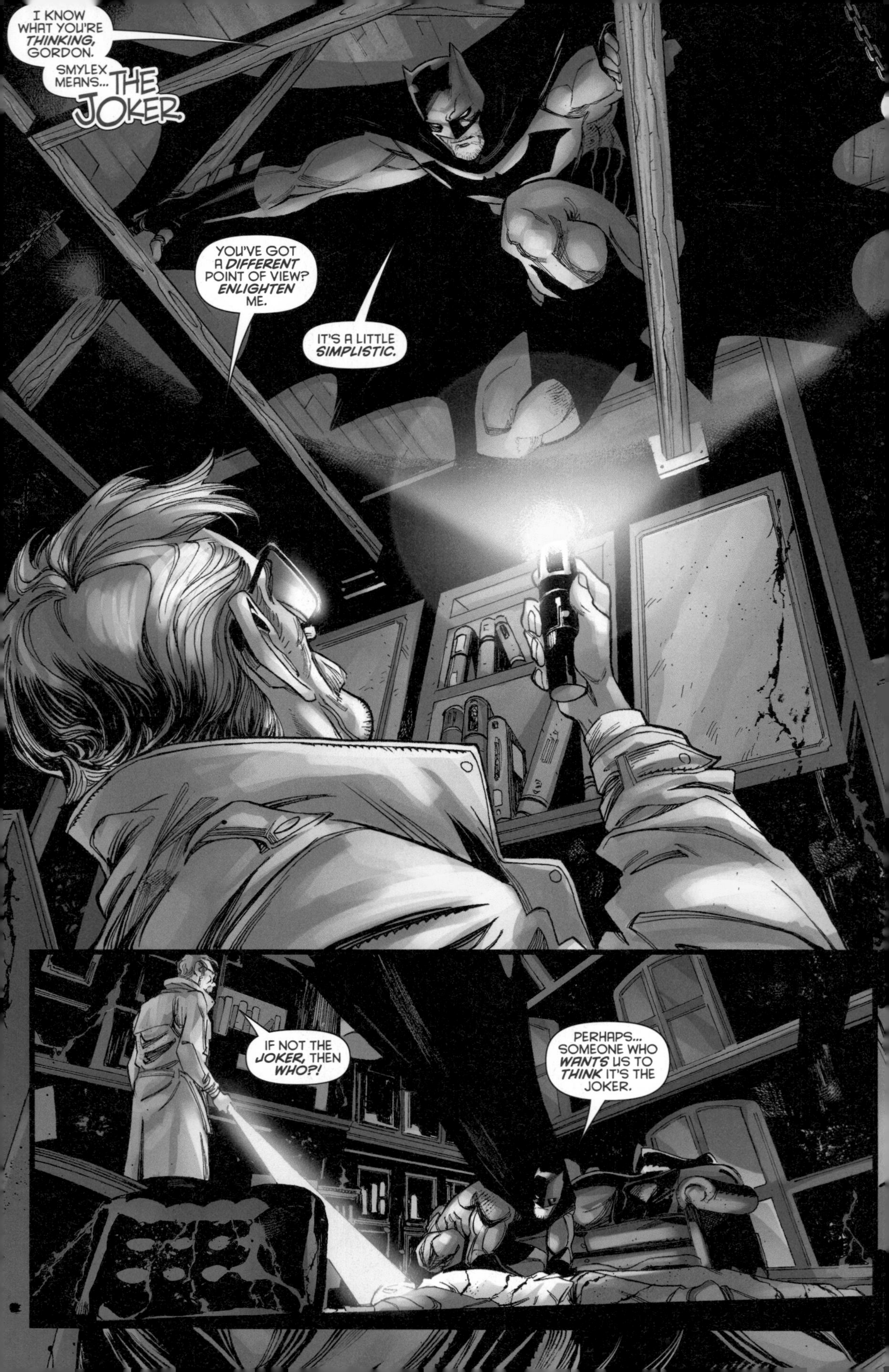
I KNOW WHAT YOU'RE THINKING, GORDON.
SMYLEX MEANS... THE JOKER.
YOU'VE GOT A DIFFERENT POINT OF VIEW? ENLIGHTEN ME.
IT'S A LITTLE SIMPLISTIC.
IF NOT THE JOKER, THEN WHO?!
PERHAPS... SOMEONE WHO WANTS US TO THINK IT'S THE JOKER.

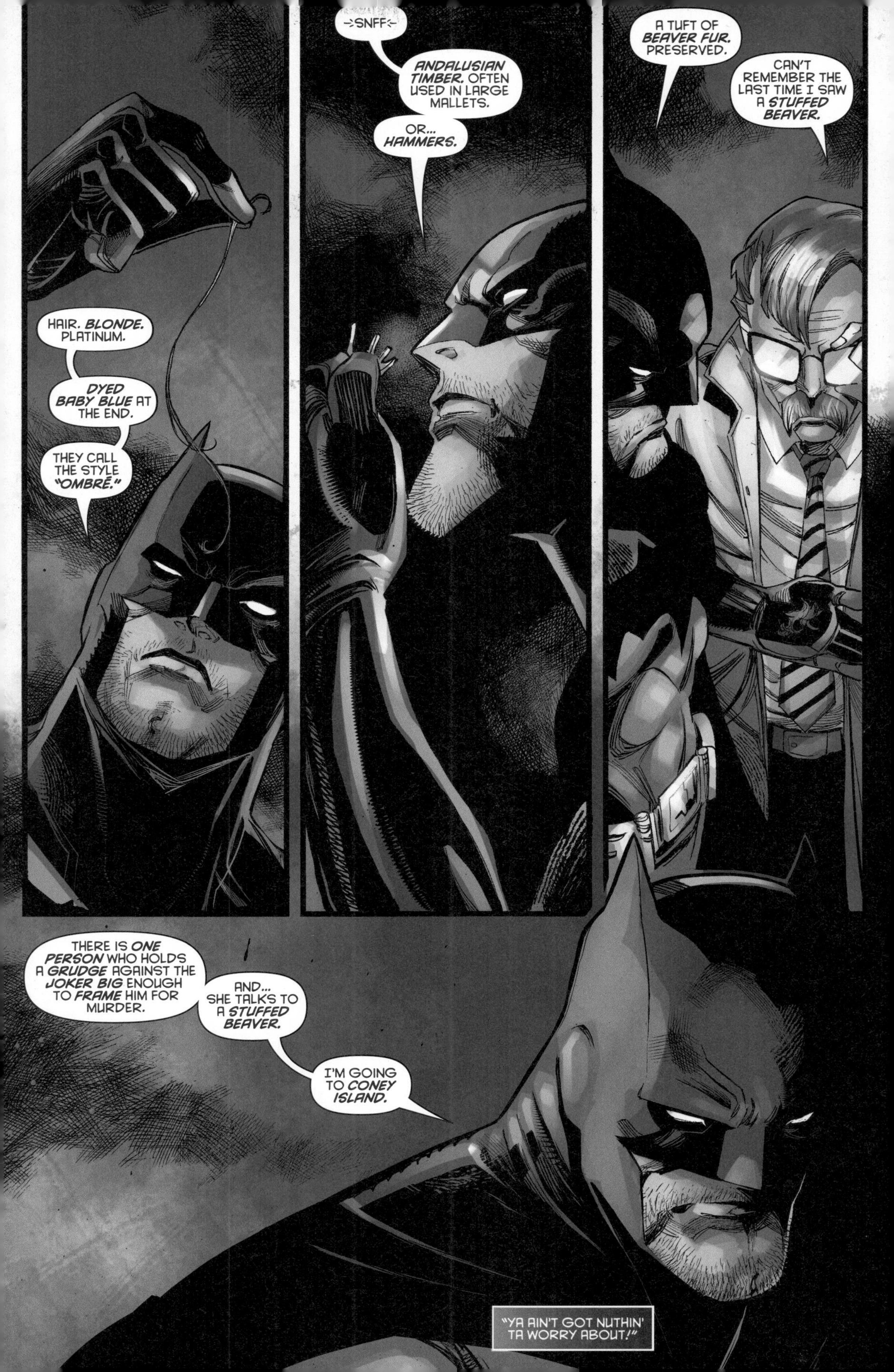
HAIR. BLONDE. PLATINUM.
DYED BABY BLUE AT THE END.
THEY CALL THE STYLE "OMBRÉ."
-SNFF-
ANDALUSIAN TIMBER. OFTEN USED IN LARGE MALLETS.
OR... HAMMERS.
A TUFT OF BEAVER FUR. PRESERVED.
CAN'T REMEMBER THE LAST TIME I SAW A STUFFED BEAVER.
THERE IS ONE PERSON WHO HOLDS A GRUDGE AGAINST THE JOKER BIG ENOUGH TO FRAME HIM FOR MURDER.
AND... SHE TALKS TO A STUFFED BEAVER.
I'M GOING TO CONEY ISLAND.
"YA AIN'T GOT NUTHIN' TA WORRY ABOUT!"

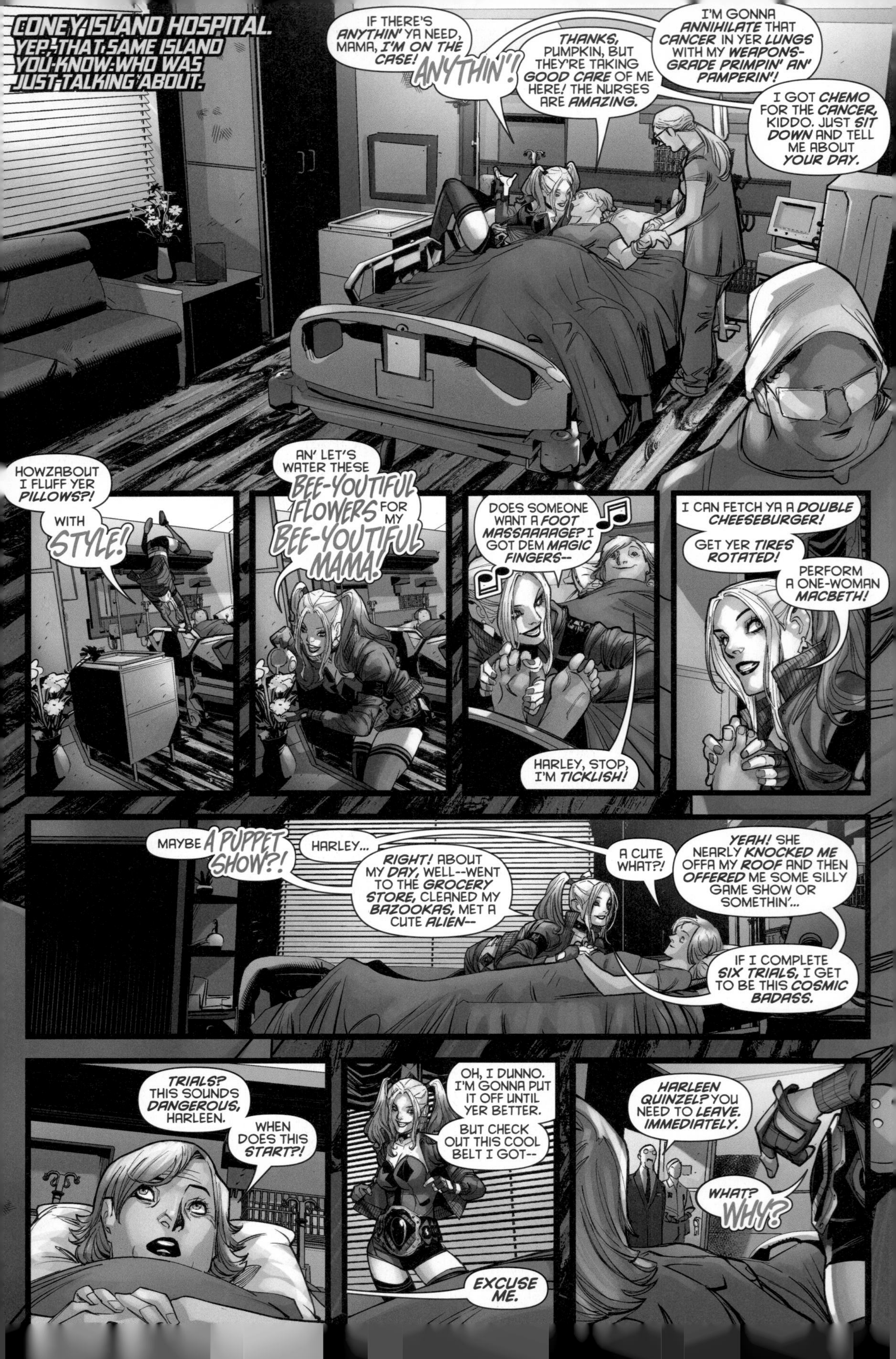
CONEY ISLAND HOSPITAL. YEP, THAT SAME ISLAND YOU-KNOW-WHO WAS JUST TALKING ABOUT.
IF THERE'S ANYTHIN' YA NEED, MAMA, I'M ON THE CASE! ANYTHIN'!
THANKS, PUMPKIN, BUT THEY'RE TAKING GOOD CARE OF ME HERE! THE NURSES ARE AMAZING.
I'M GONNA ANNIHILATE THAT CANCER IN YER LUNGS WITH MY WEAPONS-GRADE PRIMPIN' AN' PAMPERIN'!
I GOT CHEMO FOR THE CANCER, KIDDO. JUST SIT DOWN AND TELL ME ABOUT YOUR DAY.
HOWZABOUT I FLUFF YER PILLOWS?!
WITH STYLE!
AN' LET'S WATER THESE BEE-YOUTIFUL FLOWERS FOR MY BEE-YOUTIFUL MAMA!
DOES SOMEONE WANT A FOOT MASSAAAAGE? I GOT DEM MAGIC FINGERS--
HARLEY, STOP, I'M TICKLISH!
I CAN FETCH YA A DOUBLE CHEESEBURGER!
GET YER TIRES ROTATED!
PERFORM A ONE-WOMAN MACBETH!
MAYBE A PUPPET SHOW?!
HARLEY...
RIGHT! ABOUT MY DAY, WELL--WENT TO THE GROCERY STORE, CLEANED MY BAZOOKAS, MET A CUTE ALIEN--
A CUTE WHAT?!
YEAH! SHE NEARLY KNOCKED ME OFFA MY ROOF AND THEN OFFERED ME SOME SILLY GAME SHOW OR SOMETHIN'...
IF I COMPLETE SIX TRIALS, I GET TO BE THIS COSMIC BADASS.
TRIALS? THIS SOUNDS DANGEROUS, HARLEEN.
WHEN DOES THIS START?!
OH, I DUNNO. I'M GONNA PUT IT OFF UNTIL YER BETTER.
BUT CHECK OUT THIS COOL BELT I GOT--
EXCUSE ME.
HARLEEN QUINZEL? YOU NEED TO LEAVE. IMMEDIATELY.
WHAT? WHY?

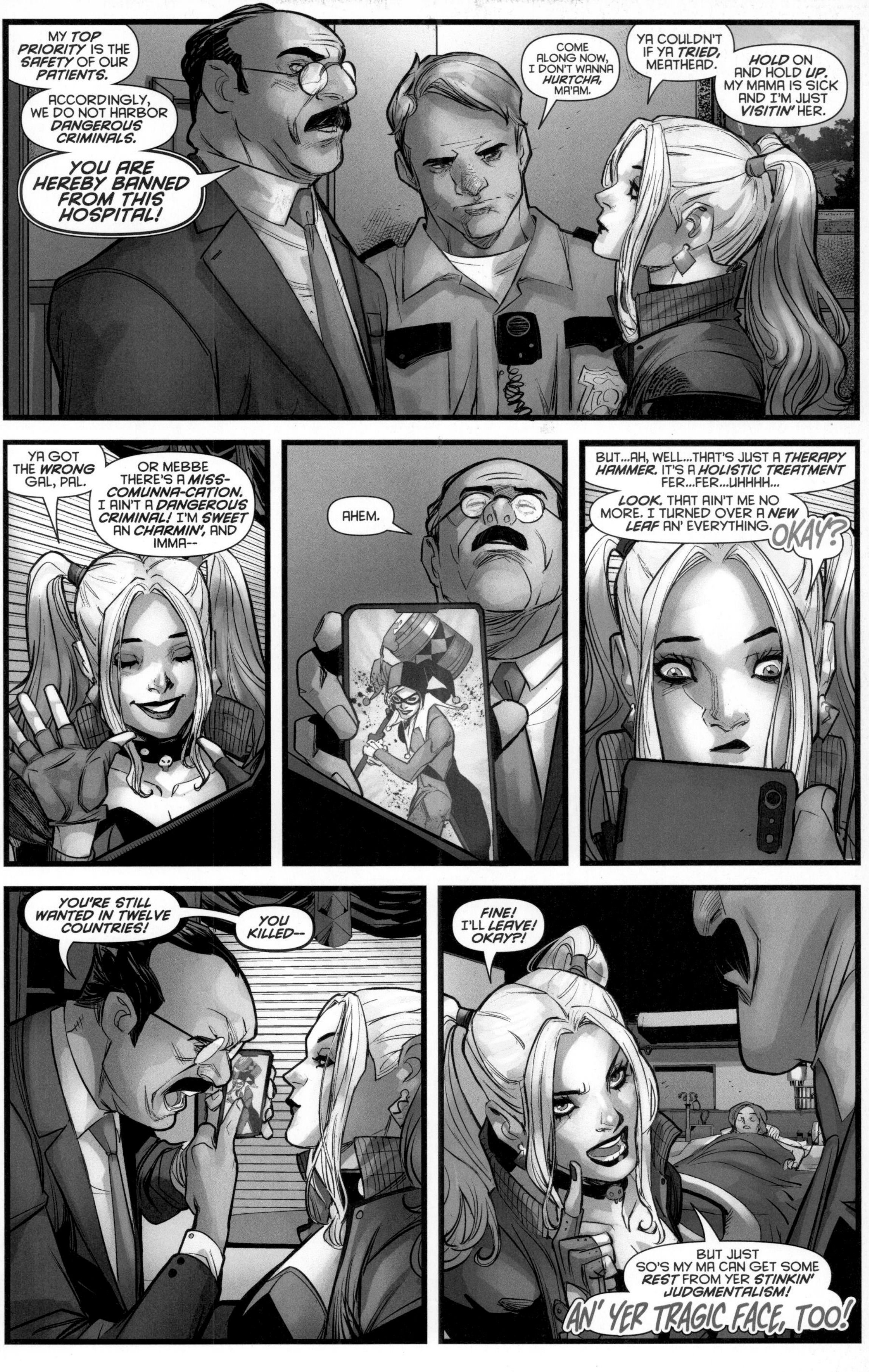
MY TOP PRIORITY IS THE SAFETY OF OUR PATIENTS.
ACCORDINGLY, WE DO NOT HARBOR DANGEROUS CRIMINALS.
YOU ARE HEREBY BANNED FROM THIS HOSPITAL!
COME ALONG NOW, I DON'T WANNA HURTCHA, MA'AM.
YA COULDN'T IF YA TRIED, MEATHEAD.
HOLD ON AND HOLD UP. MY MAMA IS SICK AND I'M JUST VISITIN' HER.
YA GOT THE WRONG GAL, PAL.
OR MEBBE THERE'S A MISS-COMUNNA-CATION. I AIN'T A DANGEROUS CRIMINAL! I'M SWEET AN CHARMIN', AND IMMA--
AHEM.
BUT...AH, WELL...THAT'S JUST A THERAPY HAMMER. IT'S A HOLISTIC TREATMENT FER...FER...UHHHH...
LOOK. THAT AIN'T ME NO MORE. I TURNED OVER A NEW LEAF AN' EVERYTHING.
OKAY?
YOU'RE STILL WANTED IN TWELVE COUNTRIES!
YOU KILLED--
FINE! I'LL LEAVE! OKAY?!
BUT JUST SO'S MY MA CAN GET SOME REST FROM YER STINKIN' JUDGMENTALISM!
AN' YER TRAGIC FACE, TOO!

HARLEY CAN'T WAIT!

By Meredith Clatterbuck

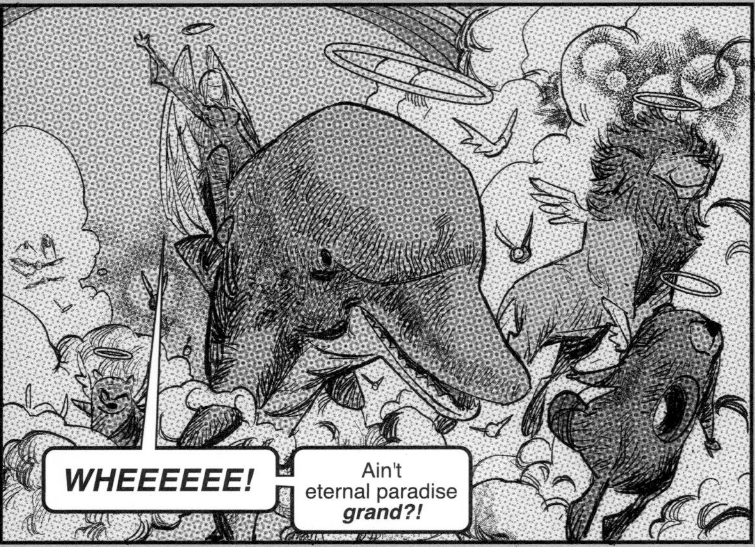
WHEEEEEE!
Ain't eternal paradise grand?!

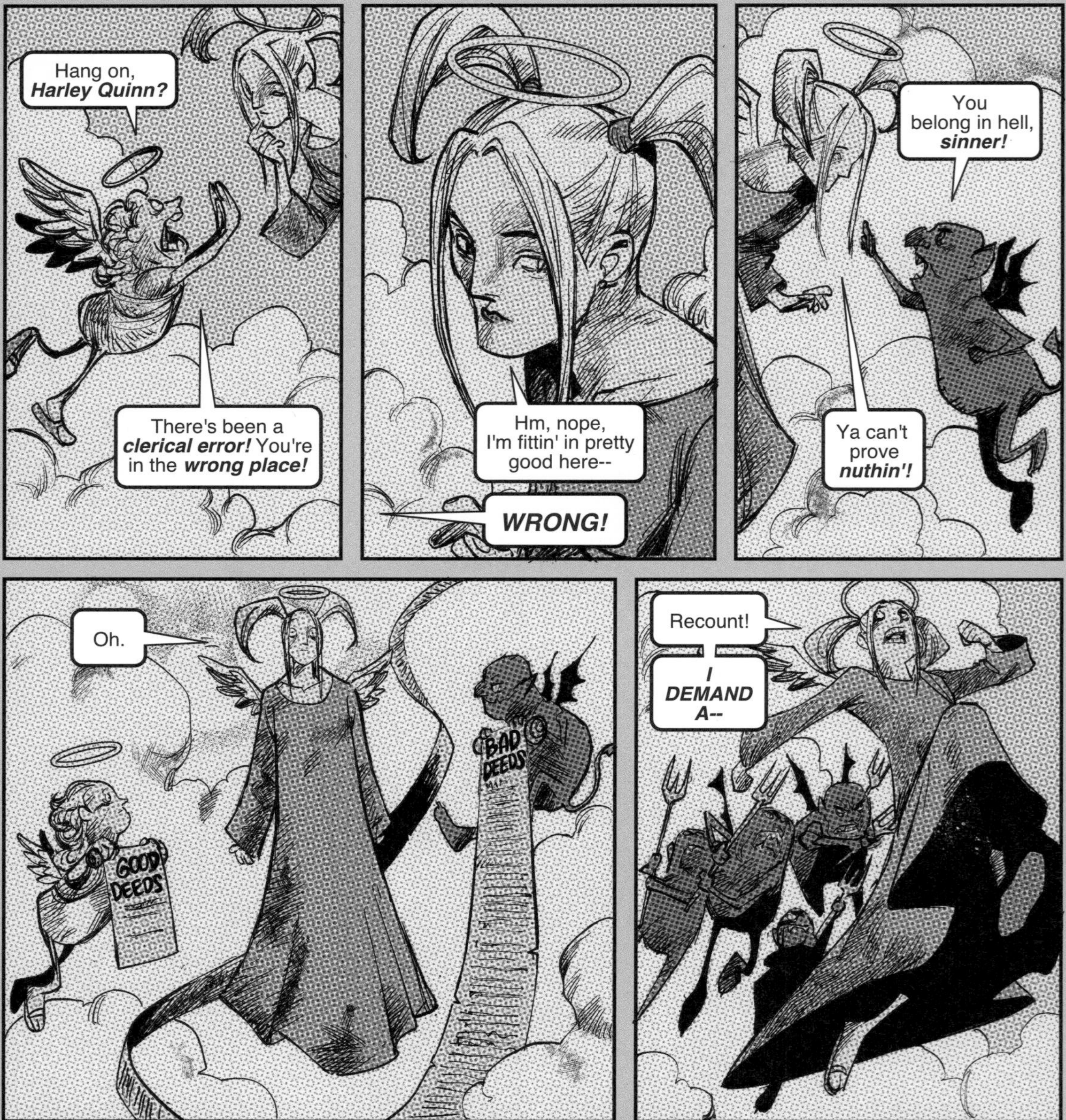
Hang on, Harley Quinn?
There's been a clerical error! You're in the wrong place!
Hm, nope, I'm fittin' in pretty good here--
WRONG!
You belong in hell, sinner!
Ya can't prove nuthin'!
Oh.
BAD DEEDS
GOOD DEEDS
Recount!
I DEMAND A--

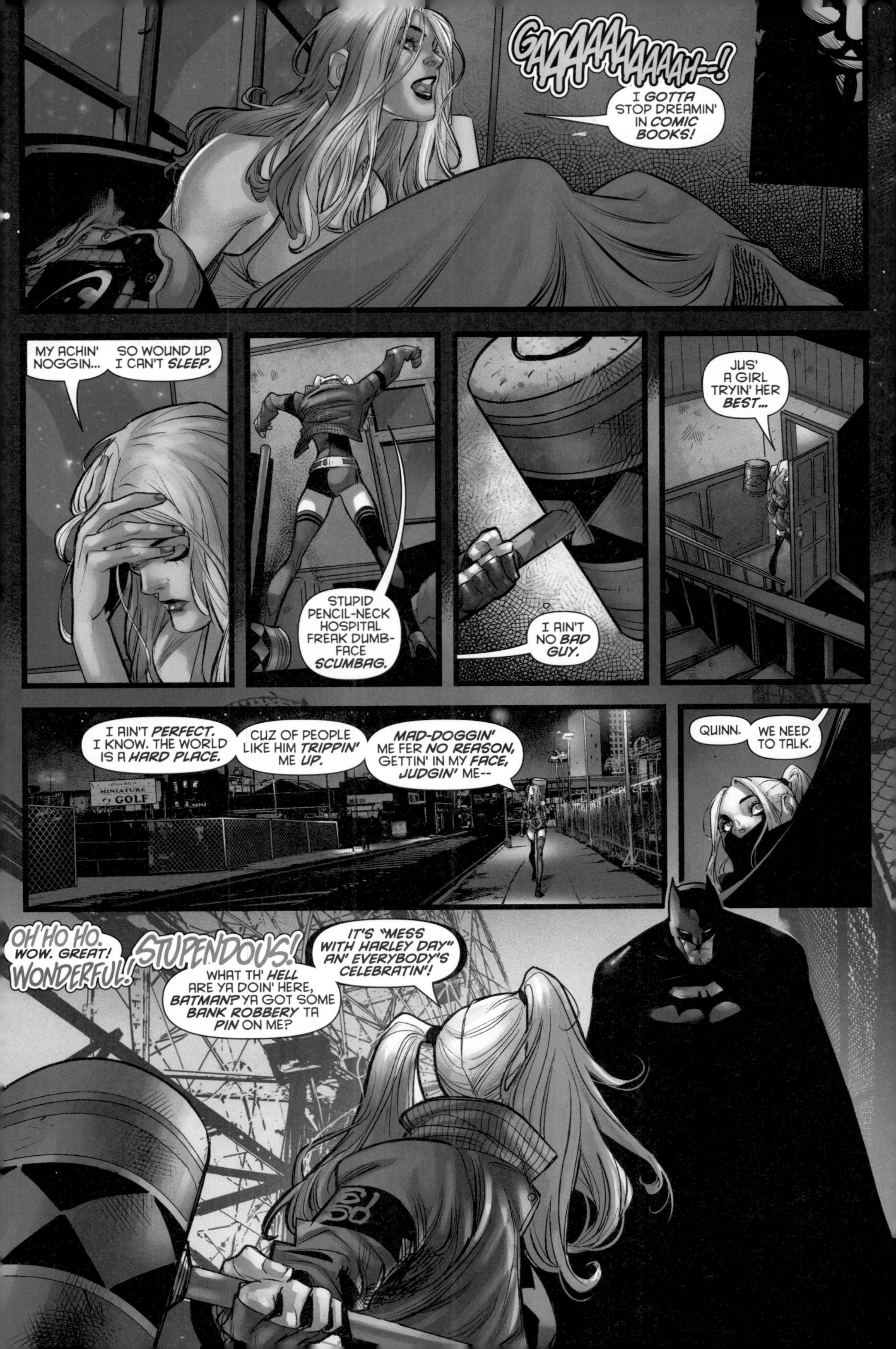

GAAAAAAAAAAH--!
I GOTTA STOP DREAMIN' IN COMIC BOOKS!
MY ACHIN' NOGGIN...
SO WOUND UP I CAN'T SLEEP.
STUPID PENCIL-NECK HOSPITAL FREAK DUMB-FACE SCUMBAG.
I AIN'T NO BAD GUY.
JUS' A GIRL TRYIN' HER BEST...
I AIN'T PERFECT. I KNOW. THE WORLD IS A HARD PLACE.
CUZ OF PEOPLE LIKE HIM TRIPPIN' ME UP.
MAD-DOGGIN' ME FER NO REASON, GETTIN' IN MY FACE, JUDGIN' ME--
MINIATURE GOLF
QUINN.
WE NEED TO TALK.
OH HO HO. WOW. GREAT! WONDERFUL!
STUPENDOUS!
IT'S "MESS WITH HARLEY DAY" AN' EVERYBODY'S CELEBRATIN'!
WHAT TH' HELL ARE YA DOIN' HERE, BATMAN? YA GOT SOME BANK ROBBERY TA PIN ON ME?

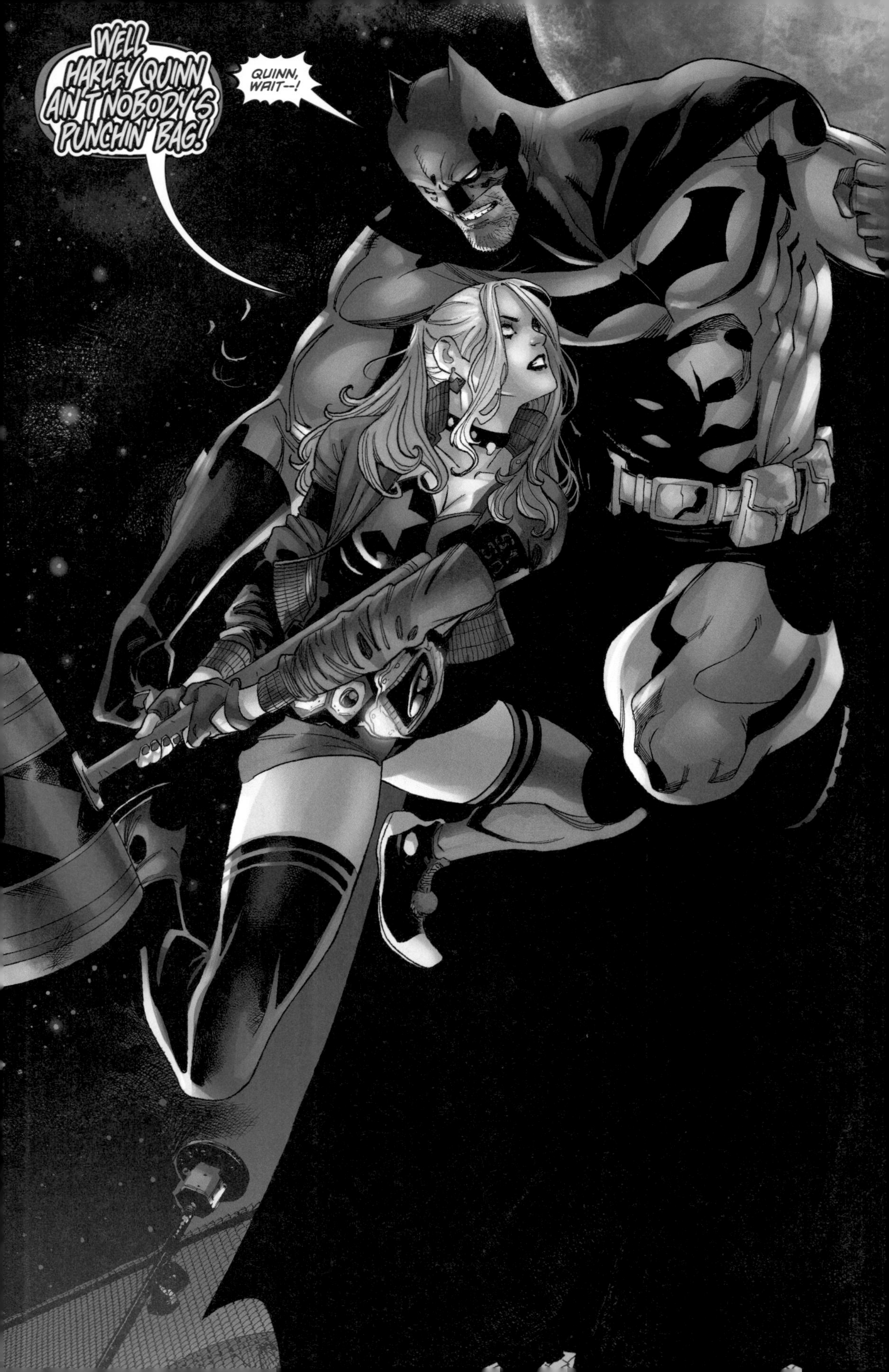
WELL HARLEY QUINN AIN'T NOBODY'S PUNCHIN' BAG!
QUINN, WAIT--!

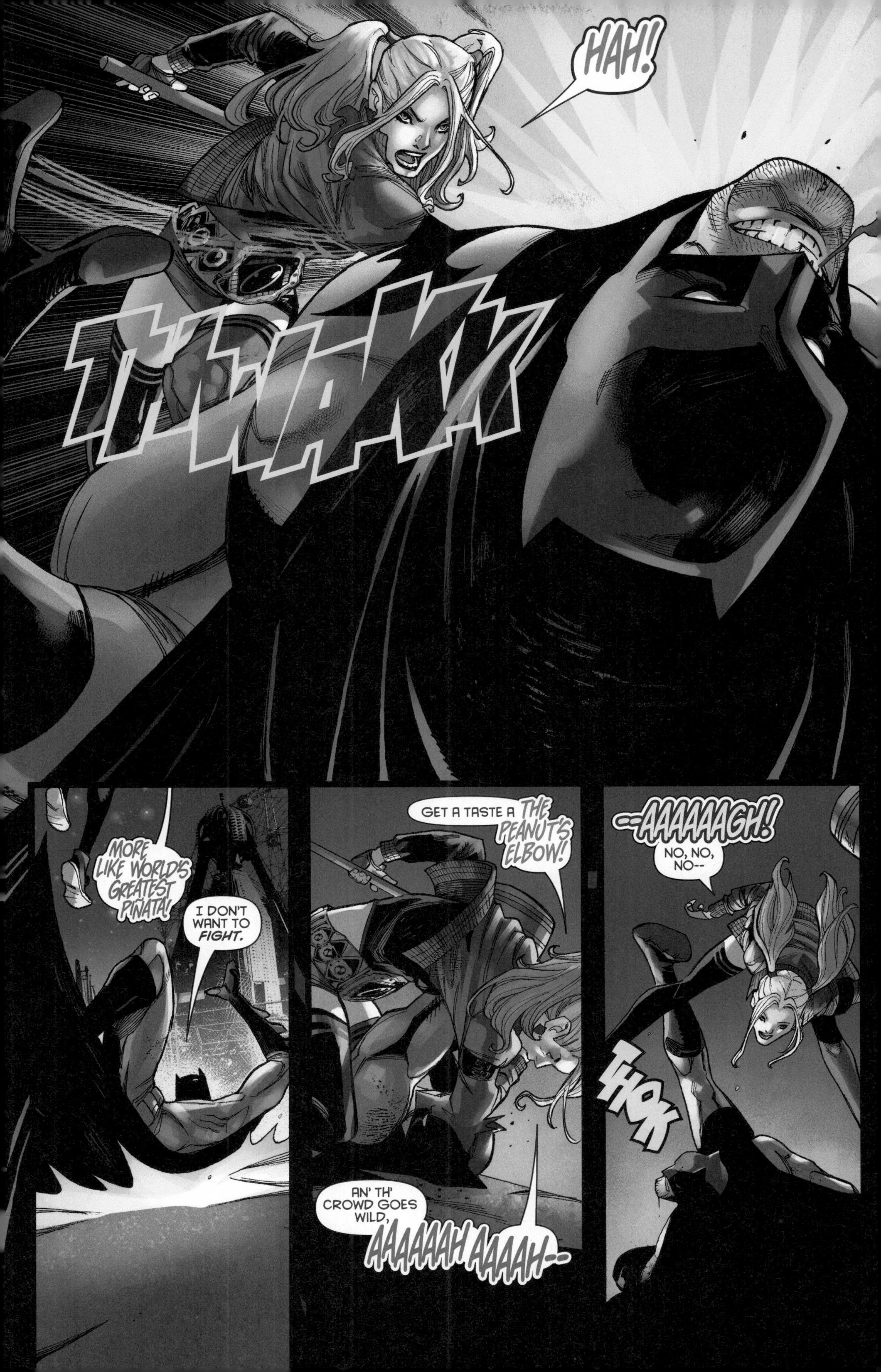
HAH!
THWAKK
MORE LIKE WORLD'S GREATEST PIÑATA!
I DON'T WANT TO FIGHT.
GET A TASTE A THE PEANUT'S ELBOW!
AN' TH' CROWD GOES WILD,
AAAAAAH AAAAH--
--AAAAAAGH!
NO, NO, NO--
THOK

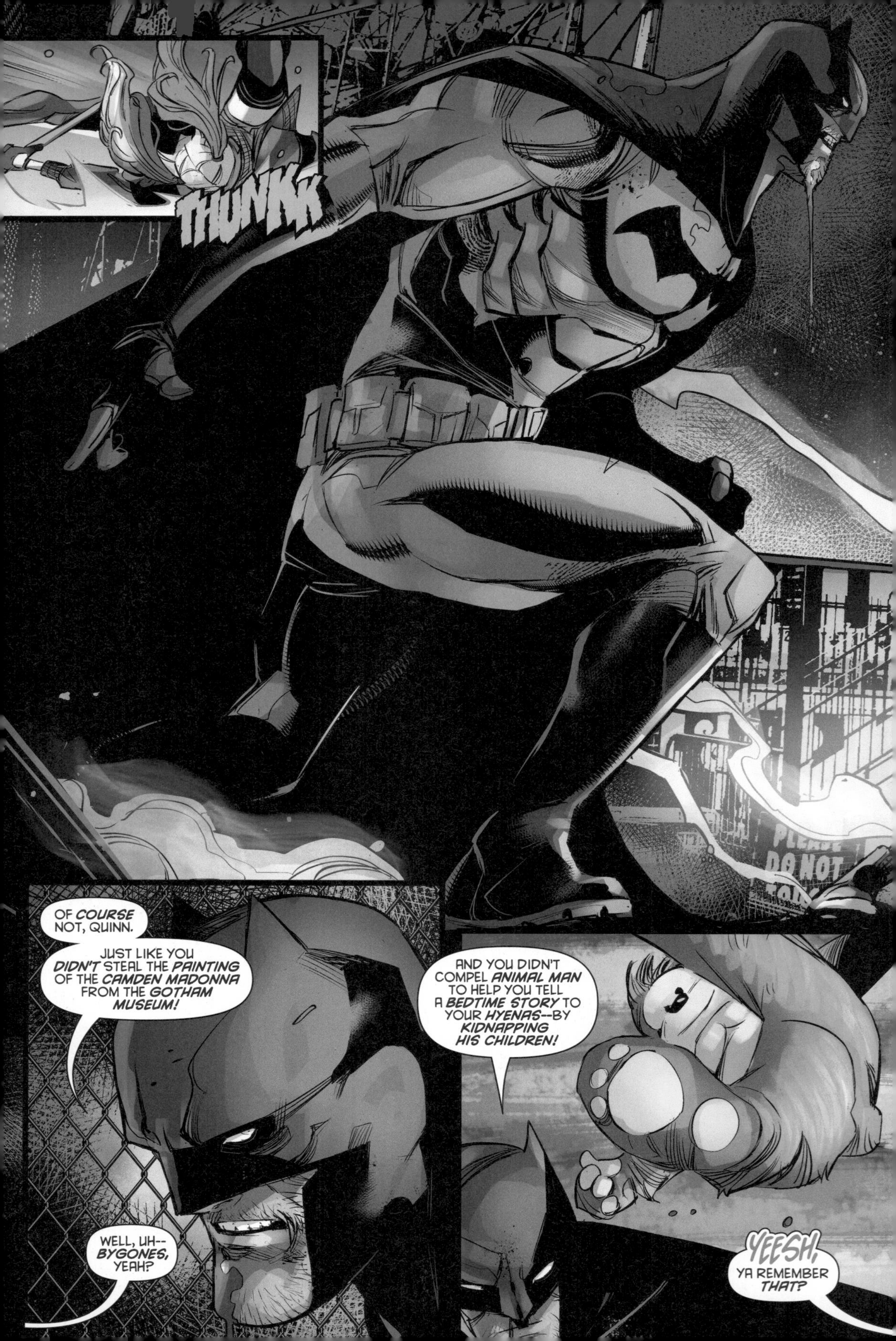
THUNKK
DO NOT
OF COURSE NOT, QUINN.
JUST LIKE YOU DIDN'T STEAL THE PAINTING OF THE CAMDEN MADONNA FROM THE GOTHAM MUSEUM!
AND YOU DIDN'T COMPEL ANIMAL MAN TO HELP YOU TELL A BEDTIME STORY TO YOUR HYENAS--BY KIDNAPPING HIS CHILDREN!
WELL, UH-- BYGONES, YEAH?
YEESH, YA REMEMBER THAT?

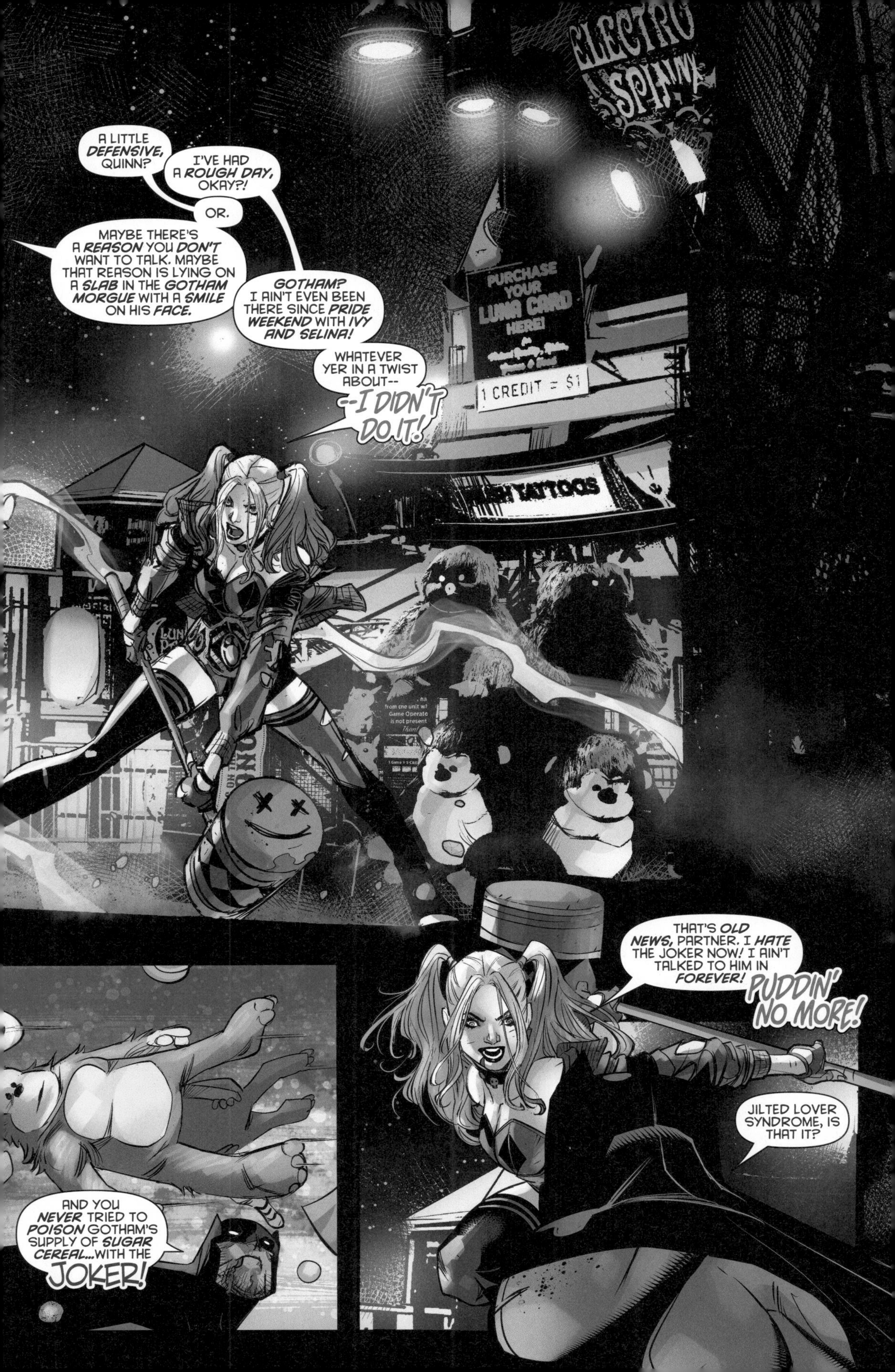
ELECTRO SPINNY
A LITTLE DEFENSIVE, QUINN?
I'VE HAD A ROUGH DAY, OKAY?!
OR.
MAYBE THERE'S A REASON YOU DON'T WANT TO TALK. MAYBE THAT REASON IS LYING ON A SLAB IN THE GOTHAM MORGUE WITH A SMILE ON HIS FACE.
GOTHAM? I AIN'T EVEN BEEN THERE SINCE PRIDE WEEKEND WITH IVY AND SELINA!
WHATEVER YER IN A TWIST ABOUT--
--I DIDN'T DO IT!
PURCHASE YOUR LUNA CARD HERE!
1 CREDIT = $1
TATTOOS
AND YOU NEVER TRIED TO POISON GOTHAM'S SUPPLY OF SUGAR CEREAL...WITH THE JOKER!
THAT'S OLD NEWS, PARTNER. I HATE THE JOKER NOW! I AIN'T TALKED TO HIM IN FOREVER!
PUDDIN' NO MORE!
JILTED LOVER SYNDROME, IS THAT IT?

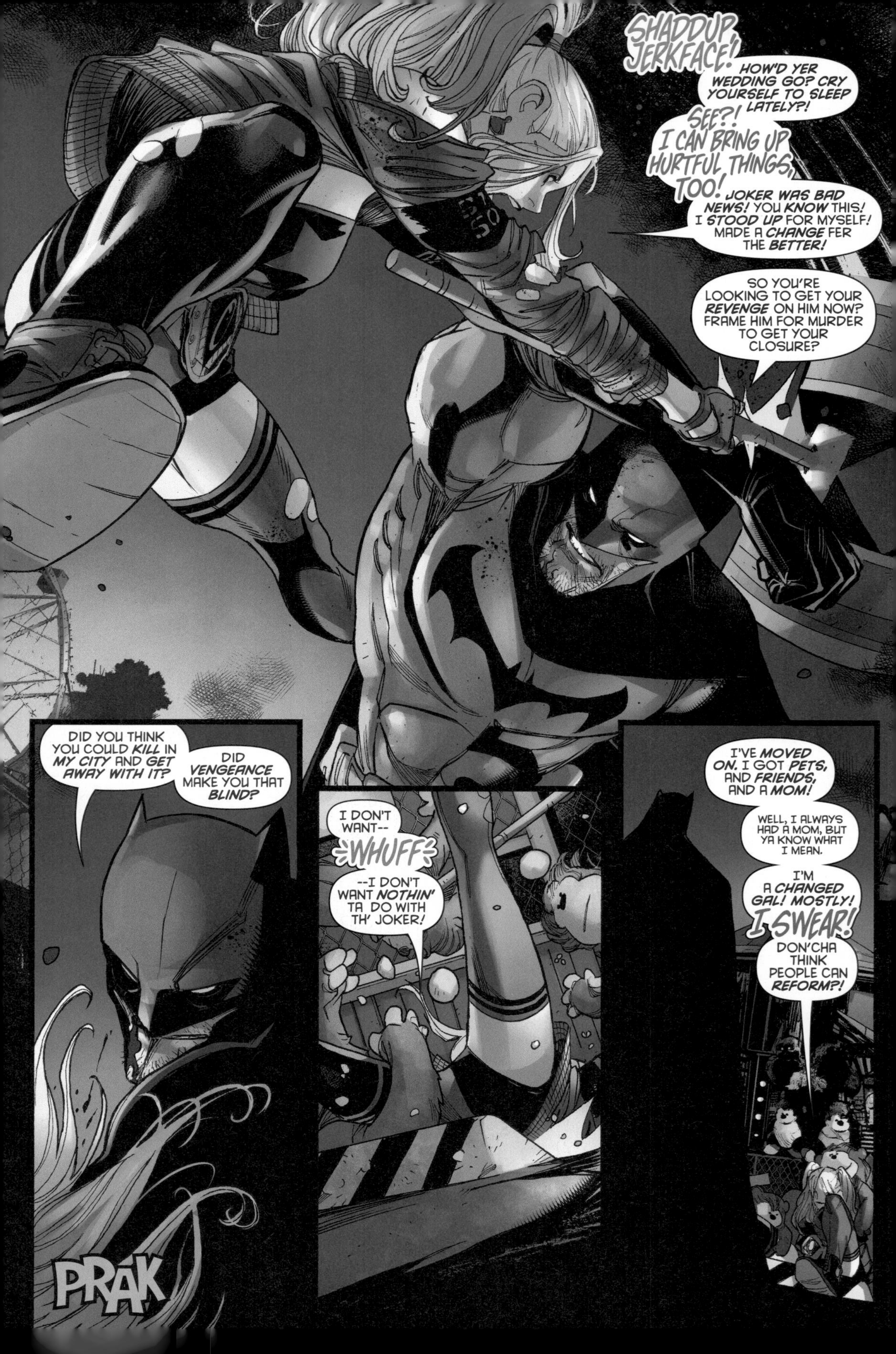
SHADDUP, JERKFACE!
HOW'D YER WEDDING GO? CRY YOURSELF TO SLEEP LATELY?!
SEE?! I CAN BRING UP HURTFUL THINGS, TOO!
JOKER WAS BAD NEWS! YOU KNOW THIS! I STOOD UP FOR MYSELF! MADE A CHANGE FER THE BETTER!
SO YOU'RE LOOKING TO GET YOUR REVENGE ON HIM NOW? FRAME HIM FOR MURDER TO GET YOUR CLOSURE?
DID YOU THINK YOU COULD KILL IN MY CITY AND GET AWAY WITH IT?
DID VENGEANCE MAKE YOU THAT BLIND?
PRAK
I DON'T WANT--
WHUFF
--I DON'T WANT NOTHIN' TA DO WITH TH' JOKER!
I'VE MOVED ON. I GOT PETS, AND FRIENDS, AND A MOM!
WELL, I ALWAYS HAD A MOM, BUT YA KNOW WHAT I MEAN.
I'M A CHANGED GAL! MOSTLY!
I SWEAR!
DON'CHA THINK PEOPLE CAN REFORM?!

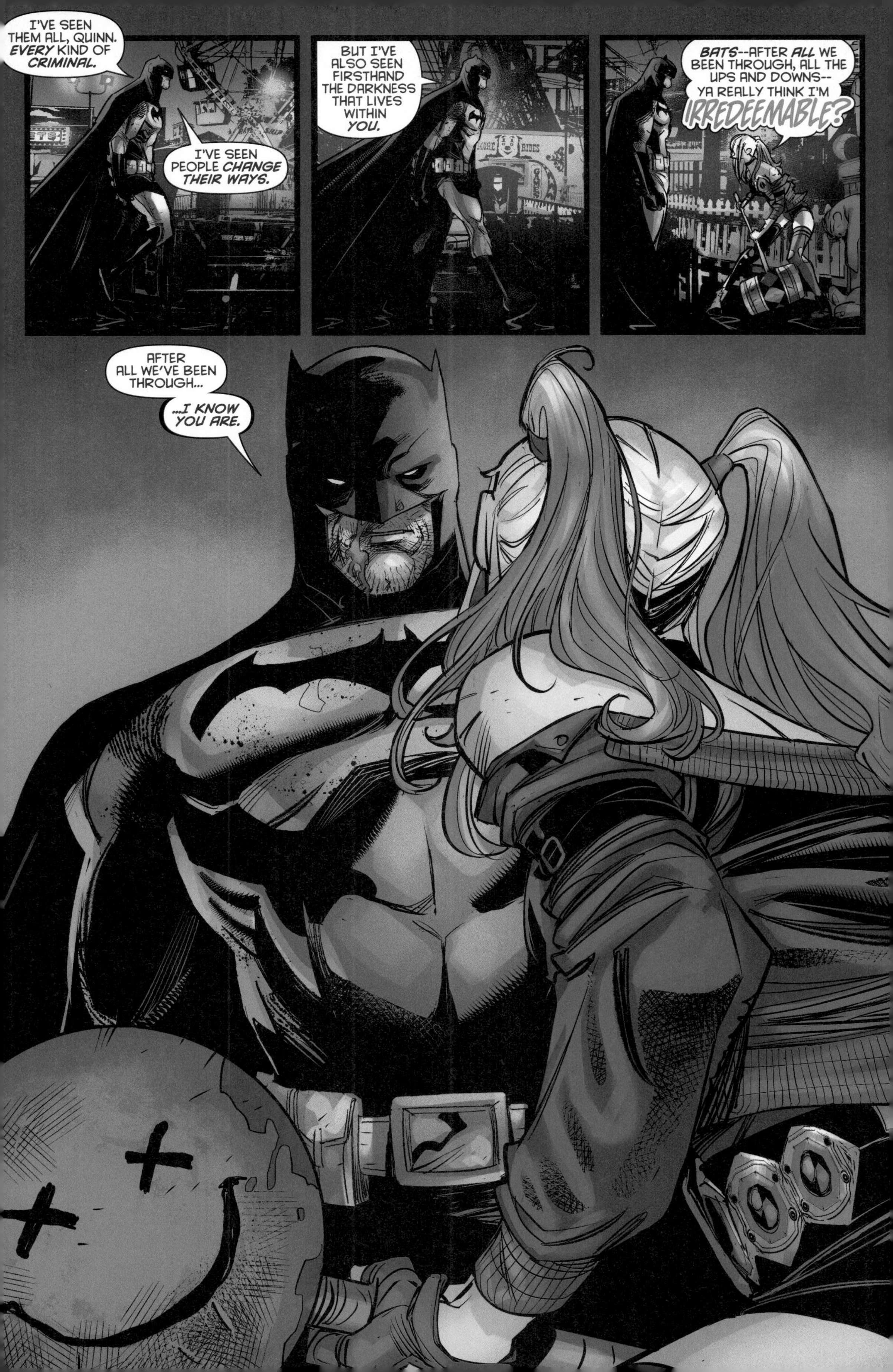
I'VE SEEN THEM ALL, QUINN. EVERY KIND OF CRIMINAL.
I'VE SEEN PEOPLE CHANGE THEIR WAYS.
BUT I'VE ALSO SEEN FIRSTHAND THE DARKNESS THAT LIVES WITHIN YOU.
BATS--AFTER ALL WE BEEN THROUGH, ALL THE UPS AND DOWNS-- YA REALLY THINK I'M IRREDEEMABLE?
AFTER ALL WE'VE BEEN THROUGH...
...I KNOW YOU ARE.

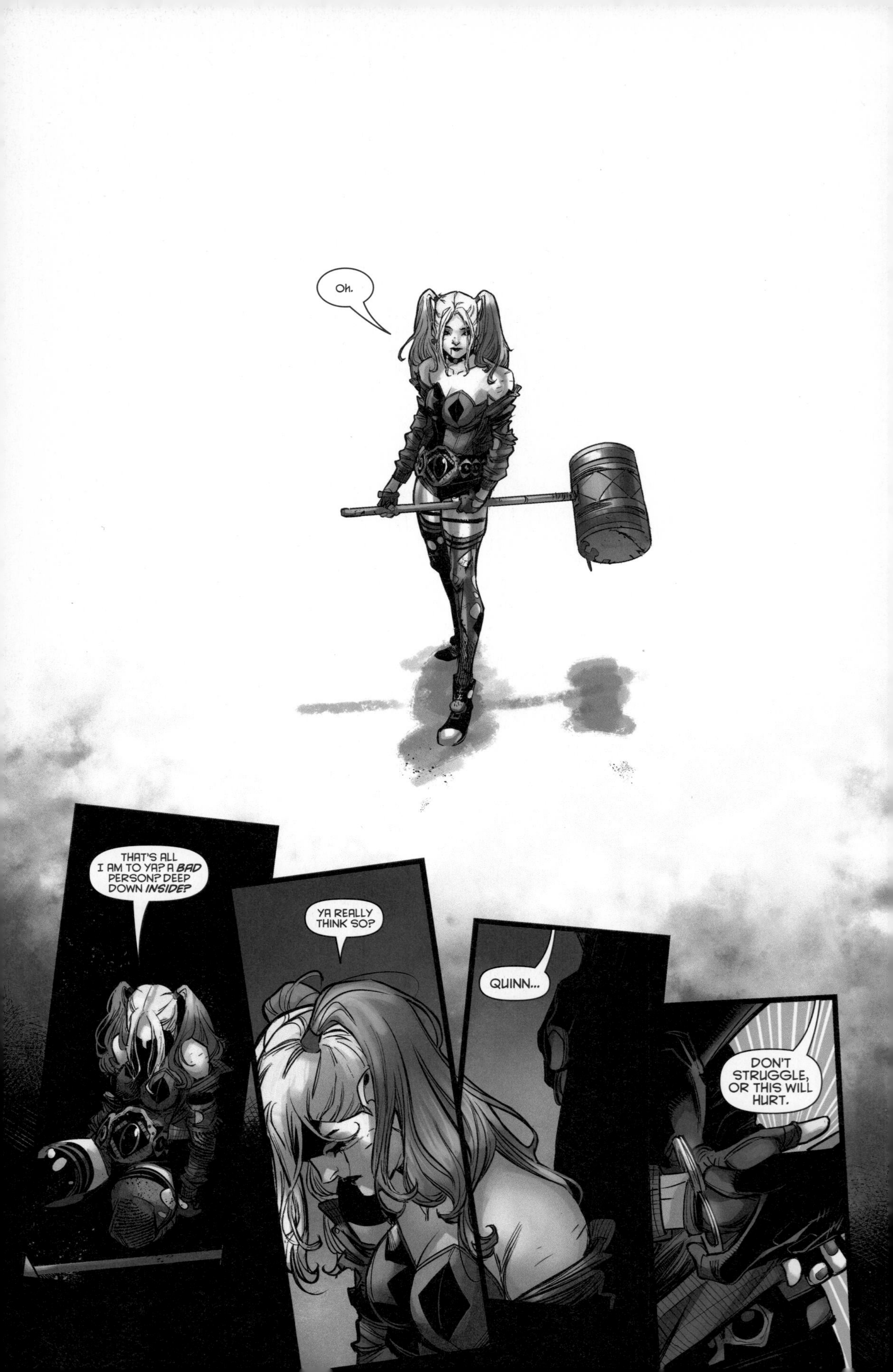
Oh.
THAT'S ALL I AM TO YA? A *BAD* PERSON? DEEP DOWN *INSIDE?*
YA REALLY THINK SO?
QUINN...
DON'T STRUGGLE, OR THIS WILL HURT.

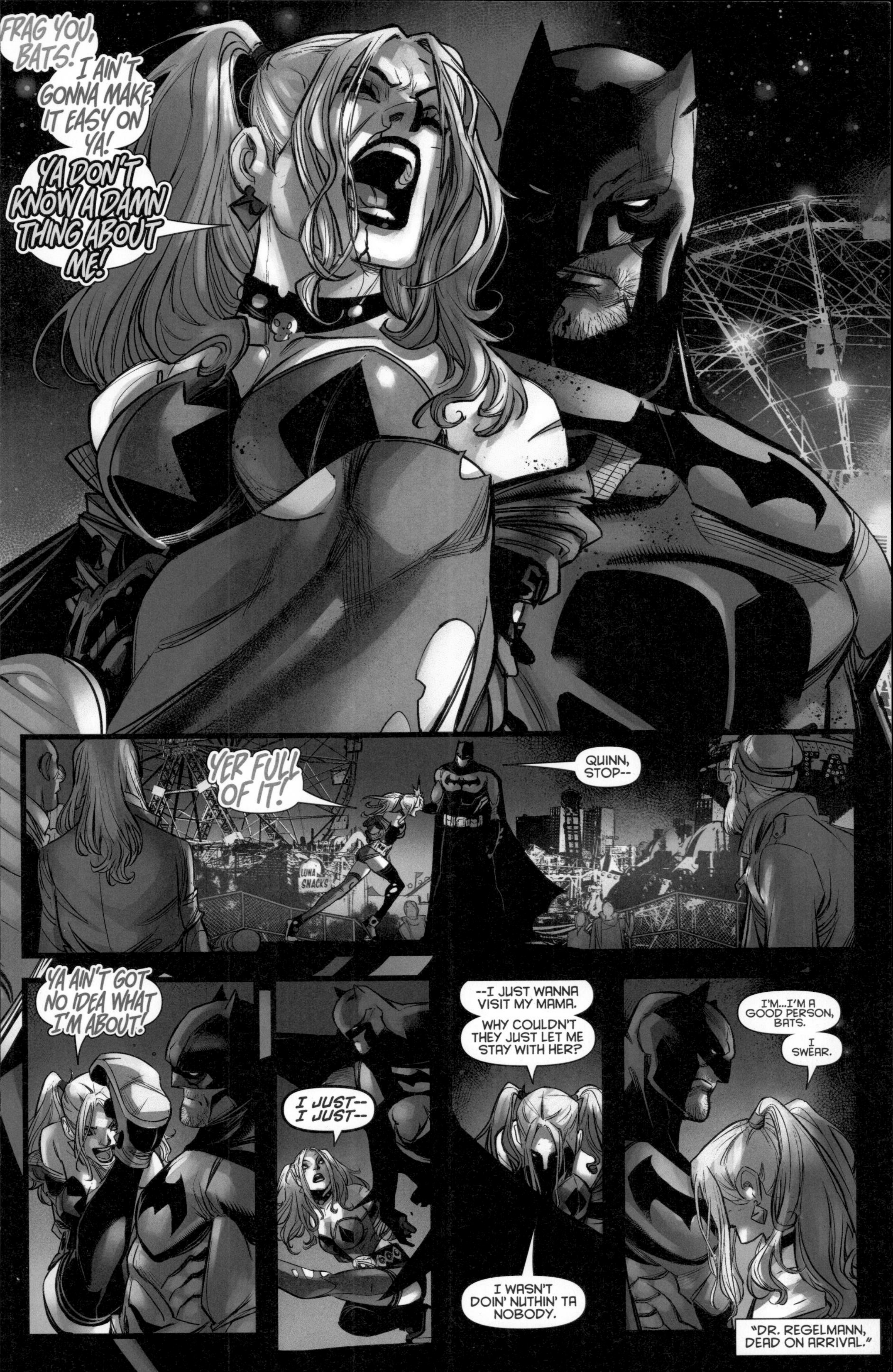
FRAG YOU, BATS!
I AIN'T GONNA MAKE IT EASY ON YA!
YA DON'T KNOW A DAMN THING ABOUT ME!
YER FULL OF IT!
QUINN, STOP--
LUNA SNACKS
YA AIN'T GOT NO IDEA WHAT I'M ABOUT!
I JUST-- I JUST--
--I JUST WANNA VISIT MY MAMA.
WHY COULDN'T THEY JUST LET ME STAY WITH HER?
I WASN'T DOIN' NUTHIN' TA NOBODY.
I'M...I'M A GOOD PERSON, BATS.
I SWEAR.
"DR. REGELMANN, DEAD ON ARRIVAL."

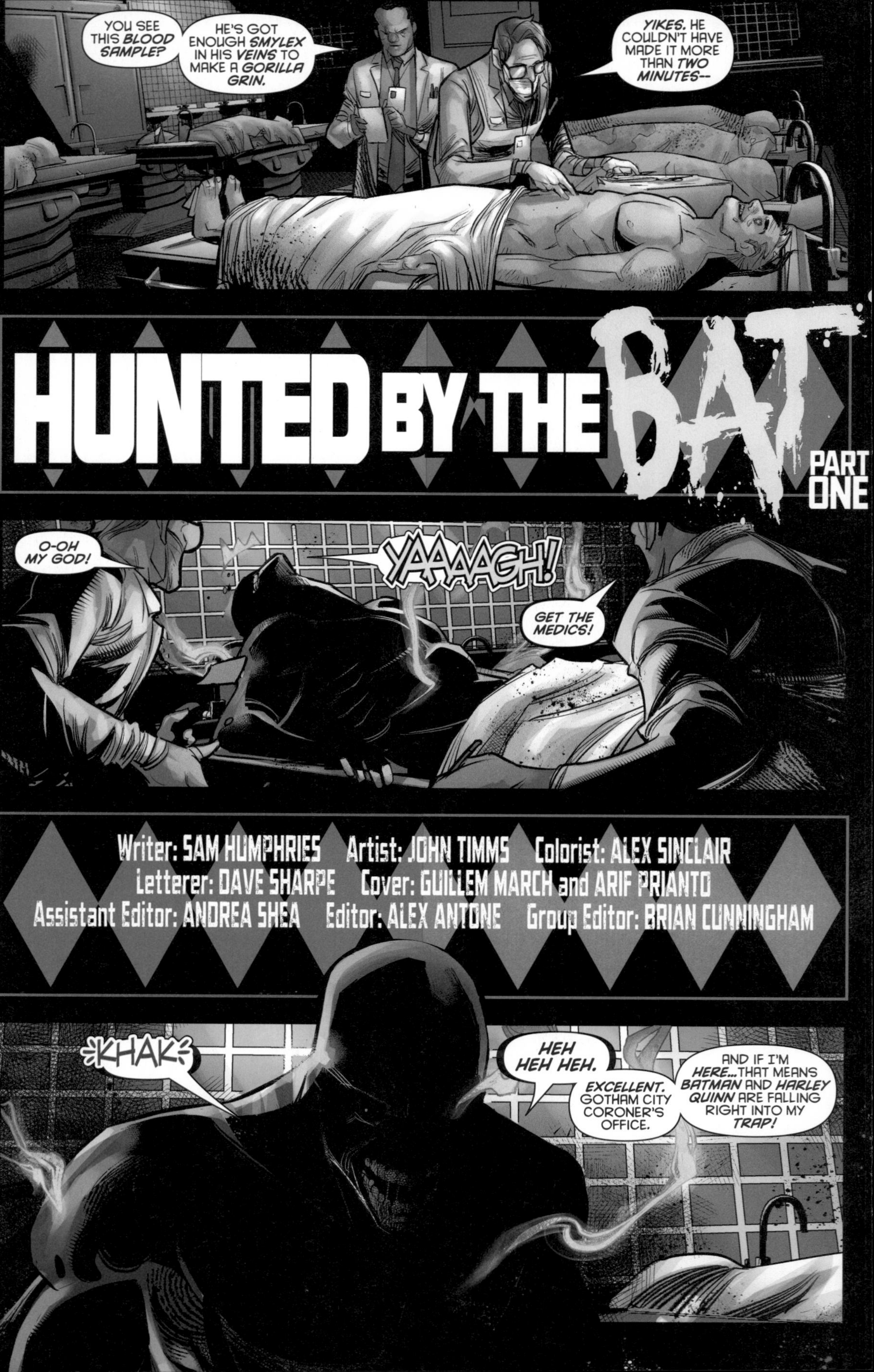
YOU SEE THIS BLOOD SAMPLE?
HE'S GOT ENOUGH SMYLEX IN HIS VEINS TO MAKE A GORILLA GRIN.
YIKES. HE COULDN'T HAVE MADE IT MORE THAN TWO MINUTES--
HUNTED BY THE BAT
PART ONE
O-OH MY GOD!
YAAAAGH!
GET THE MEDICS!
Writer: SAM HUMPHRIES Artist: JOHN TIMMS Colorist: ALEX SINCLAIR
Letterer: DAVE SHARPE Cover: GUILLEM MARCH and ARIF PRIANTO
Assistant Editor: ANDREA SHEA Editor: ALEX ANTONE Group Editor: BRIAN CUNNINGHAM
KHAK
HEH HEH HEH.
EXCELLENT. GOTHAM CITY CORONER'S OFFICE.
AND IF I'M HERE...THAT MEANS BATMAN AND HARLEY QUINN ARE FALLING RIGHT INTO MY TRAP!

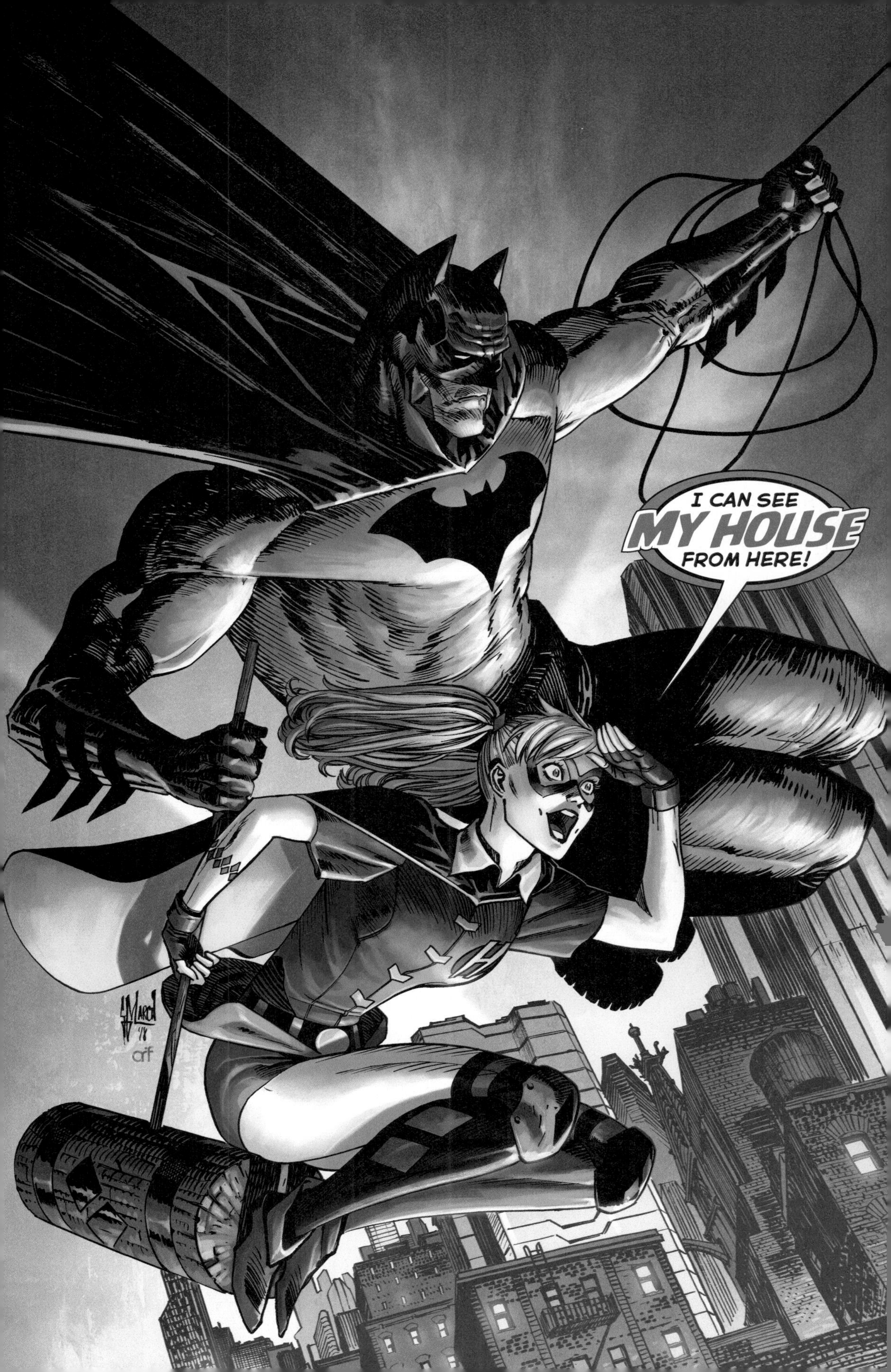
I CAN SEE MY HOUSE FROM HERE!

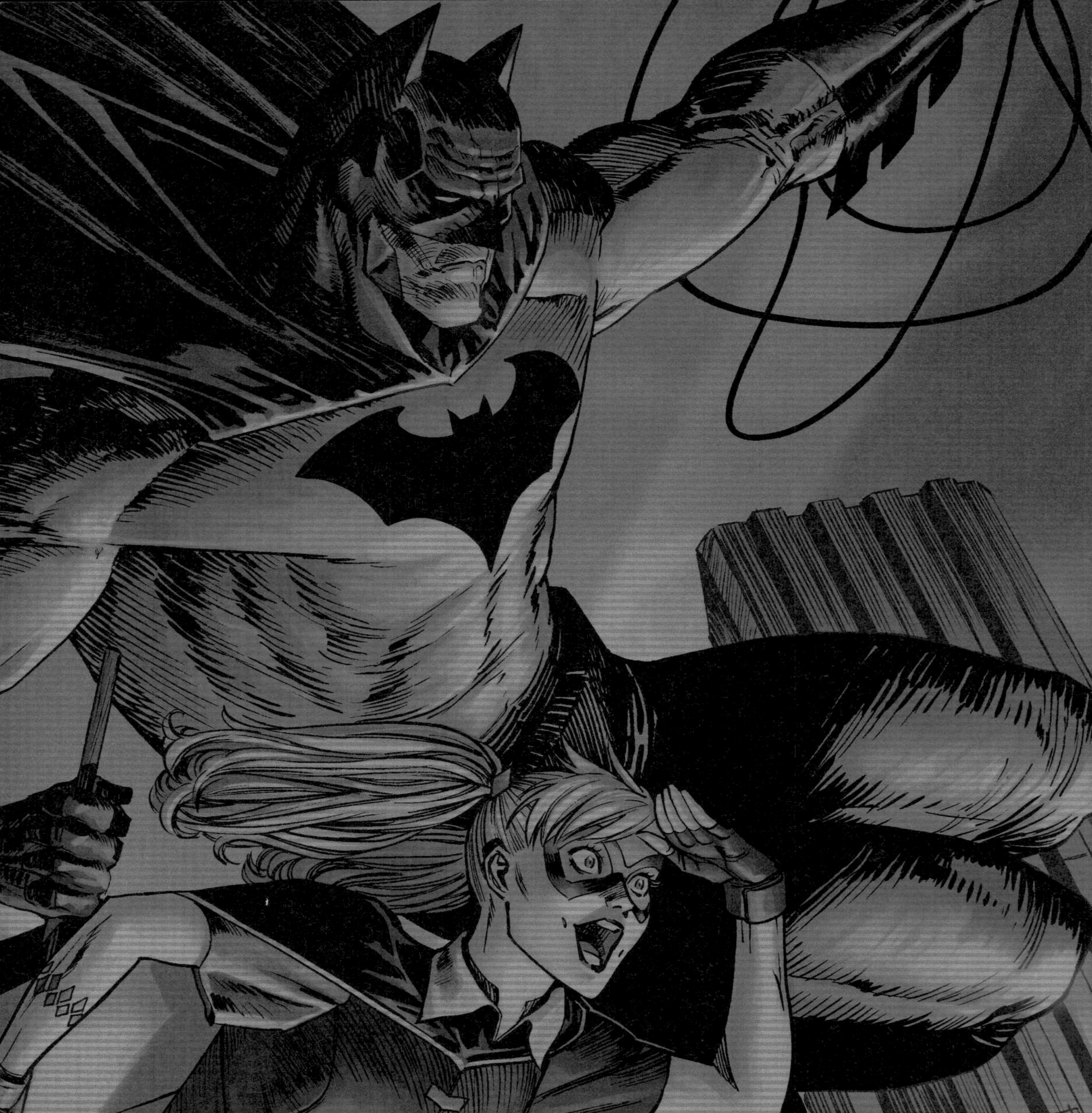

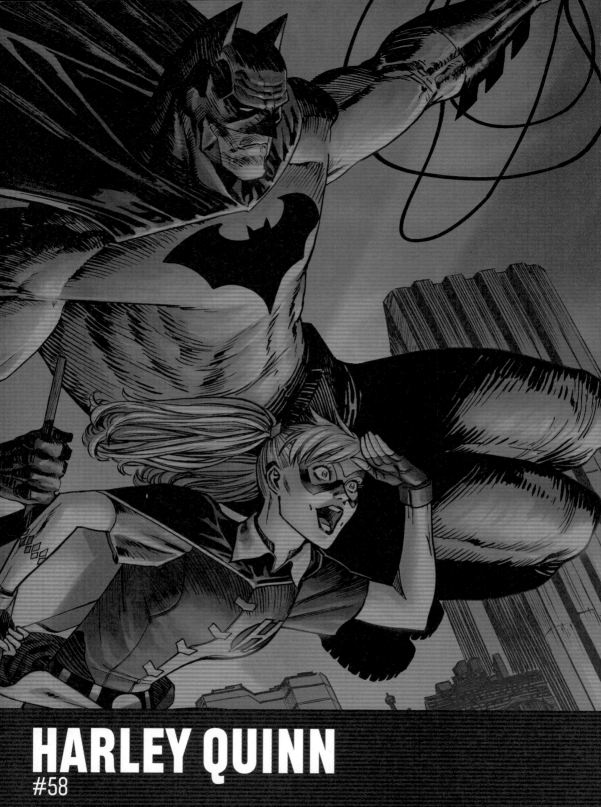

HARLEY QUINN
#58

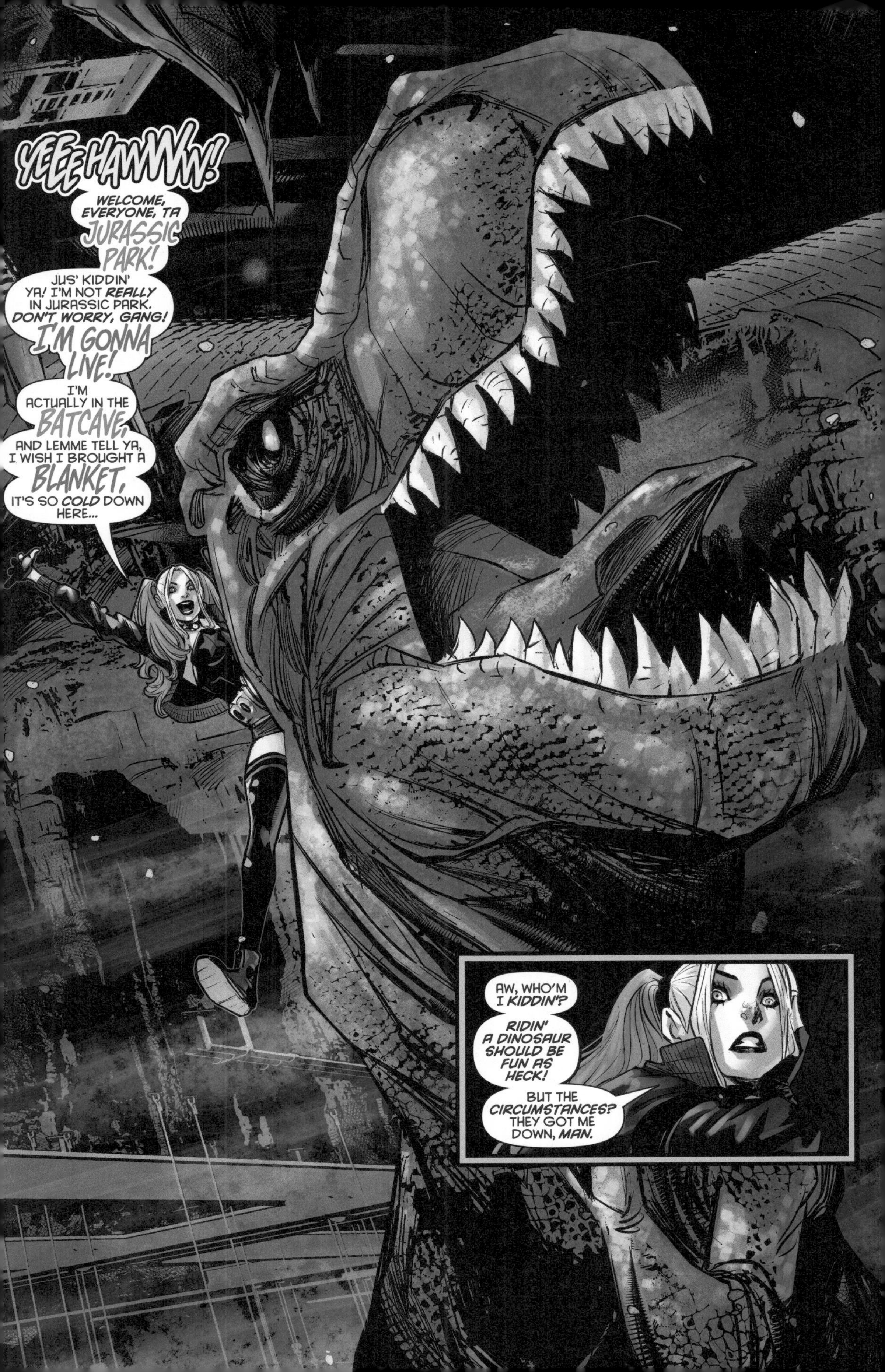
YEEEE HAWWWW!
WELCOME, EVERYONE, TA JURASSIC PARK!
JUS' KIDDIN' YA! I'M NOT REALLY IN JURASSIC PARK. DON'T WORRY, GANG! I'M GONNA LIVE!
I'M ACTUALLY IN THE BATCAVE,
AND LEMME TELL YA, I WISH I BROUGHT A BLANKET,
IT'S SO COLD DOWN HERE...
AW, WHO'M I KIDDIN'?
RIDIN' A DINOSAUR SHOULD BE FUN AS HECK!
BUT THE CIRCUMSTANCES? THEY GOT ME DOWN, MAN.

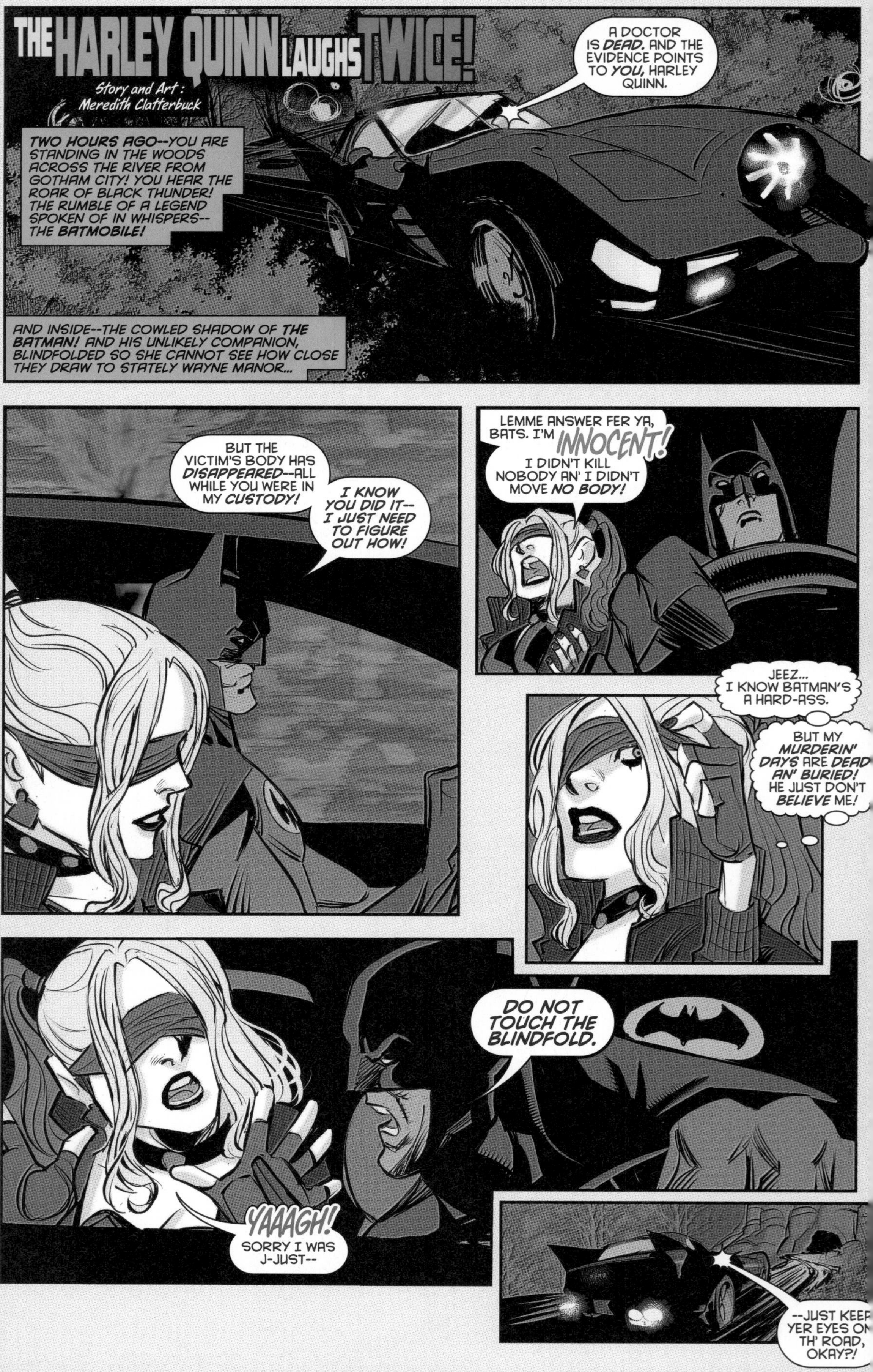
THE HARLEY QUINN LAUGHS TWICE!
Story and Art : Meredith Clatterbuck
TWO HOURS AGO--YOU ARE STANDING IN THE WOODS ACROSS THE RIVER FROM GOTHAM CITY! YOU HEAR THE ROAR OF BLACK THUNDER! THE RUMBLE OF A LEGEND SPOKEN OF IN WHISPERS-- THE BATMOBILE!
A DOCTOR IS DEAD. AND THE EVIDENCE POINTS TO YOU, HARLEY QUINN.
AND INSIDE--THE COWLED SHADOW OF THE BATMAN! AND HIS UNLIKELY COMPANION, BLINDFOLDED SO SHE CANNOT SEE HOW CLOSE THEY DRAW TO STATELY WAYNE MANOR...
BUT THE VICTIM'S BODY HAS DISAPPEARED--ALL WHILE YOU WERE IN MY CUSTODY!
I KNOW YOU DID IT-- I JUST NEED TO FIGURE OUT HOW!
LEMME ANSWER FER YA, BATS. I'M INNOCENT!
I DIDN'T KILL NOBODY AN' I DIDN'T MOVE NO BODY!
JEEZ... I KNOW BATMAN'S A HARD-ASS.
BUT MY MURDERIN' DAYS ARE DEAD AN' BURIED! HE JUST DON'T BELIEVE ME!
DO NOT TOUCH THE BLINDFOLD.
YAAAGH!
SORRY I WAS J-JUST--
--JUST KEEP YER EYES ON TH' ROAD, OKAY?!

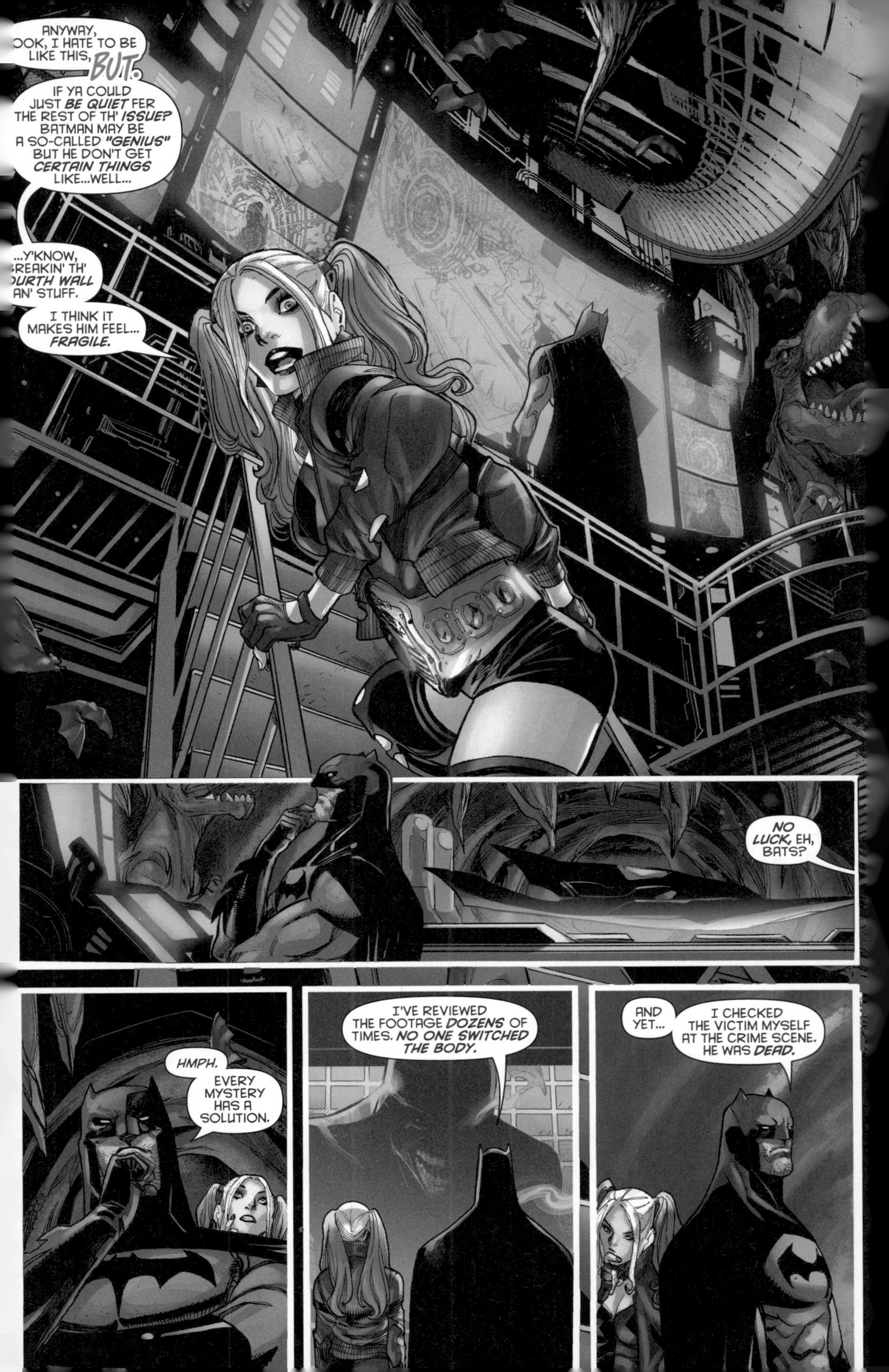
ANYWAY, OOK, I HATE TO BE LIKE THIS, BUT.
IF YA COULD JUST BE QUIET FER THE REST OF TH' ISSUE? BATMAN MAY BE A SO-CALLED "GENIUS" BUT HE DON'T GET CERTAIN THINGS LIKE...WELL...
...Y'KNOW, REAKIN' TH' OURTH WALL AN' STUFF.
I THINK IT MAKES HIM FEEL... FRAGILE.
NO LUCK, EH, BATS?
HMPH.
EVERY MYSTERY HAS A SOLUTION.
I'VE REVIEWED THE FOOTAGE DOZENS OF TIMES. NO ONE SWITCHED THE BODY.
AND YET...
I CHECKED THE VICTIM MYSELF AT THE CRIME SCENE. HE WAS DEAD.

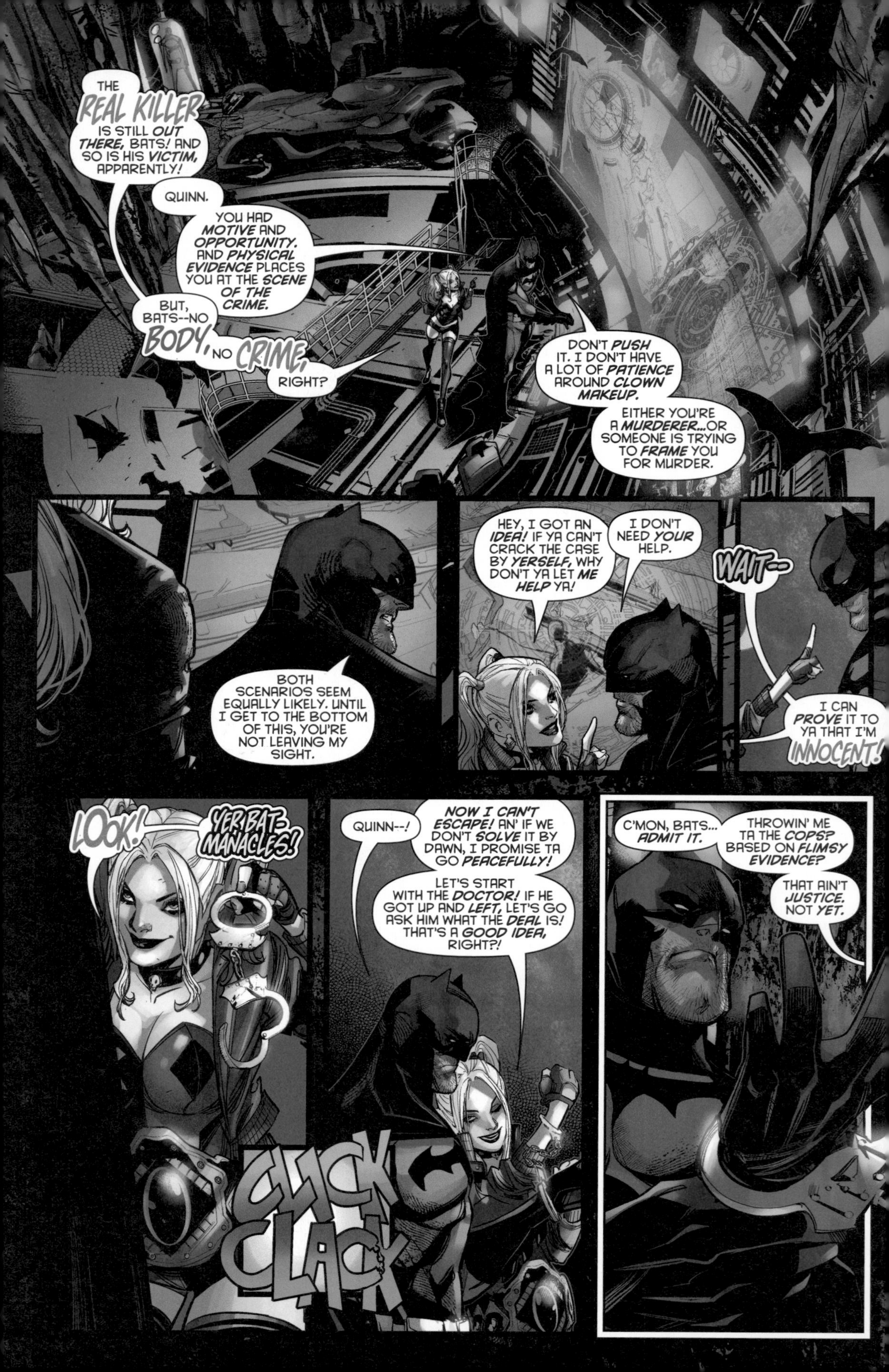
THE REAL KILLER IS STILL OUT THERE, BATS! AND SO IS HIS VICTIM, APPARENTLY!
QUINN.
YOU HAD MOTIVE AND OPPORTUNITY. AND PHYSICAL EVIDENCE PLACES YOU AT THE SCENE OF THE CRIME.
BUT, BATS--NO BODY, NO CRIME, RIGHT?
DON'T PUSH IT. I DON'T HAVE A LOT OF PATIENCE AROUND CLOWN MAKEUP.
EITHER YOU'RE A MURDERER...OR SOMEONE IS TRYING TO FRAME YOU FOR MURDER.
BOTH SCENARIOS SEEM EQUALLY LIKELY. UNTIL I GET TO THE BOTTOM OF THIS, YOU'RE NOT LEAVING MY SIGHT.
HEY, I GOT AN IDEA! IF YA CAN'T CRACK THE CASE BY YERSELF, WHY DON'T YA LET ME HELP YA!
I DON'T NEED YOUR HELP.
WAIT--
I CAN PROVE IT TO YA THAT I'M INNOCENT!
LOOK!
YER BAT-MANACLES!
CLICK
CLACK
QUINN--!
NOW I CAN'T ESCAPE! AN' IF WE DON'T SOLVE IT BY DAWN, I PROMISE TA GO PEACEFULLY!
LET'S START WITH THE DOCTOR! IF HE GOT UP AND LEFT, LET'S GO ASK HIM WHAT THE DEAL IS! THAT'S A GOOD IDEA, RIGHT?!
C'MON, BATS... ADMIT IT.
THROWIN' ME TA THE COPS? BASED ON FLIMSY EVIDENCE?
THAT AIN'T JUSTICE. NOT YET.

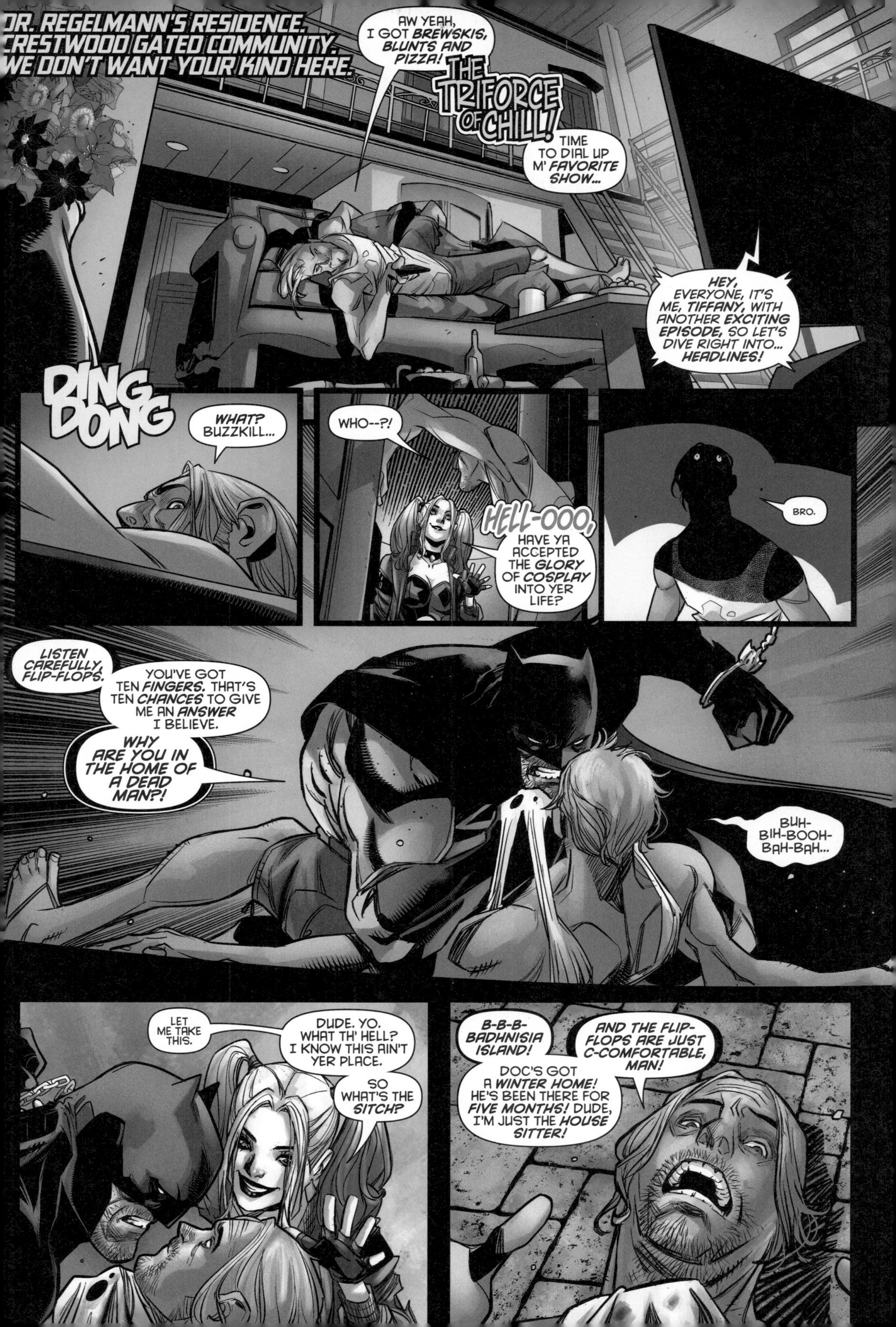
DR. REGELMANN'S RESIDENCE. CRESTWOOD GATED COMMUNITY. WE DON'T WANT YOUR KIND HERE.
AW YEAH, I GOT BREWSKIS, BLUNTS AND PIZZA!
THE TRIFORCE OF CHILL!
TIME TO DIAL UP M' FAVORITE SHOW...
HEY, EVERYONE, IT'S ME, TIFFANY, WITH ANOTHER EXCITING EPISODE, SO LET'S DIVE RIGHT INTO... HEADLINES!
DING DONG
WHAT? BUZZKILL...
WHO--?!
HELL-OOO, HAVE YA ACCEPTED THE GLORY OF COSPLAY INTO YER LIFE?
BRO.
LISTEN CAREFULLY, FLIP-FLOPS.
YOU'VE GOT TEN FINGERS. THAT'S TEN CHANCES TO GIVE ME AN ANSWER I BELIEVE.
WHY ARE YOU IN THE HOME OF A DEAD MAN?!
BUH-BIH-BOOH-BAH-BAH...
LET ME TAKE THIS.
DUDE. YO. WHAT TH' HELL? I KNOW THIS AIN'T YER PLACE.
SO WHAT'S THE SITCH?
B-B-B-BADHNISIA ISLAND!
DOC'S GOT A WINTER HOME! HE'S BEEN THERE FOR FIVE MONTHS! DUDE, I'M JUST THE HOUSE SITTER!
AND THE FLIP-FLOPS ARE JUST C-COMFORTABLE, MAN!

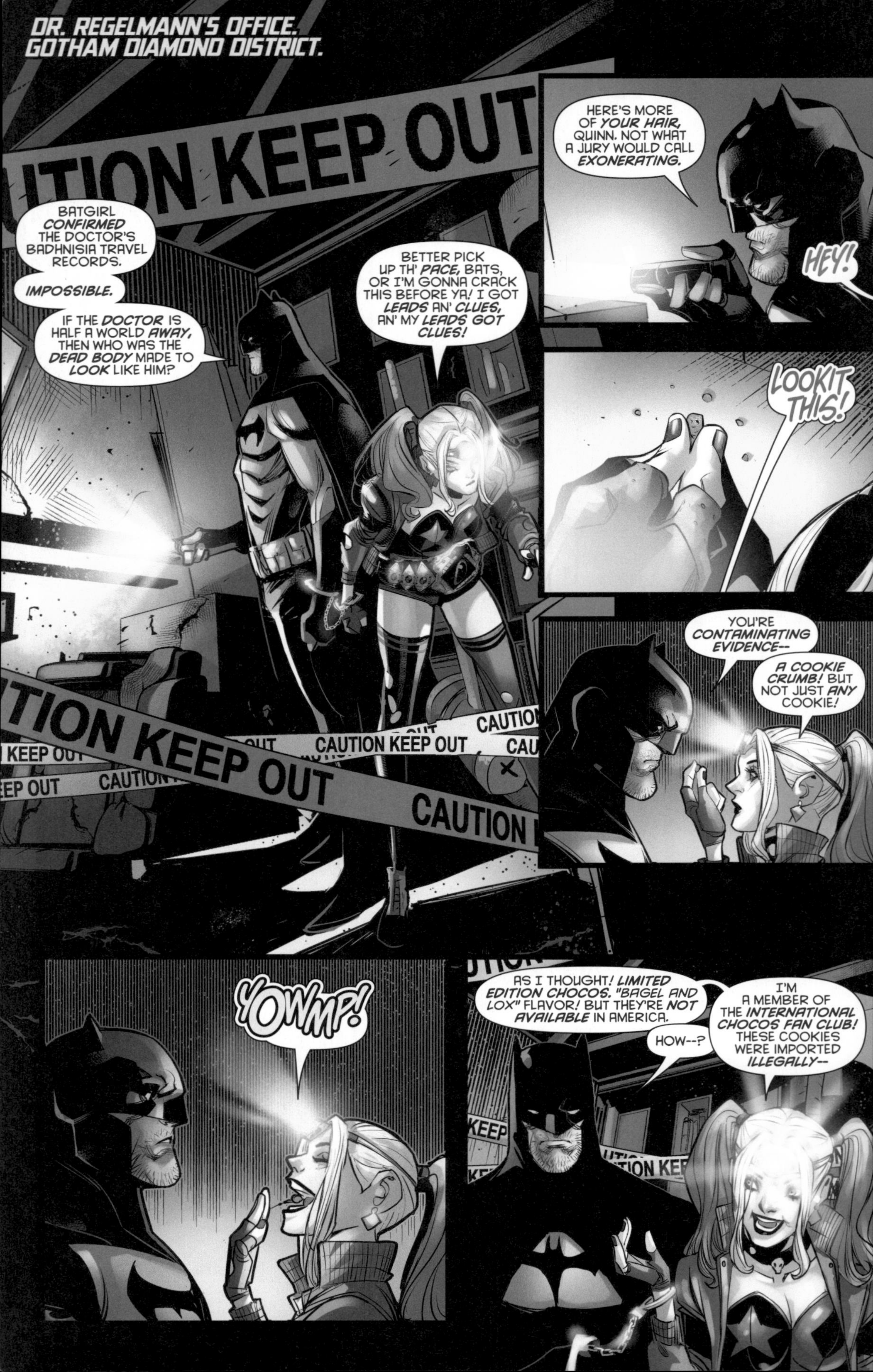
DR. REGELMANN'S OFFICE. GOTHAM DIAMOND DISTRICT.
CAUTION KEEP OUT
BATGIRL CONFIRMED THE DOCTOR'S BADHNISIA TRAVEL RECORDS.
IMPOSSIBLE.
IF THE DOCTOR IS HALF A WORLD AWAY, THEN WHO WAS THE DEAD BODY MADE TO LOOK LIKE HIM?
BETTER PICK UP TH' PACE, BATS, OR I'M GONNA CRACK THIS BEFORE YA! I GOT LEADS AN' CLUES, AN' MY LEADS GOT CLUES!
HERE'S MORE OF YOUR HAIR, QUINN. NOT WHAT A JURY WOULD CALL EXONERATING.
HEY!
LOOKIT THIS!
YOU'RE CONTAMINATING EVIDENCE--
A COOKIE CRUMB! BUT NOT JUST ANY COOKIE!
YOWMP!
AS I THOUGHT! LIMITED EDITION CHOCOS. "BAGEL AND LOX" FLAVOR! BUT THEY'RE NOT AVAILABLE IN AMERICA.
HOW--?
I'M A MEMBER OF THE INTERNATIONAL CHOCOS FAN CLUB! THESE COOKIES WERE IMPORTED ILLEGALLY--

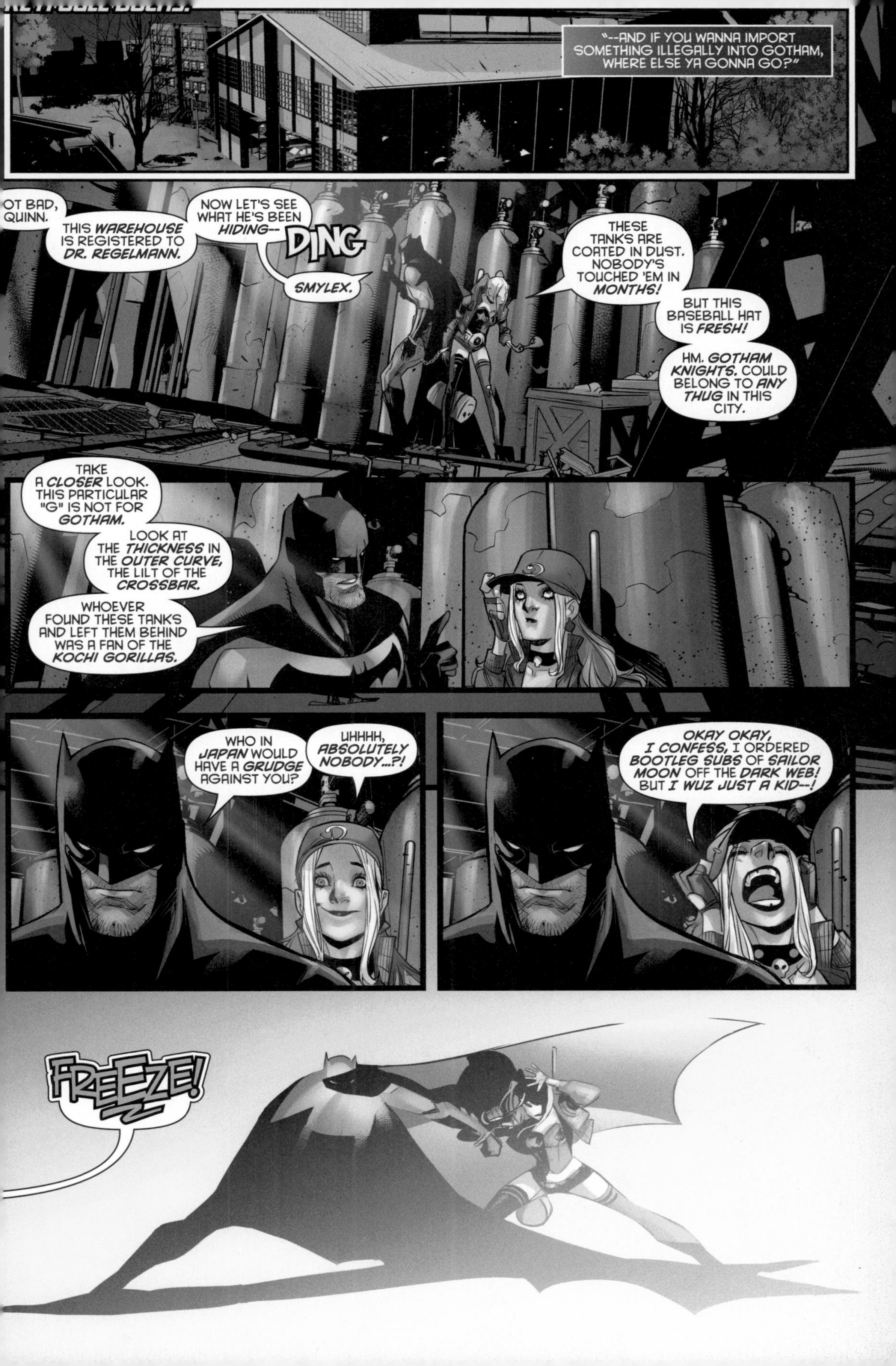
"--AND IF YOU WANNA IMPORT SOMETHING ILLEGALLY INTO GOTHAM, WHERE ELSE YA GONNA GO?"
OT BAD, QUINN.
THIS WAREHOUSE IS REGISTERED TO DR. REGELMANN.
NOW LET'S SEE WHAT HE'S BEEN HIDING--
DING
SMYLEX.
THESE TANKS ARE COATED IN DUST. NOBODY'S TOUCHED 'EM IN MONTHS!
BUT THIS BASEBALL HAT IS FRESH!
HM. GOTHAM KNIGHTS. COULD BELONG TO ANY THUG IN THIS CITY.
TAKE A CLOSER LOOK. THIS PARTICULAR "G" IS NOT FOR GOTHAM.
LOOK AT THE THICKNESS IN THE OUTER CURVE, THE LILT OF THE CROSSBAR.
WHOEVER FOUND THESE TANKS AND LEFT THEM BEHIND WAS A FAN OF THE KOCHI GORILLAS.
WHO IN JAPAN WOULD HAVE A GRUDGE AGAINST YOU?
UHHHH, ABSOLUTELY NOBODY...?!
OKAY OKAY, I CONFESS, I ORDERED BOOTLEG SUBS OF SAILOR MOON OFF THE DARK WEB! BUT I WUZ JUST A KID--!
FREEZE!

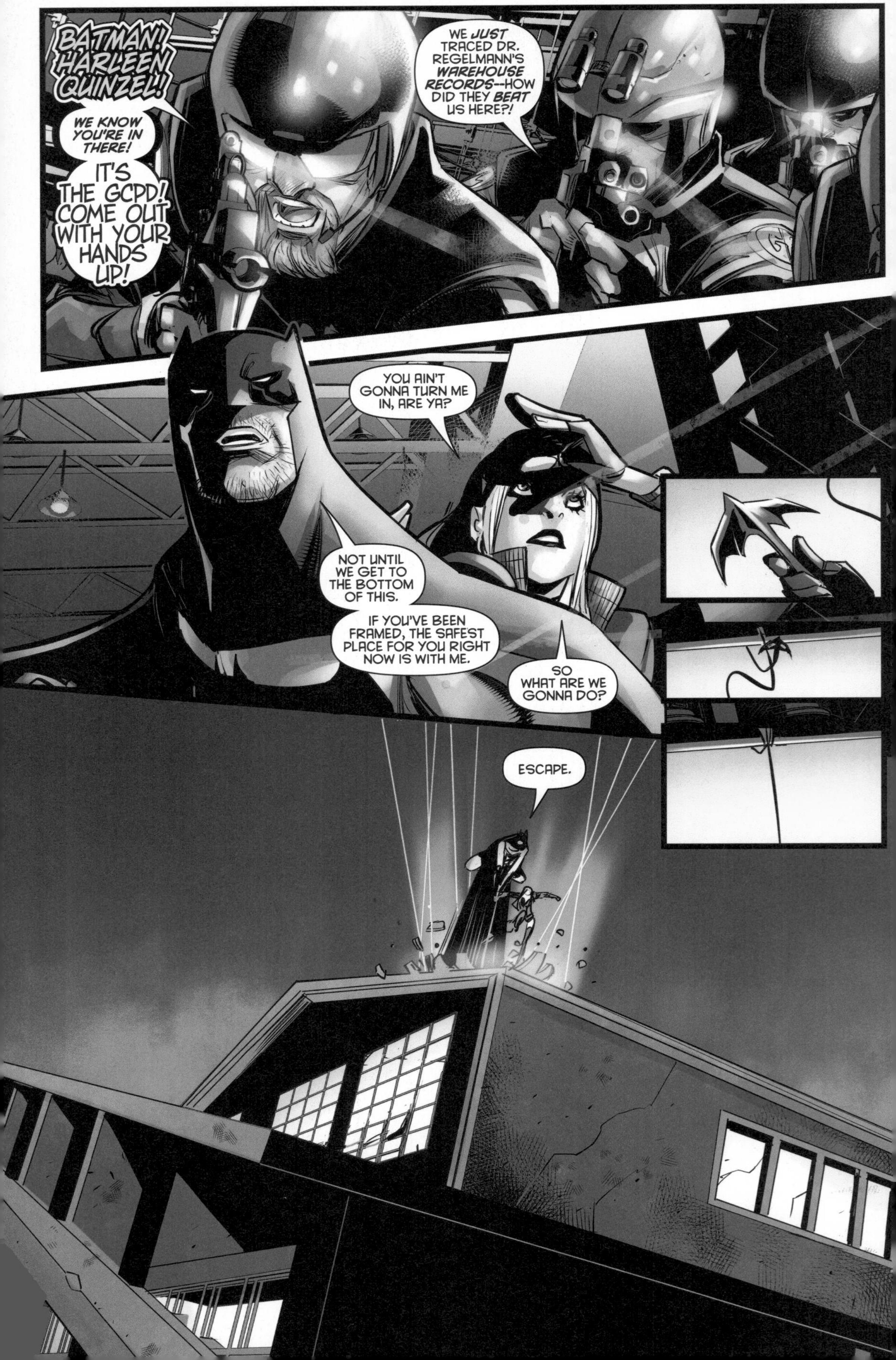
BATMAN! HARLEEN QUINZEL!
WE KNOW YOU'RE IN THERE!
IT'S THE GCPD! COME OUT WITH YOUR HANDS UP!
WE JUST TRACED DR. REGELMANN'S WAREHOUSE RECORDS--HOW DID THEY BEAT US HERE?!
YOU AIN'T GONNA TURN ME IN, ARE YA?
NOT UNTIL WE GET TO THE BOTTOM OF THIS.
IF YOU'VE BEEN FRAMED, THE SAFEST PLACE FOR YOU RIGHT NOW IS WITH ME.
SO WHAT ARE WE GONNA DO?
ESCAPE.

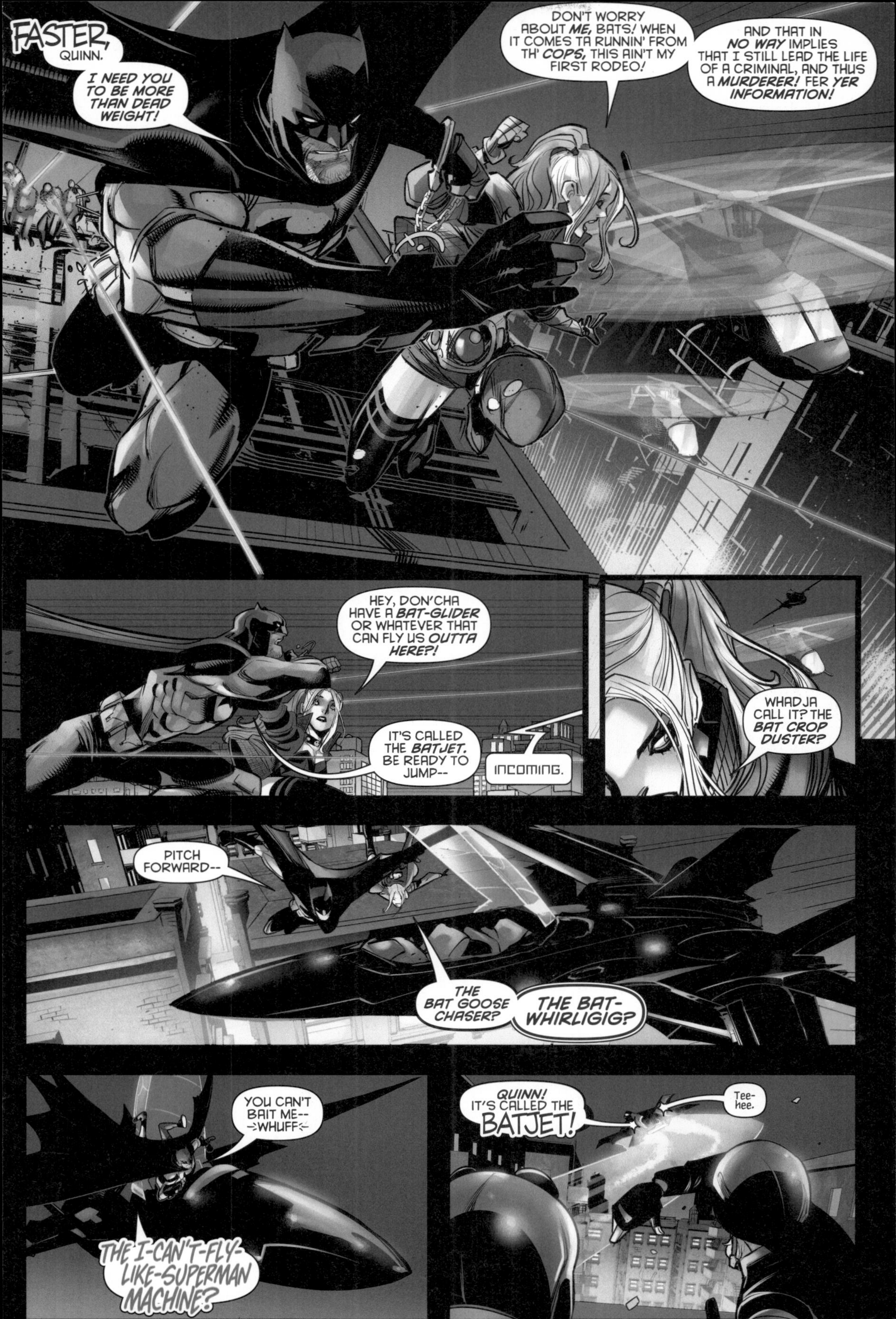
FASTER, QUINN.
I NEED YOU TO BE MORE THAN DEAD WEIGHT!
DON'T WORRY ABOUT ME, BATS! WHEN IT COMES TA RUNNIN' FROM TH' COPS, THIS AIN'T MY FIRST RODEO!
AND THAT IN NO WAY IMPLIES THAT I STILL LEAD THE LIFE OF A CRIMINAL, AND THUS A MURDERER! FER YER INFORMATION!
HEY, DON'CHA HAVE A BAT-GLIDER OR WHATEVER THAT CAN FLY US OUTTA HERE?!
IT'S CALLED THE BATJET. BE READY TO JUMP--
INCOMING.
WHADJA CALL IT? THE BAT CROP DUSTER?
PITCH FORWARD--
THE BAT GOOSE CHASER?
THE BAT-WHIRLIGIG?
YOU CAN'T BAIT ME--
-WHUFF-
THE I-CAN'T-FLY-LIKE-SUPERMAN MACHINE?
QUINN! IT'S CALLED THE BATJET!
Tee-hee.

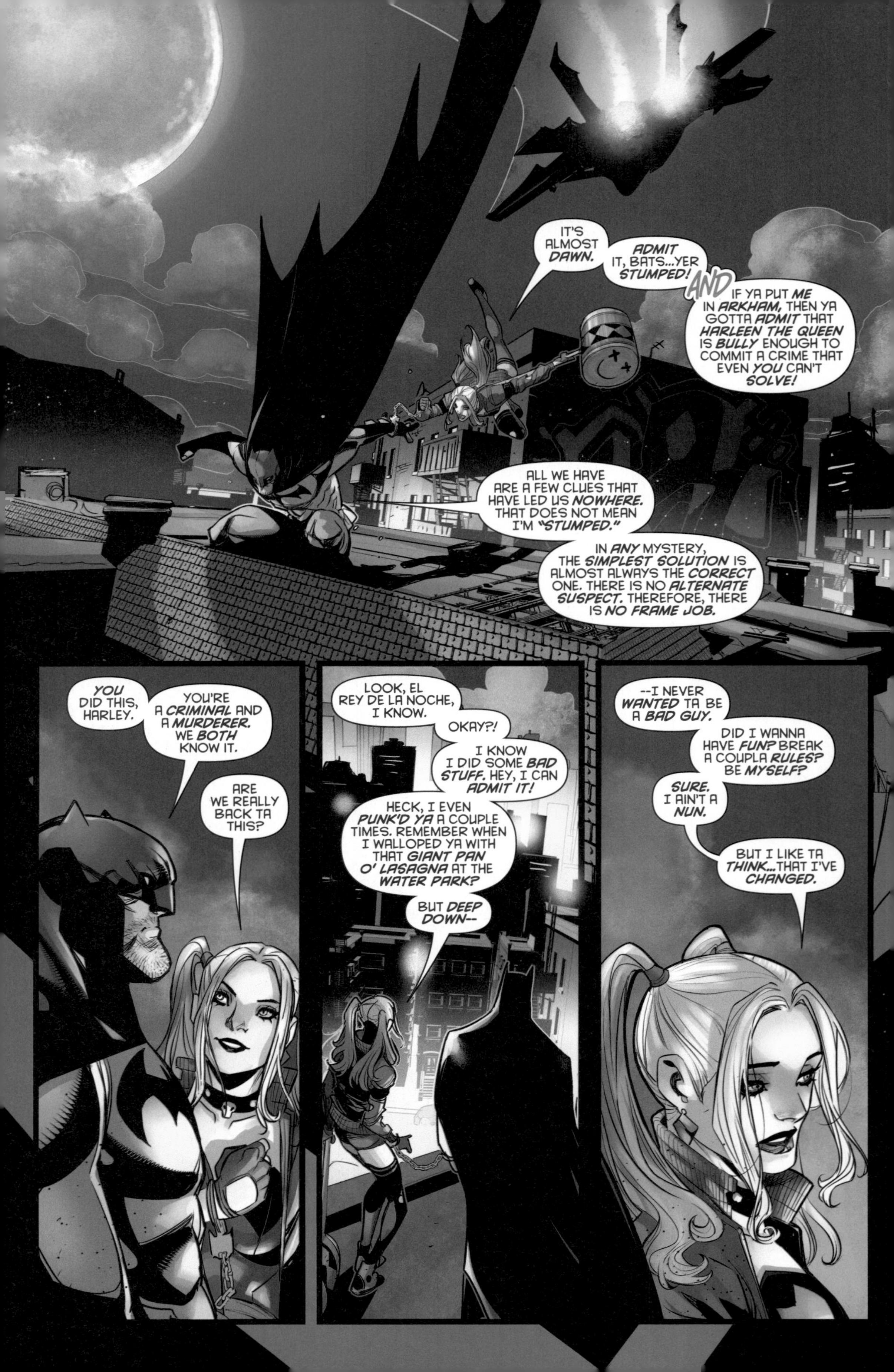
IT'S ALMOST DAWN.
ADMIT IT, BATS...YER STUMPED!
AND IF YA PUT ME IN ARKHAM, THEN YA GOTTA ADMIT THAT HARLEEN THE QUEEN IS BULLY ENOUGH TO COMMIT A CRIME THAT EVEN YOU CAN'T SOLVE!
ALL WE HAVE ARE A FEW CLUES THAT HAVE LED US NOWHERE. THAT DOES NOT MEAN I'M "STUMPED."
IN ANY MYSTERY, THE SIMPLEST SOLUTION IS ALMOST ALWAYS THE CORRECT ONE. THERE IS NO ALTERNATE SUSPECT. THEREFORE, THERE IS NO FRAME JOB.
YOU DID THIS, HARLEY.
YOU'RE A CRIMINAL AND A MURDERER. WE BOTH KNOW IT.
ARE WE REALLY BACK TA THIS?
LOOK, EL REY DE LA NOCHE, I KNOW.
OKAY?!
I KNOW I DID SOME BAD STUFF. HEY, I CAN ADMIT IT!
HECK, I EVEN PUNK'D YA A COUPLE TIMES. REMEMBER WHEN I WALLOPED YA WITH THAT GIANT PAN O' LASAGNA AT THE WATER PARK?
BUT DEEP DOWN--
--I NEVER WANTED TA BE A BAD GUY.
DID I WANNA HAVE FUN? BREAK A COUPLA RULES? BE MYSELF?
SURE. I AIN'T A NUN.
BUT I LIKE TA THINK...THAT I'VE CHANGED.

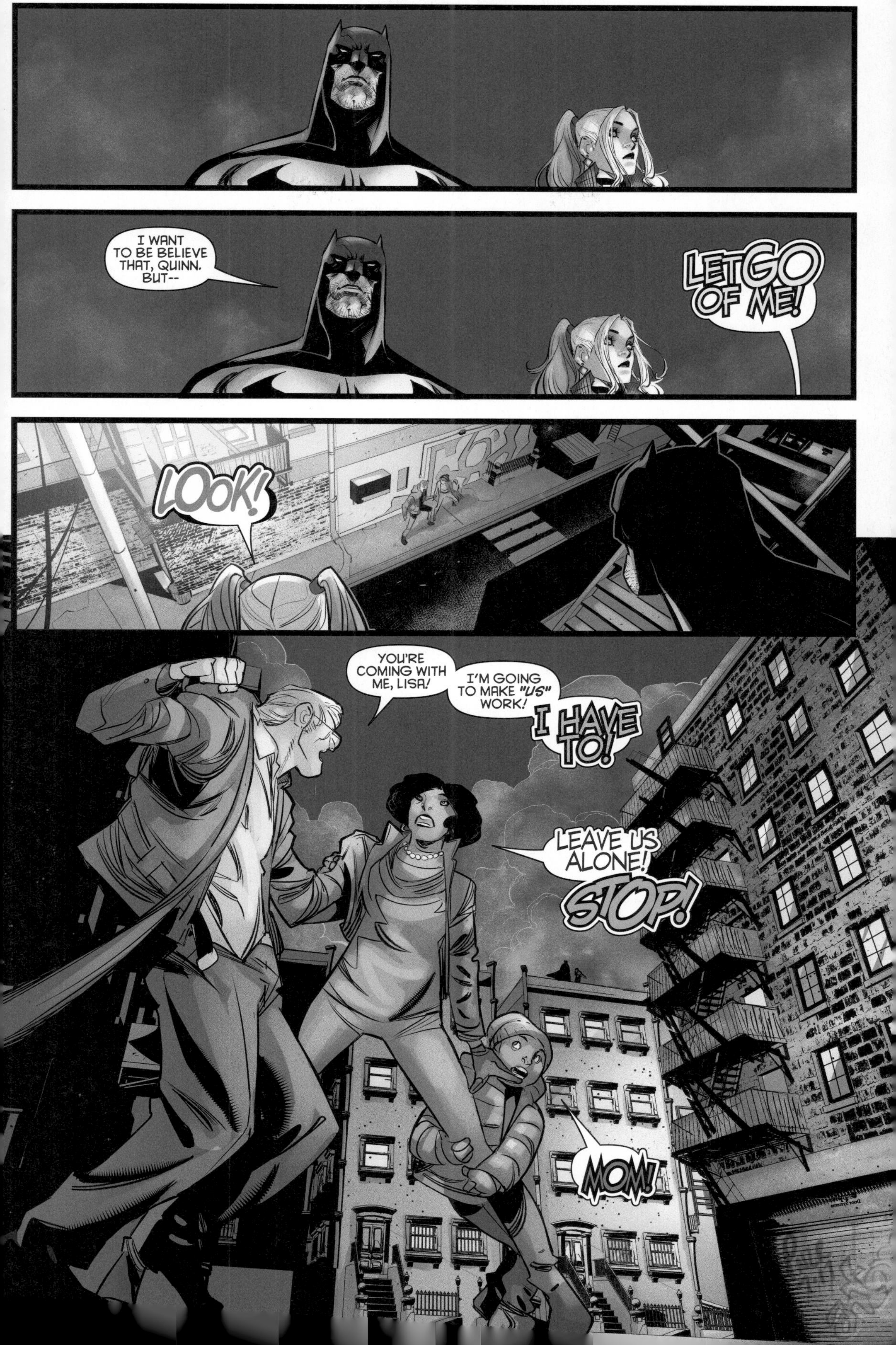
I WANT TO BE BELIEVE THAT, QUINN. BUT--
LET GO OF ME!
LOOK!
YOU'RE COMING WITH ME, LISA!
I'M GOING TO MAKE "US" WORK!
I HAVE TO!
LEAVE US ALONE!
STOP!
MOM!

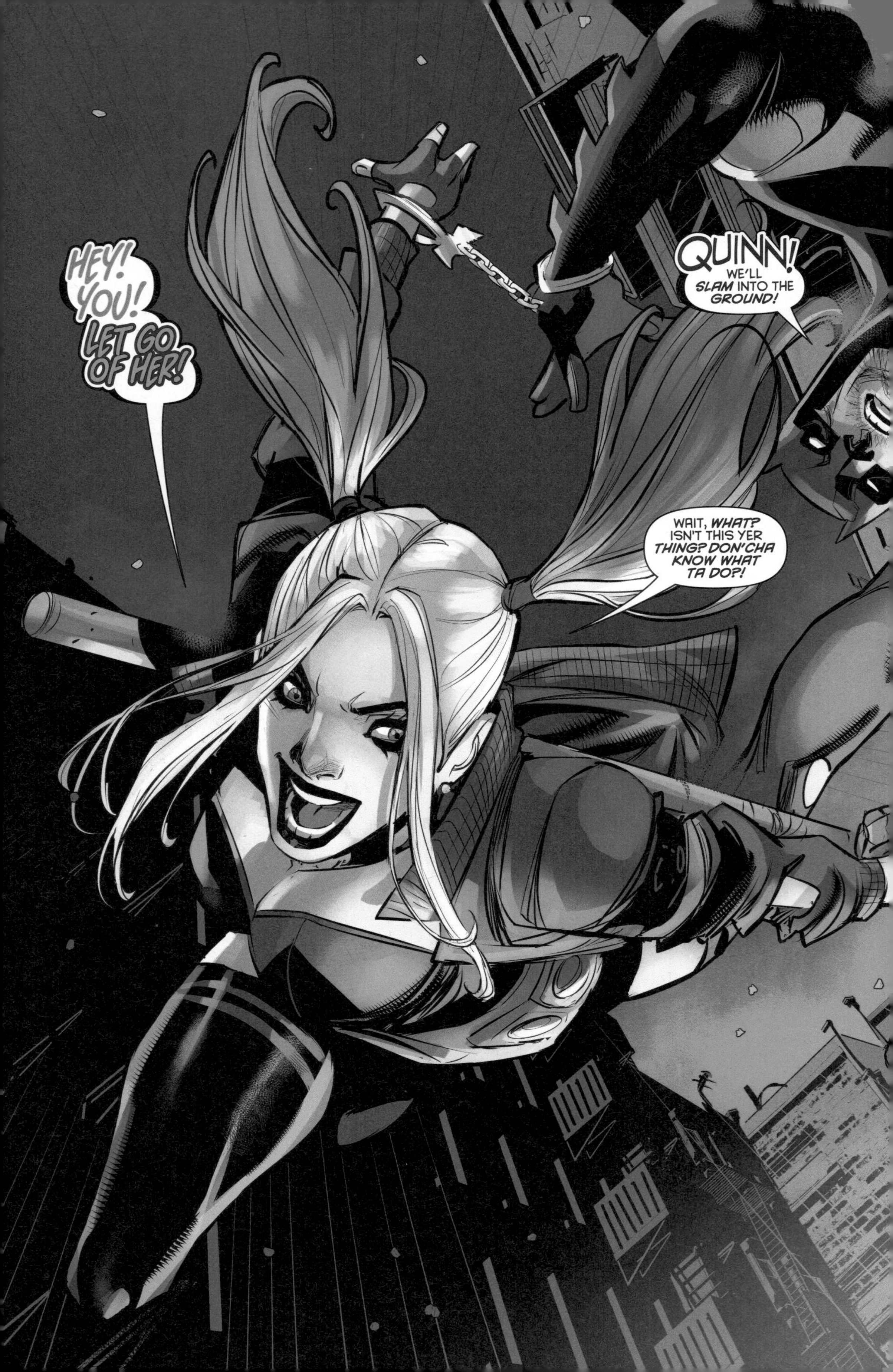
HEY! YOU! LET GO OF HER!
QUINN! WE'LL SLAM INTO THE GROUND!
WAIT, WHAT? ISN'T THIS YER THING? DON'CHA KNOW WHAT TA DO?!

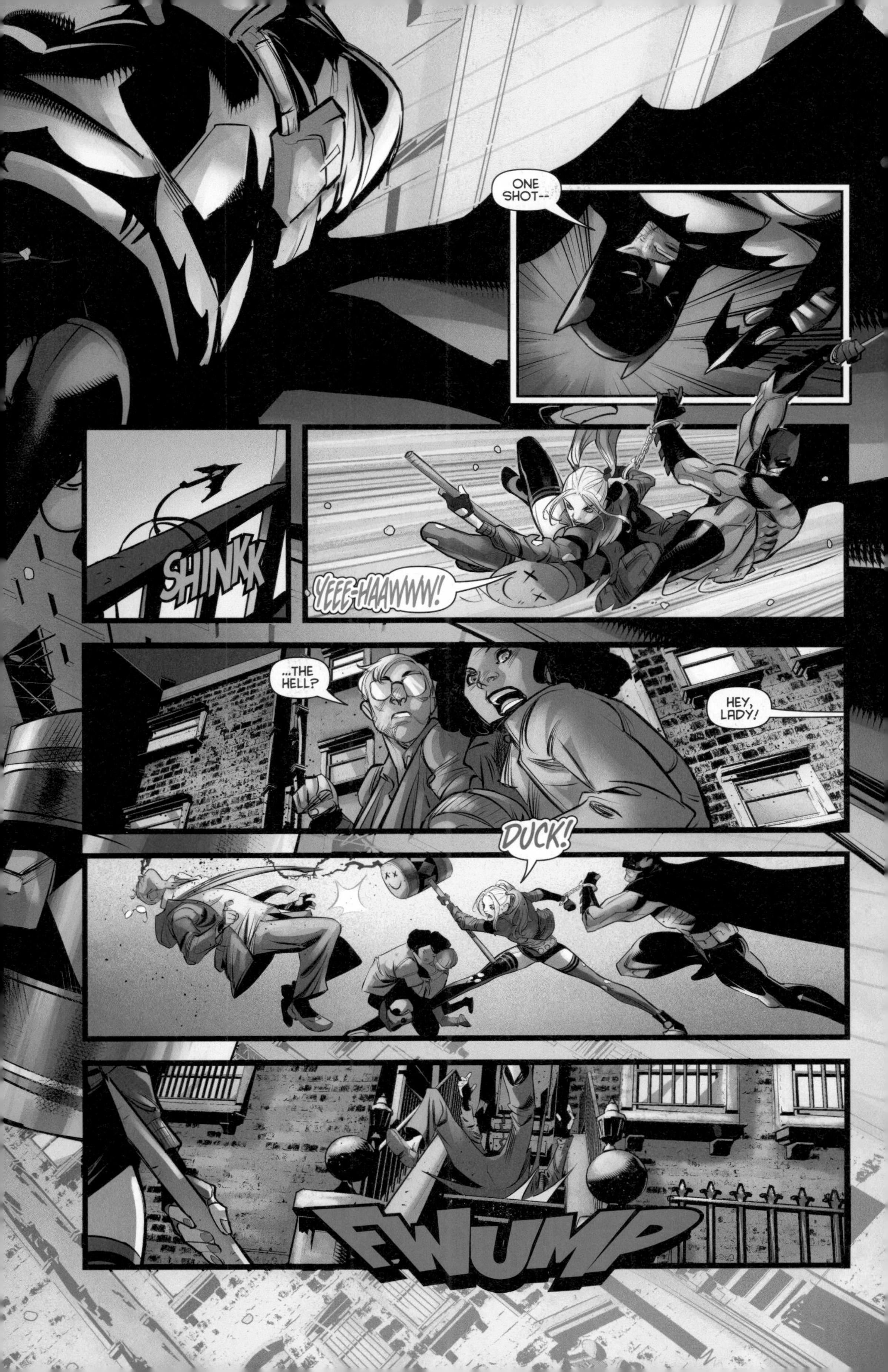

ONE SHOT--
SHINKK
YEEE-HAAWWW!
...THE HELL?
HEY, LADY!
DUCK!
FWUMP

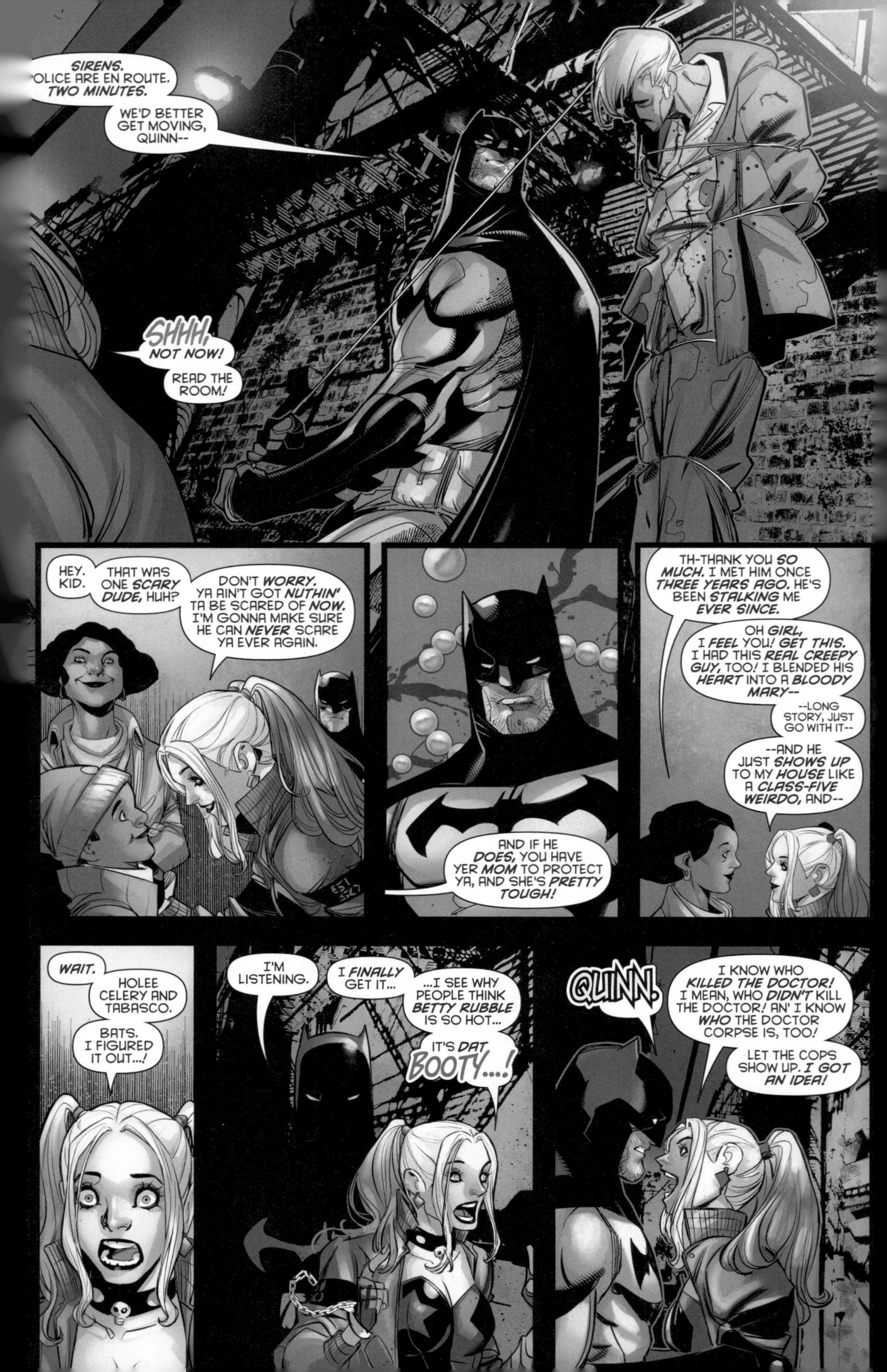
SIRENS. POLICE ARE EN ROUTE. TWO MINUTES.
WE'D BETTER GET MOVING, QUINN--
SHHH, NOT NOW!
READ THE ROOM!
HEY. KID.
THAT WAS ONE SCARY DUDE, HUH?
DON'T WORRY. YA AIN'T GOT NUTHIN' TA BE SCARED OF NOW. I'M GONNA MAKE SURE HE CAN NEVER SCARE YA EVER AGAIN.
AND IF HE DOES, YOU HAVE YER MOM TO PROTECT YA, AND SHE'S PRETTY TOUGH!
TH-THANK YOU SO MUCH. I MET HIM ONCE THREE YEARS AGO. HE'S BEEN STALKING ME EVER SINCE.
OH GIRL, I FEEL YOU! GET THIS. I HAD THIS REAL CREEPY GUY, TOO! I BLENDED HIS HEART INTO A BLOODY MARY--
--LONG STORY, JUST GO WITH IT--
--AND HE JUST SHOWS UP TO MY HOUSE LIKE A CLASS-FIVE WEIRDO, AND--
WAIT.
HOLEE CELERY AND TABASCO.
BATS. I FIGURED IT OUT...!
I'M LISTENING.
I FINALLY GET IT...
...I SEE WHY PEOPLE THINK BETTY RUBBLE IS SO HOT...
IT'S DAT BOOTY...!
QUINN.
I KNOW WHO KILLED THE DOCTOR! I MEAN, WHO DIDN'T KILL THE DOCTOR! AN' I KNOW WHO THE DOCTOR CORPSE IS, TOO!
LET THE COPS SHOW UP. I GOT AN IDEA!

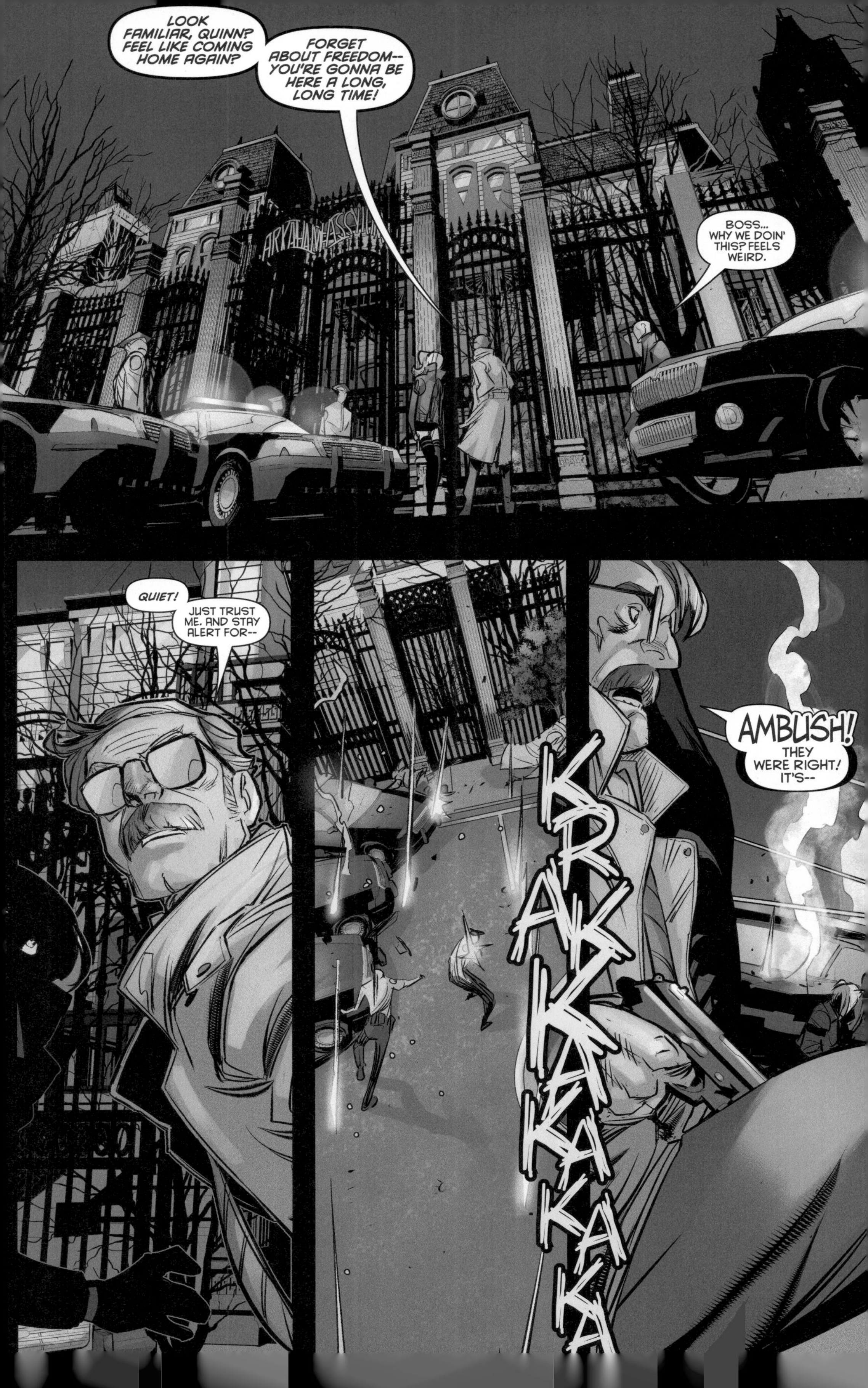
LOOK FAMILIAR, QUINN? FEEL LIKE COMING HOME AGAIN?
FORGET ABOUT FREEDOM-- YOU'RE GONNA BE HERE A LONG, LONG TIME!
ARKHAM ASYLUM
BOSS... WHY WE DOIN' THIS? FEELS WEIRD.
QUIET!
JUST TRUST ME. AND STAY ALERT FOR--
KRAKAKAKAKAKA
AMBUSH! THEY WERE RIGHT! IT'S--

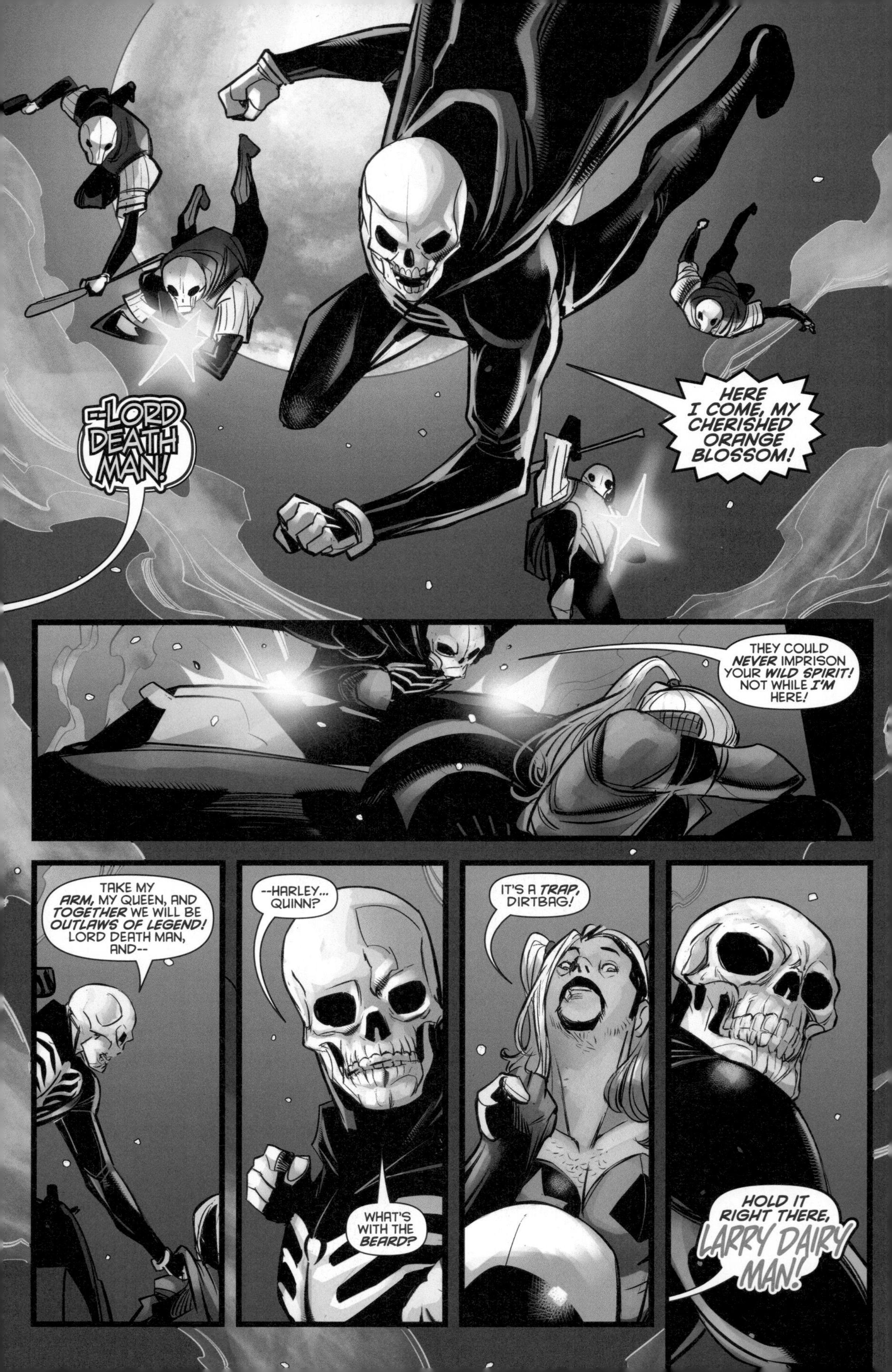
HERE I COME, MY CHERISHED ORANGE BLOSSOM!
--LORD DEATH MAN!
THEY COULD NEVER IMPRISON YOUR WILD SPIRIT! NOT WHILE I'M HERE!
TAKE MY ARM, MY QUEEN, AND TOGETHER WE WILL BE OUTLAWS OF LEGEND! LORD DEATH MAN, AND--
--HARLEY... QUINN?
WHAT'S WITH THE BEARD?
IT'S A TRAP, DIRTBAG!
HOLD IT RIGHT THERE, LARRY DAIRY MAN!

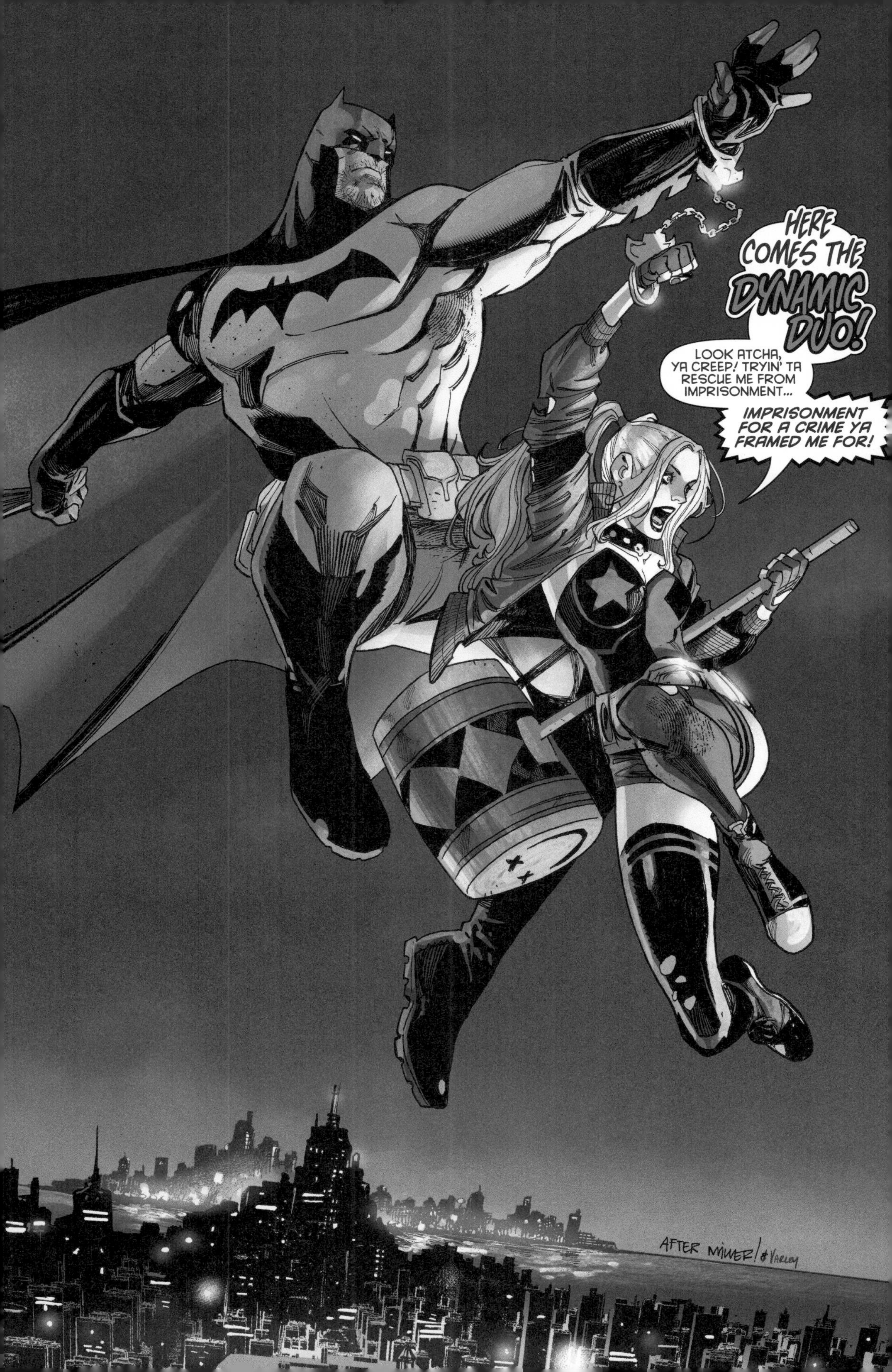
HERE COMES THE DYNAMIC DUO!
LOOK ATCHA, YA CREEP! TRYIN' TA RESCUE ME FROM IMPRISONMENT...
IMPRISONMENT FOR A CRIME YA FRAMED ME FOR!
AFTER MILLER! & VARLEY

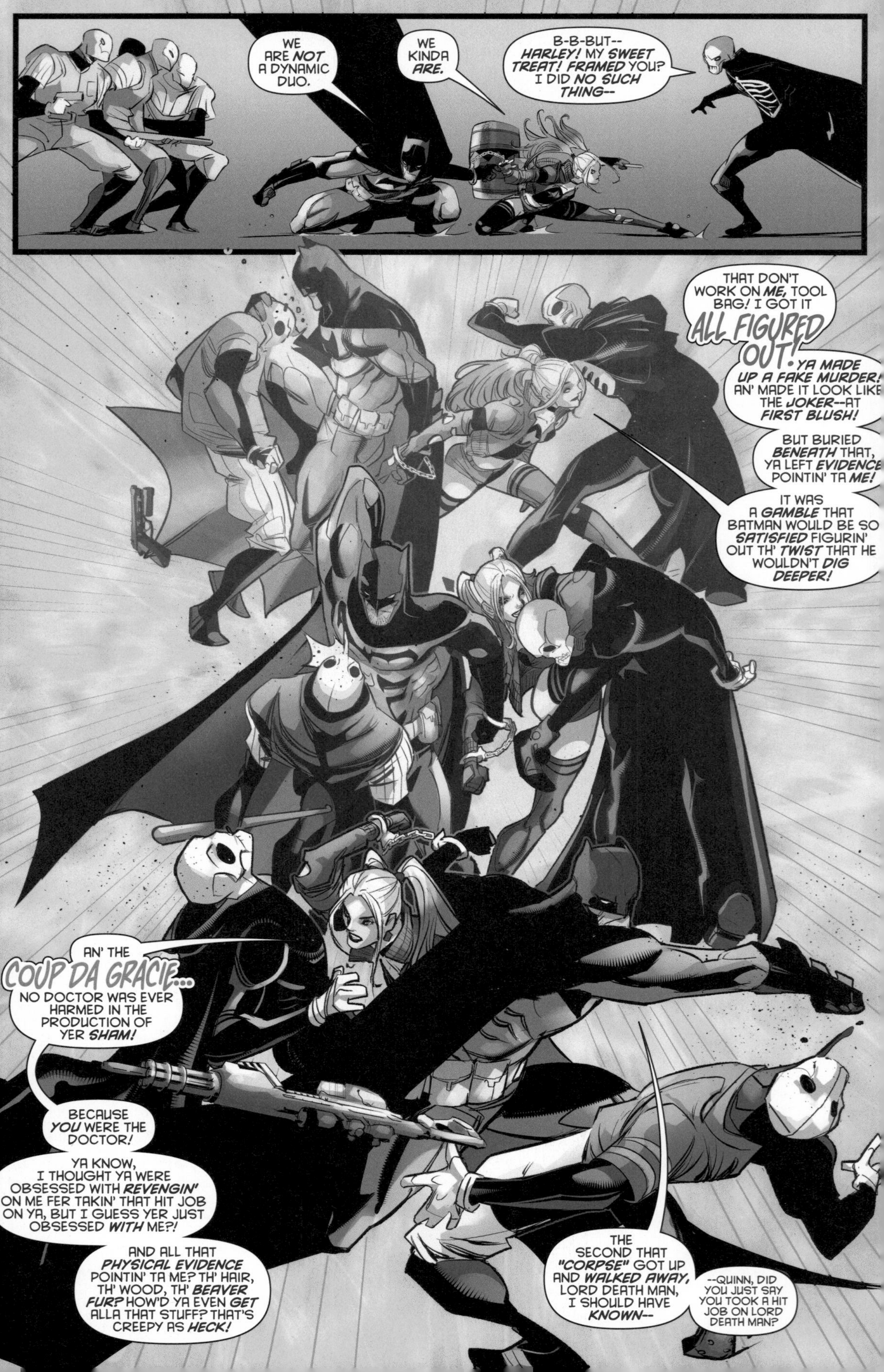

WE ARE *NOT* A DYNAMIC DUO.
WE KINDA *ARE.*
B-B-BUT-- *HARLEY!* MY *SWEET TREAT! FRAMED* YOU? I DID *NO SUCH THING--*
THAT DON'T WORK ON *ME,* TOOL BAG! I GOT IT
ALL FIGURED OUT!
YA MADE UP A FAKE MURDER! AN' MADE IT LOOK LIKE THE *JOKER*--AT *FIRST BLUSH!*
BUT BURIED *BENEATH* THAT, YA LEFT *EVIDENCE* POINTIN' TA *ME!*
IT WAS A *GAMBLE* THAT BATMAN WOULD BE SO *SATISFIED* FIGURIN' OUT TH' *TWIST* THAT HE WOULDN'T *DIG DEEPER!*
AN' THE
COUP DA GRACIE...
NO DOCTOR WAS EVER HARMED IN THE PRODUCTION OF YER *SHAM!*
BECAUSE *YOU* WERE THE *DOCTOR!*
YA KNOW, I THOUGHT YA WERE OBSESSED WITH *REVENGIN'* ON ME FER TAKIN' THAT HIT JOB ON YA, BUT I GUESS YER JUST OBSESSED *WITH* ME?!
AND ALL THAT *PHYSICAL EVIDENCE* POINTIN' TA ME? TH' HAIR, TH' WOOD, TH' *BEAVER FUR?* HOW'D YA EVEN *GET* ALLA THAT STUFF? THAT'S CREEPY AS *HECK!*
THE SECOND THAT *"CORPSE"* GOT UP AND *WALKED AWAY,* LORD DEATH MAN, I SHOULD HAVE *KNOWN--*
--QUINN, DID YOU JUST SAY YOU TOOK A HIT JOB ON LORD DEATH MAN?

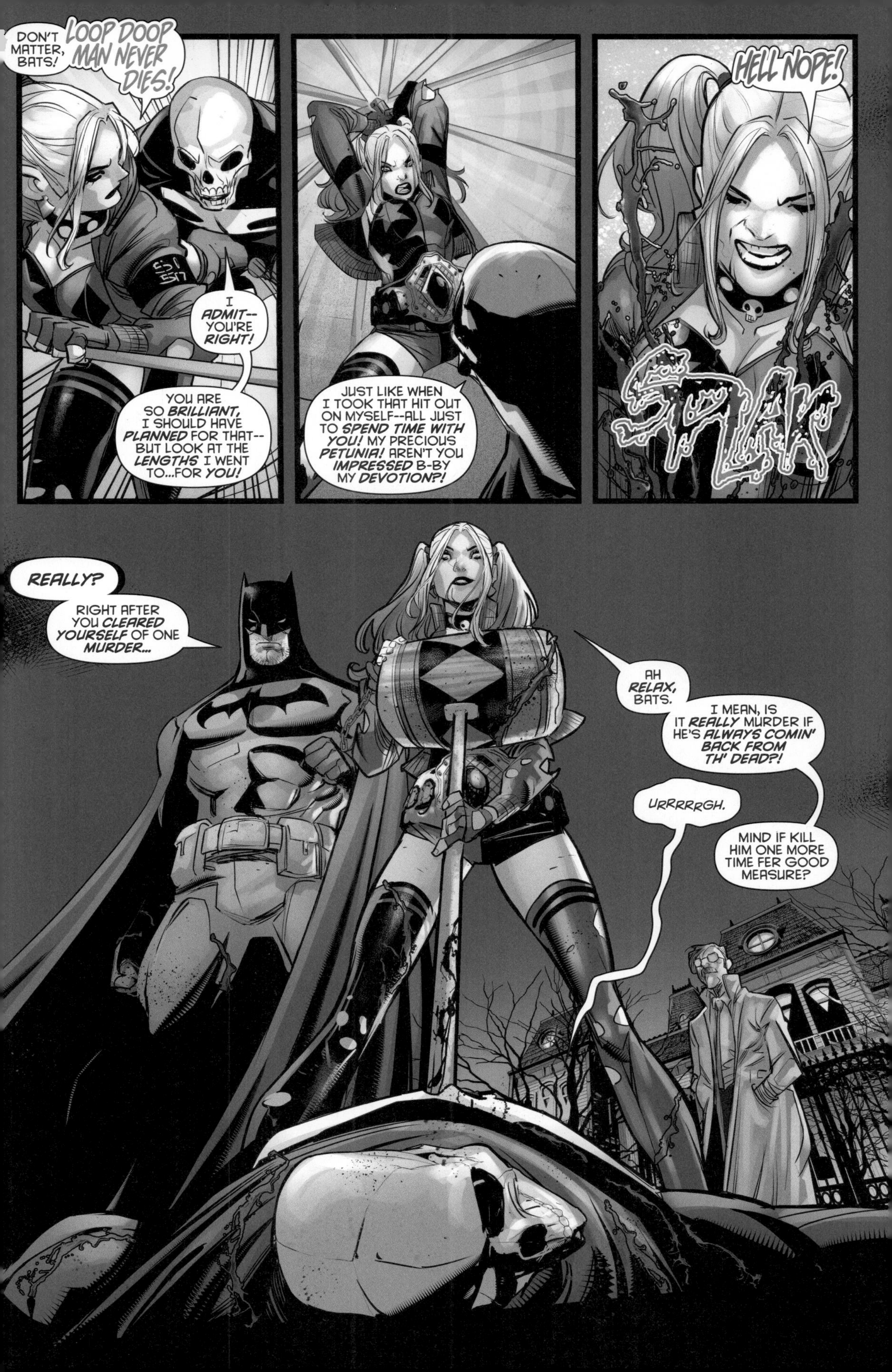
DON'T MATTER, BATS!
LOOP DOOP MAN NEVER DIES!
I ADMIT--YOU'RE RIGHT!
YOU ARE SO BRILLIANT, I SHOULD HAVE PLANNED FOR THAT--BUT LOOK AT THE LENGTHS I WENT TO...FOR YOU!
JUST LIKE WHEN I TOOK THAT HIT OUT ON MYSELF--ALL JUST TO SPEND TIME WITH YOU! MY PRECIOUS PETUNIA! AREN'T YOU IMPRESSED B-BY MY DEVOTION?!
HELL NOPE!
SPLAK
REALLY?
RIGHT AFTER YOU CLEARED YOURSELF OF ONE MURDER...
AH RELAX, BATS.
I MEAN, IS IT REALLY MURDER IF HE'S ALWAYS COMIN' BACK FROM TH' DEAD?!
URRRRRGH.
MIND IF KILL HIM ONE MORE TIME FER GOOD MEASURE?

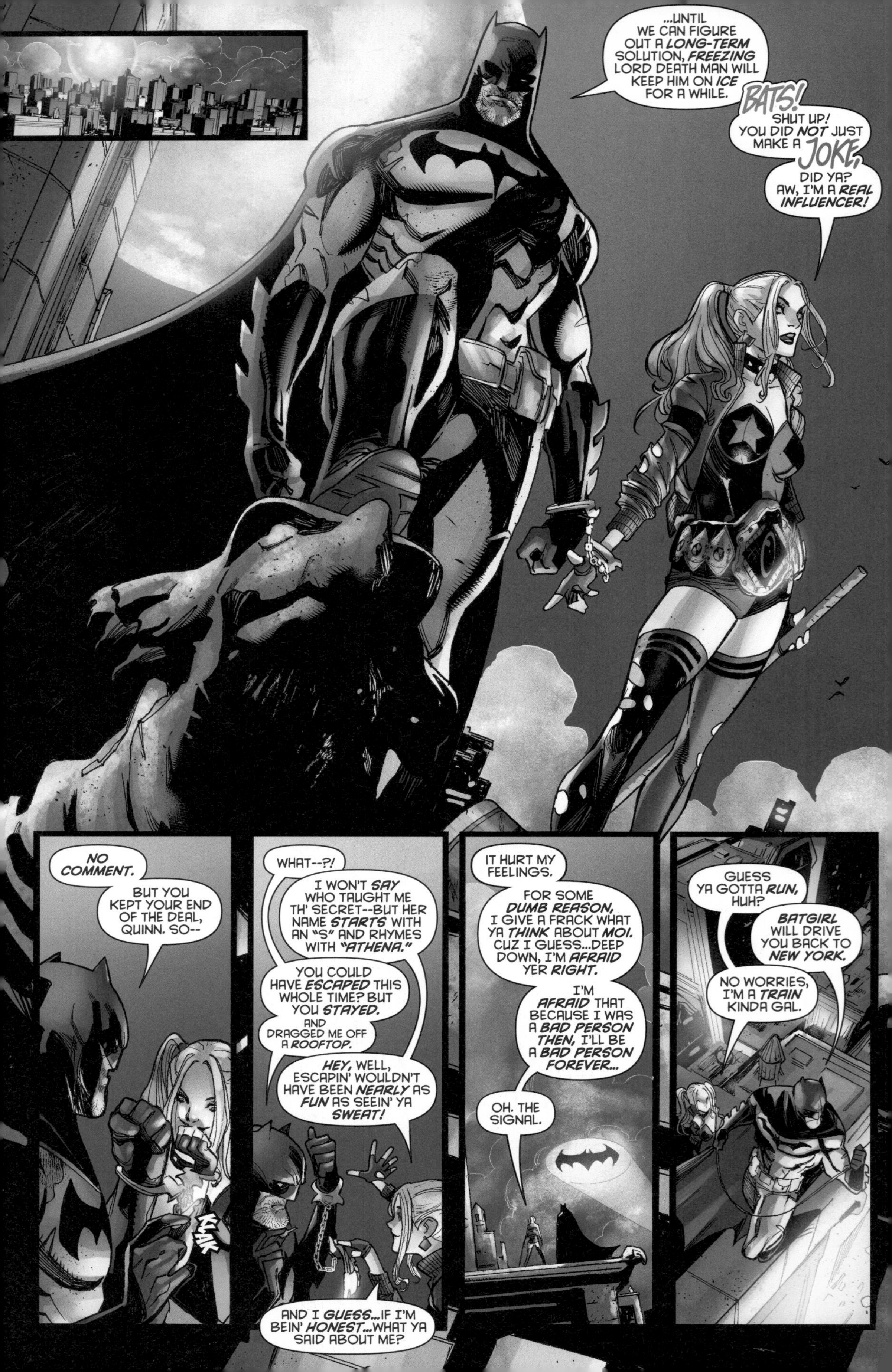
...UNTIL WE CAN FIGURE OUT A LONG-TERM SOLUTION, FREEZING LORD DEATH MAN WILL KEEP HIM ON ICE FOR A WHILE.
BATS! SHUT UP! YOU DID NOT JUST MAKE A JOKE,
DID YA? AW, I'M A REAL INFLUENCER!
NO COMMENT.
BUT YOU KEPT YOUR END OF THE DEAL, QUINN. SO--
KLAK
WHAT--?!
I WON'T SAY WHO TAUGHT ME TH' SECRET--BUT HER NAME STARTS WITH AN "S" AND RHYMES WITH "ATHENA."
YOU COULD HAVE ESCAPED THIS WHOLE TIME? BUT YOU STAYED.
AND DRAGGED ME OFF A ROOFTOP.
HEY, WELL, ESCAPIN' WOULDN'T HAVE BEEN NEARLY AS FUN AS SEEIN' YA SWEAT!
AND I GUESS...IF I'M BEIN' HONEST...WHAT YA SAID ABOUT ME?
IT HURT MY FEELINGS.
FOR SOME DUMB REASON, I GIVE A FRACK WHAT YA THINK ABOUT MOI. CUZ I GUESS...DEEP DOWN, I'M AFRAID YER RIGHT.
I'M AFRAID THAT BECAUSE I WAS A BAD PERSON THEN, I'LL BE A BAD PERSON FOREVER...
OH. THE SIGNAL.
GUESS YA GOTTA RUN, HUH?
BATGIRL WILL DRIVE YOU BACK TO NEW YORK.
NO WORRIES, I'M A TRAIN KINDA GAL.

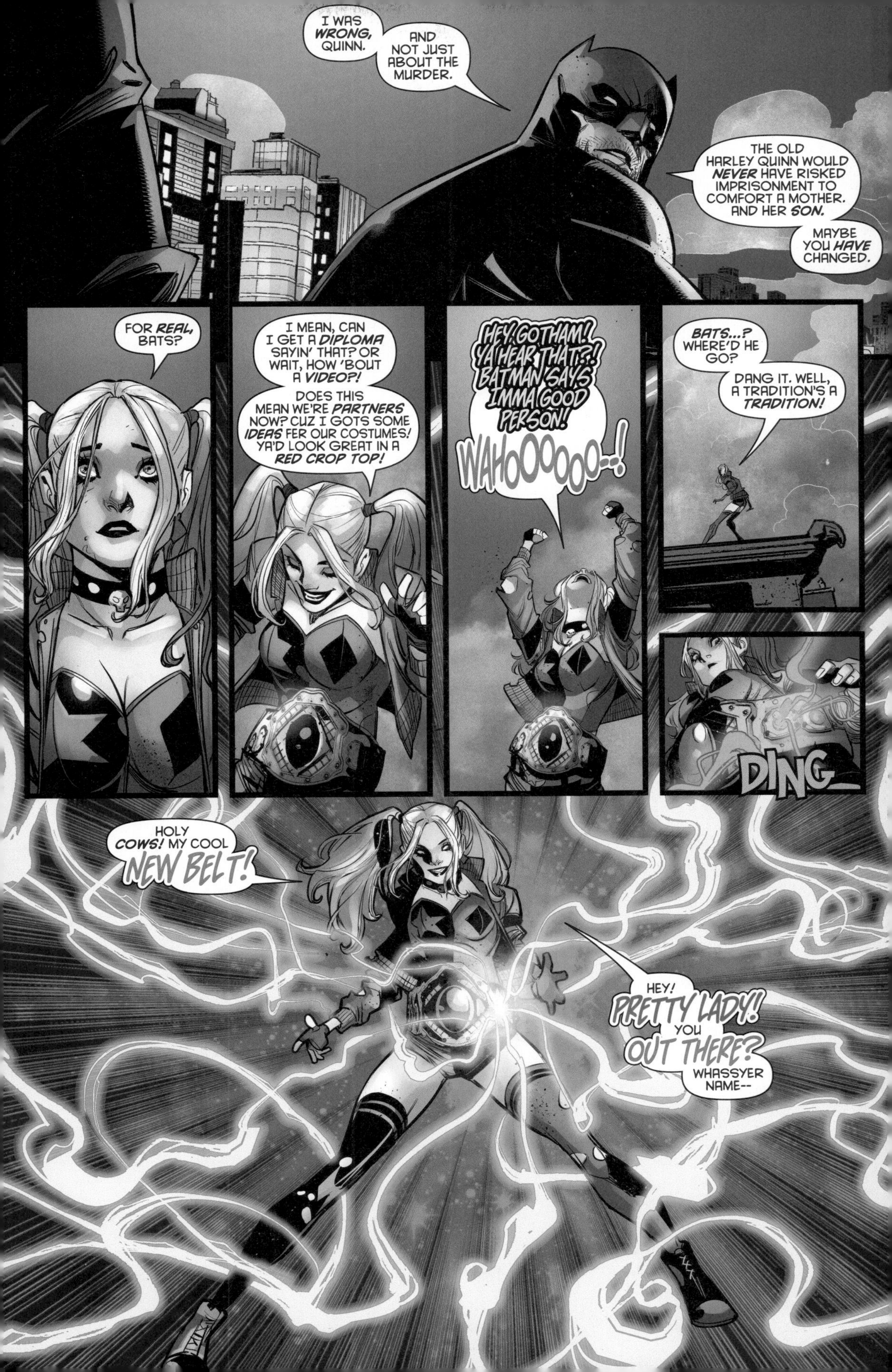

I WAS WRONG, QUINN.
AND NOT JUST ABOUT THE MURDER.
THE OLD HARLEY QUINN WOULD NEVER HAVE RISKED IMPRISONMENT TO COMFORT A MOTHER. AND HER SON.
MAYBE YOU HAVE CHANGED.
FOR REAL, BATS?
I MEAN, CAN I GET A DIPLOMA SAYIN' THAT? OR WAIT, HOW 'BOUT A VIDEO?!
DOES THIS MEAN WE'RE PARTNERS NOW? CUZ I GOTS SOME IDEAS FER OUR COSTUMES! YA'D LOOK GREAT IN A RED CROP TOP!
HEY GOTHAM! YA HEAR THAT?! BATMAN SAYS IMMA GOOD PERSON!
WAHOOOOOO--!
BATS...? WHERE'D HE GO?
DANG IT. WELL, A TRADITION'S A TRADITION!
DING
HOLY COWS! MY COOL NEW BELT!
HEY! PRETTY LADY! YOU OUT THERE? WHASSYER NAME--

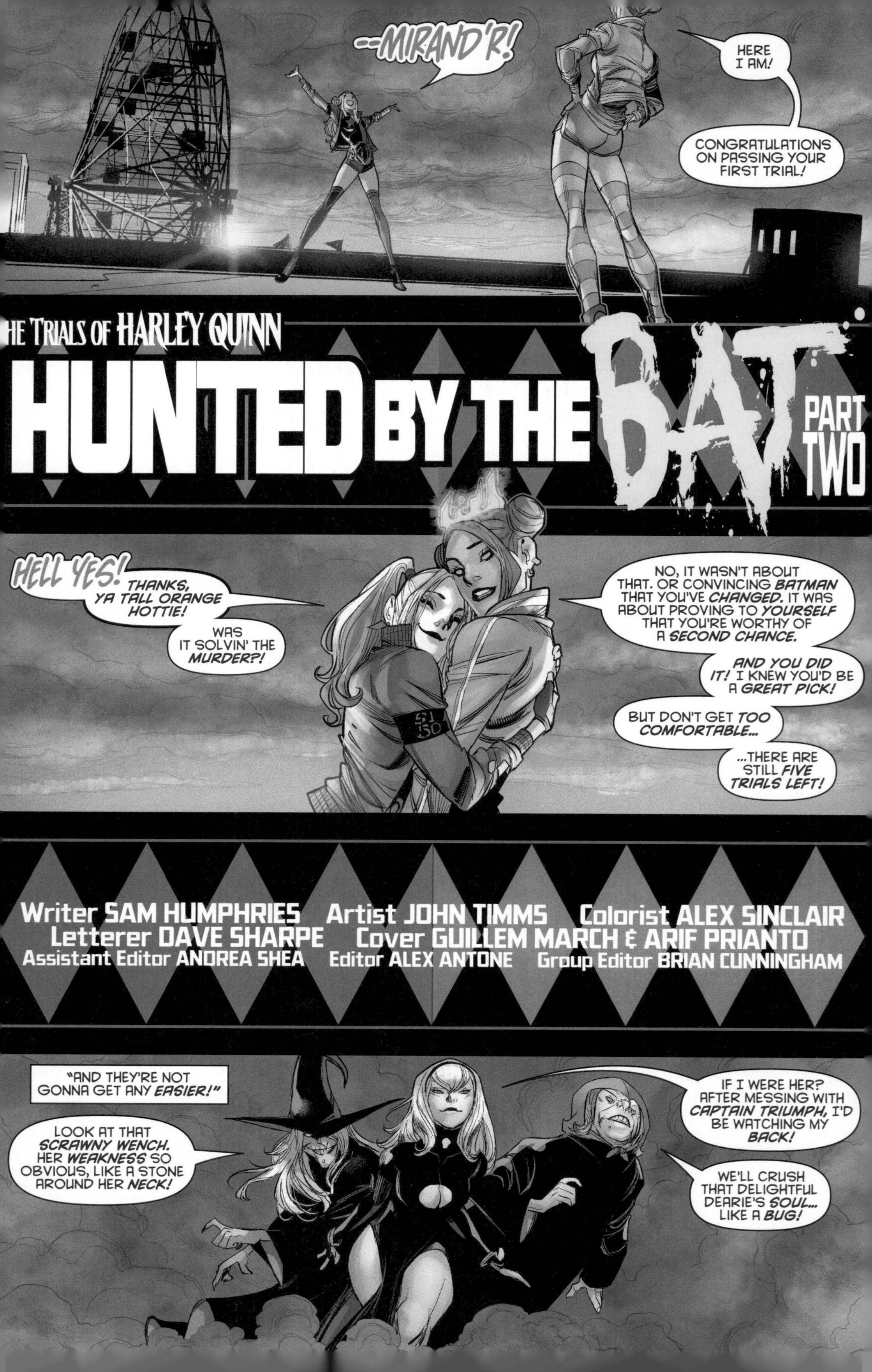
--MIRAND'R!
HERE I AM!
CONGRATULATIONS ON PASSING YOUR FIRST TRIAL!
HE TRIALS OF HARLEY QUINN
HUNTED BY THE BAT PART TWO
HELL YES!
THANKS, YA TALL ORANGE HOTTIE!
WAS IT SOLVIN' THE MURDER?!
NO, IT WASN'T ABOUT THAT. OR CONVINCING BATMAN THAT YOU'VE CHANGED. IT WAS ABOUT PROVING TO YOURSELF THAT YOU'RE WORTHY OF A SECOND CHANCE.
AND YOU DID IT! I KNEW YOU'D BE A GREAT PICK!
BUT DON'T GET TOO COMFORTABLE...
...THERE ARE STILL FIVE TRIALS LEFT!
Writer SAM HUMPHRIES Artist JOHN TIMMS Colorist ALEX SINCLAIR
Letterer DAVE SHARPE Cover GUILLEM MARCH & ARIF PRIANTO
Assistant Editor ANDREA SHEA Editor ALEX ANTONE Group Editor BRIAN CUNNINGHAM
"AND THEY'RE NOT GONNA GET ANY EASIER!"
LOOK AT THAT SCRAWNY WENCH. HER WEAKNESS SO OBVIOUS, LIKE A STONE AROUND HER NECK!
IF I WERE HER? AFTER MESSING WITH CAPTAIN TRIUMPH, I'D BE WATCHING MY BACK!
WE'LL CRUSH THAT DELIGHTFUL DEARIE'S SOUL... LIKE A BUG!

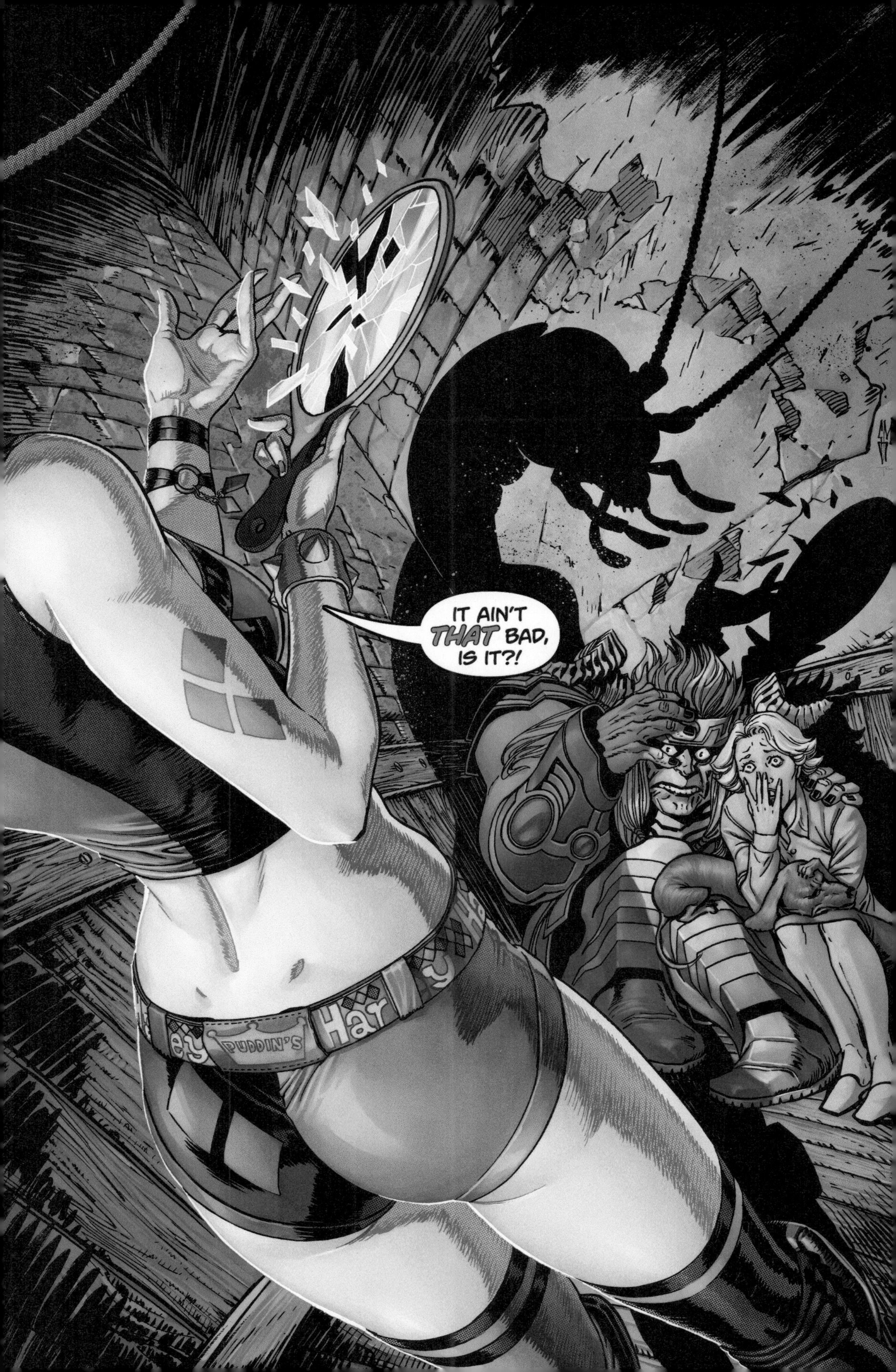
IT AIN'T THAT BAD, IS IT?!
PUDDIN'S

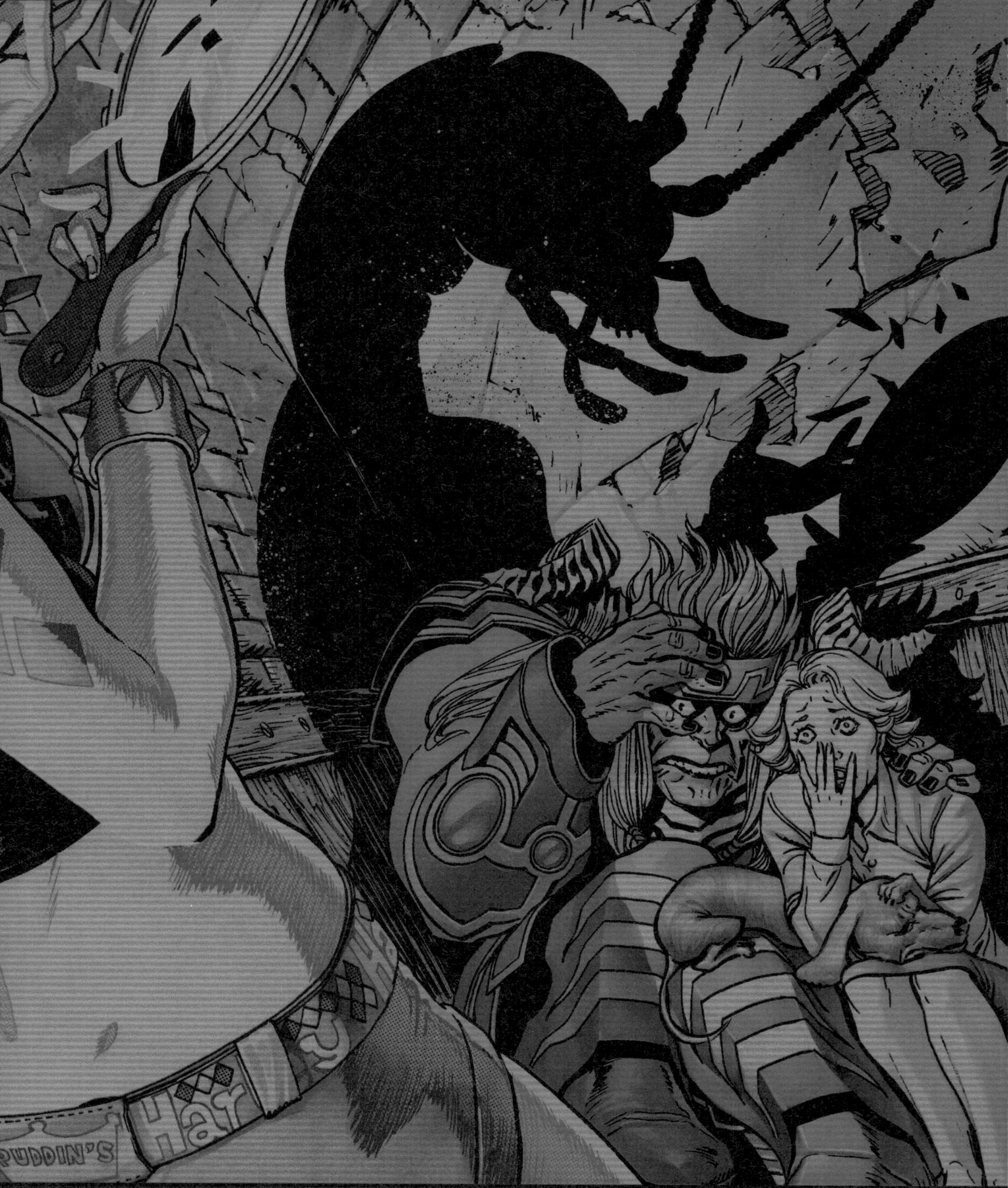
PUDDIN'S

HARLEY QUINN
#59

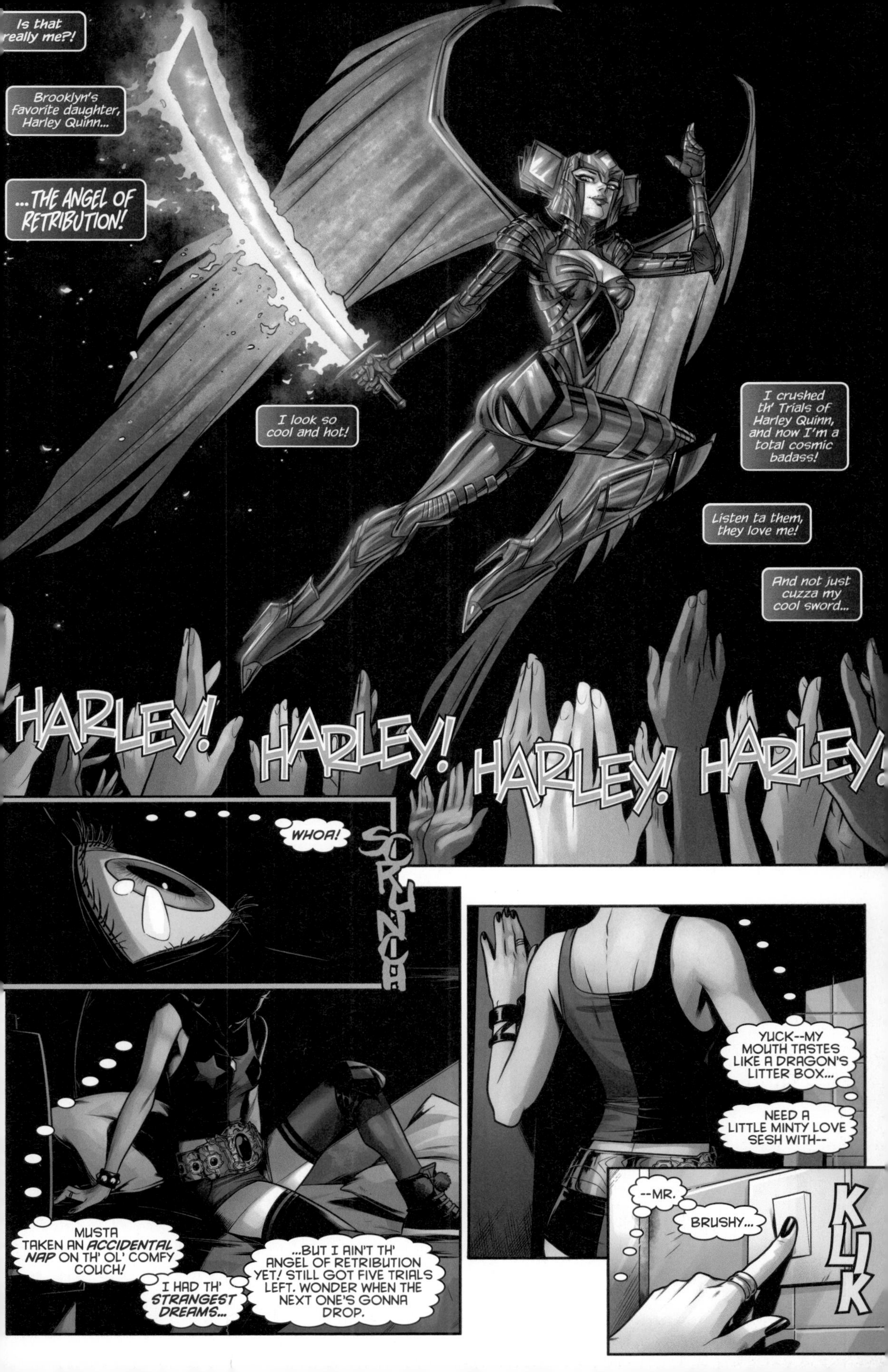
Is that really me?!
Brooklyn's favorite daughter, Harley Quinn...
...THE ANGEL OF RETRIBUTION!
I look so cool and hot!
I crushed th' Trials of Harley Quinn, and now I'm a total cosmic badass!
Listen ta them, they love me!
And not just cuzza my cool sword...
HARLEY! HARLEY! HARLEY! HARLEY!
WHOA!
SCRUNCH
MUSTA TAKEN AN ACCIDENTAL NAP ON TH' OL' COMFY COUCH!
I HAD TH' STRANGEST DREAMS...
...BUT I AIN'T TH' ANGEL OF RETRIBUTION YET! STILL GOT FIVE TRIALS LEFT. WONDER WHEN THE NEXT ONE'S GONNA DROP.
YUCK--MY MOUTH TASTES LIKE A DRAGON'S LITTER BOX...
NEED A LITTLE MINTY LOVE SESH WITH--
--MR.
BRUSHY...
KLIK

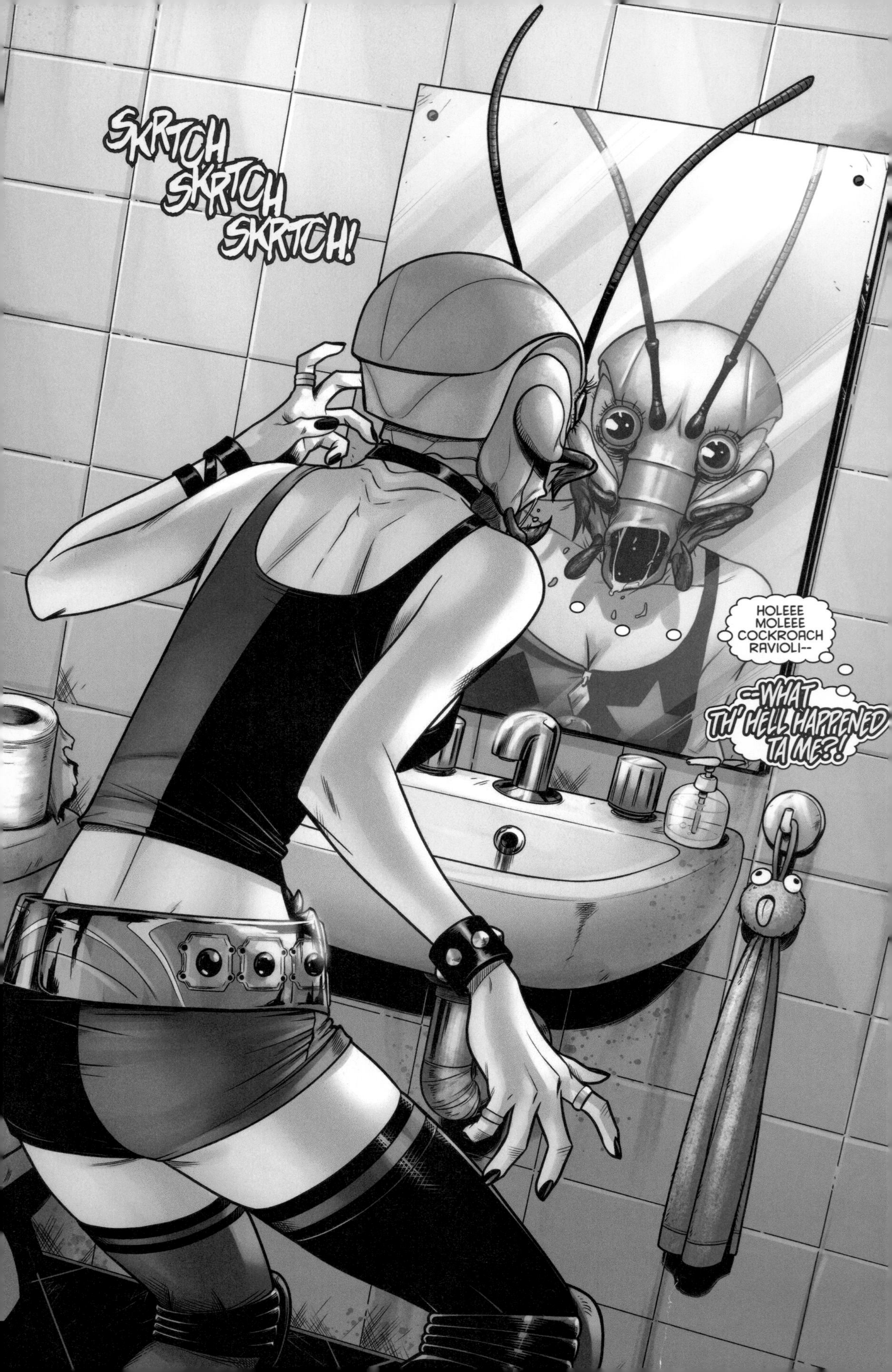
SKRTCH SKRTCH SKRTCH!
HOLEEE MOLEEE COCKROACH RAVIOLI--
--WHAT TH' HELL HAPPENED TA ME?!

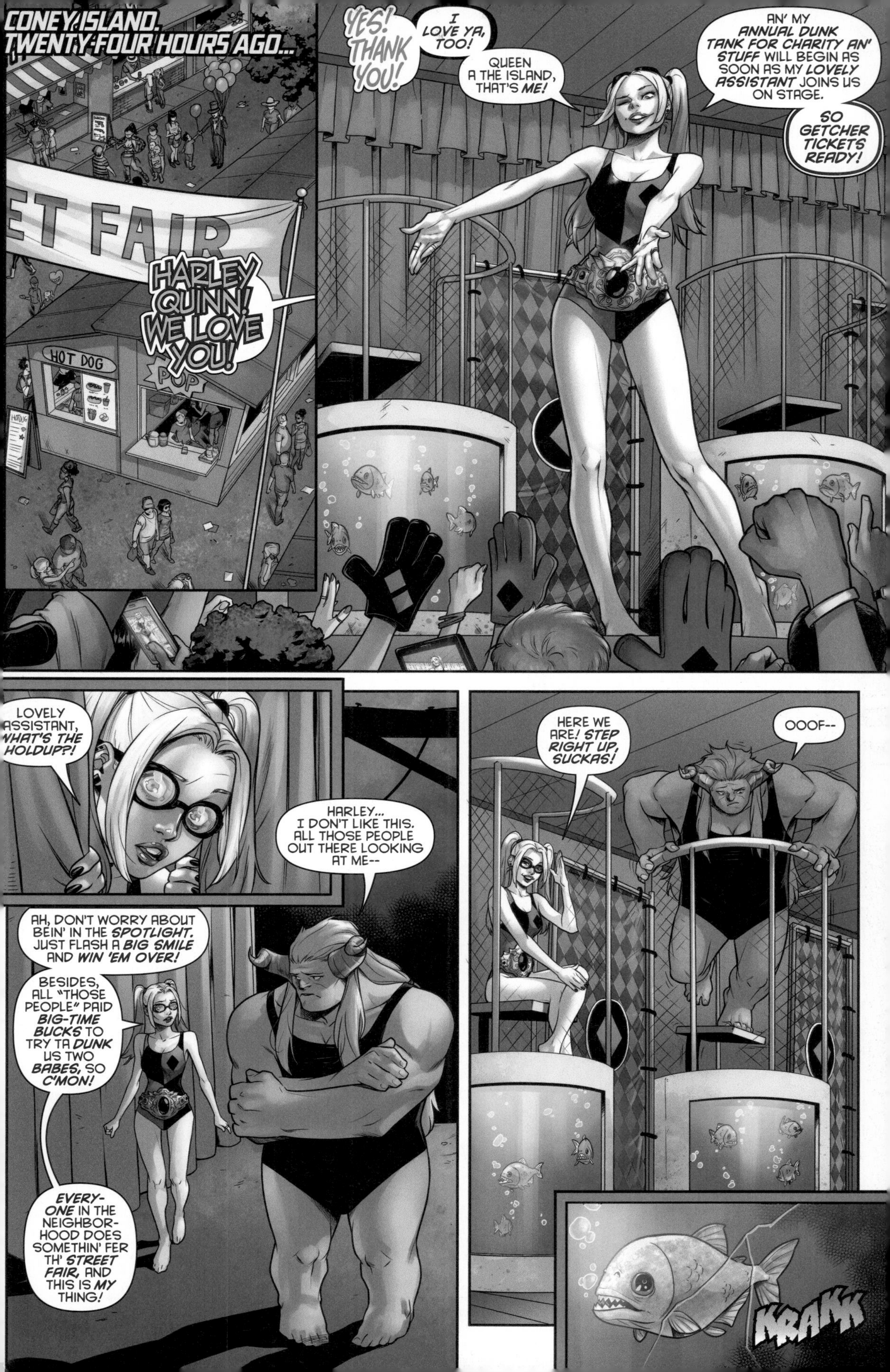

CONEY ISLAND. TWENTY-FOUR HOURS AGO...
ET FAIR
HARLEY QUINN! WE LOVE YOU!
HOT DOG
POP
YES! THANK YOU!
I LOVE YA, TOO!
QUEEN A THE ISLAND, THAT'S ME!
AN' MY ANNUAL DUNK TANK FOR CHARITY AN' STUFF WILL BEGIN AS SOON AS MY LOVELY ASSISTANT JOINS US ON STAGE.
SO GETCHER TICKETS READY!
LOVELY ASSISTANT, WHAT'S THE HOLDUP?!
HARLEY... I DON'T LIKE THIS. ALL THOSE PEOPLE OUT THERE LOOKING AT ME--
AH, DON'T WORRY ABOUT BEIN' IN THE SPOTLIGHT. JUST FLASH A BIG SMILE AND WIN 'EM OVER!
BESIDES, ALL "THOSE PEOPLE" PAID BIG-TIME BUCKS TO TRY TA DUNK US TWO BABES, SO C'MON!
EVERY-ONE IN THE NEIGHBOR-HOOD DOES SOMETHIN' FER TH' STREET FAIR, AND THIS IS MY THING!
HERE WE ARE! STEP RIGHT UP, SUCKAS!
OOOF--
KRAKK

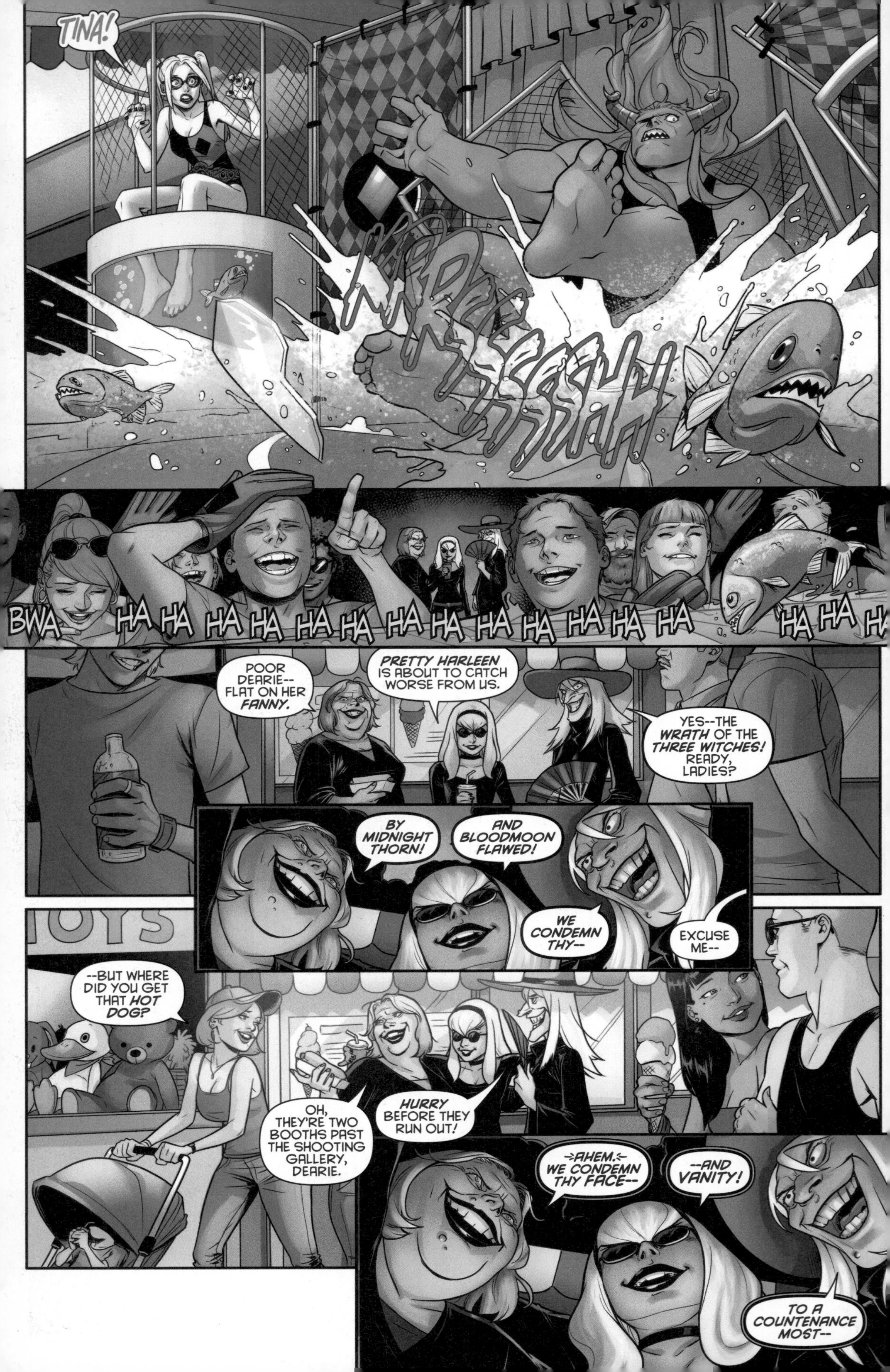
TINA!
BWA HA HA HA HA HA HA HA HA HA HA HA HA HA HA HA HA
POOR DEARIE-- FLAT ON HER FANNY.
PRETTY HARLEEN IS ABOUT TO CATCH WORSE FROM US.
YES--THE WRATH OF THE THREE WITCHES! READY, LADIES?
BY MIDNIGHT THORN!
AND BLOODMOON FLAWED!
WE CONDEMN THY--
EXCUSE ME--
--BUT WHERE DID YOU GET THAT HOT DOG?
OH, THEY'RE TWO BOOTHS PAST THE SHOOTING GALLERY, DEARIE.
HURRY BEFORE THEY RUN OUT!
AHEM. WE CONDEMN THY FACE--
--AND VANITY!
TO A COUNTENANCE MOST--
TOYS

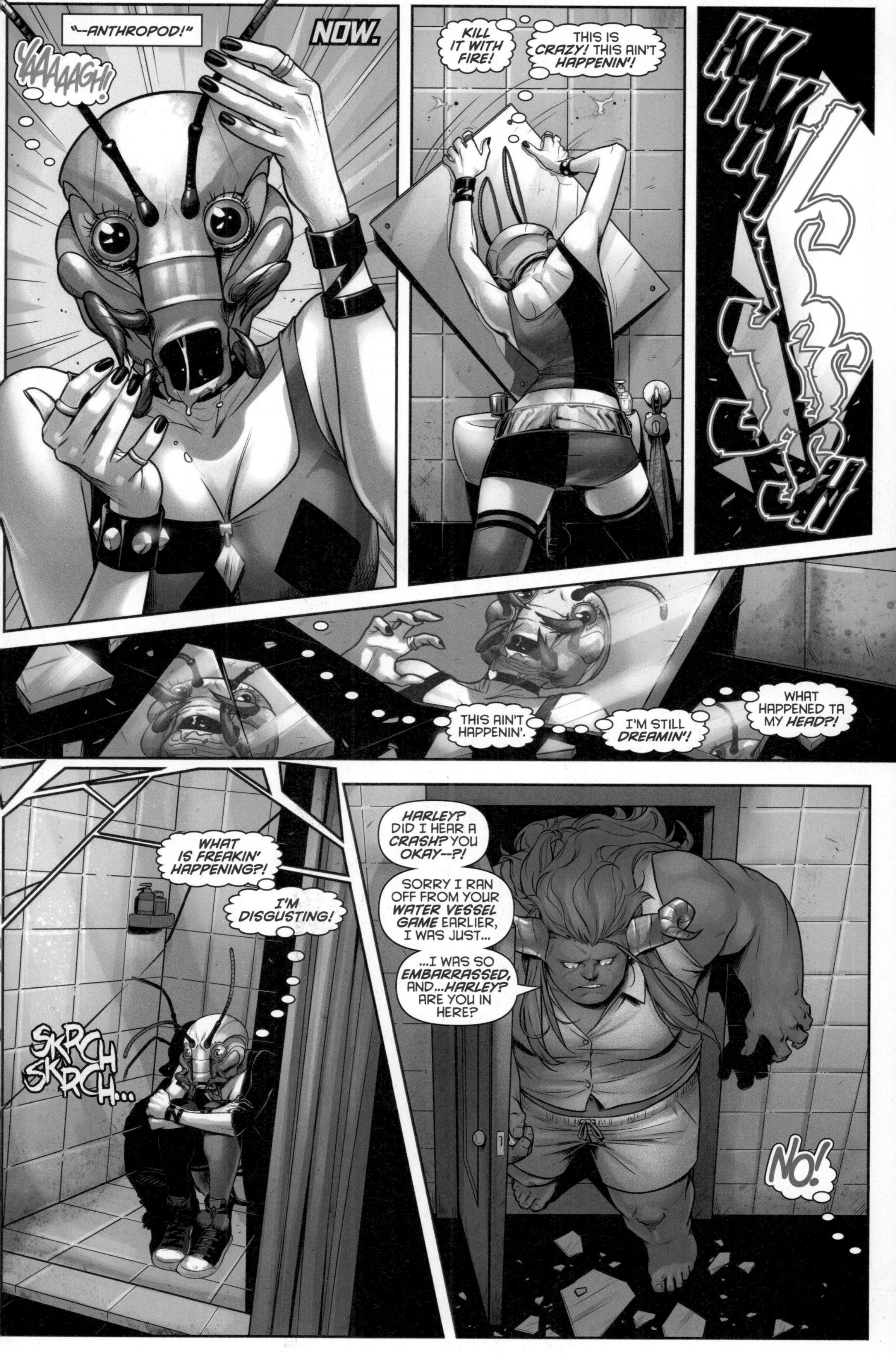
"--ANTHROPOD!"
NOW.
YAAAAAGH!
KILL IT WITH FIRE!
THIS IS CRAZY! THIS AIN'T HAPPENIN'!
KKKKRASSHH
THIS AIN'T HAPPENIN'.
I'M STILL DREAMIN'!
WHAT HAPPENED TA MY HEAD?!
WHAT IS FREAKIN' HAPPENING?!
I'M DISGUSTING!
SKRCH SKRCH...
HARLEY? DID I HEAR A CRASH? YOU OKAY--?!
SORRY I RAN OFF FROM YOUR WATER VESSEL GAME EARLIER, I WAS JUST...
...I WAS SO EMBARRASSED, AND...HARLEY? ARE YOU IN HERE?
NO!

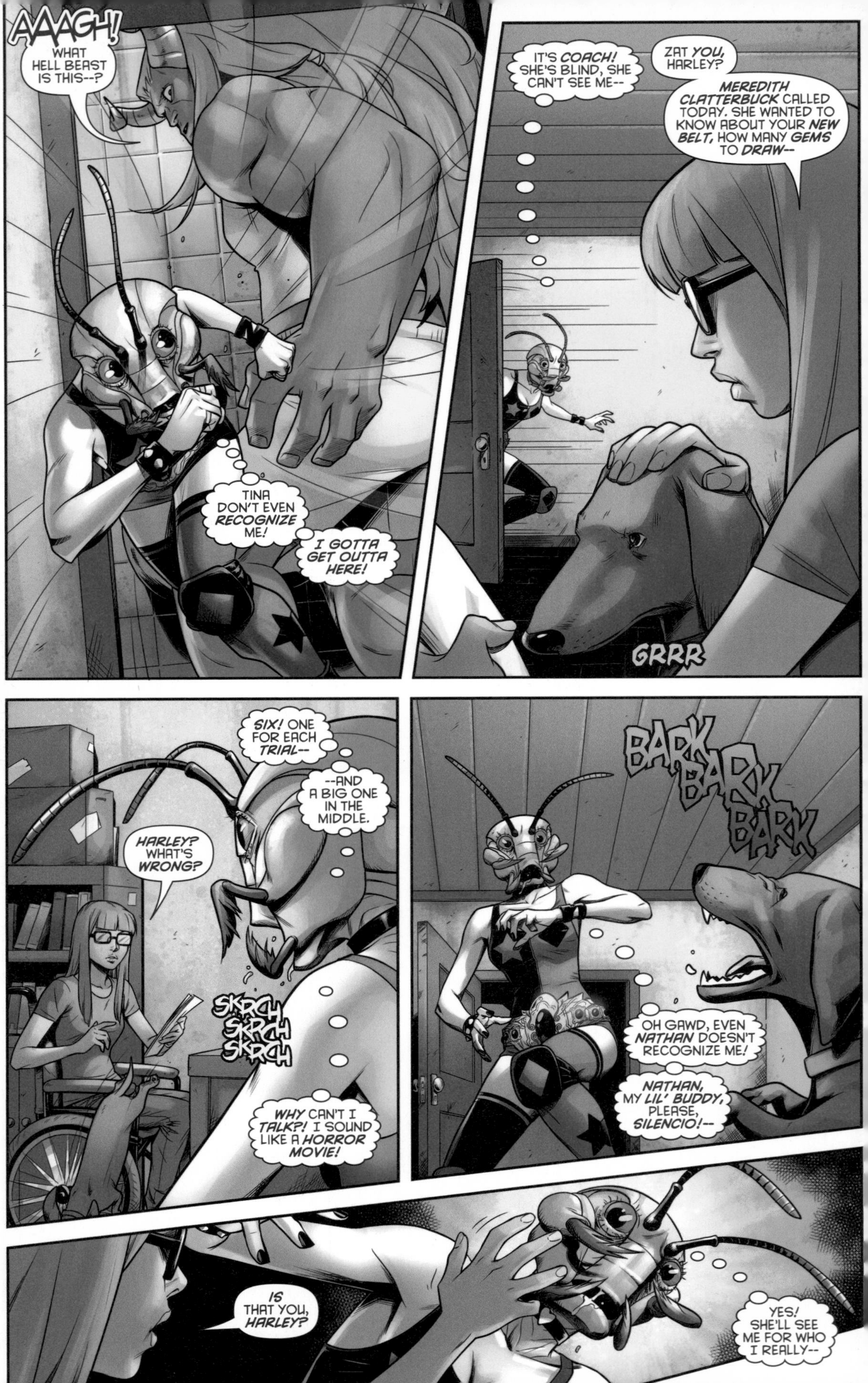

AAAGH!
WHAT HELL BEAST IS THIS--?
TINA DON'T EVEN RECOGNIZE ME!
I GOTTA GET OUTTA HERE!
IT'S COACH! SHE'S BLIND, SHE CAN'T SEE ME--
ZAT YOU, HARLEY?
MEREDITH CLATTERBUCK CALLED TODAY. SHE WANTED TO KNOW ABOUT YOUR NEW BELT, HOW MANY GEMS TO DRAW--
GRRR
SIX! ONE FOR EACH TRIAL--
--AND A BIG ONE IN THE MIDDLE.
HARLEY? WHAT'S WRONG?
SKRCH SKRCH SKRCH
WHY CAN'T I TALK?! I SOUND LIKE A HORROR MOVIE!
BARK BARK BARK
OH GAWD, EVEN NATHAN DOESN'T RECOGNIZE ME!
NATHAN, MY LIL' BUDDY, PLEASE, SILENCIO!--
IS THAT YOU, HARLEY?
YES! SHE'LL SEE ME FOR WHO I REALLY--

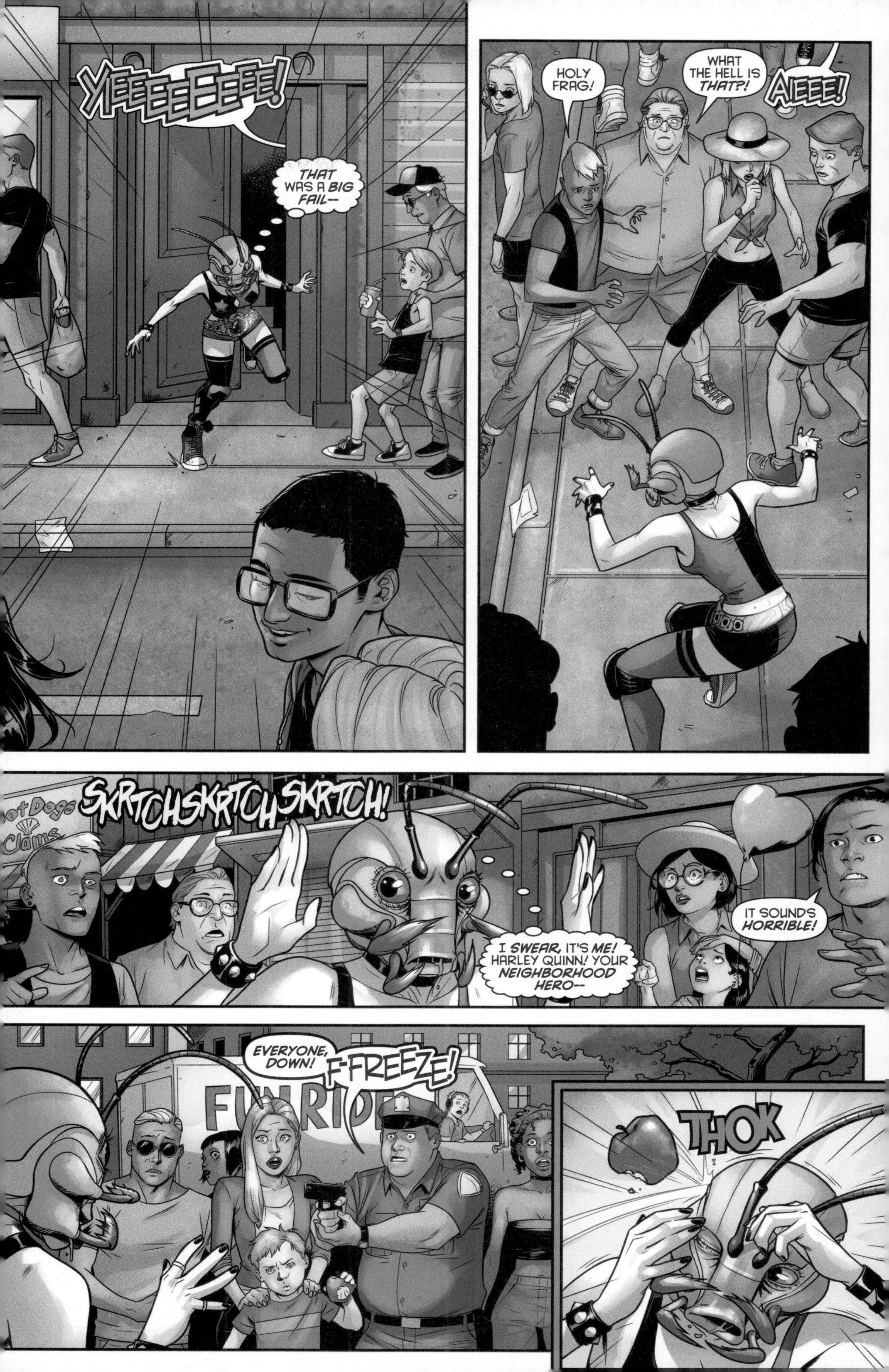
YIEEEEEEEEE!
THAT WAS A BIG FAIL--
HOLY FRAG!
WHAT THE HELL IS THAT?!
AIEEE!
SKRTCHSKRTCHSKRTCH!
Hot Dogs
Clams
I SWEAR, IT'S ME! HARLEY QUINN! YOUR NEIGHBORHOOD HERO--
IT SOUNDS HORRIBLE!
EVERYONE, DOWN!
F-FREEZE!
FUN RIDE
THOK

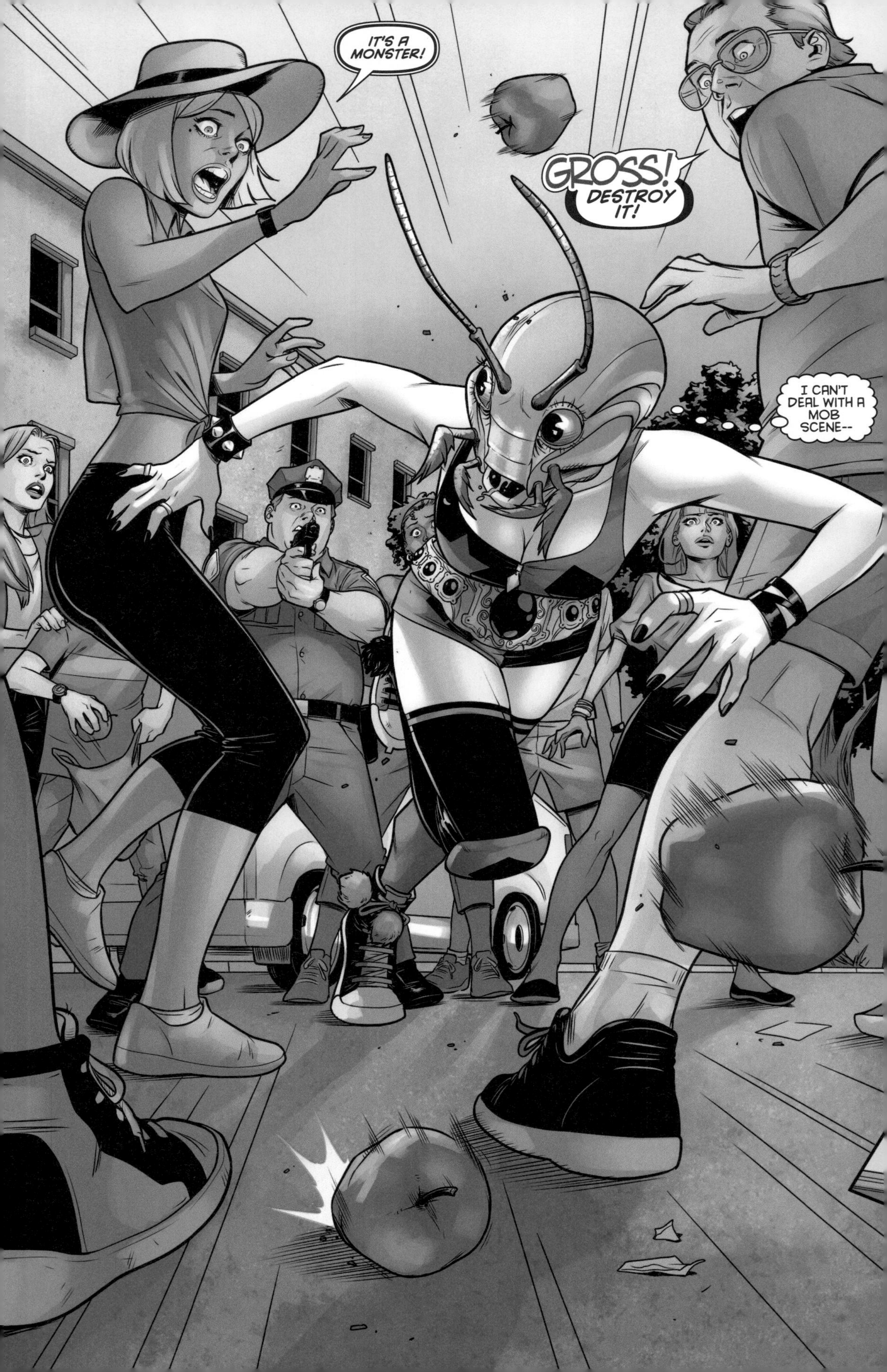
IT'S A MONSTER!
GROSS! DESTROY IT!
I CAN'T DEAL WITH A MOB SCENE--

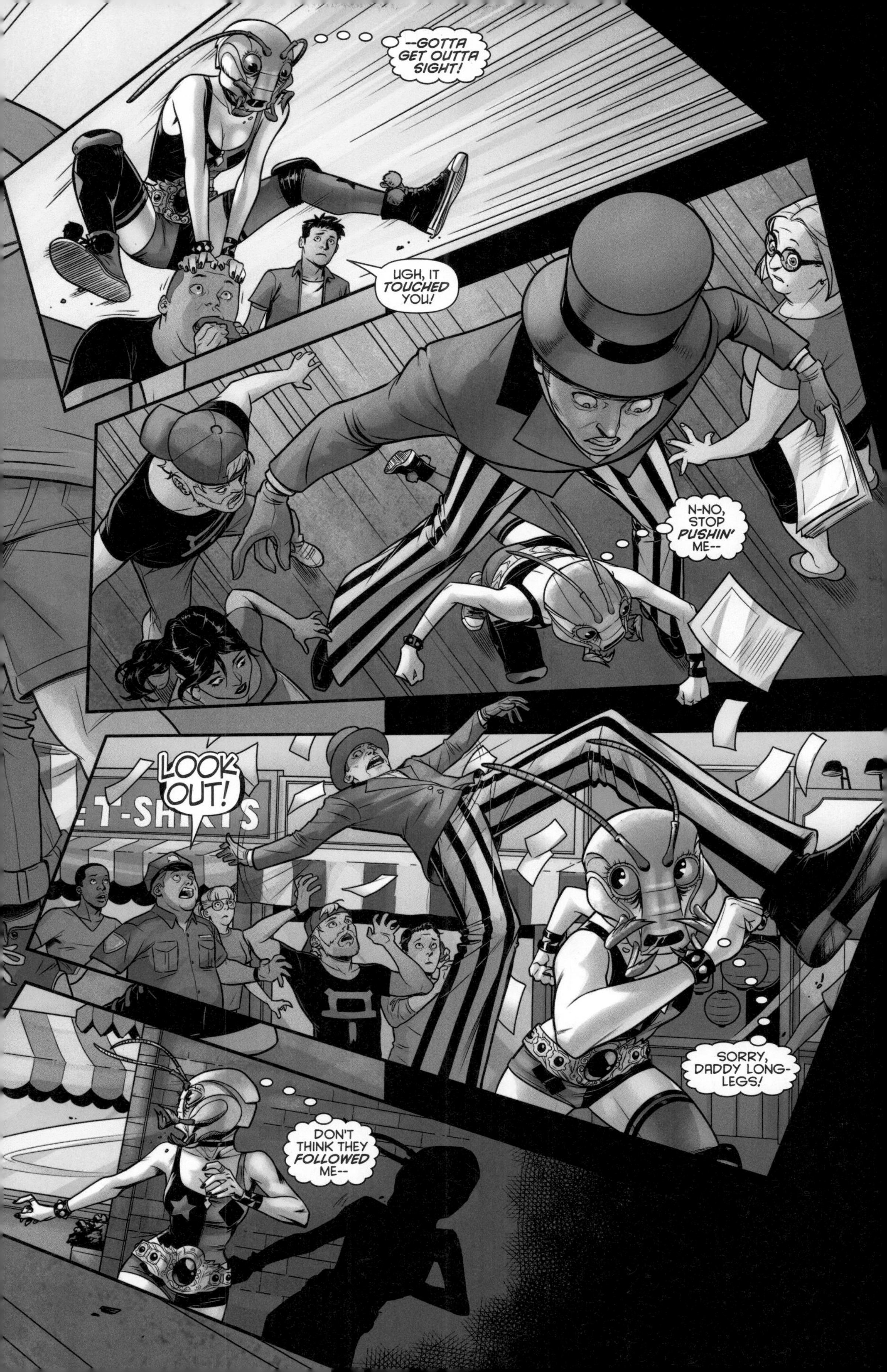

--GOTTA GET OUTTA SIGHT!
UGH, IT TOUCHED YOU!
N-NO, STOP PUSHIN' ME--
LOOK OUT!
T-SHIRTS
SORRY, DADDY LONG-LEGS!
DON'T THINK THEY FOLLOWED ME--

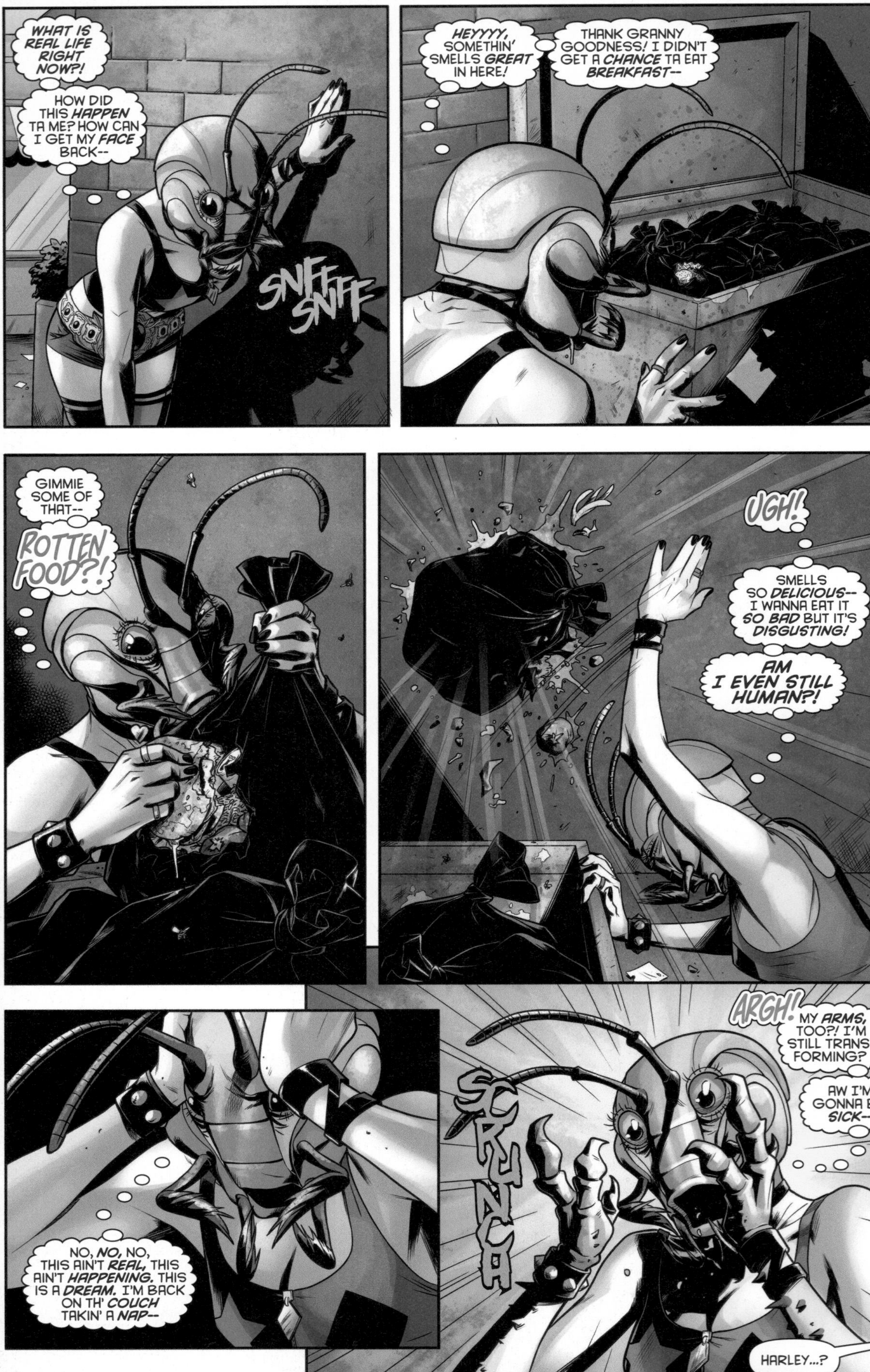

WHAT IS REAL LIFE RIGHT NOW?!
HOW DID THIS HAPPEN TA ME? HOW CAN I GET MY FACE BACK--
SNIFF SNIFF
HEYYYY, SOMETHIN' SMELLS GREAT IN HERE!
THANK GRANNY GOODNESS! I DIDN'T GET A CHANCE TA EAT BREAKFAST--
GIMMIE SOME OF THAT--
ROTTEN FOOD?!
UGH!
SMELLS SO DELICIOUS-- I WANNA EAT IT SO BAD BUT IT'S DISGUSTING!
AM I EVEN STILL HUMAN?!
NO, NO, NO, THIS AIN'T REAL, THIS AIN'T HAPPENING. THIS IS A DREAM. I'M BACK ON TH' COUCH TAKIN' A NAP--
ARGH!
MY ARMS, TOO?! I'M STILL TRANS-FORMING?
SCRUNCH
AW I'M GONNA BE SICK--
HARLEY...?

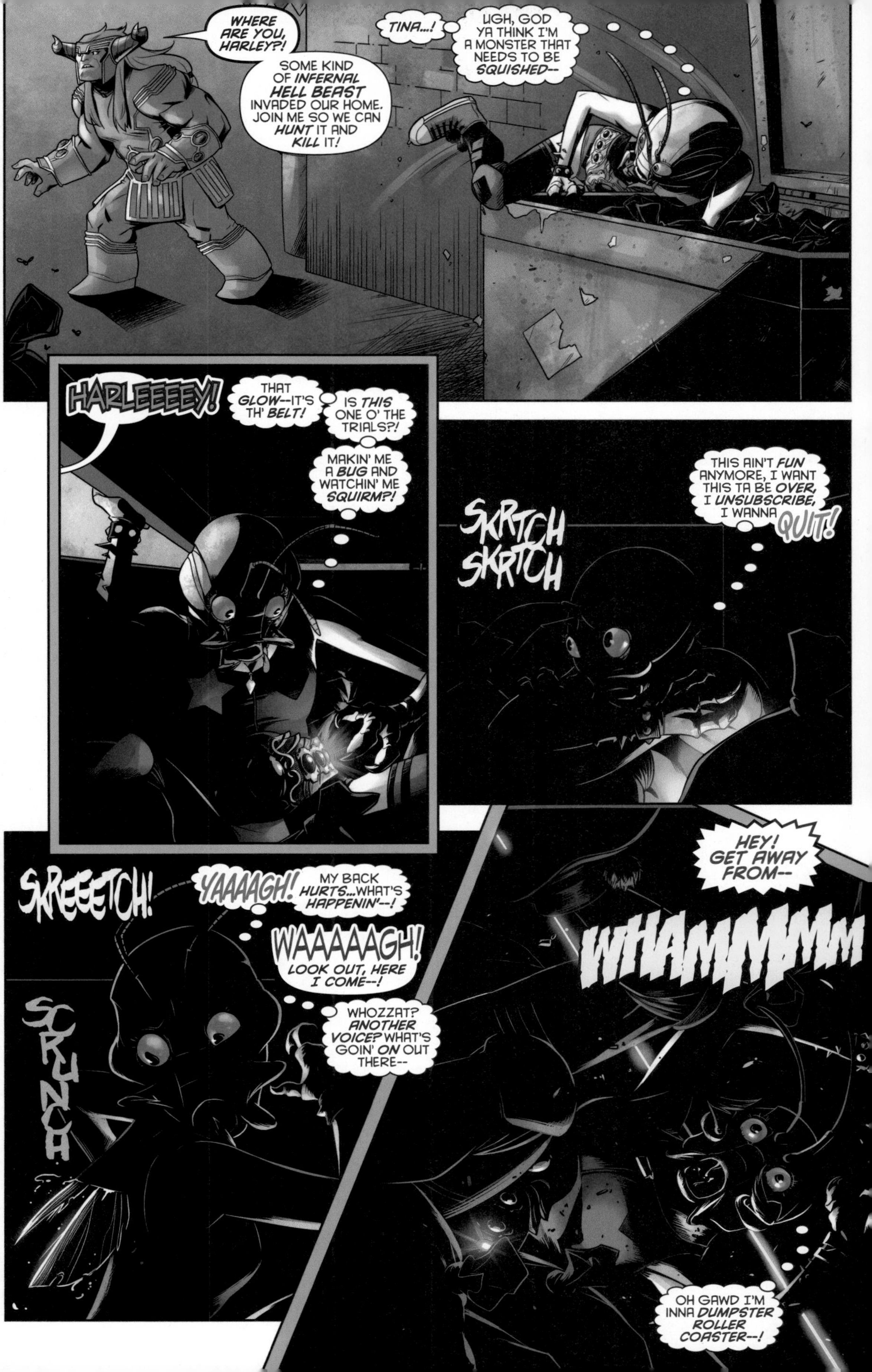
WHERE ARE YOU, HARLEY?!
SOME KIND OF INFERNAL HELL BEAST INVADED OUR HOME. JOIN ME SO WE CAN HUNT IT AND KILL IT!
TINA...!
UGH, GOD YA THINK I'M A MONSTER THAT NEEDS TO BE SQUISHED--
HARLEEEEEY!
THAT GLOW--IT'S TH' BELT!
IS THIS ONE O' THE TRIALS?!
MAKIN' ME A BUG AND WATCHIN' ME SQUIRM?!
SKRTCH SKRTCH
THIS AIN'T FUN ANYMORE, I WANT THIS TA BE OVER, I UNSUBSCRIBE, I WANNA QUIT!
SKREEEETCH!
YAAAAGH!
MY BACK HURTS...WHAT'S HAPPENIN'--!
WAAAAAGH!
LOOK OUT, HERE I COME--!
SCRUNCH
WHOZZAT? ANOTHER VOICE? WHAT'S GOIN' ON OUT THERE--
HEY! GET AWAY FROM--
WHAMMMMM
OH GAWD I'M INNA DUMPSTER ROLLER COASTER--!

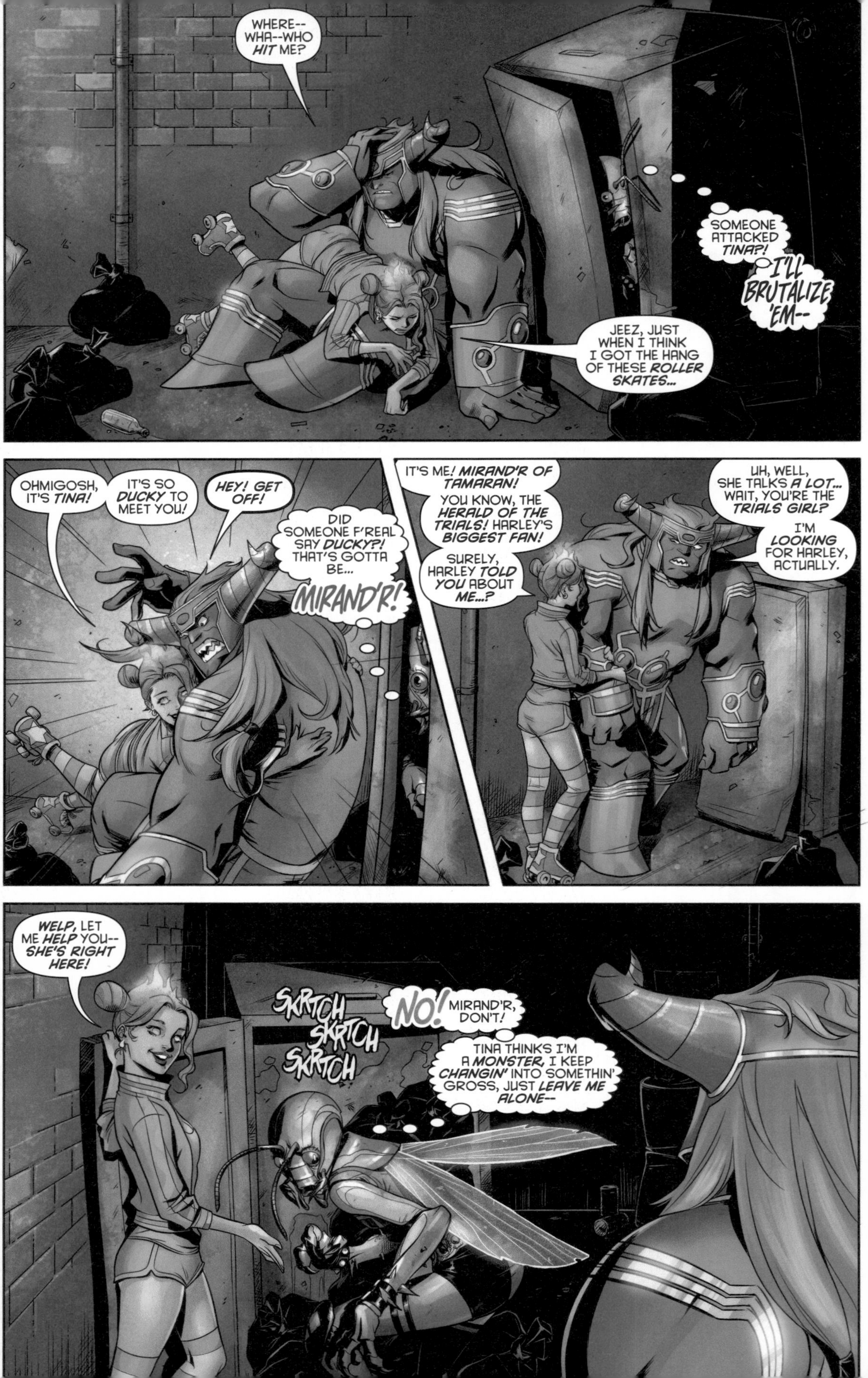
WHERE--
WHA--WHO
HIT ME?
SOMEONE ATTACKED TINA?!
I'LL BRUTALIZE 'EM--
JEEZ, JUST WHEN I THINK I GOT THE HANG OF THESE ROLLER SKATES...
OHMIGOSH, IT'S TINA!
IT'S SO DUCKY TO MEET YOU!
HEY! GET OFF!
DID SOMEONE F'REAL SAY DUCKY?! THAT'S GOTTA BE...
MIRAND'R!
IT'S ME! MIRAND'R OF TAMARAN!
YOU KNOW, THE HERALD OF THE TRIALS! HARLEY'S BIGGEST FAN!
SURELY, HARLEY TOLD YOU ABOUT ME...?
UH, WELL, SHE TALKS A LOT... WAIT, YOU'RE THE TRIALS GIRL?
I'M LOOKING FOR HARLEY, ACTUALLY.
WELP, LET ME HELP YOU-- SHE'S RIGHT HERE!
SKRTCH SKRTCH SKRTCH
NO! MIRAND'R, DON'T!
TINA THINKS I'M A MONSTER, I KEEP CHANGIN' INTO SOMETHIN' GROSS, JUST LEAVE ME ALONE--

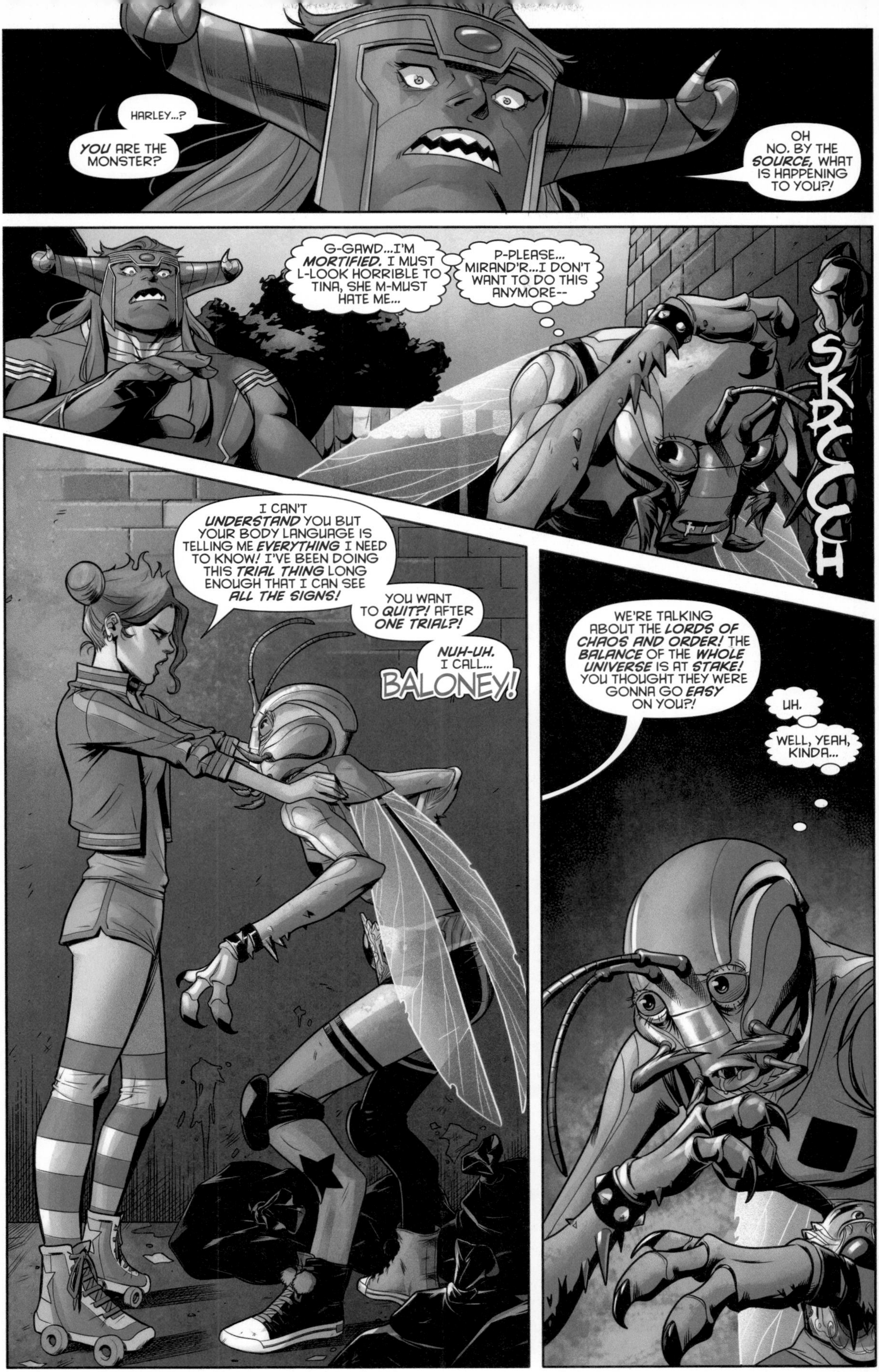

HARLEY...?
YOU ARE THE MONSTER?
OH NO. BY THE SOURCE, WHAT IS HAPPENING TO YOU?!
G-GAWD...I'M MORTIFIED. I MUST L-LOOK HORRIBLE TO TINA, SHE M-MUST HATE ME...
P-PLEASE... MIRAND'R...I DON'T WANT TO DO THIS ANYMORE--
SKRCCH
I CAN'T UNDERSTAND YOU BUT YOUR BODY LANGUAGE IS TELLING ME EVERYTHING I NEED TO KNOW! I'VE BEEN DOING THIS TRIAL THING LONG ENOUGH THAT I CAN SEE ALL THE SIGNS!
YOU WANT TO QUIT?! AFTER ONE TRIAL?!
NUH-UH. I CALL...
BALONEY!
WE'RE TALKING ABOUT THE LORDS OF CHAOS AND ORDER! THE BALANCE OF THE WHOLE UNIVERSE IS AT STAKE! YOU THOUGHT THEY WERE GONNA GO EASY ON YOU?!
UH.
WELL, YEAH, KINDA...

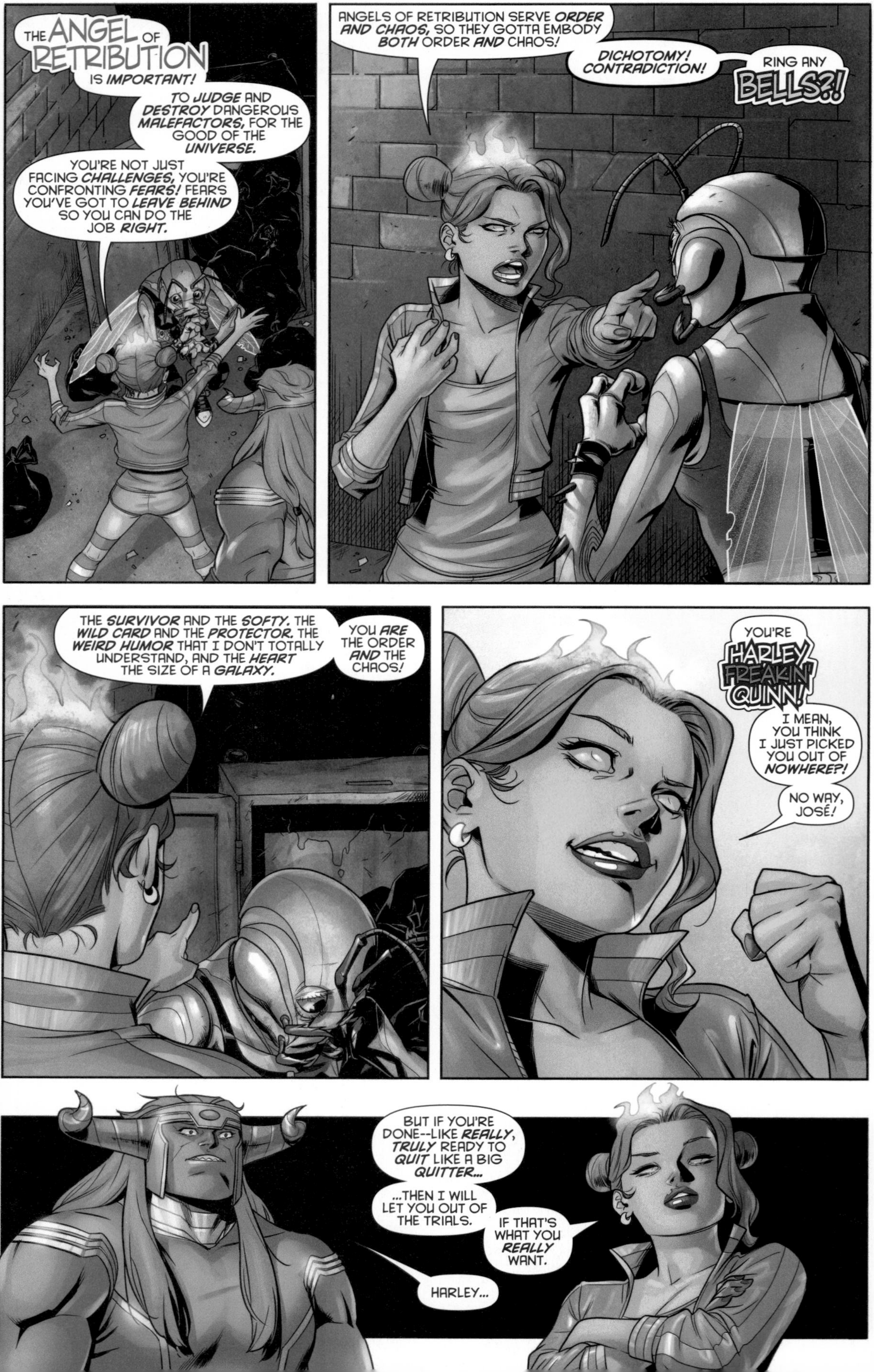
THE ANGEL OF RETRIBUTION IS IMPORTANT!
TO JUDGE AND DESTROY DANGEROUS MALEFACTORS, FOR THE GOOD OF THE UNIVERSE.
YOU'RE NOT JUST FACING CHALLENGES, YOU'RE CONFRONTING FEARS! FEARS YOU'VE GOT TO LEAVE BEHIND SO YOU CAN DO THE JOB RIGHT.
ANGELS OF RETRIBUTION SERVE ORDER AND CHAOS, SO THEY GOTTA EMBODY BOTH ORDER AND CHAOS!
DICHOTOMY! CONTRADICTION!
RING ANY BELLS?!
THE SURVIVOR AND THE SOFTY. THE WILD CARD AND THE PROTECTOR. THE WEIRD HUMOR THAT I DON'T TOTALLY UNDERSTAND, AND THE HEART THE SIZE OF A GALAXY.
YOU ARE THE ORDER AND THE CHAOS!
YOU'RE HARLEY FREAKIN' QUINN!
I MEAN, YOU THINK I JUST PICKED YOU OUT OF NOWHERE?!
NO WAY, JOSÉ!
BUT IF YOU'RE DONE--LIKE REALLY, TRULY READY TO QUIT LIKE A BIG QUITTER...
...THEN I WILL LET YOU OUT OF THE TRIALS.
IF THAT'S WHAT YOU REALLY WANT.
HARLEY...

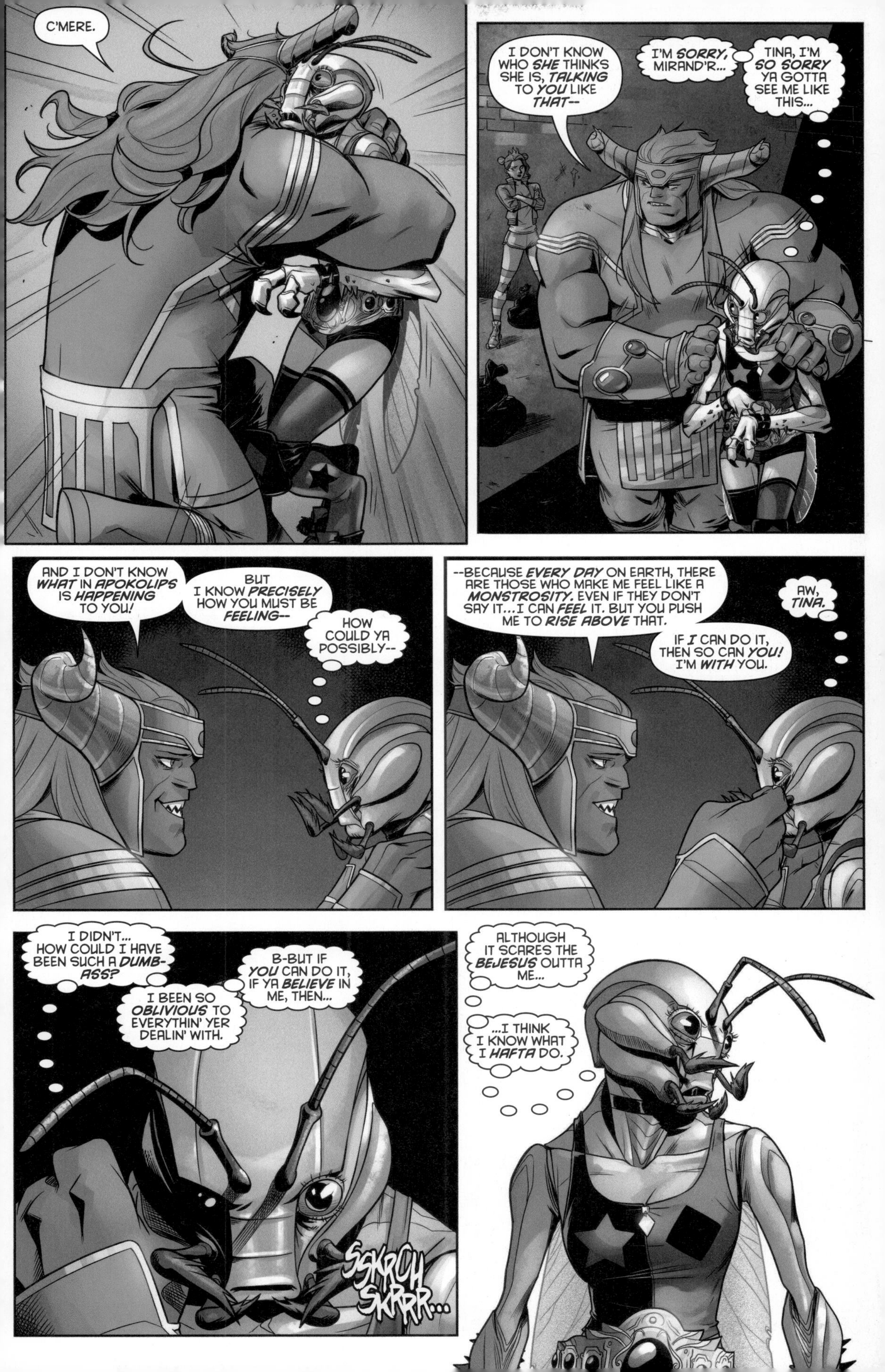
C'MERE.
I DON'T KNOW WHO SHE THINKS SHE IS, TALKING TO YOU LIKE THAT--
I'M SORRY, MIRAND'R...
TINA, I'M SO SORRY YA GOTTA SEE ME LIKE THIS...
AND I DON'T KNOW WHAT IN APOKOLIPS IS HAPPENING TO YOU!
BUT I KNOW PRECISELY HOW YOU MUST BE FEELING--
HOW COULD YA POSSIBLY--
--BECAUSE EVERY DAY ON EARTH, THERE ARE THOSE WHO MAKE ME FEEL LIKE A MONSTROSITY. EVEN IF THEY DON'T SAY IT... I CAN FEEL IT. BUT YOU PUSH ME TO RISE ABOVE THAT.
AW, TINA.
IF I CAN DO IT, THEN SO CAN YOU! I'M WITH YOU.
I DIDN'T... HOW COULD I HAVE BEEN SUCH A DUMB-ASS?
I BEEN SO OBLIVIOUS TO EVERYTHIN' YER DEALIN' WITH.
B-BUT IF YOU CAN DO IT, IF YA BELIEVE IN ME, THEN...
SSKRCH SKRRR...
ALTHOUGH IT SCARES THE BEJESUS OUTTA ME...
...I THINK I KNOW WHAT I HAFTA DO.

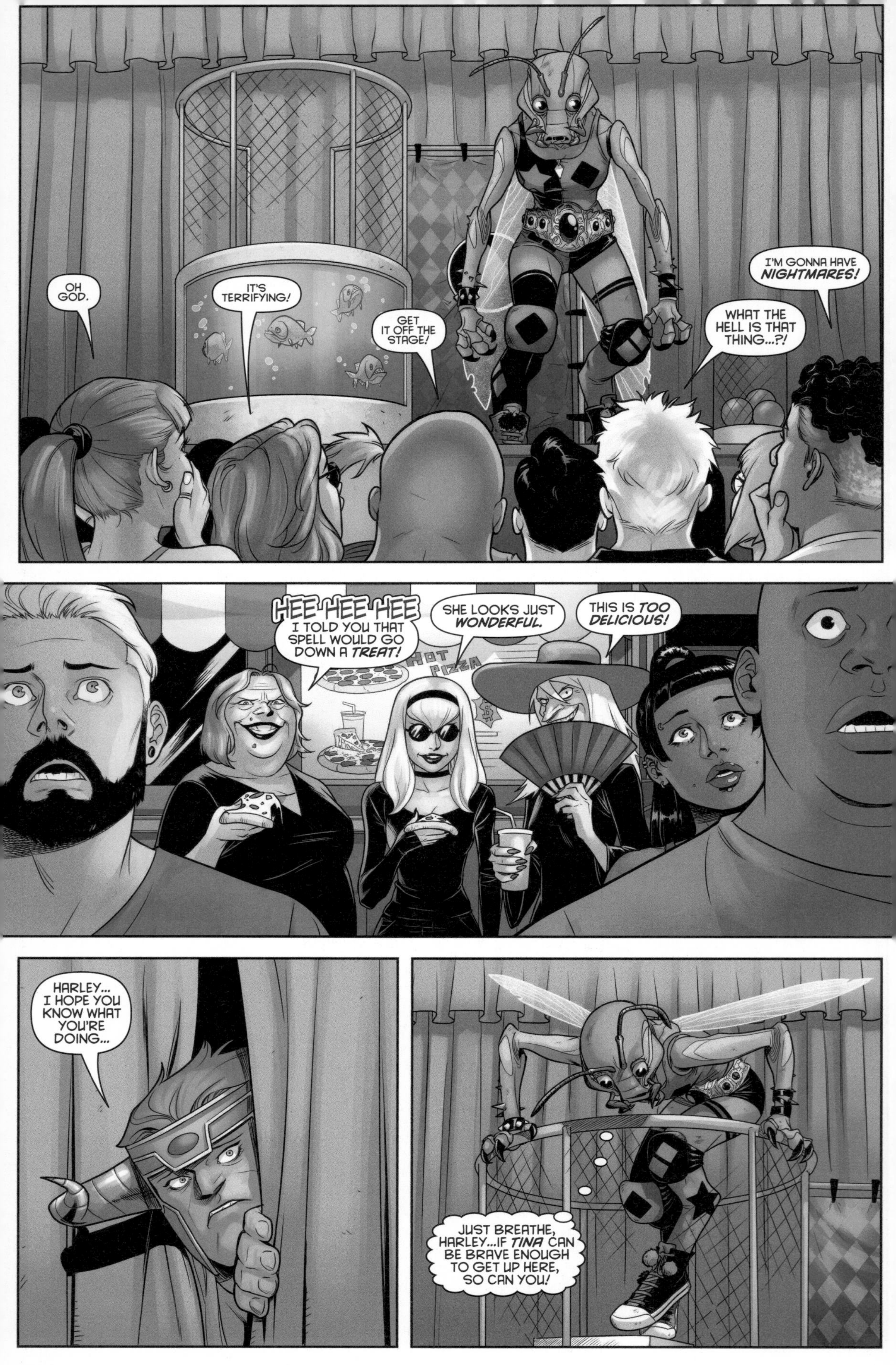
OH GOD.
IT'S TERRIFYING!
GET IT OFF THE STAGE!
I'M GONNA HAVE NIGHTMARES!
WHAT THE HELL IS THAT THING...?!
HEE HEE HEE I TOLD YOU THAT SPELL WOULD GO DOWN A TREAT!
HOT PIZZA
SHE LOOKS JUST WONDERFUL.
THIS IS TOO DELICIOUS!
HARLEY... I HOPE YOU KNOW WHAT YOU'RE DOING...
JUST BREATHE, HARLEY...IF TINA CAN BE BRAVE ENOUGH TO GET UP HERE, SO CAN YOU!

HAW HAW! LOOK AT THE *FREAK*!

CAN'T LET MYSELF GET TWISTED BY THE HATERS. I'VE HAD IT EASY, BEIN' IN FRONT OF PEOPLE WHEN THEY LIKE WHAT THEY SEE...

YA GOTTA BE KIDDING ME!

CALL THE EXTERMINATOR!

MY EYES ARE BURNING!

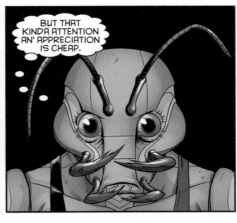

BUT THAT KINDA ATTENTION AN' APPRECIATION IS CHEAP.

ME FIRST!

HERE WE GO--

AN' IF THAT'S ALL THESE PEOPLE GOT FER ME, WELL--

WHAM

--THEN I DON'T NEED THEIR APPROVAL IN THE FIRST PLACE!

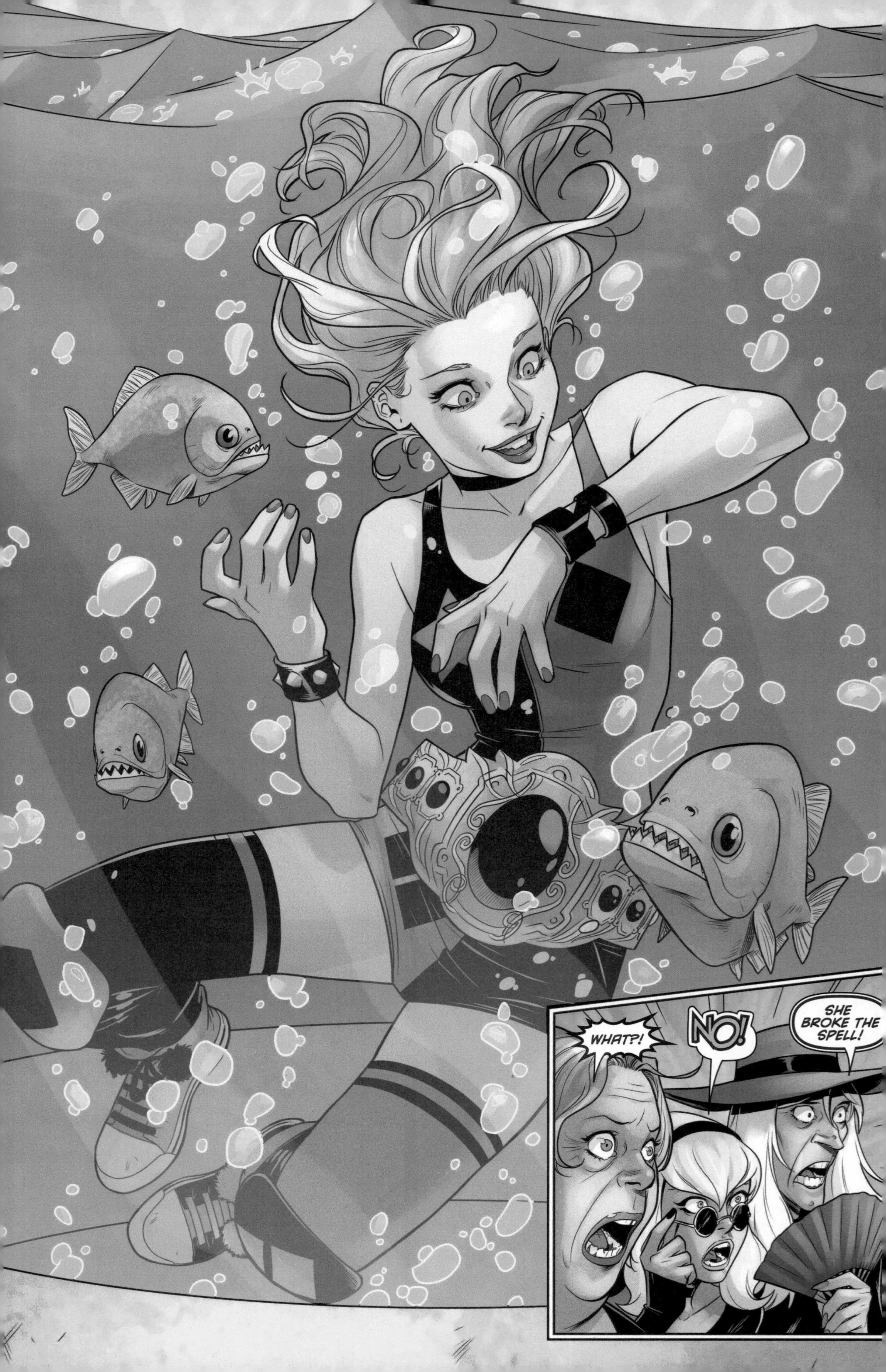
WHAT?!
NO!
SHE BROKE THE SPELL!

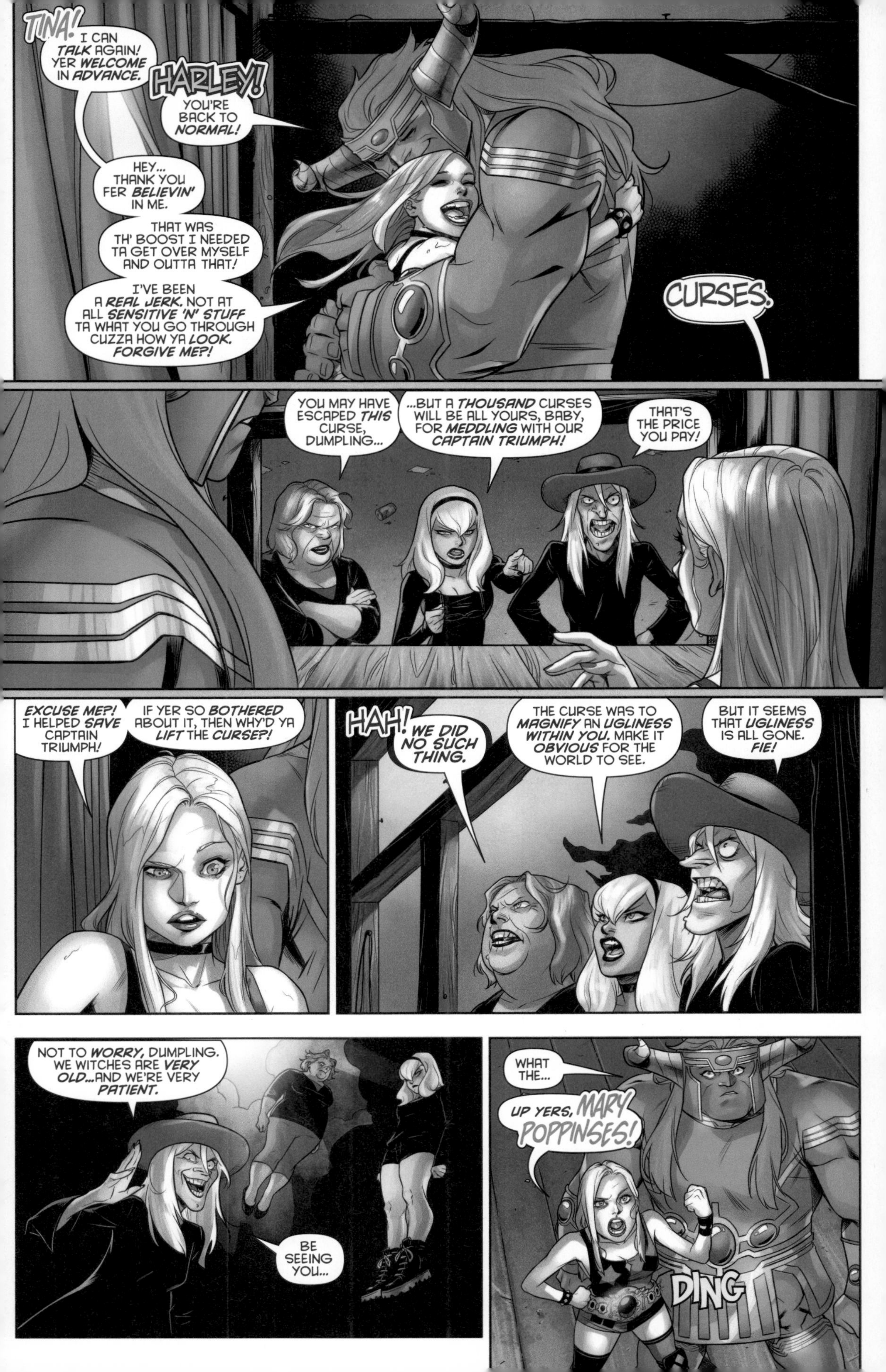
TINA!
I CAN TALK AGAIN! YER WELCOME IN ADVANCE.
HARLEY!
YOU'RE BACK TO NORMAL!
HEY... THANK YOU FER BELIEVIN' IN ME.
THAT WAS TH' BOOST I NEEDED TA GET OVER MYSELF AND OUTTA THAT!
I'VE BEEN A REAL JERK. NOT AT ALL SENSITIVE 'N' STUFF TA WHAT YOU GO THROUGH CUZZA HOW YA LOOK. FORGIVE ME?!
CURSES.
YOU MAY HAVE ESCAPED THIS CURSE, DUMPLING...
...BUT A THOUSAND CURSES WILL BE ALL YOURS, BABY, FOR MEDDLING WITH OUR CAPTAIN TRIUMPH!
THAT'S THE PRICE YOU PAY!
EXCUSE ME?! I HELPED SAVE CAPTAIN TRIUMPH!
IF YER SO BOTHERED ABOUT IT, THEN WHY'D YA LIFT THE CURSE?!
HAH!
WE DID NO SUCH THING.
THE CURSE WAS TO MAGNIFY AN UGLINESS WITHIN YOU. MAKE IT OBVIOUS FOR THE WORLD TO SEE.
BUT IT SEEMS THAT UGLINESS IS ALL GONE. FIE!
NOT TO WORRY, DUMPLING. WE WITCHES ARE VERY OLD...AND WE'RE VERY PATIENT.
BE SEEING YOU...
WHAT THE...
UP YERS, MARY POPPINSES!
DING

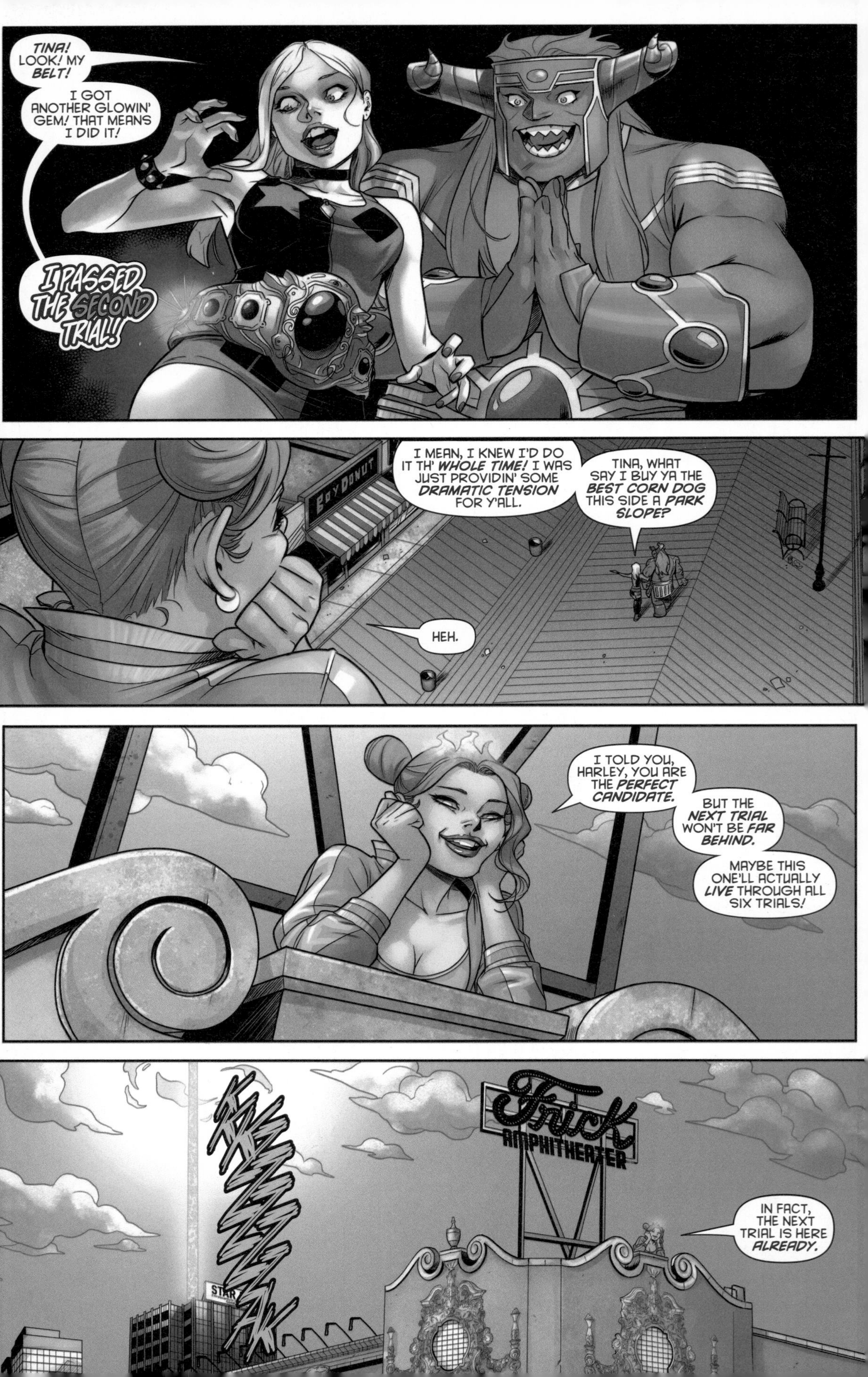
TINA! LOOK! MY BELT!
I GOT ANOTHER GLOWIN' GEM! THAT MEANS I DID IT!
I PASSED THE SECOND TRIAL!
I MEAN, I KNEW I'D DO IT TH' WHOLE TIME! I WAS JUST PROVIDIN' SOME DRAMATIC TENSION FOR Y'ALL.
TINA, WHAT SAY I BUY YA THE BEST CORN DOG THIS SIDE A PARK SLOPE?
HEH.
I TOLD YOU, HARLEY, YOU ARE THE PERFECT CANDIDATE.
BUT THE NEXT TRIAL WON'T BE FAR BEHIND.
MAYBE THIS ONE'LL ACTUALLY LIVE THROUGH ALL SIX TRIALS!
Frick
AMPHITHEATER
IN FACT, THE NEXT TRIAL IS HERE ALREADY.

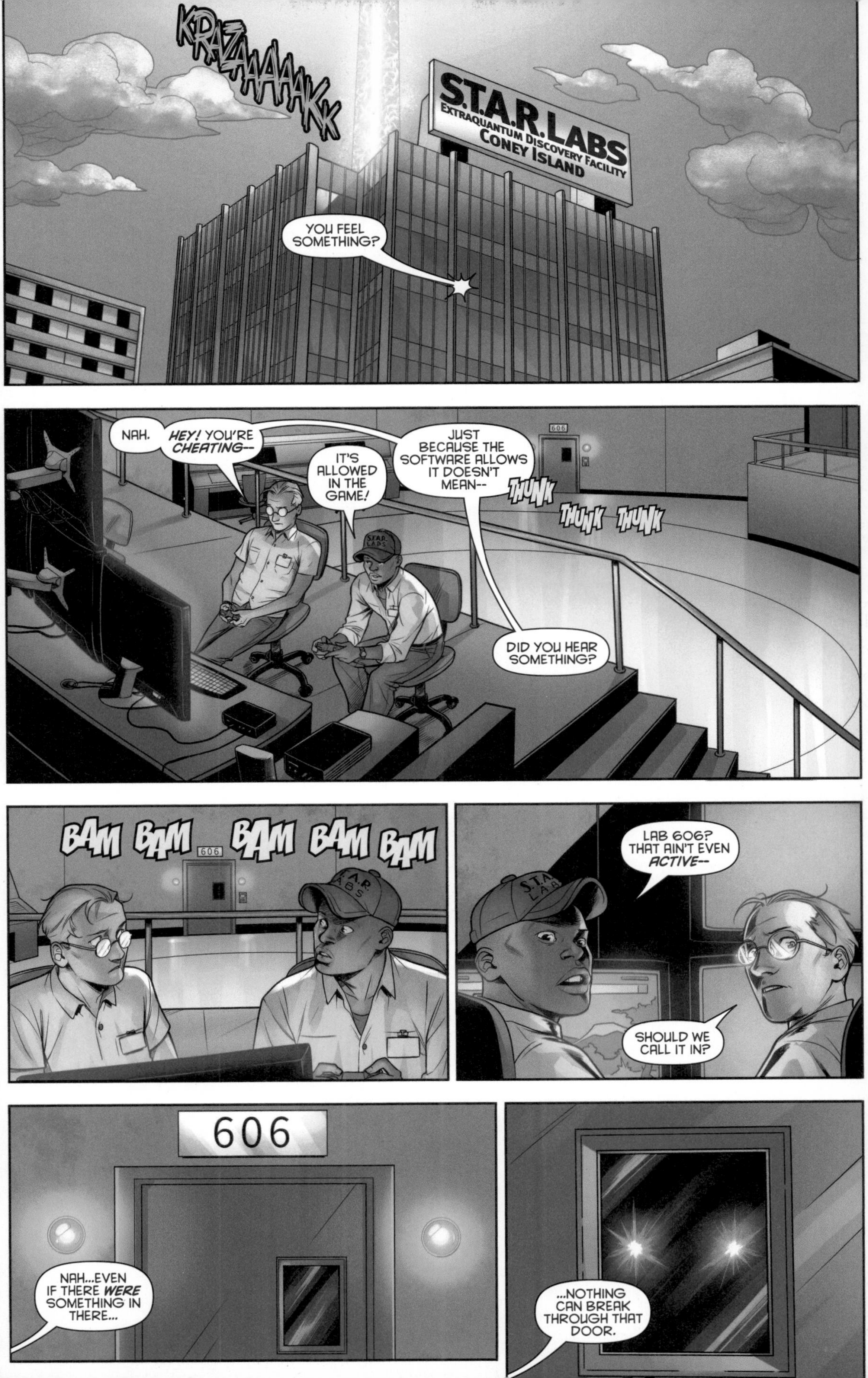
KRAZAAAAAKK
S.T.A.R. LABS
EXTRAQUANTUM DISCOVERY FACILITY
CONEY ISLAND
YOU FEEL SOMETHING?
NAH.
HEY! YOU'RE CHEATING--
IT'S ALLOWED IN THE GAME!
JUST BECAUSE THE SOFTWARE ALLOWS IT DOESN'T MEAN--
THUNK
THUNK THUNK
DID YOU HEAR SOMETHING?
BAM BAM BAM BAM BAM
606
LAB 606? THAT AIN'T EVEN ACTIVE--
SHOULD WE CALL IT IN?
606
NAH...EVEN IF THERE WERE SOMETHING IN THERE...
...NOTHING CAN BREAK THROUGH THAT DOOR.

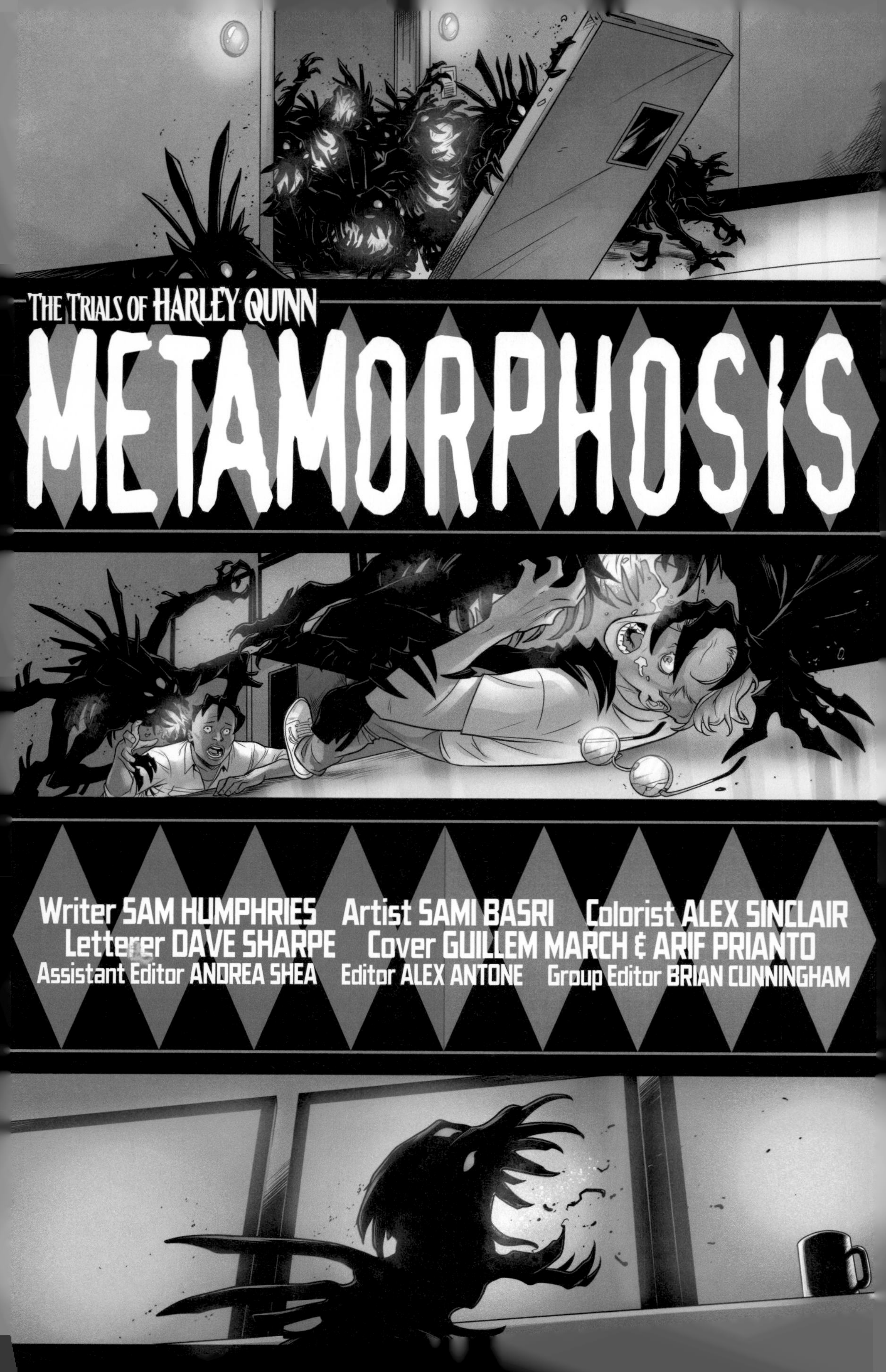
THE TRIALS OF HARLEY QUINN
METAMORPHOSIS
Writer SAM HUMPHRIES Artist SAMI BASRI Colorist ALEX SINCLAIR
Letterer DAVE SHARPE Cover GUILLEM MARCH & ARIF PRIANTO
Assistant Editor ANDREA SHEA Editor ALEX ANTONE Group Editor BRIAN CUNNINGHAM

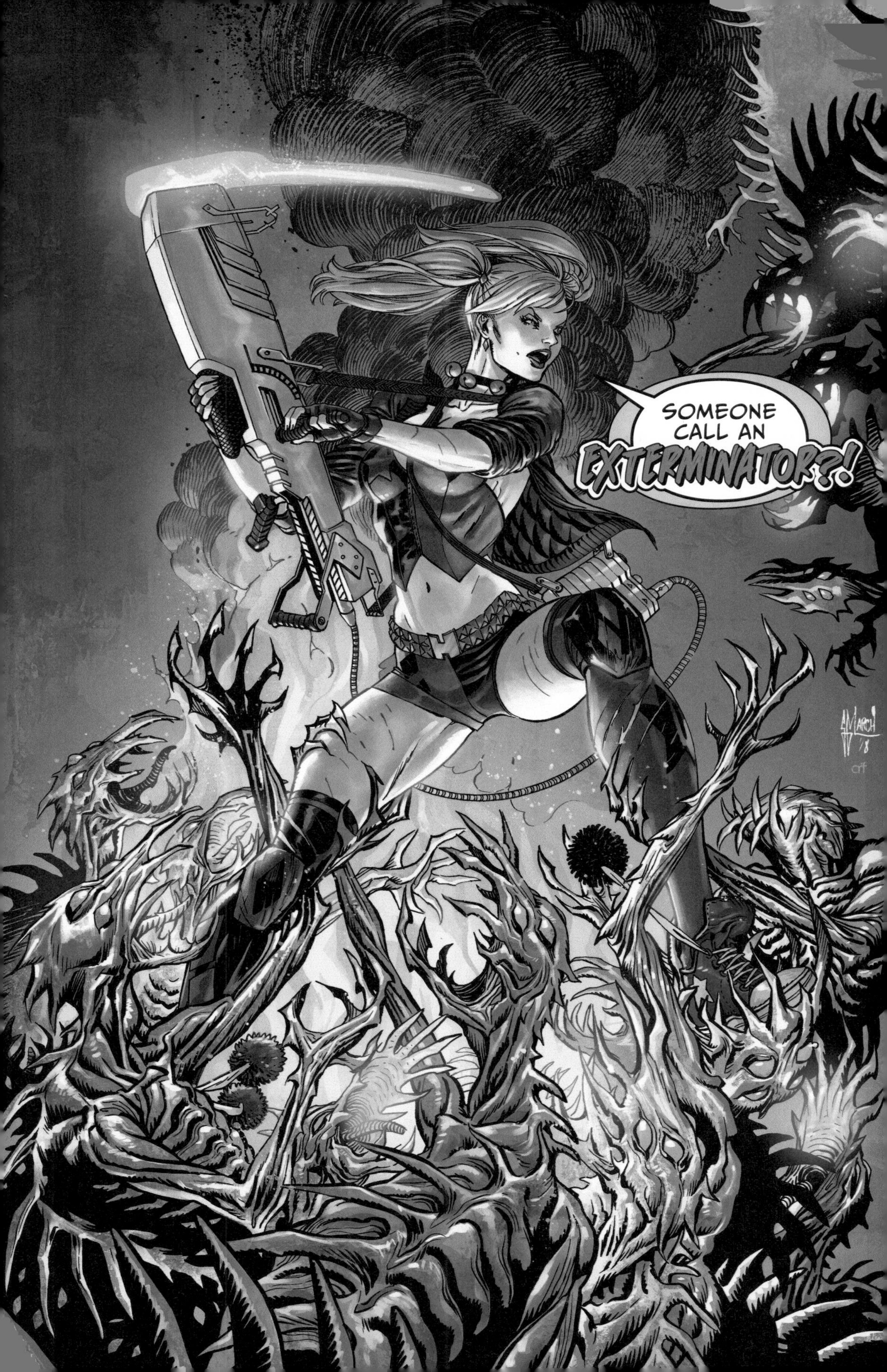
SOMEONE CALL AN EXTERMINATOR?!

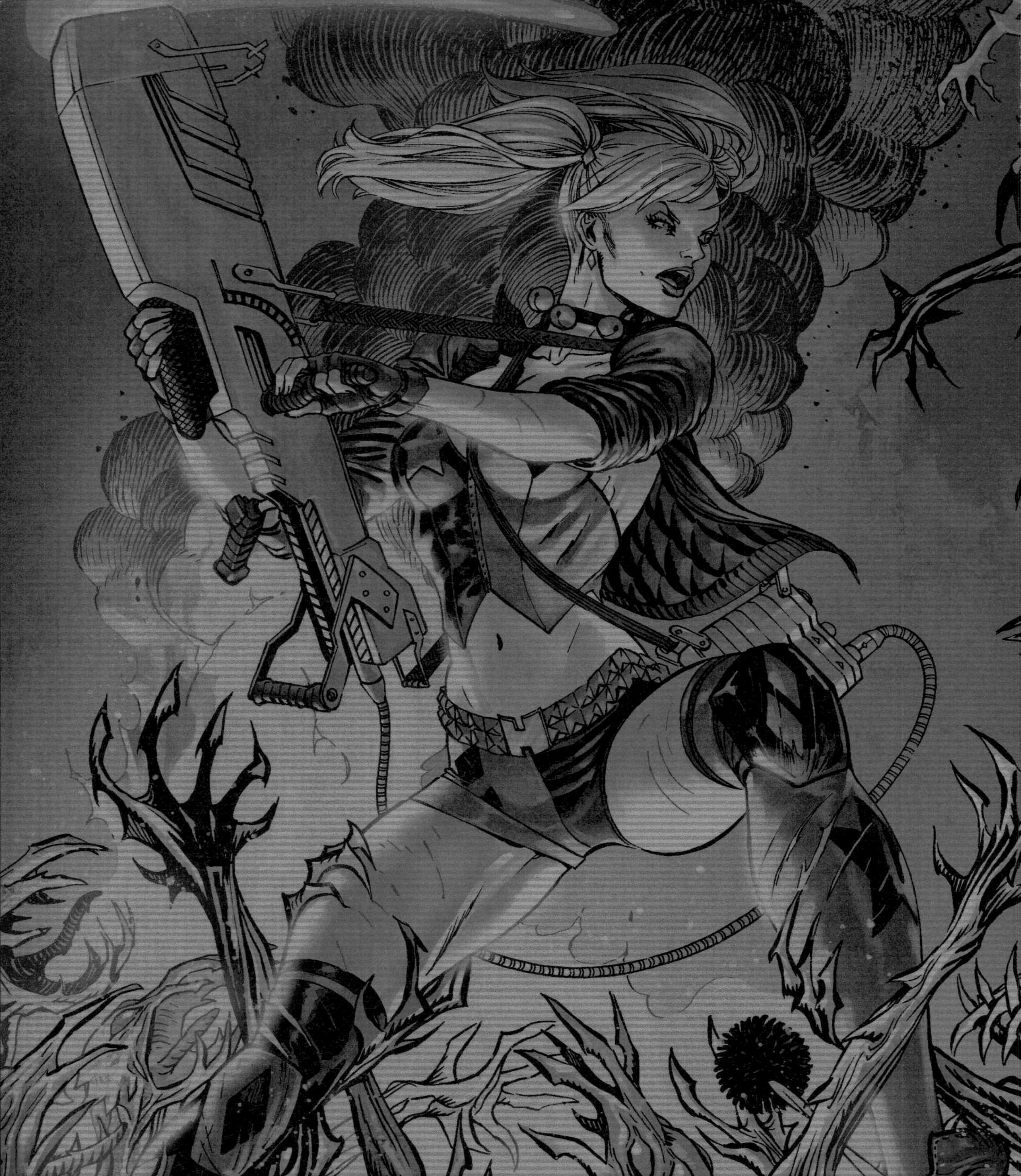

HARLEY QUINN

#60

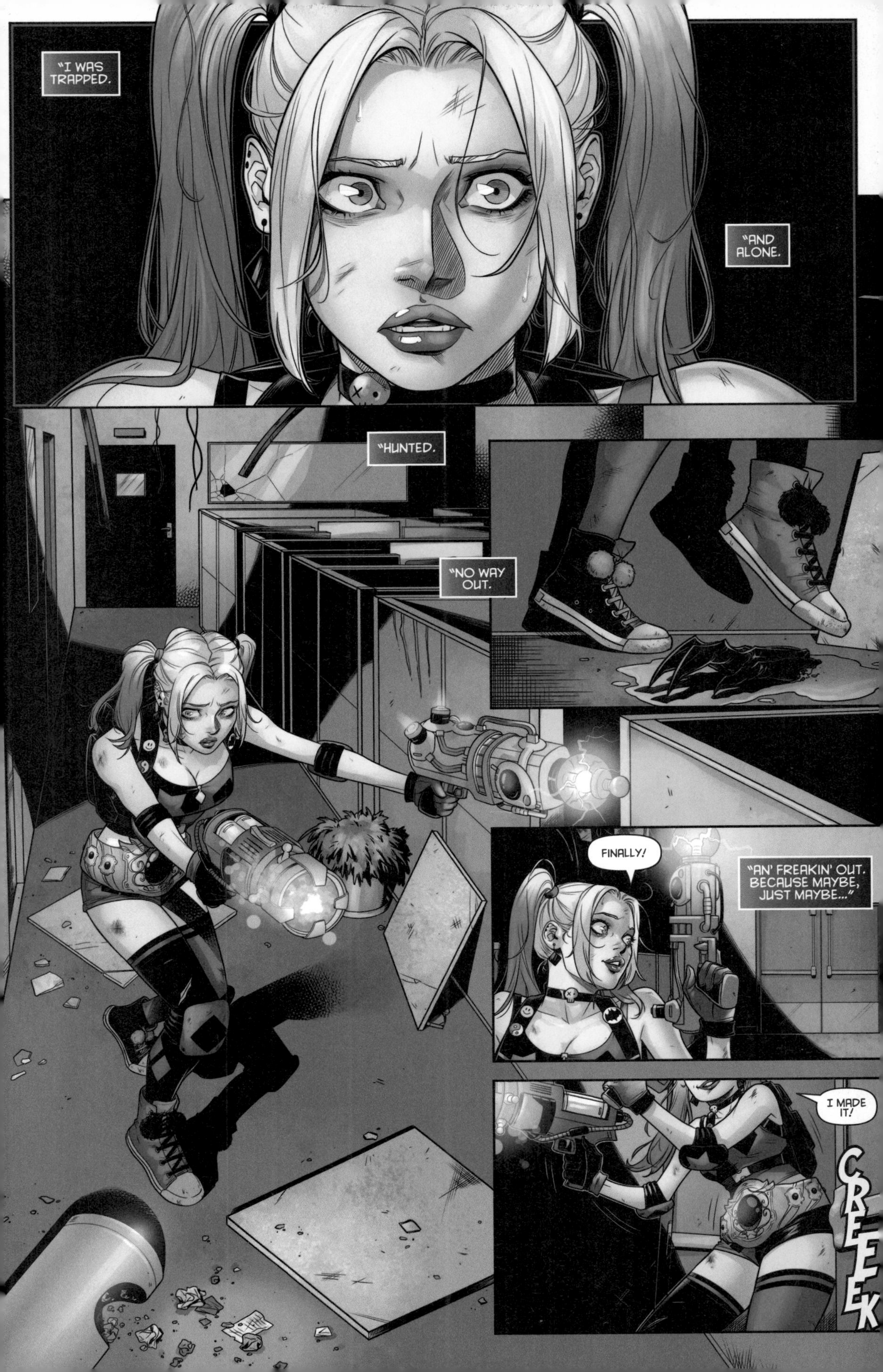
"I WAS TRAPPED.
"AND ALONE.
"HUNTED.
"NO WAY OUT.
FINALLY!
"AN' FREAKIN' OUT. BECAUSE MAYBE, JUST MAYBE..."
I MADE IT!
CREEEK

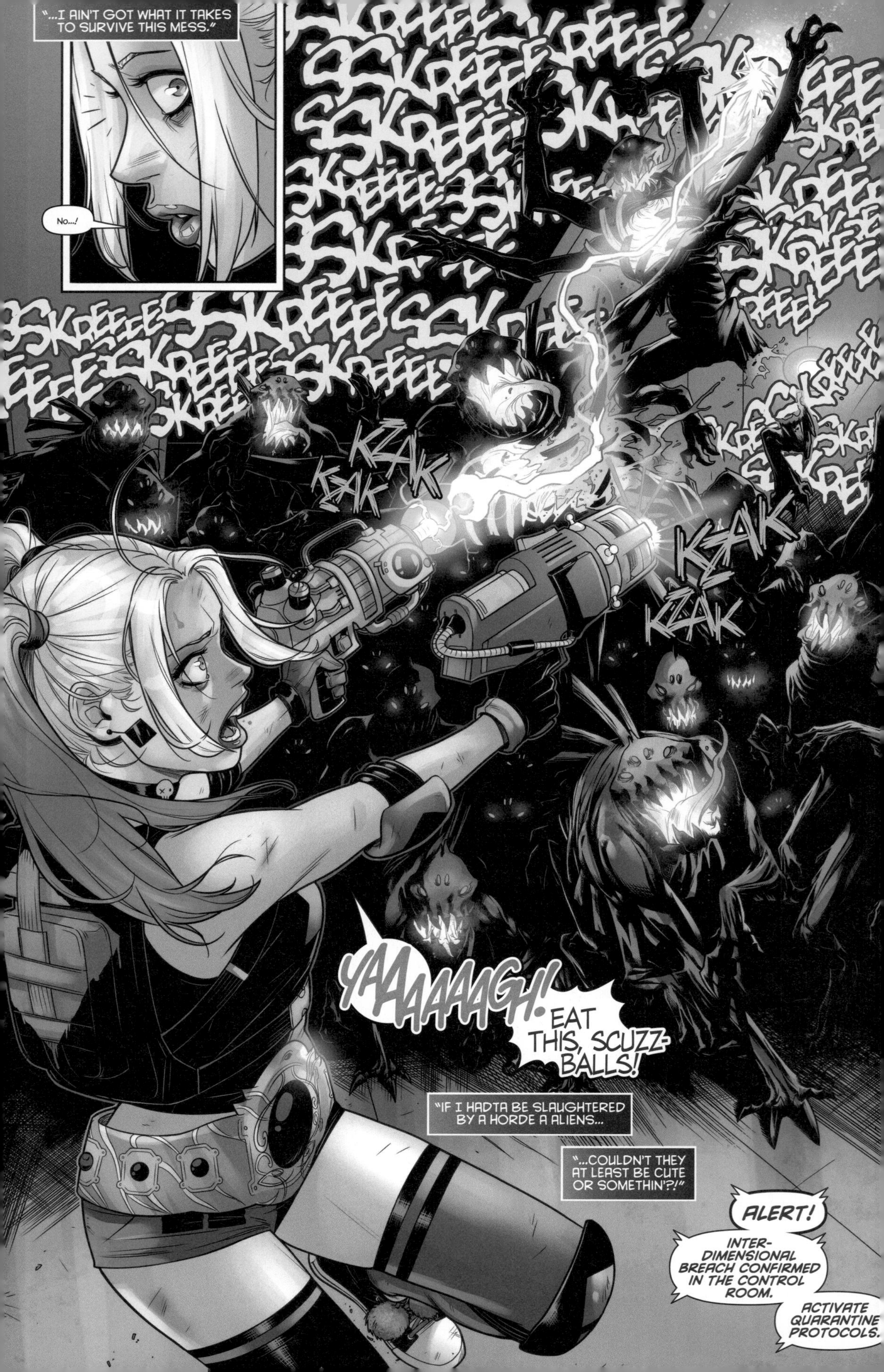

"...I AIN'T GOT WHAT IT TAKES TO SURVIVE THIS MESS."
No...!
SKREEEE SKREEEE SKREEEE
KZAK KZAK KZAK
KZAK KZAK
YAAAAAAAGH! EAT THIS, SCUZZ-BALLS!
"IF I HADTA BE SLAUGHTERED BY A HORDE A ALIENS...
"...COULDN'T THEY AT LEAST BE CUTE OR SOMETHIN'?!"
ALERT!
INTER-DIMENSIONAL BREACH CONFIRMED IN THE CONTROL ROOM.
ACTIVATE QUARANTINE PROTOCOLS.

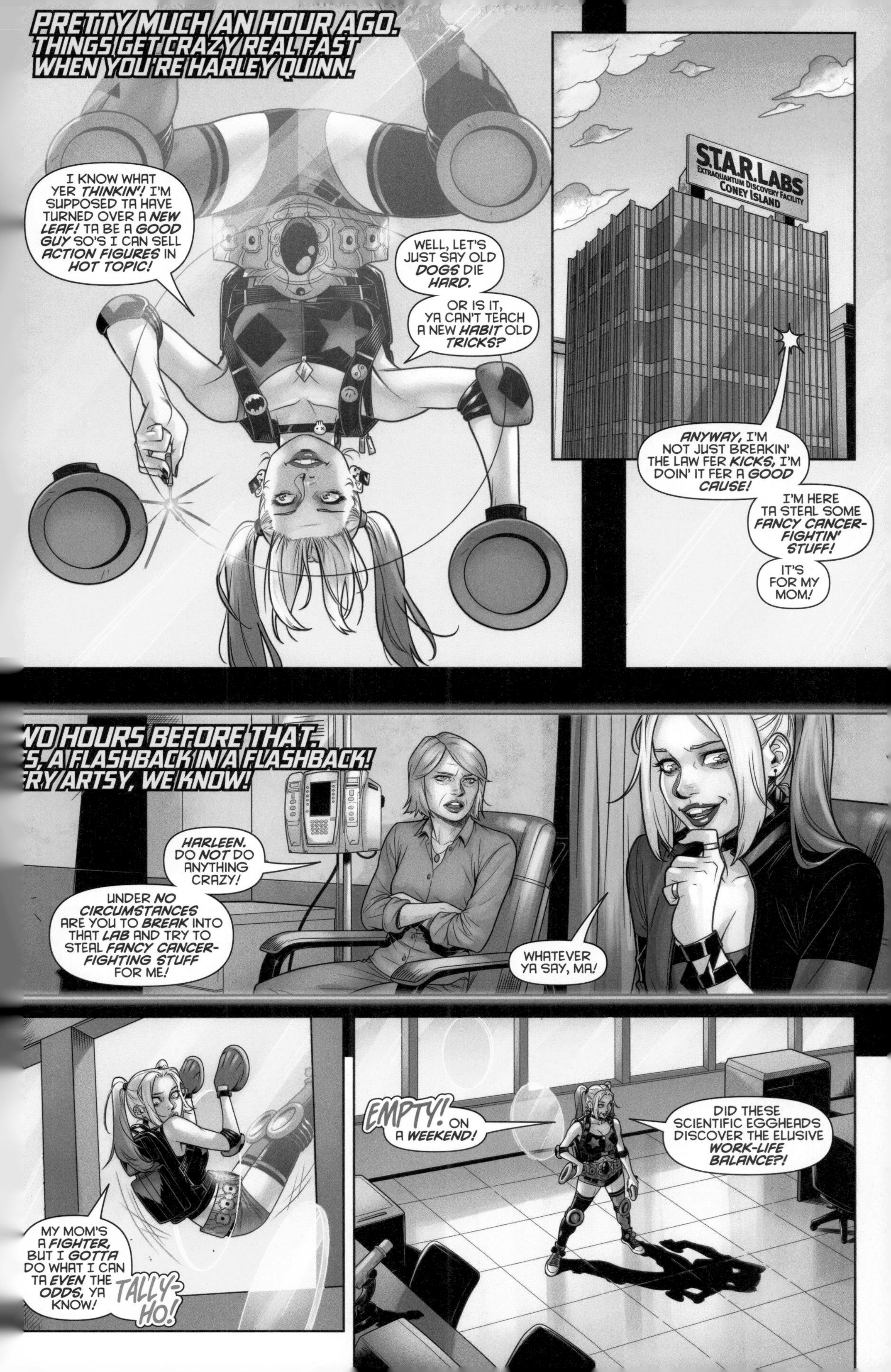

PRETTY MUCH AN HOUR AGO. THINGS GET CRAZY REAL FAST WHEN YOU'RE HARLEY QUINN.
I KNOW WHAT YER THINKIN'! I'M SUPPOSED TA HAVE TURNED OVER A NEW LEAF! TA BE A GOOD GUY SO'S I CAN SELL ACTION FIGURES IN HOT TOPIC!
WELL, LET'S JUST SAY OLD DOGS DIE HARD.
OR IS IT, YA CAN'T TEACH A NEW HABIT OLD TRICKS?
S.T.A.R. LABS EXTRAQUANTUM DISCOVERY FACILITY CONEY ISLAND
ANYWAY, I'M NOT JUST BREAKIN' THE LAW FER KICKS, I'M DOIN' IT FER A GOOD CAUSE!
I'M HERE TA STEAL SOME FANCY CANCER-FIGHTIN' STUFF!
IT'S FOR MY MOM!
WO HOURS BEFORE THAT. S, A FLASHBACK IN A FLASHBACK! RY ARTSY, WE KNOW!
HARLEEN. DO NOT DO ANYTHING CRAZY!
UNDER NO CIRCUMSTANCES ARE YOU TO BREAK INTO THAT LAB AND TRY TO STEAL FANCY CANCER-FIGHTING STUFF FOR ME!
WHATEVER YA SAY, MA!
MY MOM'S A FIGHTER, BUT I GOTTA DO WHAT I CAN TA EVEN THE ODDS, YA KNOW!
TALLY-HO!
EMPTY! ON A WEEKEND!
DID THESE SCIENTIFIC EGGHEADS DISCOVER THE ELUSIVE WORK-LIFE BALANCE?!

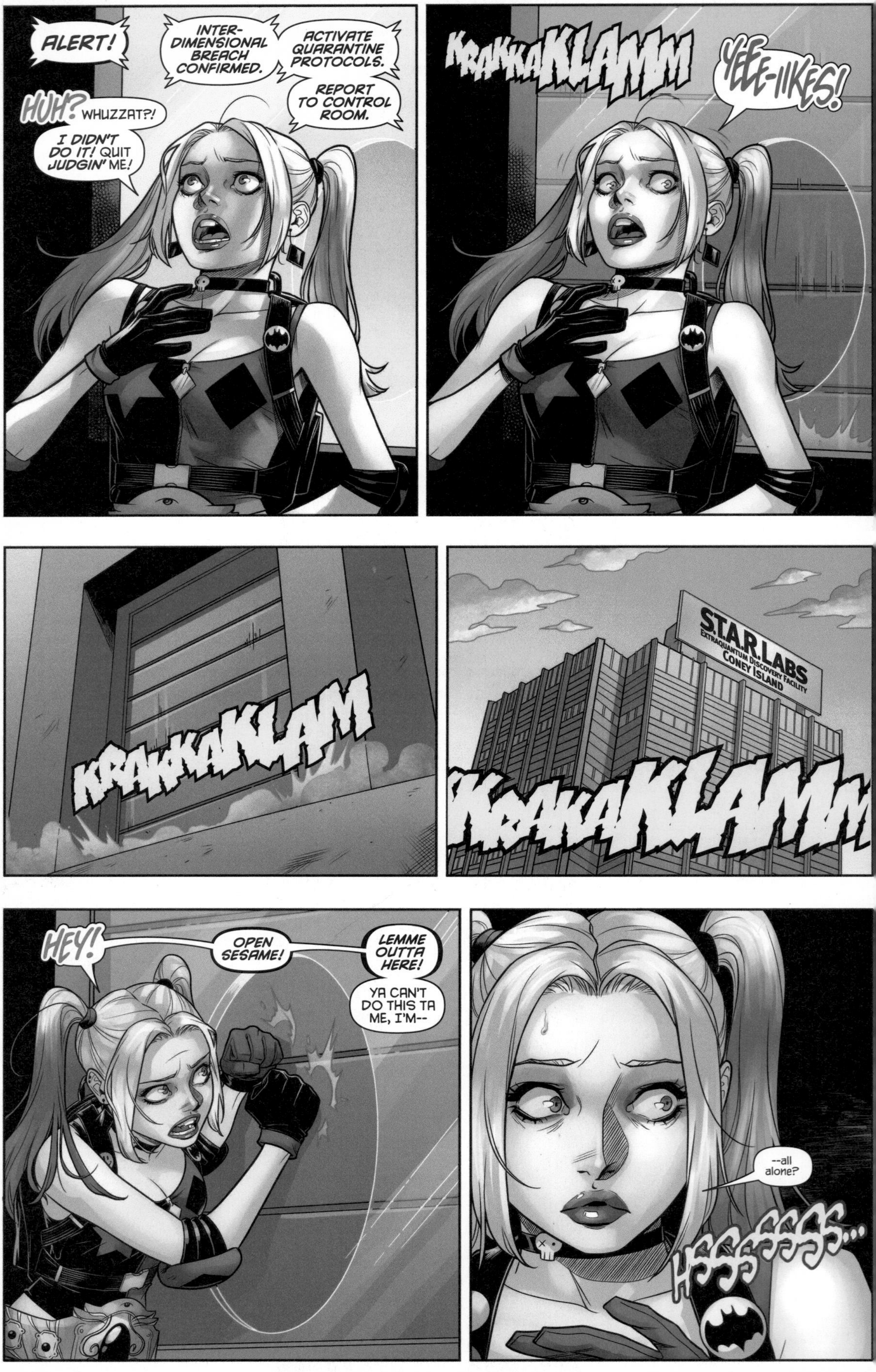
ALERT!
INTER-DIMENSIONAL BREACH CONFIRMED.
ACTIVATE QUARANTINE PROTOCOLS.
REPORT TO CONTROL ROOM.
HUH? WHUZZAT?!
I DIDN'T DO IT! QUIT JUDGIN' ME!
KRAKKAKLAMM
YEEE-IIKES!
KRAKKAKLAM
S.T.A.R. LABS
EXTRAQUANTUM DISCOVERY FACILITY
CONEY ISLAND
KRAKKAKLAMM
HEY!
OPEN SESAME!
LEMME OUTTA HERE!
YA CAN'T DO THIS TA ME, I'M--
--all alone?
HSSSSSSS...

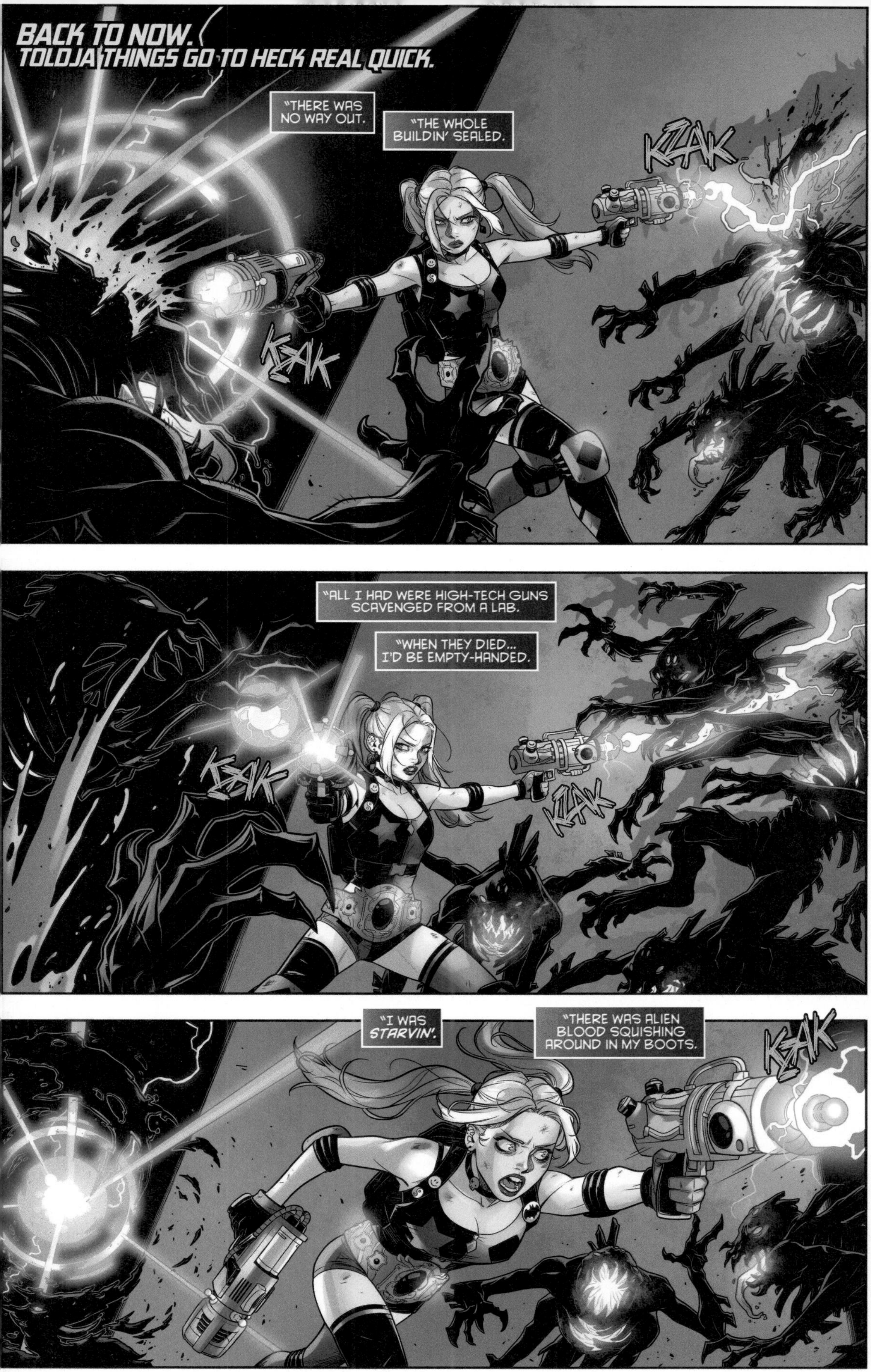
BACK TO NOW.
TOLDJA THINGS GO TO HECK REAL QUICK.
"THERE WAS NO WAY OUT.
"THE WHOLE BUILDIN' SEALED.
KZAK
KZAK
"ALL I HAD WERE HIGH-TECH GUNS SCAVENGED FROM A LAB.
"WHEN THEY DIED... I'D BE EMPTY-HANDED.
KZAK
KZAK
"I WAS STARVIN'.
"THERE WAS ALIEN BLOOD SQUISHING AROUND IN MY BOOTS.
KZAK

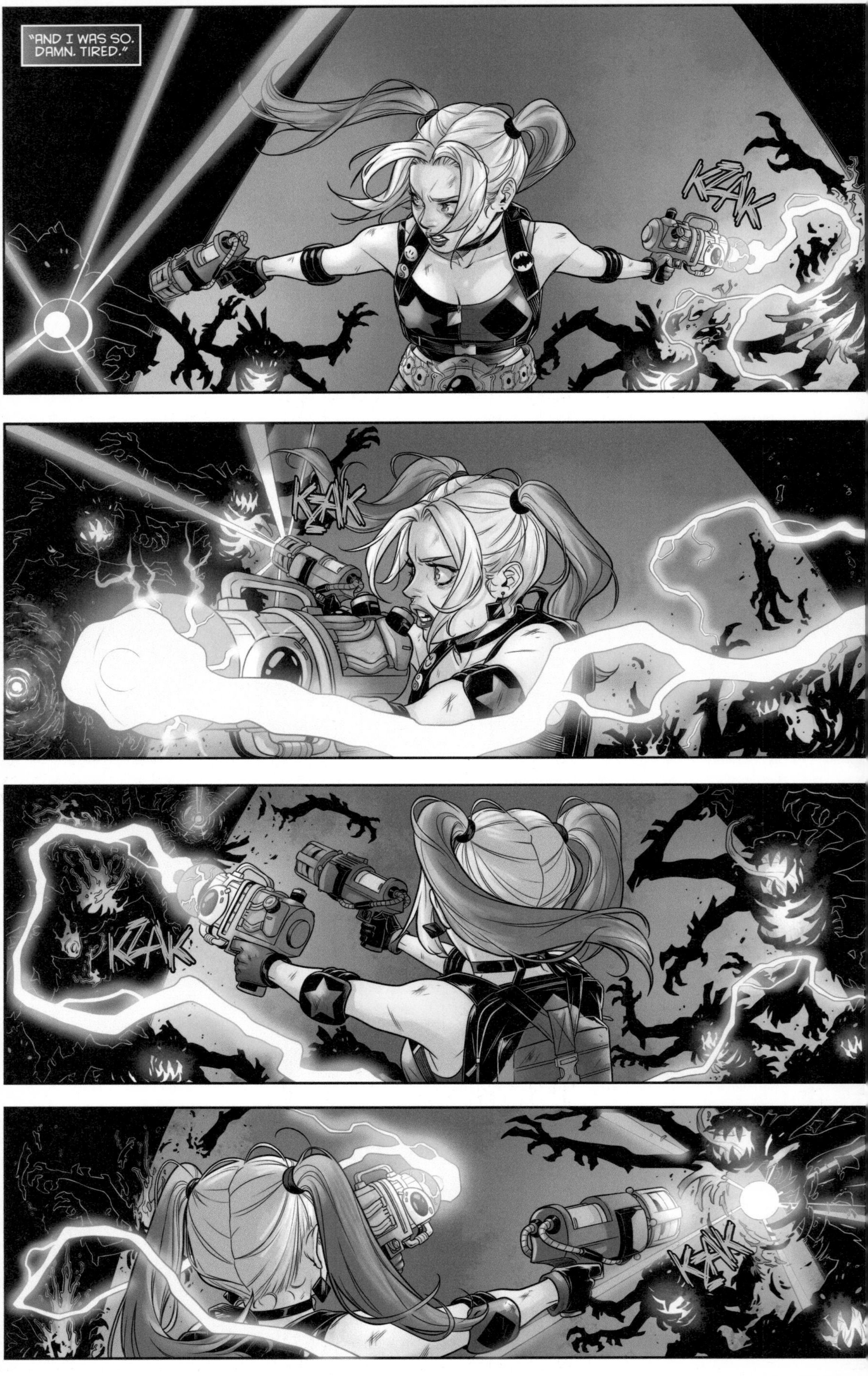
"AND I WAS SO. DAMN. TIRED."
KZAK
KZAK
KZAK
KZAK

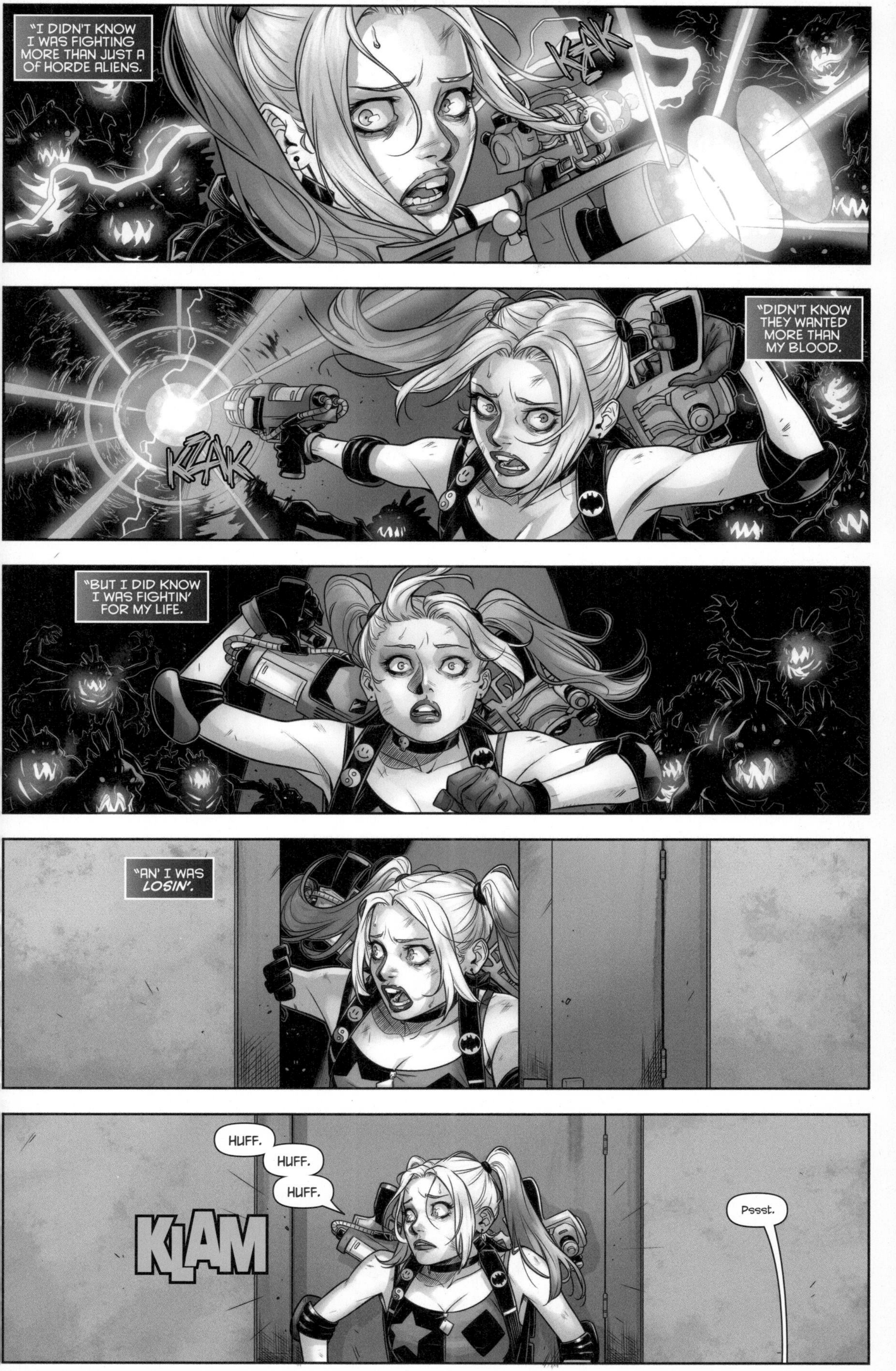
"I DIDN'T KNOW I WAS FIGHTING MORE THAN JUST A OF HORDE ALIENS.
KZAK
"DIDN'T KNOW THEY WANTED MORE THAN MY BLOOD.
KZAK
"BUT I DID KNOW I WAS FIGHTIN' FOR MY LIFE.
"AN' I WAS *LOSIN'*.
HUFF.
HUFF.
HUFF.
KLAM
Pssst.

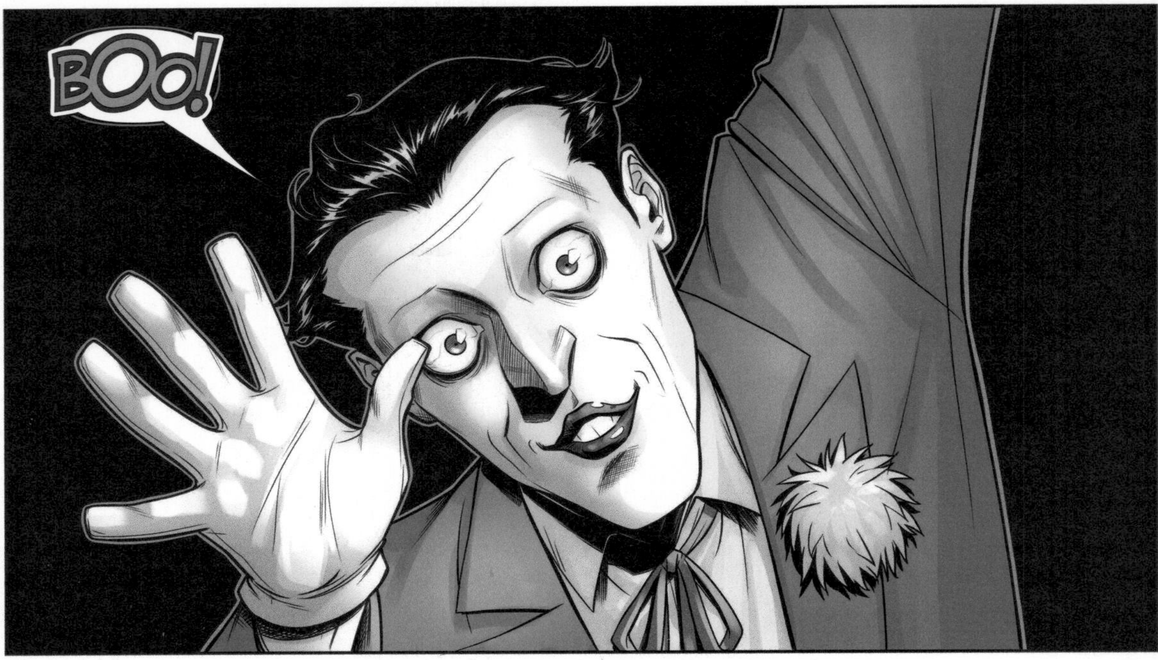
BOO!

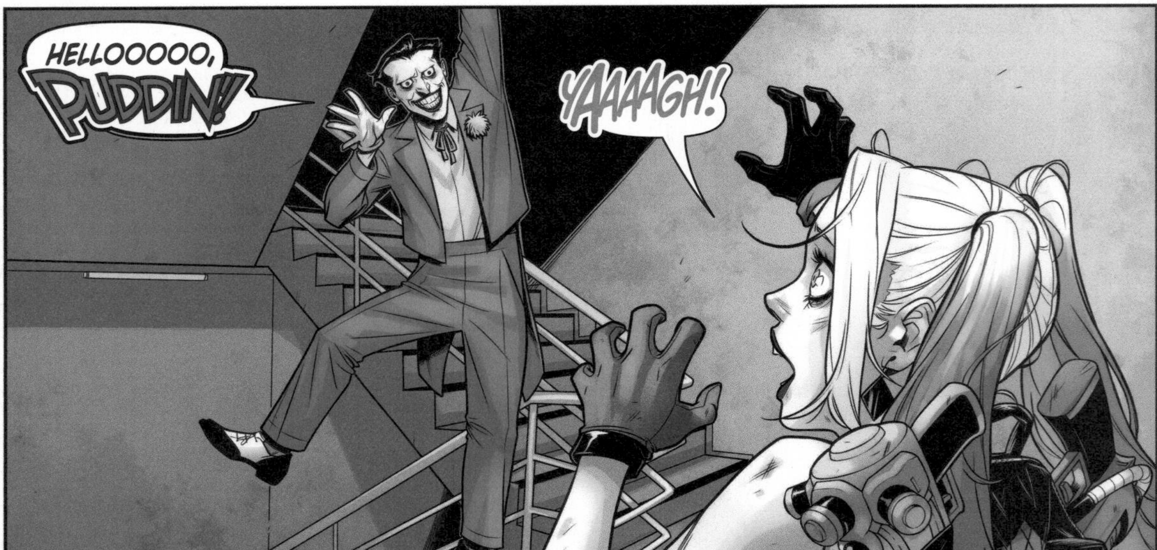
HELLOOOOO, PUDDIN'!
YAAAAGH!

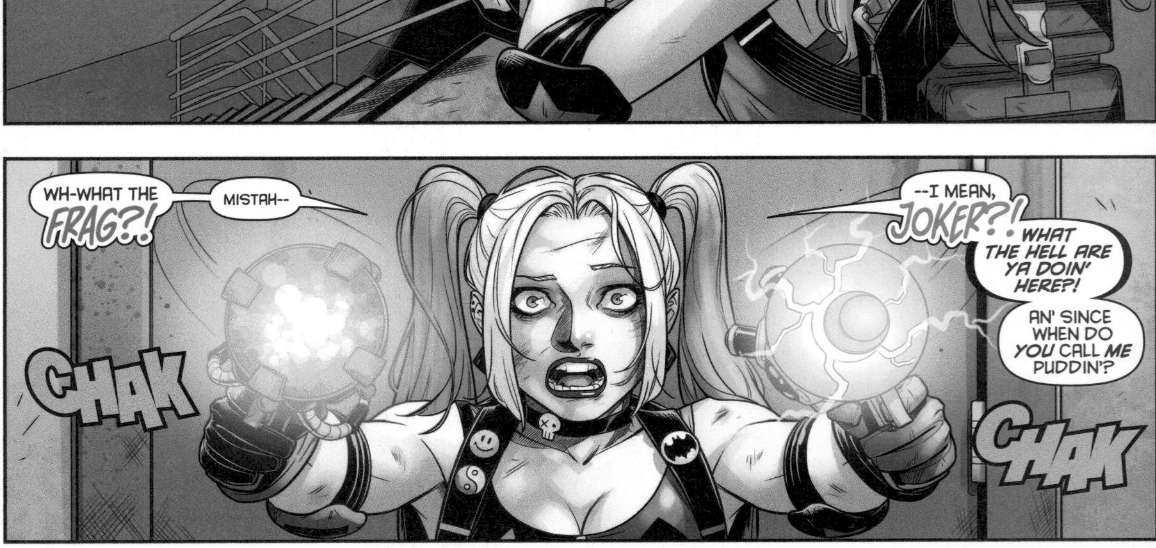
WH-WHAT THE FRAG?!
MISTAH--
--I MEAN, JOKER?!
WHAT THE HELL ARE YA DOIN' HERE?!
AN' SINCE WHEN DO YOU CALL ME PUDDIN'?
CHAK
CHAK

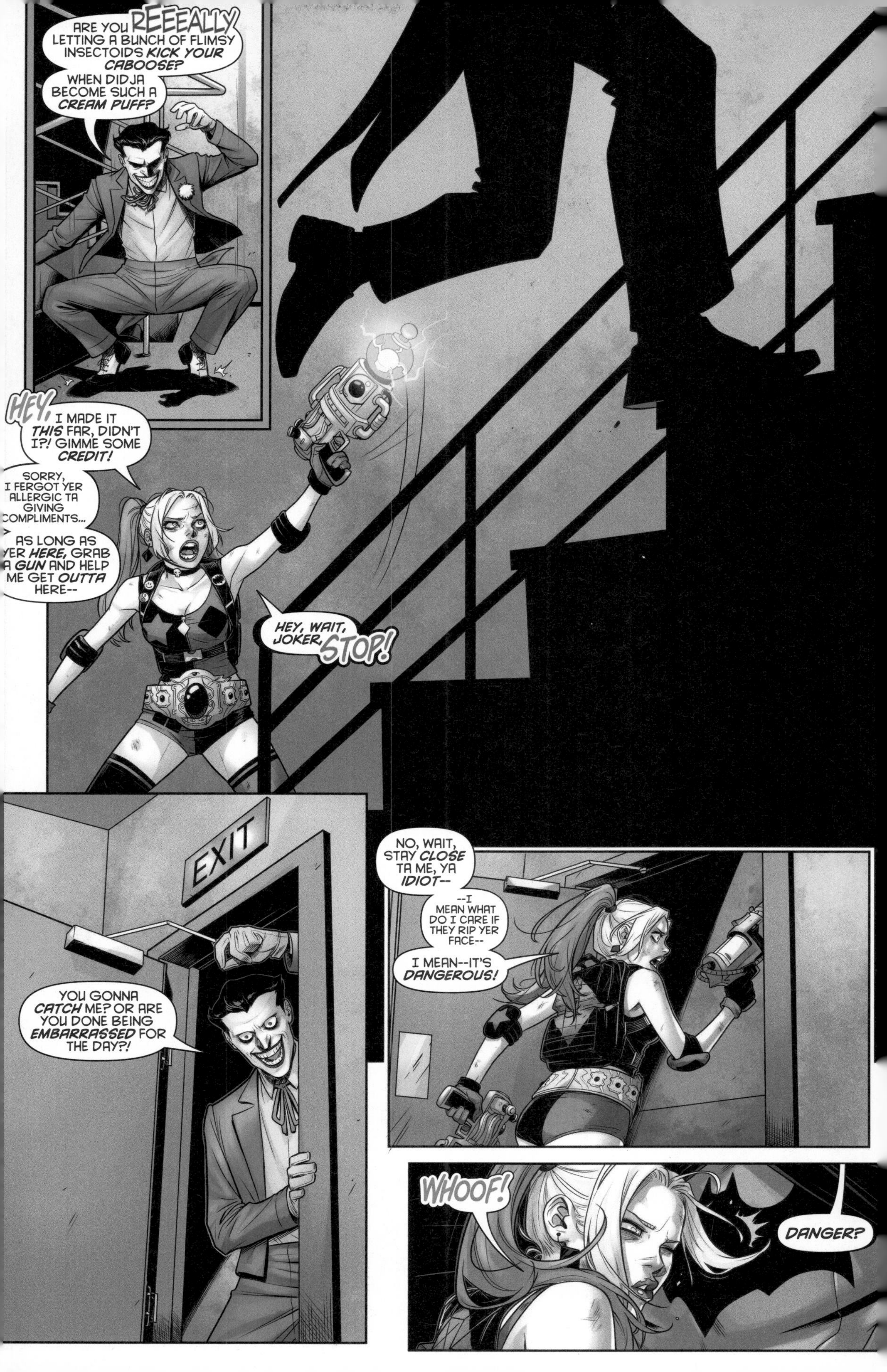
ARE YOU REEEALLY LETTING A BUNCH OF FLIMSY INSECTOIDS KICK YOUR CABOOSE?
WHEN DIDJA BECOME SUCH A CREAM PUFF?
HEY, I MADE IT THIS FAR, DIDN'T I?! GIMME SOME CREDIT!
SORRY, I FERGOT YER ALLERGIC TA GIVING COMPLIMENTS...
AS LONG AS YER HERE, GRAB A GUN AND HELP ME GET OUTTA HERE--
HEY, WAIT, JOKER, STOP!
EXIT
YOU GONNA CATCH ME? OR ARE YOU DONE BEING EMBARRASSED FOR THE DAY?!
NO, WAIT, STAY CLOSE TA ME, YA IDIOT--
--I MEAN WHAT DO I CARE IF THEY RIP YER FACE--
I MEAN--IT'S DANGEROUS!
WHOOF!
DANGER?

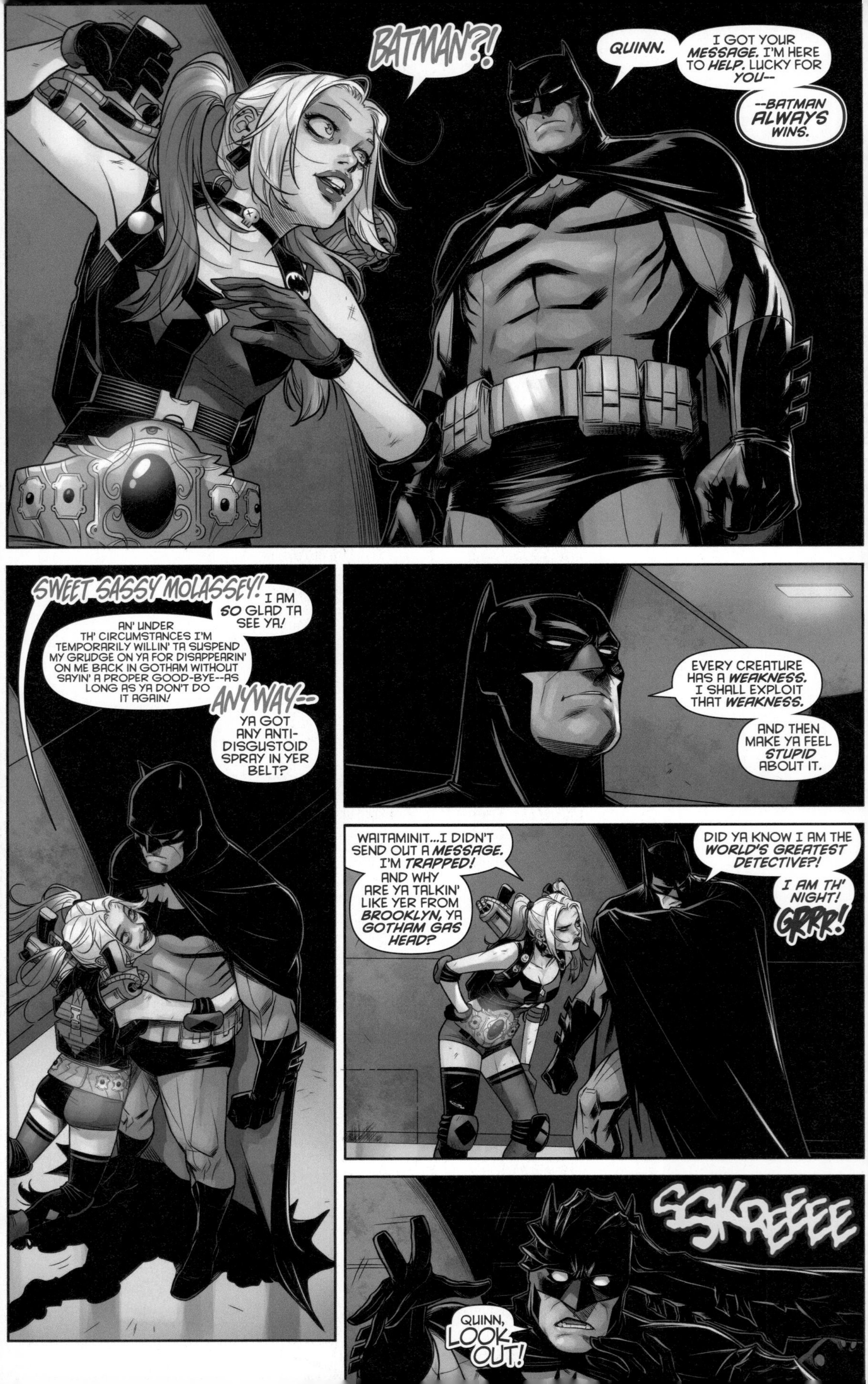
BATMAN?!
QUINN.
I GOT YOUR MESSAGE. I'M HERE TO HELP. LUCKY FOR YOU--
--BATMAN ALWAYS WINS.
SWEET SASSY MOLASSEY!
I AM SO GLAD TA SEE YA!
AN' UNDER TH' CIRCUMSTANCES I'M TEMPORARILY WILLIN' TA SUSPEND MY GRUDGE ON YA FOR DISAPPEARIN' ON ME BACK IN GOTHAM WITHOUT SAYIN' A PROPER GOOD-BYE--AS LONG AS YA DON'T DO IT AGAIN!
ANYWAY--
YA GOT ANY ANTI-DISGUSTOID SPRAY IN YER BELT?
EVERY CREATURE HAS A WEAKNESS. I SHALL EXPLOIT THAT WEAKNESS.
AND THEN MAKE YA FEEL STUPID ABOUT IT.
WAITAMINIT...I DIDN'T SEND OUT A MESSAGE. I'M TRAPPED! AND WHY ARE YA TALKIN' LIKE YER FROM BROOKLYN, YA GOTHAM GAS HEAD?
DID YA KNOW I AM THE WORLD'S GREATEST DETECTIVE?!
I AM TH' NIGHT!
GRRR!
SKREEEE
QUINN, LOOK OUT!

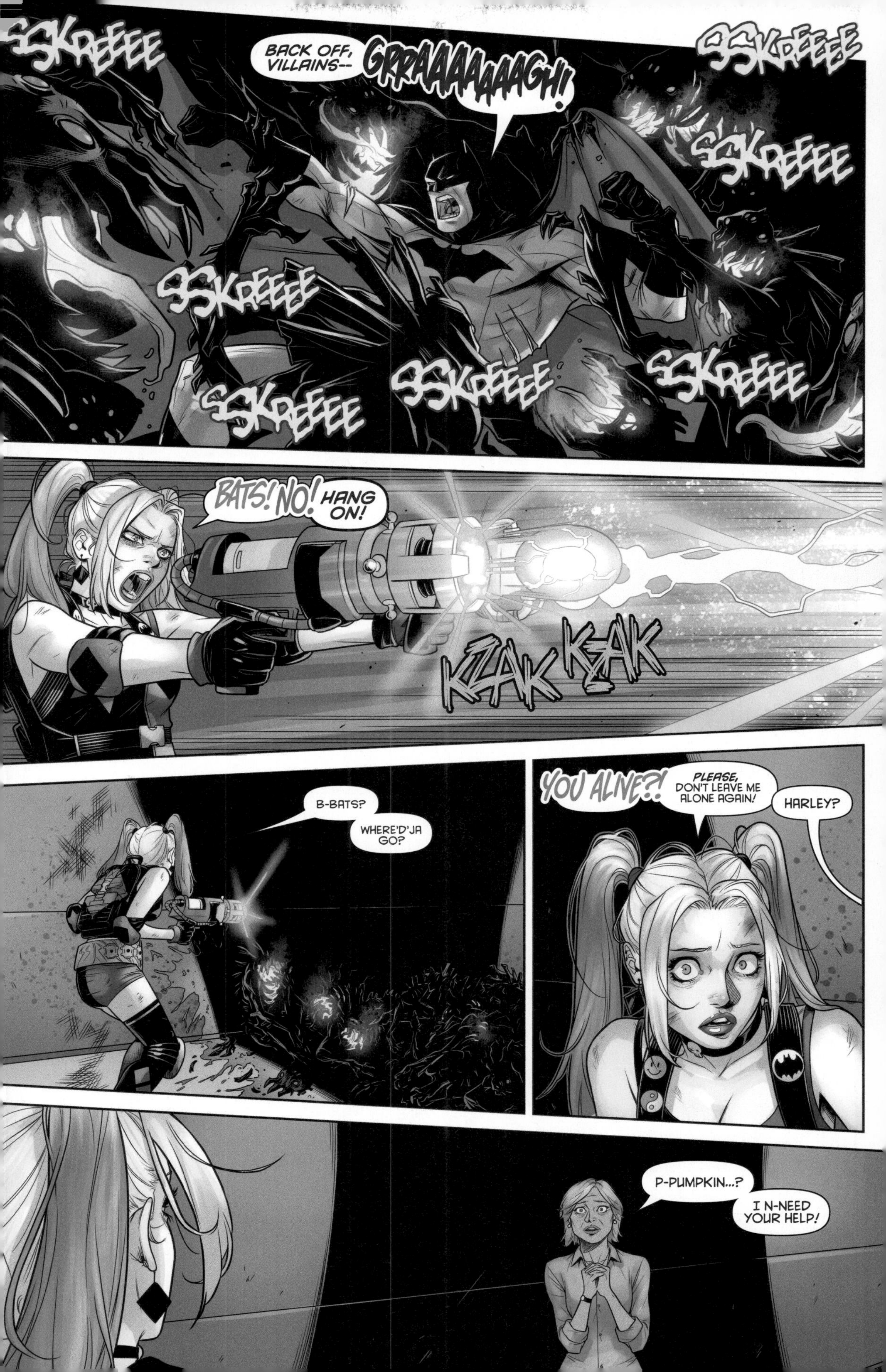
SSKREEEEE
BACK OFF, VILLAINS--
GRRAAAAAAAAGH!
SSKREEEEE
SSKREEEEE
SSKREEEEE
SSKREEEEE
SSKREEEEE
SSKREEEEE
BATS! NO! HANG ON!
KZAK
KZAK
B-BATS?
WHERE'D'JA GO?
YOU ALIVE?!
PLEASE, DON'T LEAVE ME ALONE AGAIN!
HARLEY?
P-PUMPKIN...?
I N-NEED YOUR HELP!

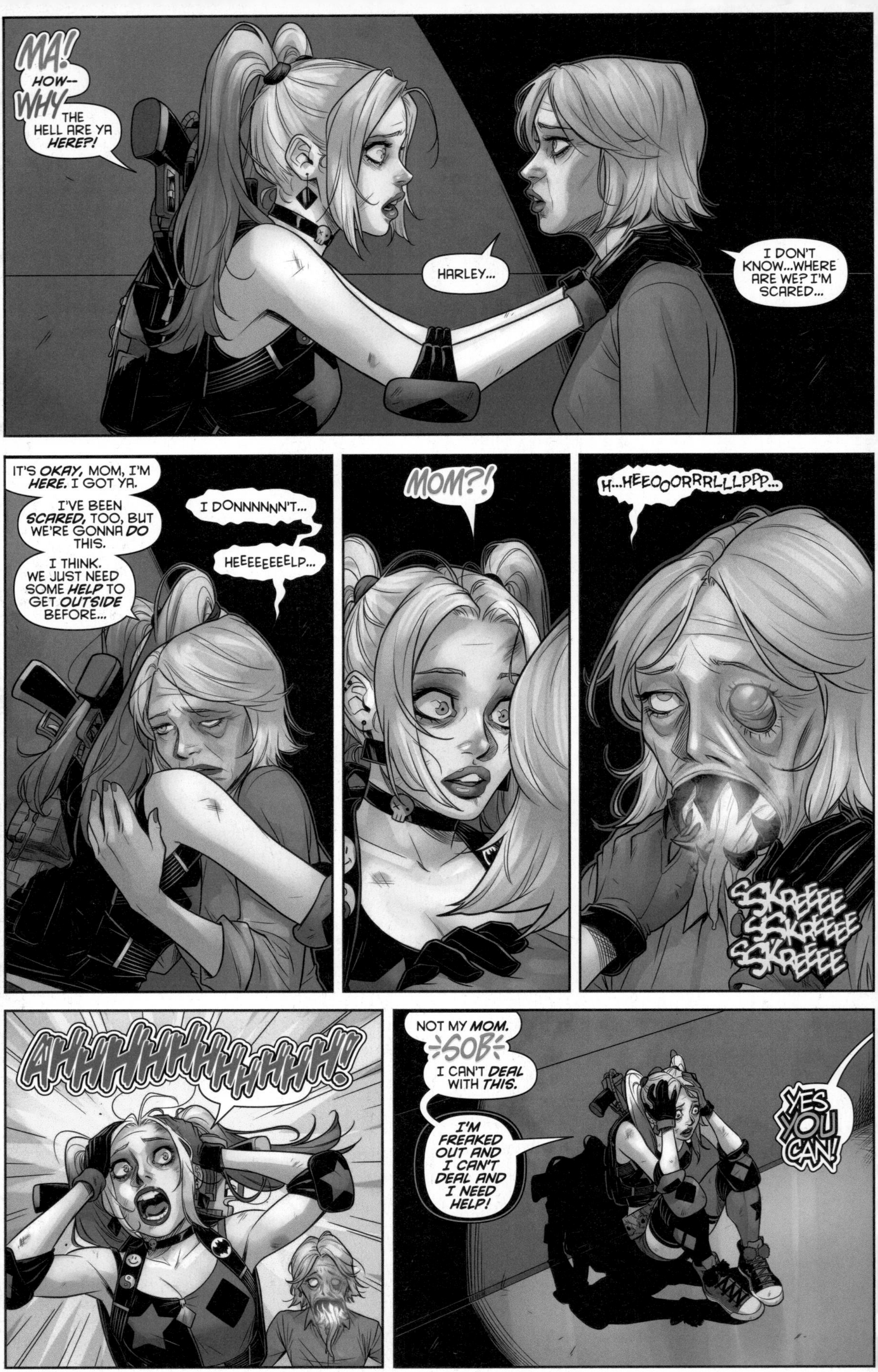
MA! HOW-- WHY THE HELL ARE YA HERE?!
HARLEY...
I DON'T KNOW...WHERE ARE WE? I'M SCARED...
IT'S OKAY, MOM, I'M HERE. I GOT YA.
I'VE BEEN SCARED, TOO, BUT WE'RE GONNA DO THIS.
I THINK. WE JUST NEED SOME HELP TO GET OUTSIDE BEFORE...
I DONNNNNN'T...
HEEEEEEEELP...
MOM?!
H...HEEOOORRRLLLPPP...
SSKREEEE SSKREEEE SSKREEEE
AHHHHHHHHHHHHH!
NOT MY MOM. SOB I CAN'T DEAL WITH THIS.
I'M FREAKED OUT AND I CAN'T DEAL AND I NEED HELP!
YES YOU CAN!

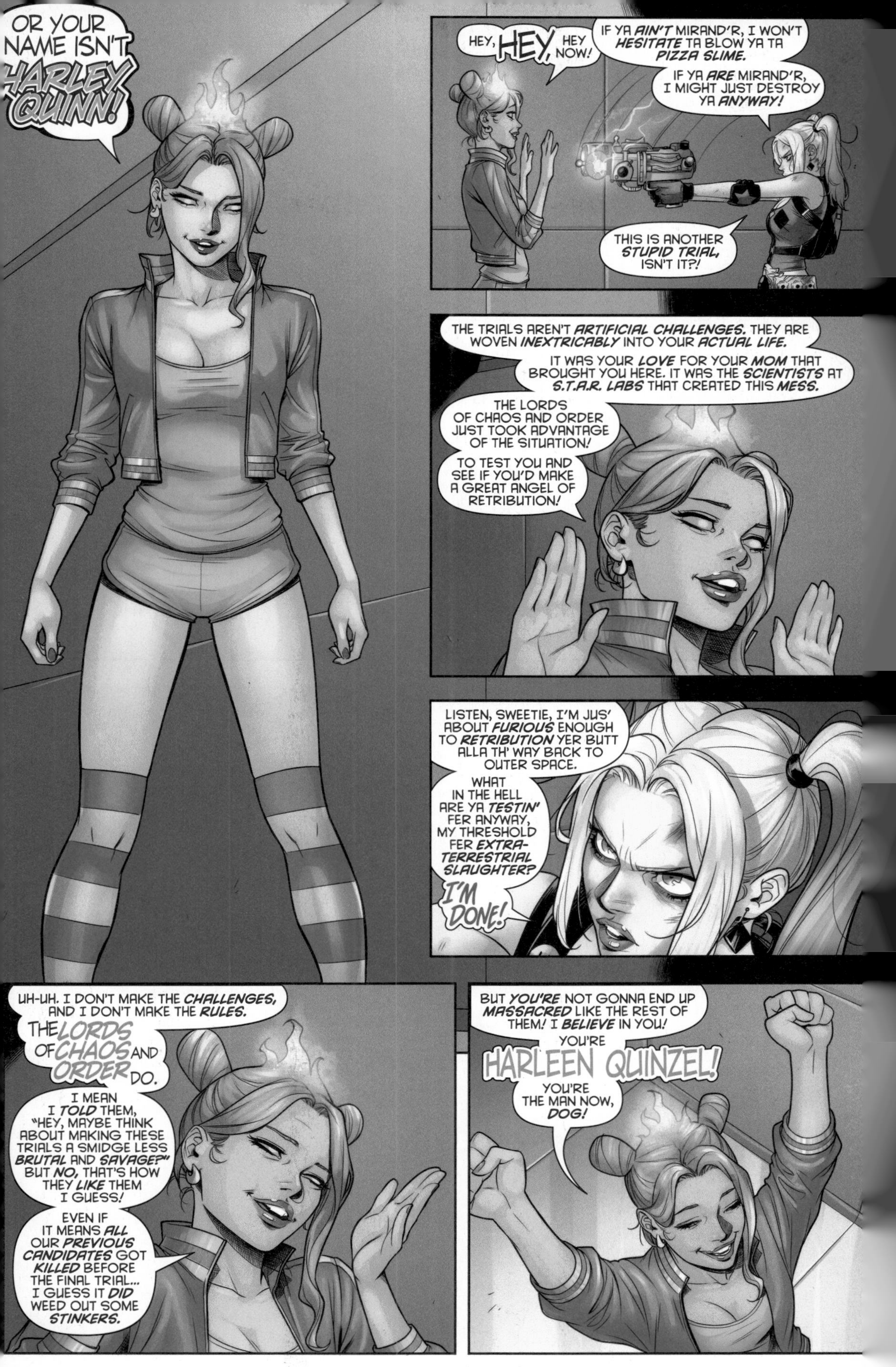
OR YOUR NAME ISN'T HARLEY QUINN!
HEY, HEY, HEY NOW!
IF YA AIN'T MIRAND'R, I WON'T HESITATE TA BLOW YA TA PIZZA SLIME.
IF YA ARE MIRAND'R, I MIGHT JUST DESTROY YA ANYWAY!
THIS IS ANOTHER STUPID TRIAL, ISN'T IT?!
THE TRIALS AREN'T ARTIFICIAL CHALLENGES. THEY ARE WOVEN INEXTRICABLY INTO YOUR ACTUAL LIFE.
IT WAS YOUR LOVE FOR YOUR MOM THAT BROUGHT YOU HERE. IT WAS THE SCIENTISTS AT S.T.A.R. LABS THAT CREATED THIS MESS.
THE LORDS OF CHAOS AND ORDER JUST TOOK ADVANTAGE OF THE SITUATION!
TO TEST YOU AND SEE IF YOU'D MAKE A GREAT ANGEL OF RETRIBUTION!
LISTEN, SWEETIE, I'M JUS' ABOUT FURIOUS ENOUGH TO RETRIBUTION YER BUTT ALLA TH' WAY BACK TO OUTER SPACE.
WHAT IN THE HELL ARE YA TESTIN' FER ANYWAY, MY THRESHOLD FER EXTRA-TERRESTRIAL SLAUGHTER?
I'M DONE!
UH-UH. I DON'T MAKE THE CHALLENGES, AND I DON'T MAKE THE RULES.
THE LORDS OF CHAOS AND ORDER DO.
I MEAN I TOLD THEM, "HEY, MAYBE THINK ABOUT MAKING THESE TRIALS A SMIDGE LESS BRUTAL AND SAVAGE?" BUT NO, THAT'S HOW THEY LIKE THEM I GUESS!
EVEN IF IT MEANS ALL OUR PREVIOUS CANDIDATES GOT KILLED BEFORE THE FINAL TRIAL... I GUESS IT DID WEED OUT SOME STINKERS.
BUT YOU'RE NOT GONNA END UP MASSACRED LIKE THE REST OF THEM! I BELIEVE IN YOU!
YOU'RE HARLEEN QUINZEL!
YOU'RE THE MAN NOW, DOG!

HOLD UP... YOU MEAN THESE TRIALS COULD BE **LETHAL?!**

AND I CAN'T BELIEVE I JUST GOT **YOU'RE-THE-MAN-NOW-DOG'D.**

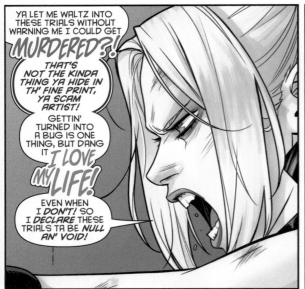

YA LET ME WALTZ INTO THESE TRIALS WITHOUT WARNING ME I COULD GET **MURDERED?!**

THAT'S NOT THE KINDA THING YA HIDE IN TH' FINE PRINT, YA SCAM ARTIST!

GETTIN' TURNED INTO A BUG IS ONE THING, BUT DANG IT **I LOVE MY LIFE!**

EVEN WHEN I **DON'T!** SO I **DECLARE** THESE TRIALS TA BE **NULL AN' VOID!**

NOT OUR FAULT YOU DIDN'T **BOTHER** TO LISTEN TO THE **RULES.** YOU **ACCEPTED,** FAIR AND SQUARE.

YOU KNOW...I FIRST **NOTICED** YOU WHEN YOU TOOK ON ALL OF **APOKOLIPS.** ON YOUR OWN!

I THOUGHT YOU HAD **GUTS.** I THOUGHT YOU HAD WHAT IT **TAKES.**

GUESS I WAS **WRONG.**

GIRL, IF I DIDN'T NEED YER **HELP** SO BAD...I'D **POP** YA IN THAT CUTE **FACE** FOR TALKIN' THAT WAY TA ME--

MIRAND'R?

MIRAND'R?!

OH, JUST **DELIGHTFUL!**

YA SWOOP IN JUST IN TIME TA SEE ME **CRYIN',** READ ME TA **FILTH** AND THEN YA **DISAPPEAR!**

WELL, I CAN INSULT **YOU** AS WELL! YER TEETH ARE TOO PERFECT!

DANG, THAT'S NOT IT--

HSSSSS

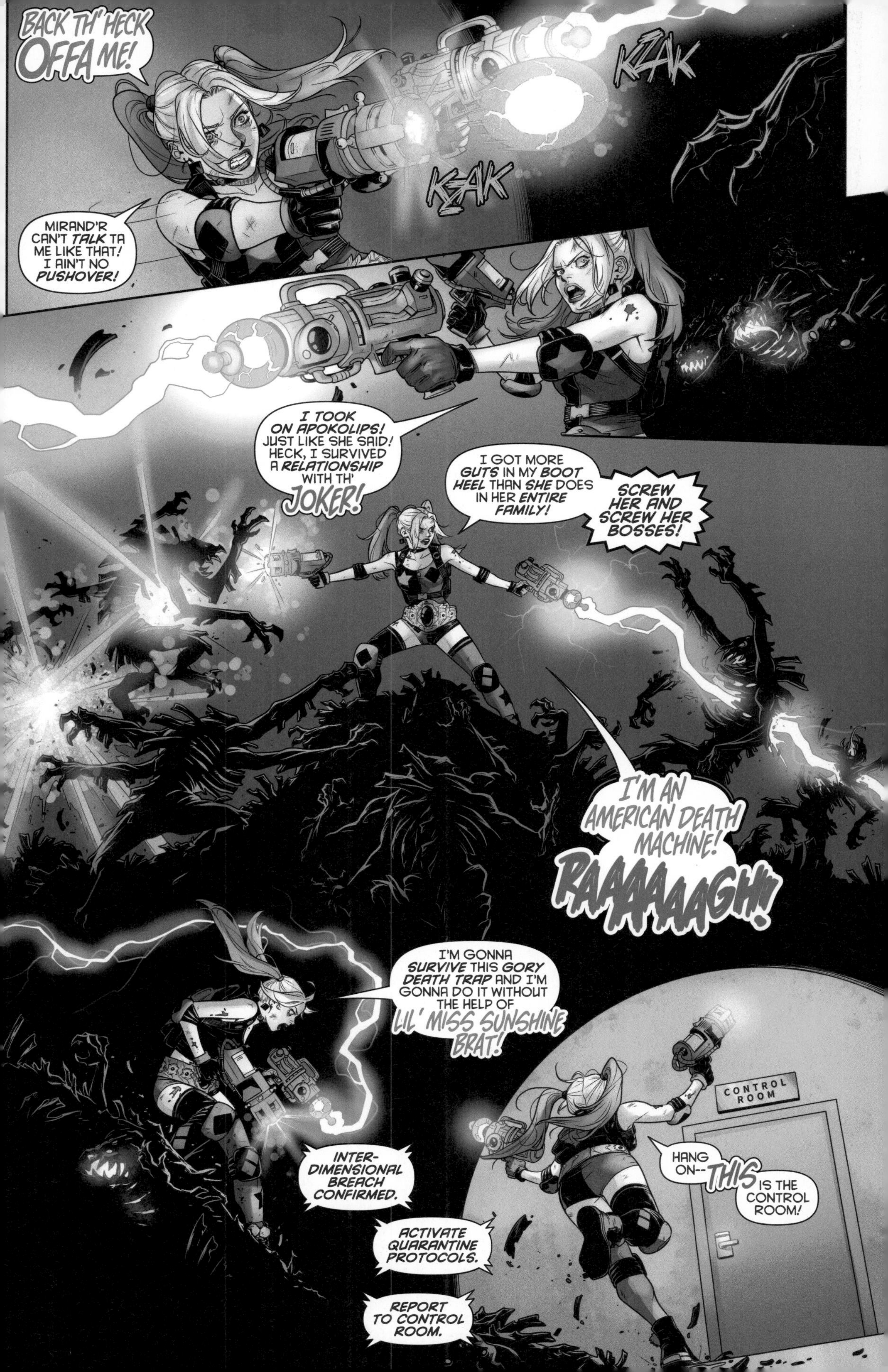
BACK TH' HECK OFFA ME!
KZAK
KZAK
MIRAND'R CAN'T TALK TA ME LIKE THAT! I AIN'T NO PUSHOVER!
I TOOK ON APOKOLIPS! JUST LIKE SHE SAID! HECK, I SURVIVED A RELATIONSHIP WITH TH' JOKER!
I GOT MORE GUTS IN MY BOOT HEEL THAN SHE DOES IN HER ENTIRE FAMILY!
SCREW HER AND SCREW HER BOSSES!
I'M AN AMERICAN DEATH MACHINE! RAAAAAAAGH!!
I'M GONNA SURVIVE THIS GORY DEATH TRAP AND I'M GONNA DO IT WITHOUT THE HELP OF LIL' MISS SUNSHINE BRAT!
INTER-DIMENSIONAL BREACH CONFIRMED.
ACTIVATE QUARANTINE PROTOCOLS.
REPORT TO CONTROL ROOM.
CONTROL ROOM
HANG ON-- THIS IS THE CONTROL ROOM!

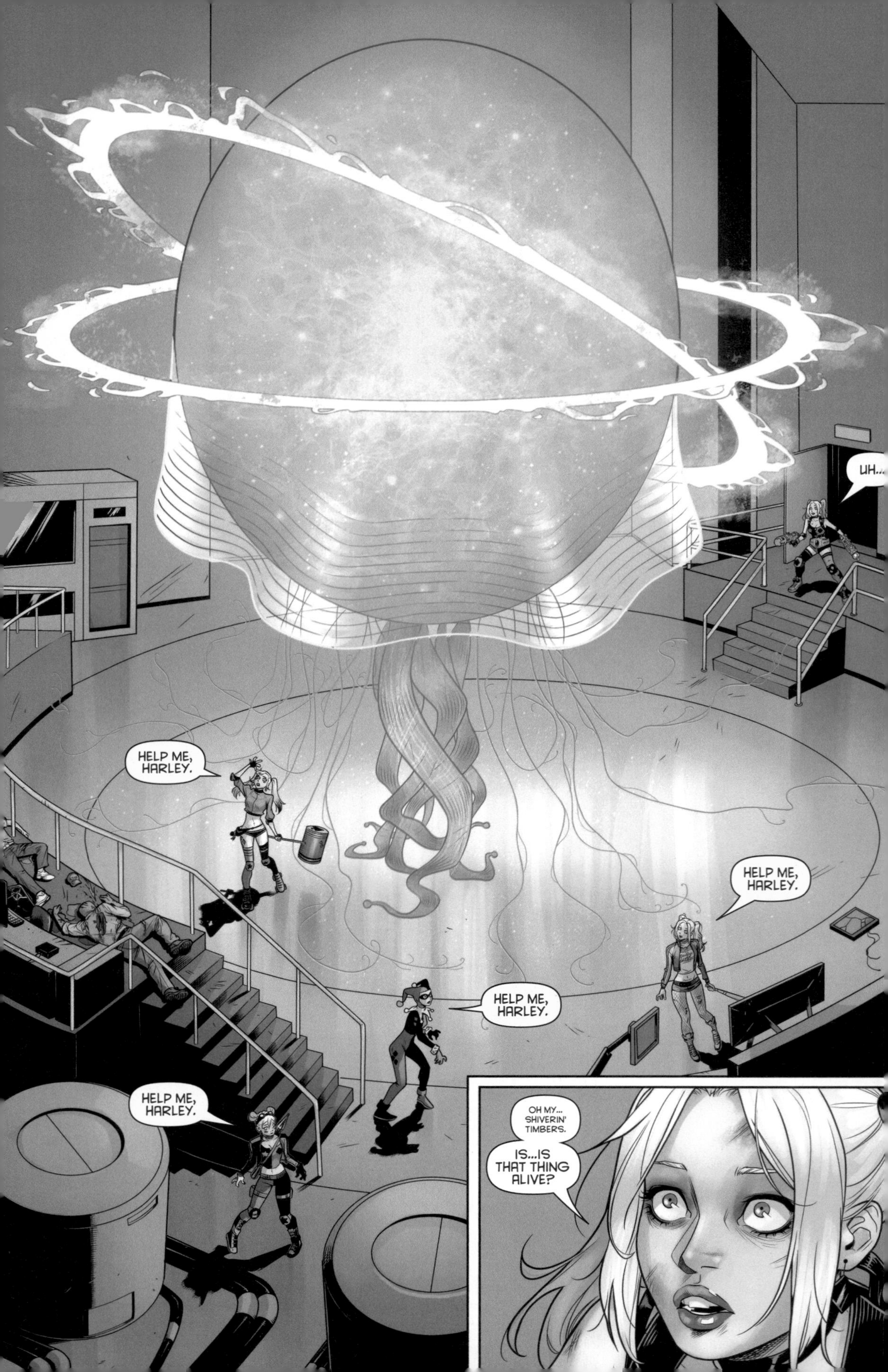
UH...
HELP ME, HARLEY.
HELP ME, HARLEY.
HELP ME, HARLEY.
HELP ME, HARLEY.
OH MY... SHIVERIN' TIMBERS.
IS...IS THAT THING ALIVE?

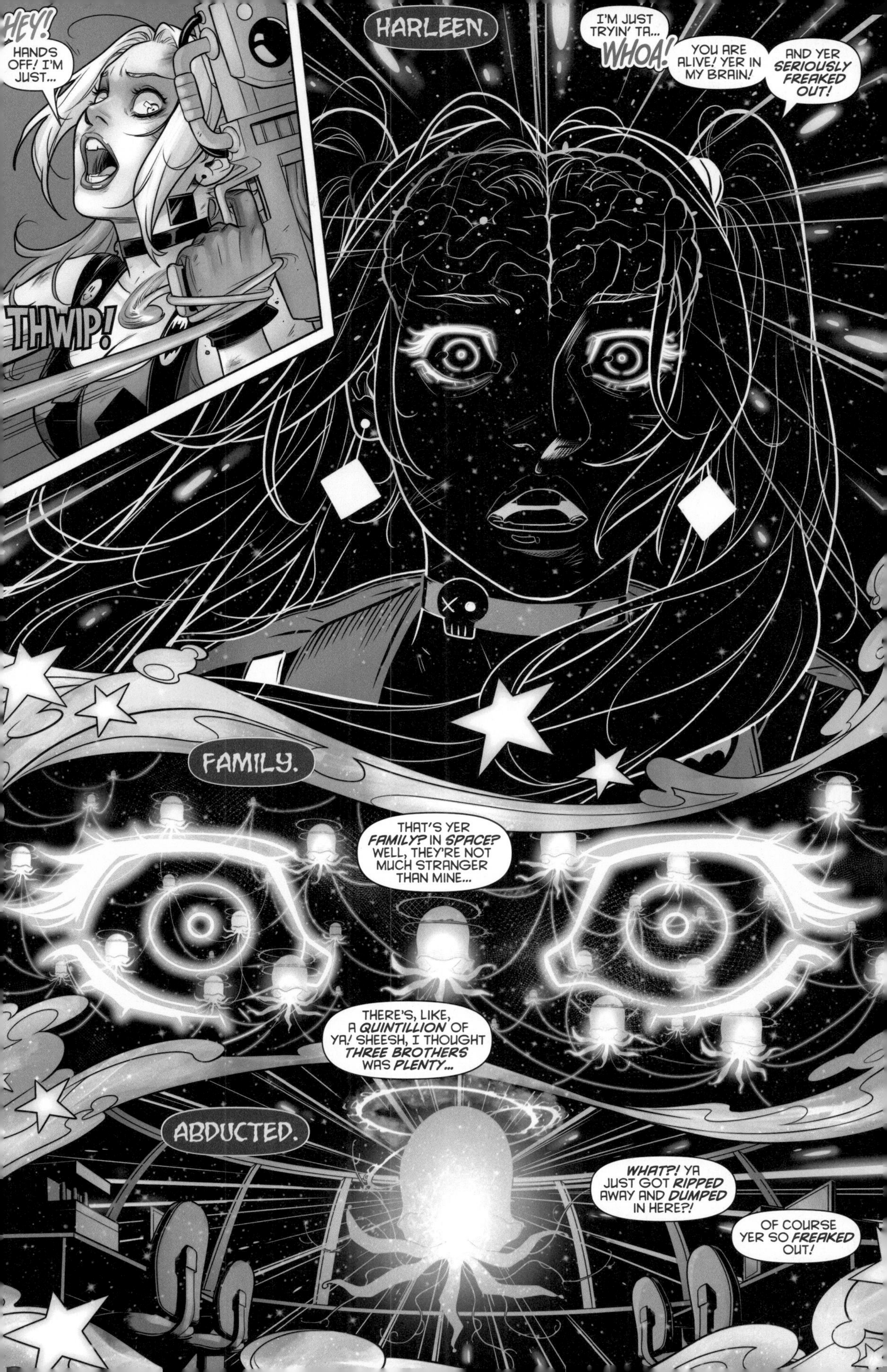
HEY!
HANDS OFF! I'M JUST...
THWIP!
HARLEEN.
I'M JUST TRYIN' TA... WHOA!
YOU ARE ALIVE! YER IN MY BRAIN!
AND YER SERIOUSLY FREAKED OUT!
FAMILY.
THAT'S YER FAMILY? IN SPACE? WELL, THEY'RE NOT MUCH STRANGER THAN MINE...
THERE'S, LIKE, A QUINTILLION OF YA! SHEESH, I THOUGHT THREE BROTHERS WAS PLENTY...
ABDUCTED.
WHAT?! YA JUST GOT RIPPED AWAY AND DUMPED IN HERE?!
OF COURSE YER SO FREAKED OUT!

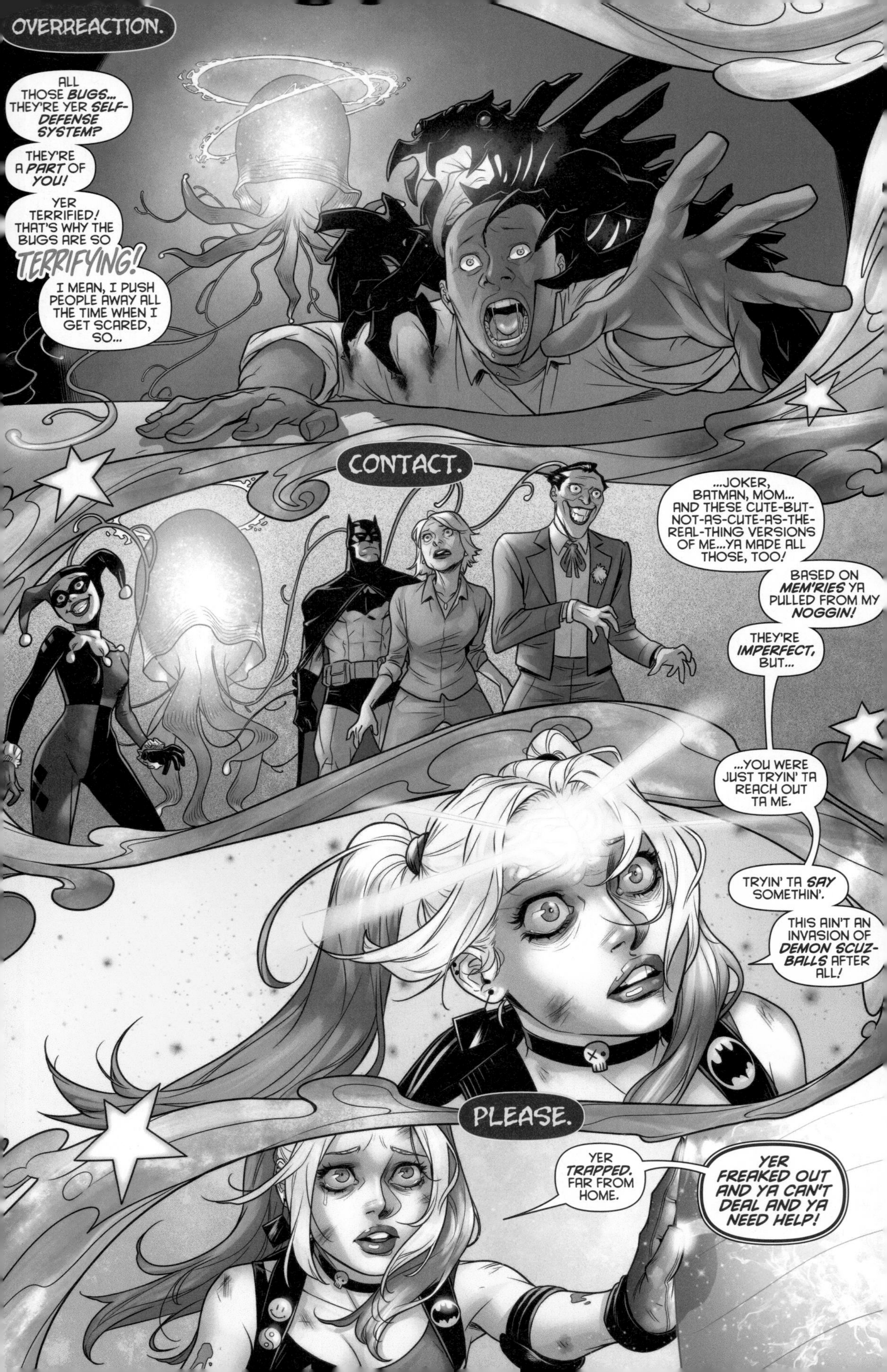
OVERREACTION.
ALL THOSE BUGS... THEY'RE YER SELF-DEFENSE SYSTEM?
THEY'RE A PART OF YOU!
YER TERRIFIED! THAT'S WHY THE BUGS ARE SO
TERRIFYING!
I MEAN, I PUSH PEOPLE AWAY ALL THE TIME WHEN I GET SCARED, SO...
CONTACT.
...JOKER, BATMAN, MOM... AND THESE CUTE-BUT-NOT-AS-CUTE-AS-THE-REAL-THING VERSIONS OF ME...YA MADE ALL THOSE, TOO!
BASED ON MEM'RIES YA PULLED FROM MY NOGGIN!
THEY'RE IMPERFECT, BUT...
...YOU WERE JUST TRYIN' TA REACH OUT TA ME.
TRYIN' TA SAY SOMETHIN'.
THIS AIN'T AN INVASION OF DEMON SCUZ-BALLS AFTER ALL!
PLEASE.
YER TRAPPED. FAR FROM HOME.
YER FREAKED OUT AND YA CAN'T DEAL AND YA NEED HELP!

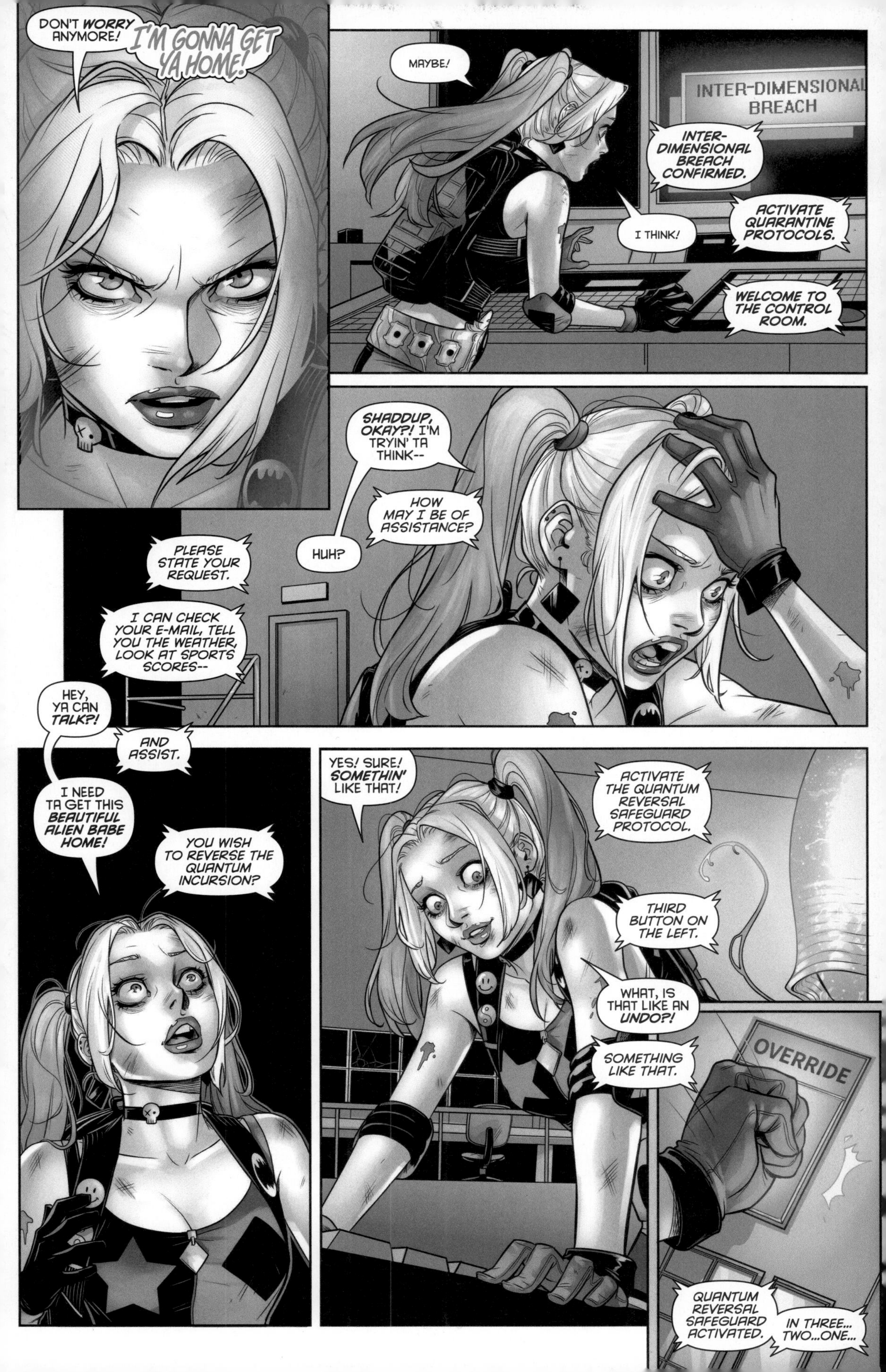
DON'T WORRY ANYMORE!
I'M GONNA GET YA HOME!
MAYBE!
INTER-DIMENSIONAL BREACH
INTER-DIMENSIONAL BREACH CONFIRMED.
I THINK!
ACTIVATE QUARANTINE PROTOCOLS.
WELCOME TO THE CONTROL ROOM.
SHADDUP, OKAY?! I'M TRYIN' TA THINK--
HOW MAY I BE OF ASSISTANCE?
HUH?
PLEASE STATE YOUR REQUEST.
I CAN CHECK YOUR E-MAIL, TELL YOU THE WEATHER, LOOK AT SPORTS SCORES--
HEY, YA CAN TALK?!
AND ASSIST.
I NEED TA GET THIS BEAUTIFUL ALIEN BABE HOME!
YOU WISH TO REVERSE THE QUANTUM INCURSION?
YES! SURE! SOMETHIN' LIKE THAT!
ACTIVATE THE QUANTUM REVERSAL SAFEGUARD PROTOCOL.
THIRD BUTTON ON THE LEFT.
WHAT, IS THAT LIKE AN UNDO?!
SOMETHING LIKE THAT.
OVERRIDE
QUANTUM REVERSAL SAFEGUARD ACTIVATED.
IN THREE... TWO...ONE...

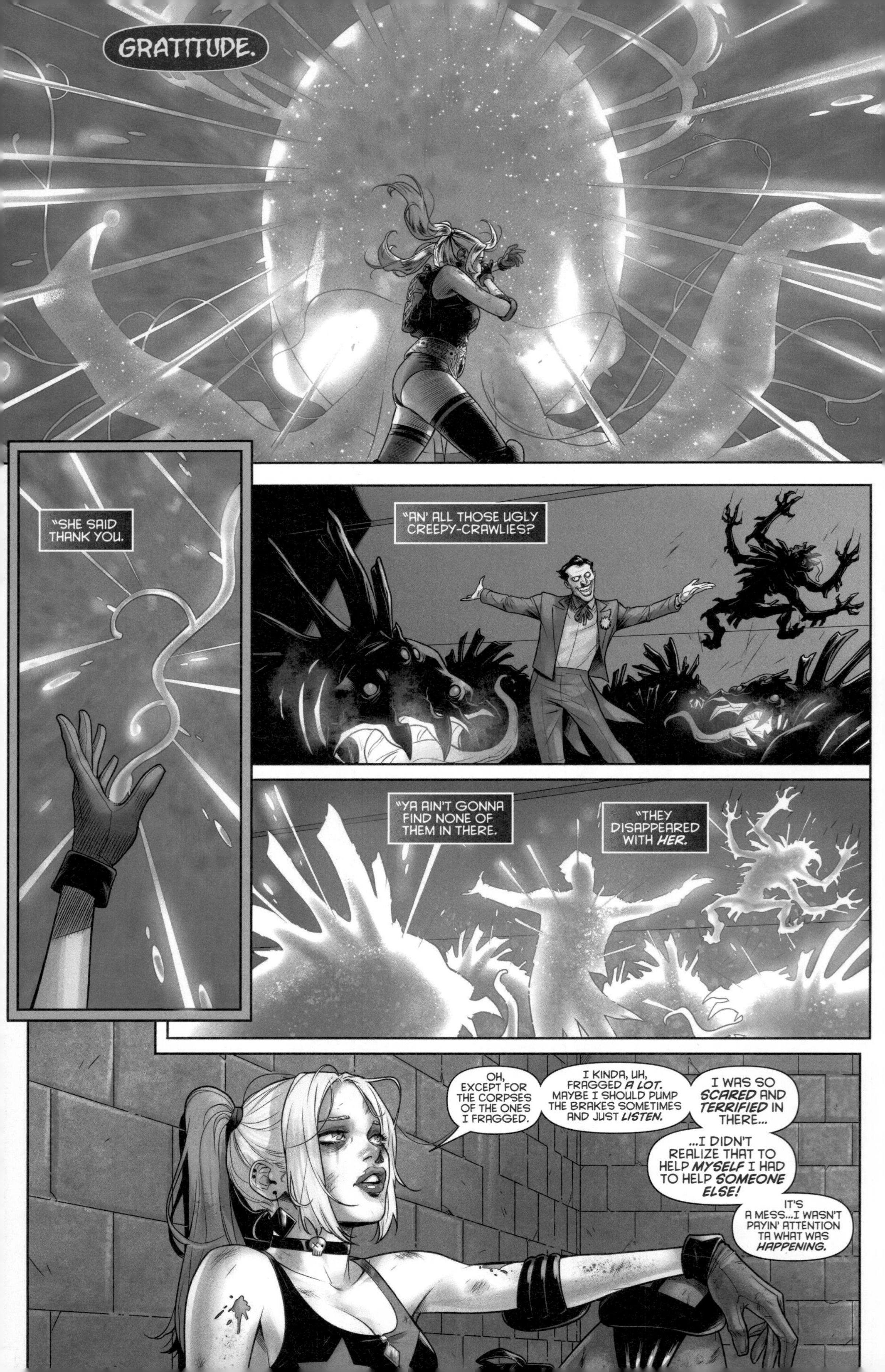
GRATITUDE.
"SHE SAID THANK YOU.
"AN' ALL THOSE UGLY CREEPY-CRAWLIES?
"YA AIN'T GONNA FIND NONE OF THEM IN THERE.
"THEY DISAPPEARED WITH *HER*.
OH, EXCEPT FOR THE CORPSES OF THE ONES I FRAGGED.
I KINDA, UH, FRAGGED *A LOT*. MAYBE I SHOULD PUMP THE BRAKES SOMETIMES AND JUST *LISTEN*.
I WAS SO *SCARED* AND *TERRIFIED* IN THERE...
...I DIDN'T REALIZE THAT TO HELP *MYSELF* I HAD TO HELP *SOMEONE ELSE!*
IT'S A MESS...I WASN'T PAYIN' ATTENTION TA WHAT WAS *HAPPENING*.

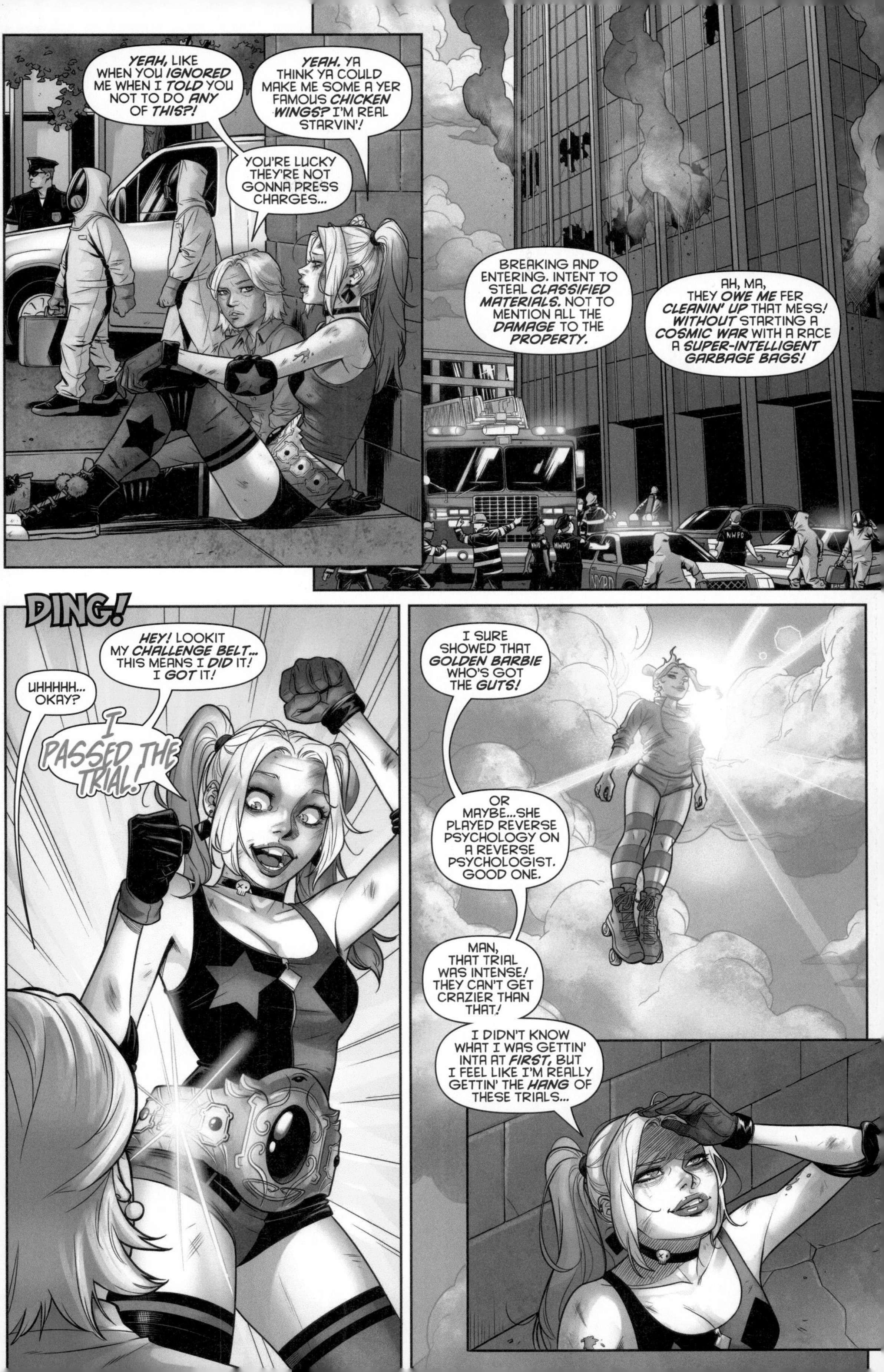

YEAH, LIKE WHEN YOU IGNORED ME WHEN I TOLD YOU NOT TO DO ANY OF THIS?!
YEAH. YA THINK YA COULD MAKE ME SOME A YER FAMOUS CHICKEN WINGS? I'M REAL STARVIN'!
YOU'RE LUCKY THEY'RE NOT GONNA PRESS CHARGES...
BREAKING AND ENTERING. INTENT TO STEAL CLASSIFIED MATERIALS. NOT TO MENTION ALL THE DAMAGE TO THE PROPERTY.
AH, MA, THEY OWE ME FER CLEANIN' UP THAT MESS! WITHOUT STARTING A COSMIC WAR WITH A RACE A SUPER-INTELLIGENT GARBAGE BAGS!
DING!
HEY! LOOKIT MY CHALLENGE BELT... THIS MEANS I DID IT! I GOT IT!
UHHHHH... OKAY?
I PASSED THE TRIAL!
I SURE SHOWED THAT GOLDEN BARBIE WHO'S GOT THE GUTS!
OR MAYBE...SHE PLAYED REVERSE PSYCHOLOGY ON A REVERSE PSYCHOLOGIST. GOOD ONE.
MAN, THAT TRIAL WAS INTENSE! THEY CAN'T GET CRAZIER THAN THAT!
I DIDN'T KNOW WHAT I WAS GETTIN' INTA AT FIRST, BUT I FEEL LIKE I'M REALLY GETTIN' THE HANG OF THESE TRIALS...

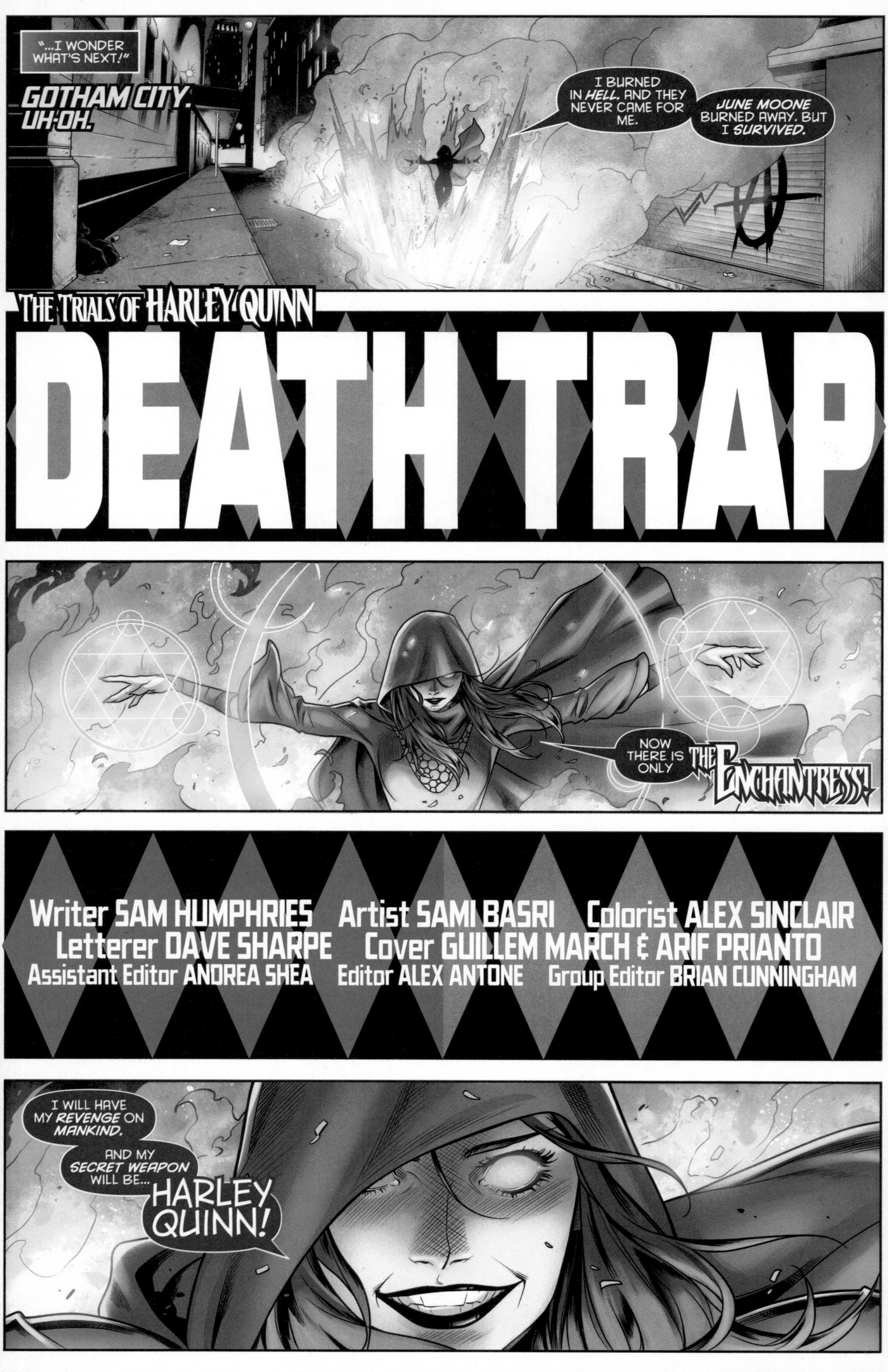
"...I WONDER WHAT'S NEXT!"
GOTHAM CITY. UH-OH.
I BURNED IN HELL, AND THEY NEVER CAME FOR ME.
JUNE MOONE BURNED AWAY. BUT I SURVIVED.
THE TRIALS OF HARLEY QUINN
DEATH TRAP
NOW THERE IS ONLY THE ENCHANTRESS!
Writer SAM HUMPHRIES Artist SAMI BASRI Colorist ALEX SINCLAIR
Letterer DAVE SHARPE Cover GUILLEM MARCH & ARIF PRIANTO
Assistant Editor ANDREA SHEA Editor ALEX ANTONE Group Editor BRIAN CUNNINGHAM
I WILL HAVE MY REVENGE ON MANKIND.
AND MY SECRET WEAPON WILL BE...
HARLEY QUINN!

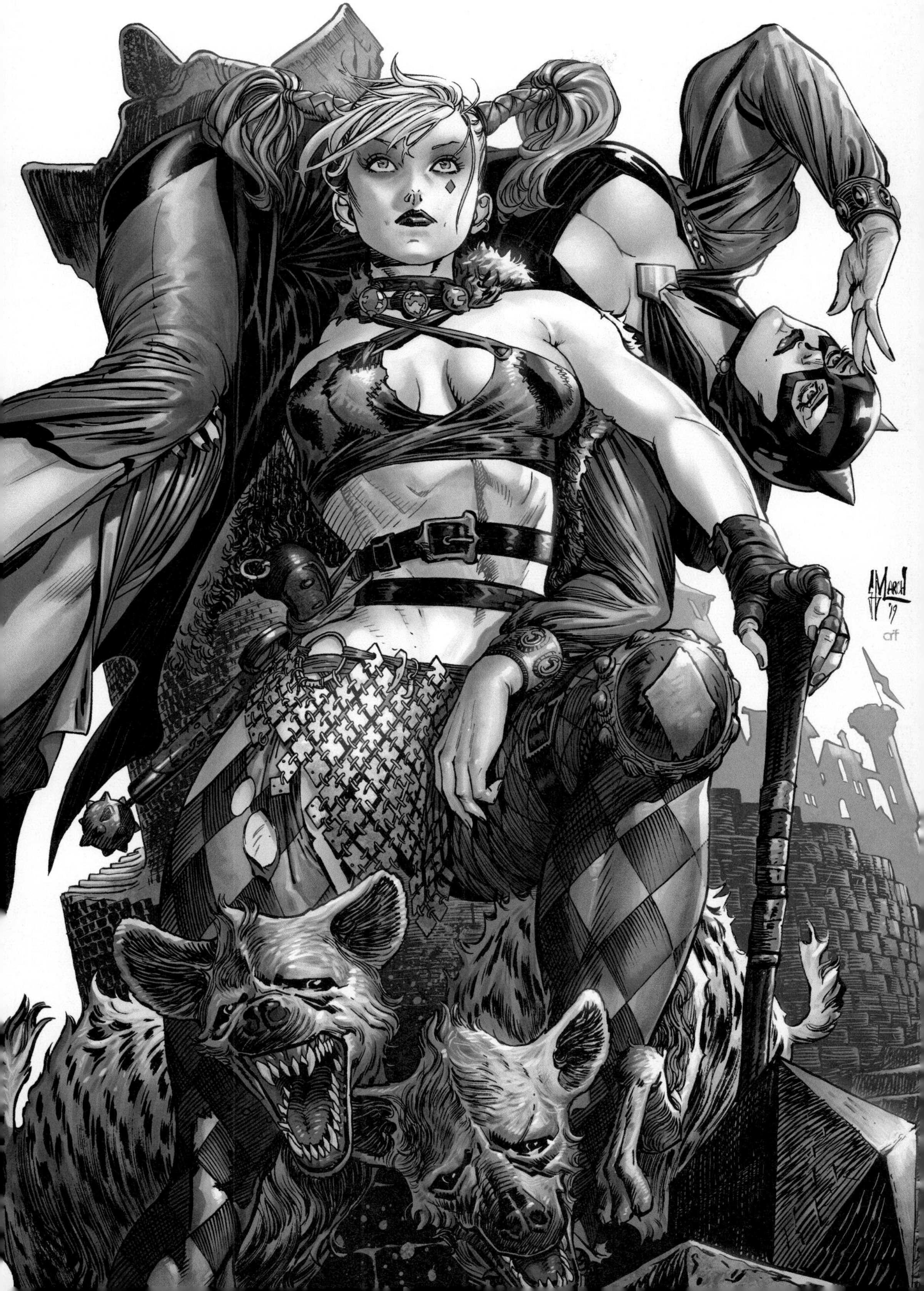

HARLEY QUINN
#61

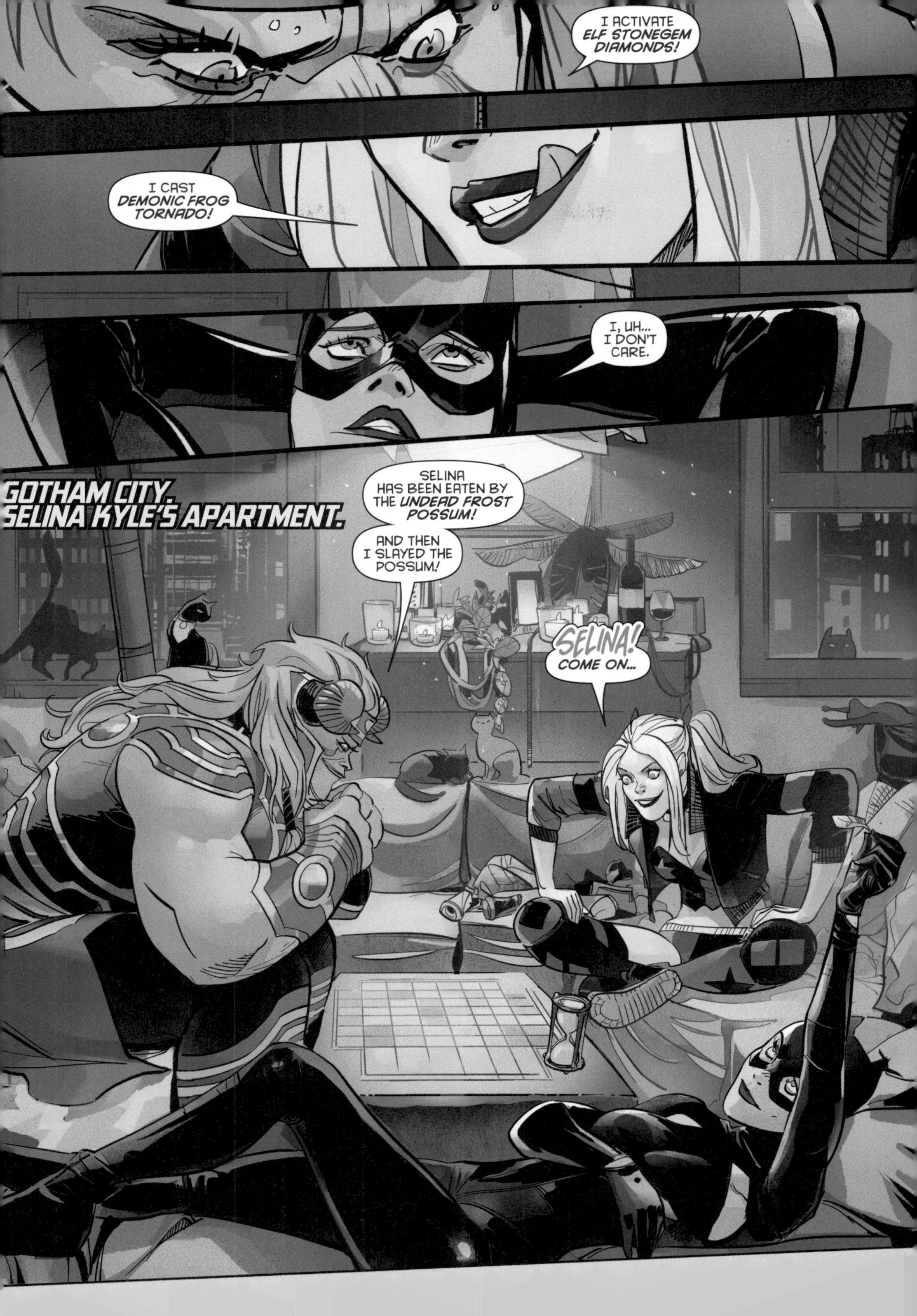
I ACTIVATE ELF STONEGEM DIAMONDS!
I CAST DEMONIC FROG TORNADO!
I, UH... I DON'T CARE.
GOTHAM CITY. SELINA KYLE'S APARTMENT.
SELINA HAS BEEN EATEN BY THE UNDEAD FROST POSSUM!
AND THEN I SLAYED THE POSSUM!
SELINA! COME ON...

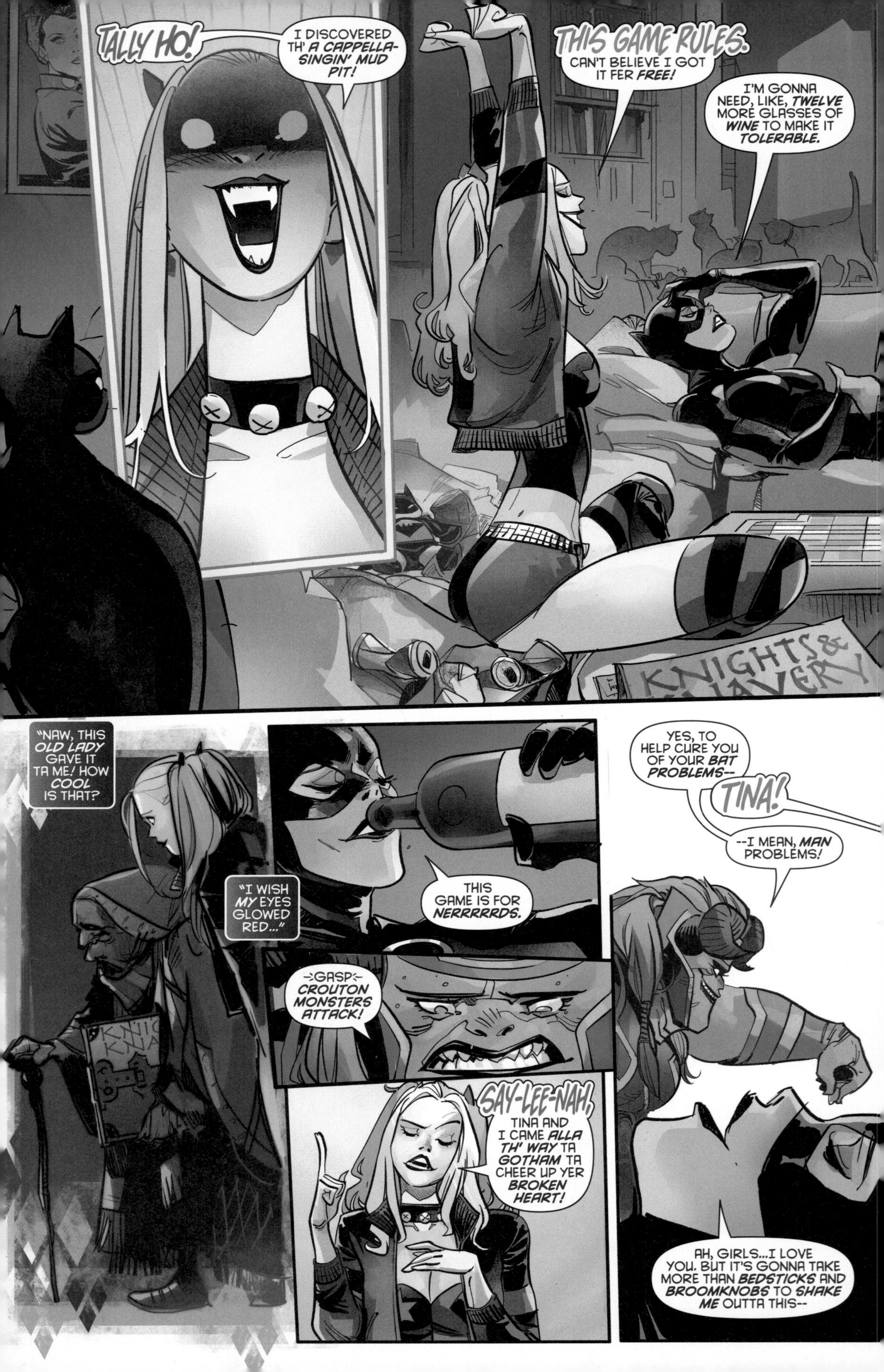
TALLY HO!
I DISCOVERED TH' A CAPPELLA-SINGIN' MUD PIT!
THIS GAME RULES.
CAN'T BELIEVE I GOT IT FER FREE!
I'M GONNA NEED, LIKE, TWELVE MORE GLASSES OF WINE TO MAKE IT TOLERABLE.
KNIGHTS & KNAVERY
"NAW, THIS OLD LADY GAVE IT TA ME! HOW COOL IS THAT?
"I WISH MY EYES GLOWED RED..."
THIS GAME IS FOR NERRRRRDS.
GASP CROUTON MONSTERS ATTACK!
YES, TO HELP CURE YOU OF YOUR BAT PROBLEMS--
TINA!
--I MEAN, MAN PROBLEMS!
SAY-LEE-NAH, TINA AND I CAME ALLA TH' WAY TA GOTHAM TA CHEER UP YER BROKEN HEART!
AH, GIRLS...I LOVE YOU. BUT IT'S GONNA TAKE MORE THAN BEDSTICKS AND BROOMKNOBS TO SHAKE ME OUTTA THIS--

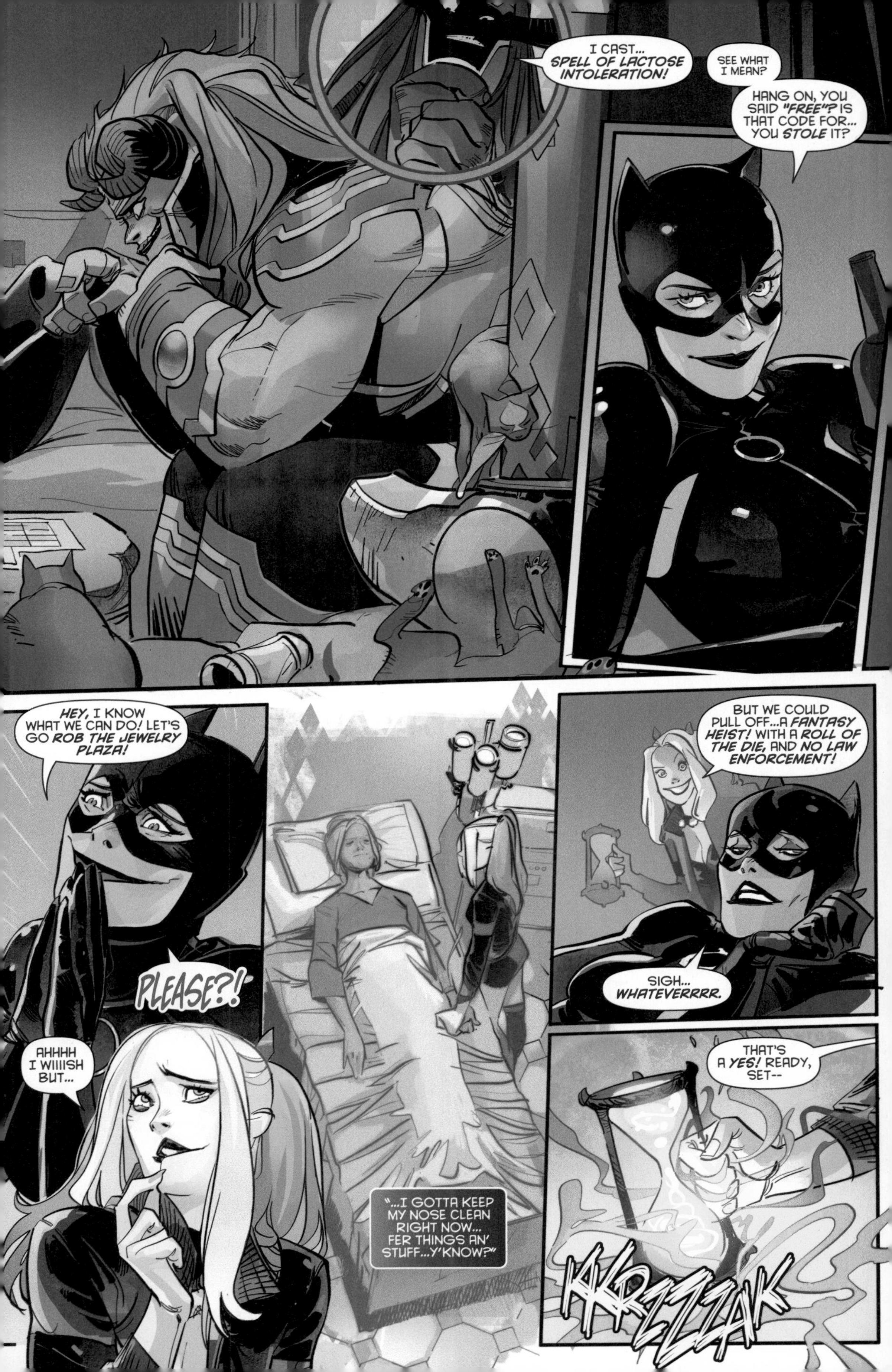

I CAST... SPELL OF LACTOSE INTOLERATION!
SEE WHAT I MEAN?
HANG ON, YOU SAID "FREE"? IS THAT CODE FOR... YOU STOLE IT?
HEY, I KNOW WHAT WE CAN DO! LET'S GO ROB THE JEWELRY PLAZA!
PLEASE?!
AHHHH I WIIIISH BUT...
"...I GOTTA KEEP MY NOSE CLEAN RIGHT NOW... FER THINGS AN' STUFF...Y'KNOW?"
BUT WE COULD PULL OFF...A FANTASY HEIST! WITH A ROLL OF THE DIE, AND NO LAW ENFORCEMENT!
SIGH... WHATEVERRRR.
THAT'S A YES! READY, SET--
KKRZZZAK

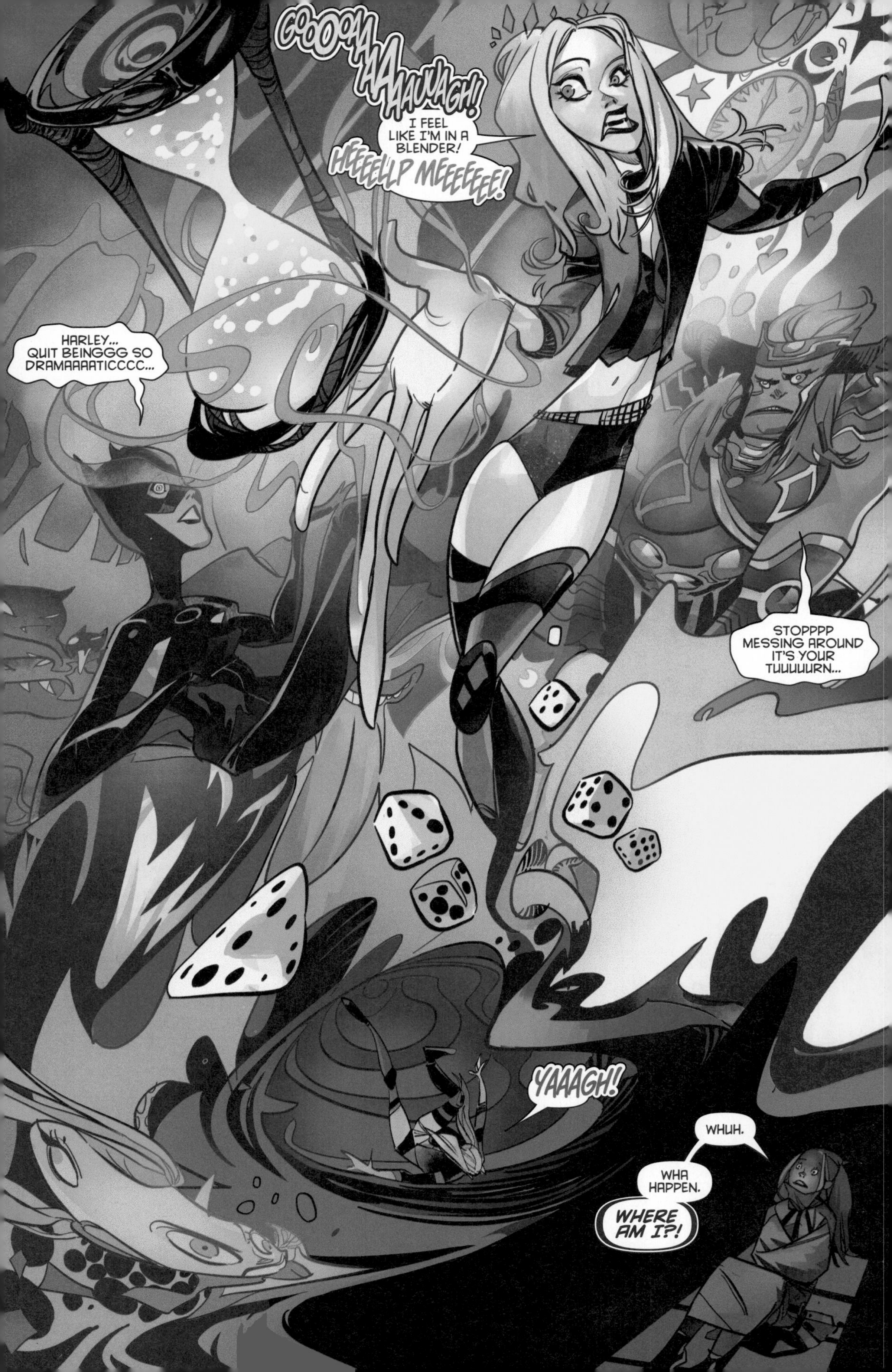
GOOOOAAAAAAUUAGH!
I FEEL LIKE I'M IN A BLENDER!
HEEEELLP MEEEEEEE!
HARLEY... QUIT BEINGGG SO DRAMAAAAATICCCC...
STOPPPP MESSING AROUND IT'S YOUR TUUUUURN...
YAAAGH!
WHUH.
WHA HAPPEN.
WHERE AM I?!

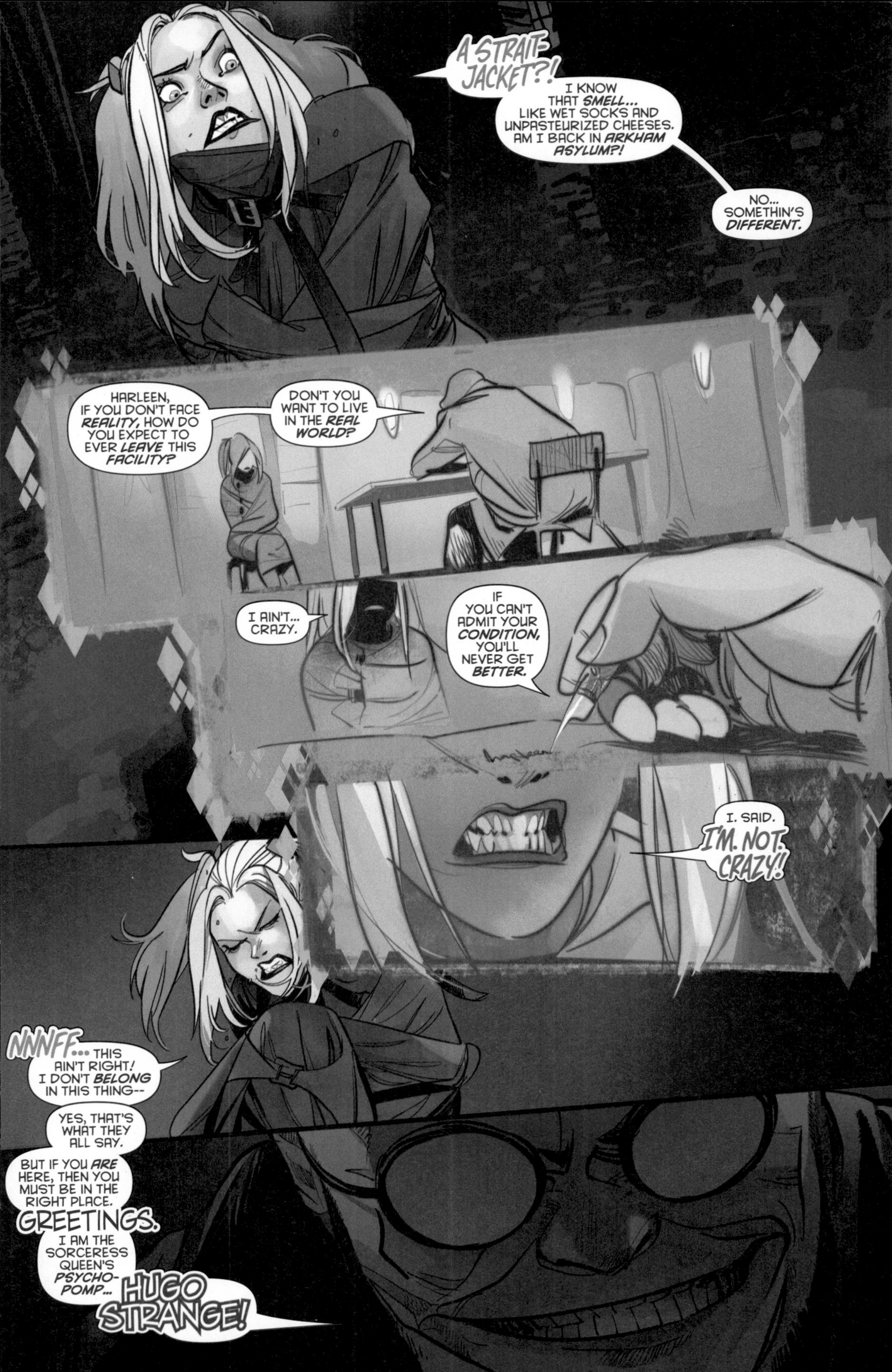
A STRAIT-JACKET?!
I KNOW THAT SMELL... LIKE WET SOCKS AND UNPASTEURIZED CHEESES. AM I BACK IN ARKHAM ASYLUM?!
NO... SOMETHIN'S DIFFERENT.
HARLEEN, IF YOU DON'T FACE REALITY, HOW DO YOU EXPECT TO EVER LEAVE THIS FACILITY?
DON'T YOU WANT TO LIVE IN THE REAL WORLD?
I AIN'T... CRAZY.
IF YOU CAN'T ADMIT YOUR CONDITION, YOU'LL NEVER GET BETTER.
I. SAID. I'M. NOT. CRAZY!
NNNFF... THIS AIN'T RIGHT! I DON'T BELONG IN THIS THING--
YES, THAT'S WHAT THEY ALL SAY.
BUT IF YOU ARE HERE, THEN YOU MUST BE IN THE RIGHT PLACE.
GREETINGS.
I AM THE SORCERESS QUEEN'S PSYCHO-POMP... HUGO STRANGE!

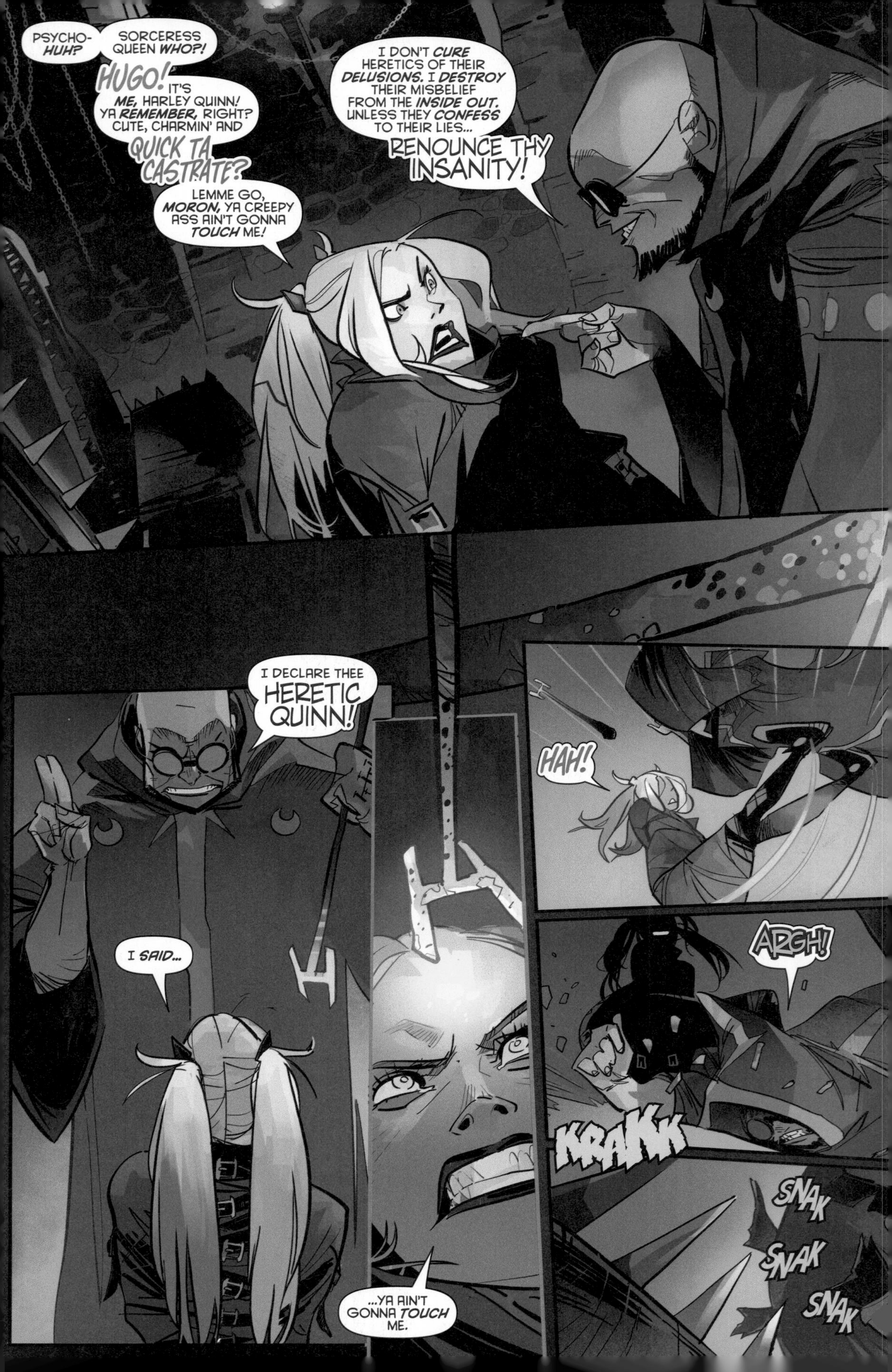

PSYCHO-HUH?
SORCERESS QUEEN WHO?!
HUGO! IT'S ME, HARLEY QUINN! YA REMEMBER, RIGHT? CUTE, CHARMIN' AND QUICK TA CASTRATE?
LEMME GO, MORON, YA CREEPY ASS AIN'T GONNA TOUCH ME!
I DON'T CURE HERETICS OF THEIR DELUSIONS. I DESTROY THEIR MISBELIEF FROM THE INSIDE OUT. UNLESS THEY CONFESS TO THEIR LIES...
RENOUNCE THY INSANITY!
I DECLARE THEE HERETIC QUINN!
I SAID...
...YA AIN'T GONNA TOUCH ME.
HAH!
ARGH!
KRAKK
SNAK
SNAK
SNAK

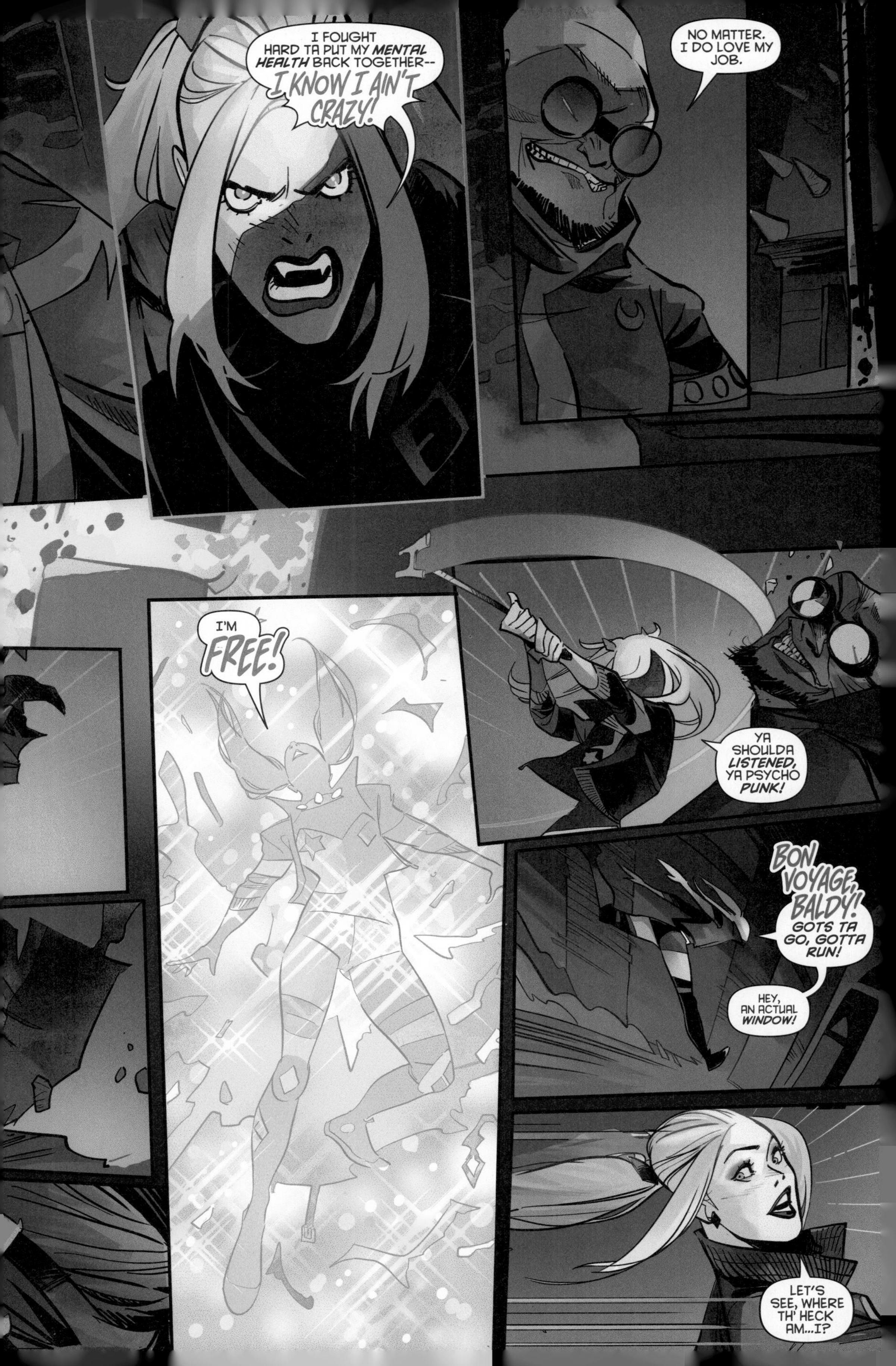
I FOUGHT HARD TA PUT MY MENTAL HEALTH BACK TOGETHER-- I KNOW I AIN'T CRAZY!
NO MATTER. I DO LOVE MY JOB.
I'M FREE!
YA SHOULDA LISTENED, YA PSYCHO PUNK!
BON VOYAGE, BALDY! GOTS TA GO, GOTTA RUN!
HEY, AN ACTUAL WINDOW!
LET'S SEE, WHERE TH' HECK AM...I?

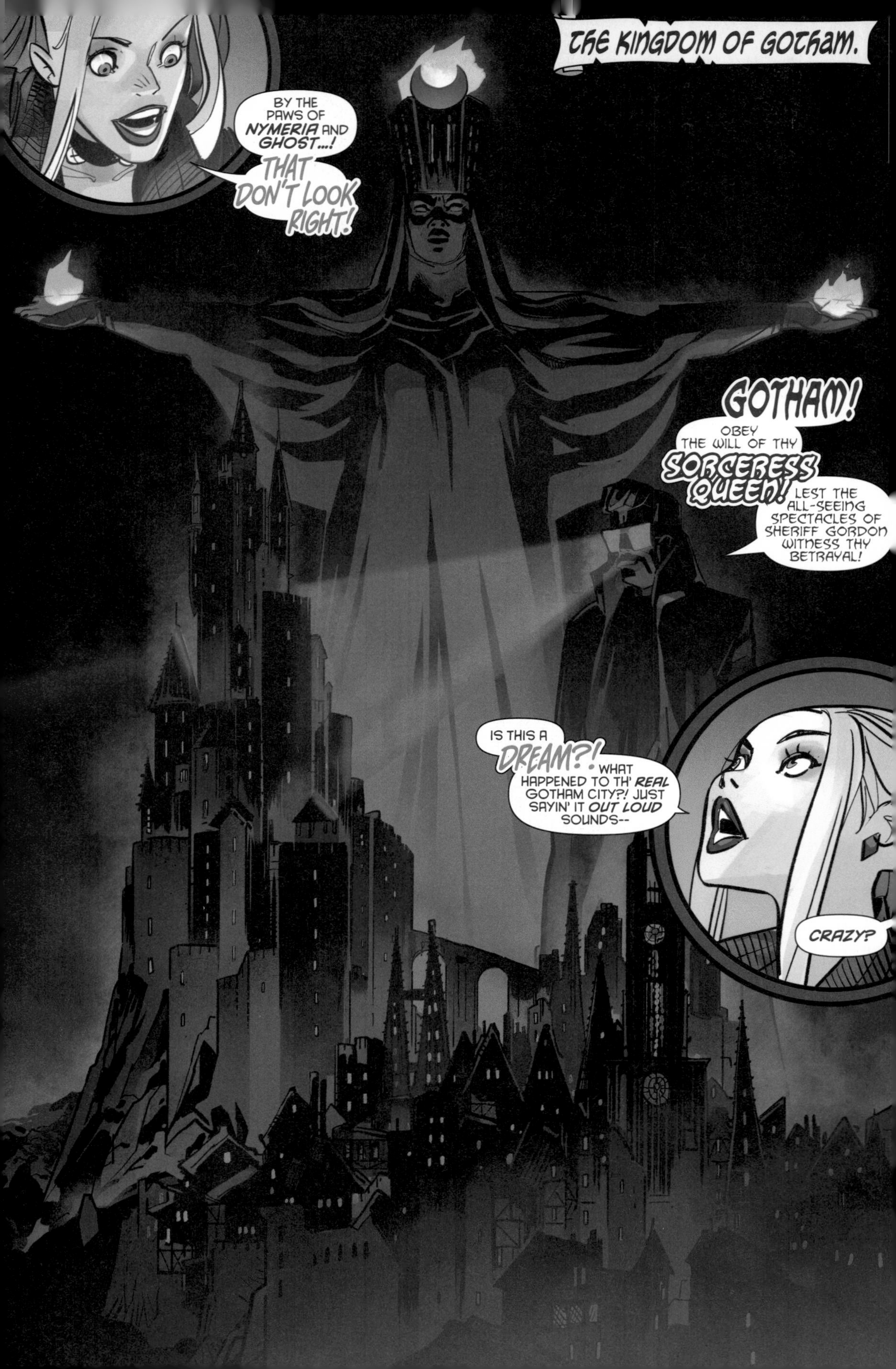

THE KINGDOM OF GOTHAM.
BY THE PAWS OF NYMERIA AND GHOST...!
THAT DON'T LOOK RIGHT!
GOTHAM!
OBEY THE WILL OF THY SORCERESS QUEEN!
LEST THE ALL-SEEING SPECTACLES OF SHERIFF GORDON WITNESS THY BETRAYAL!
IS THIS A DREAM?! WHAT HAPPENED TO TH' REAL GOTHAM CITY?! JUST SAYIN' IT OUT LOUD SOUNDS--
CRAZY?

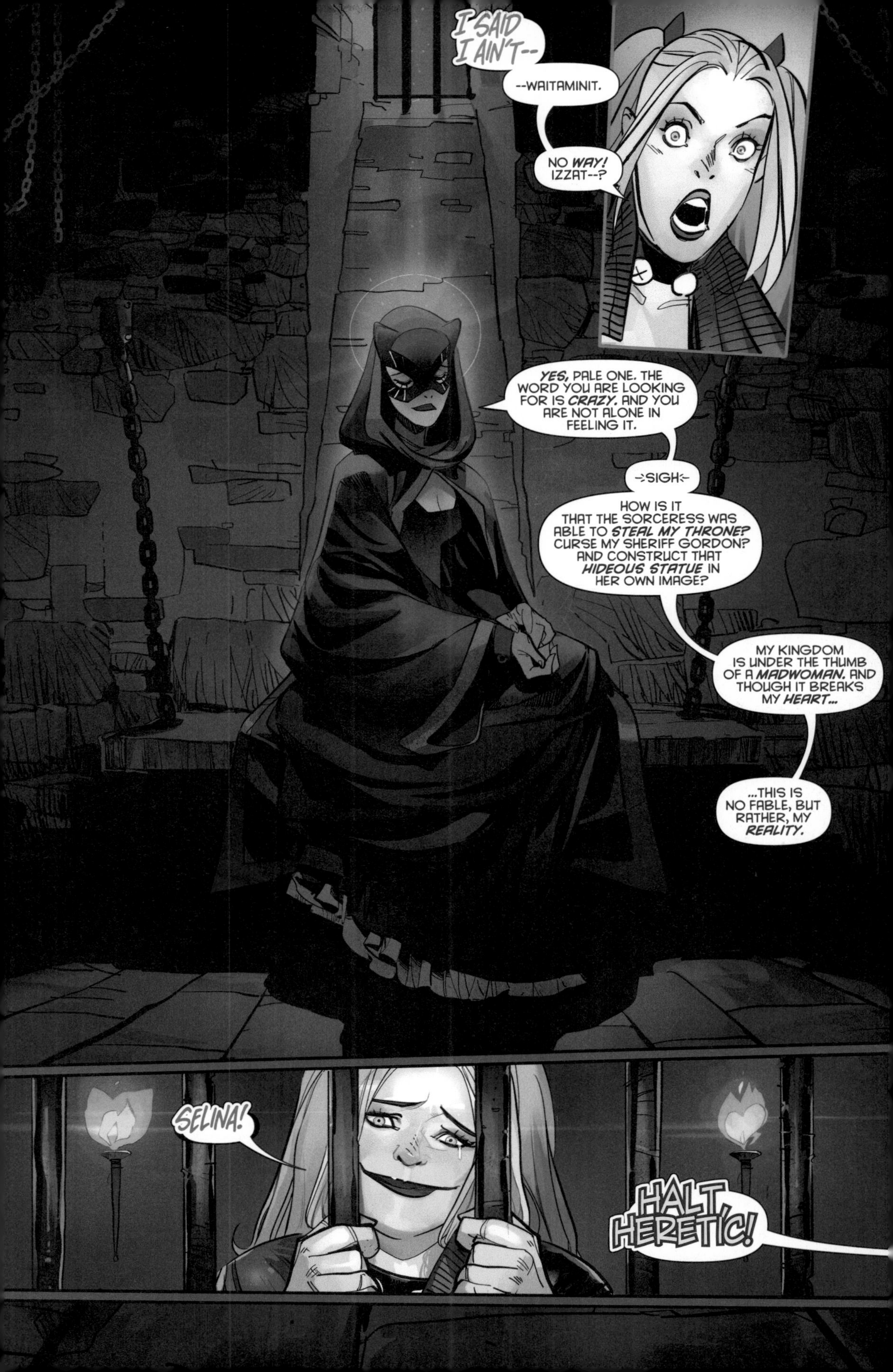
I SAID I AIN'T--
--WAITAMINIT.
NO WAY! IZZAT--?
YES, PALE ONE. THE WORD YOU ARE LOOKING FOR IS CRAZY. AND YOU ARE NOT ALONE IN FEELING IT.
SIGH
HOW IS IT THAT THE SORCERESS WAS ABLE TO STEAL MY THRONE? CURSE MY SHERIFF GORDON? AND CONSTRUCT THAT HIDEOUS STATUE IN HER OWN IMAGE?
MY KINGDOM IS UNDER THE THUMB OF A MADWOMAN. AND THOUGH IT BREAKS MY HEART...
...THIS IS NO FABLE, BUT RATHER, MY REALITY.
SELINA!
HALT, HERETIC!

Woof!

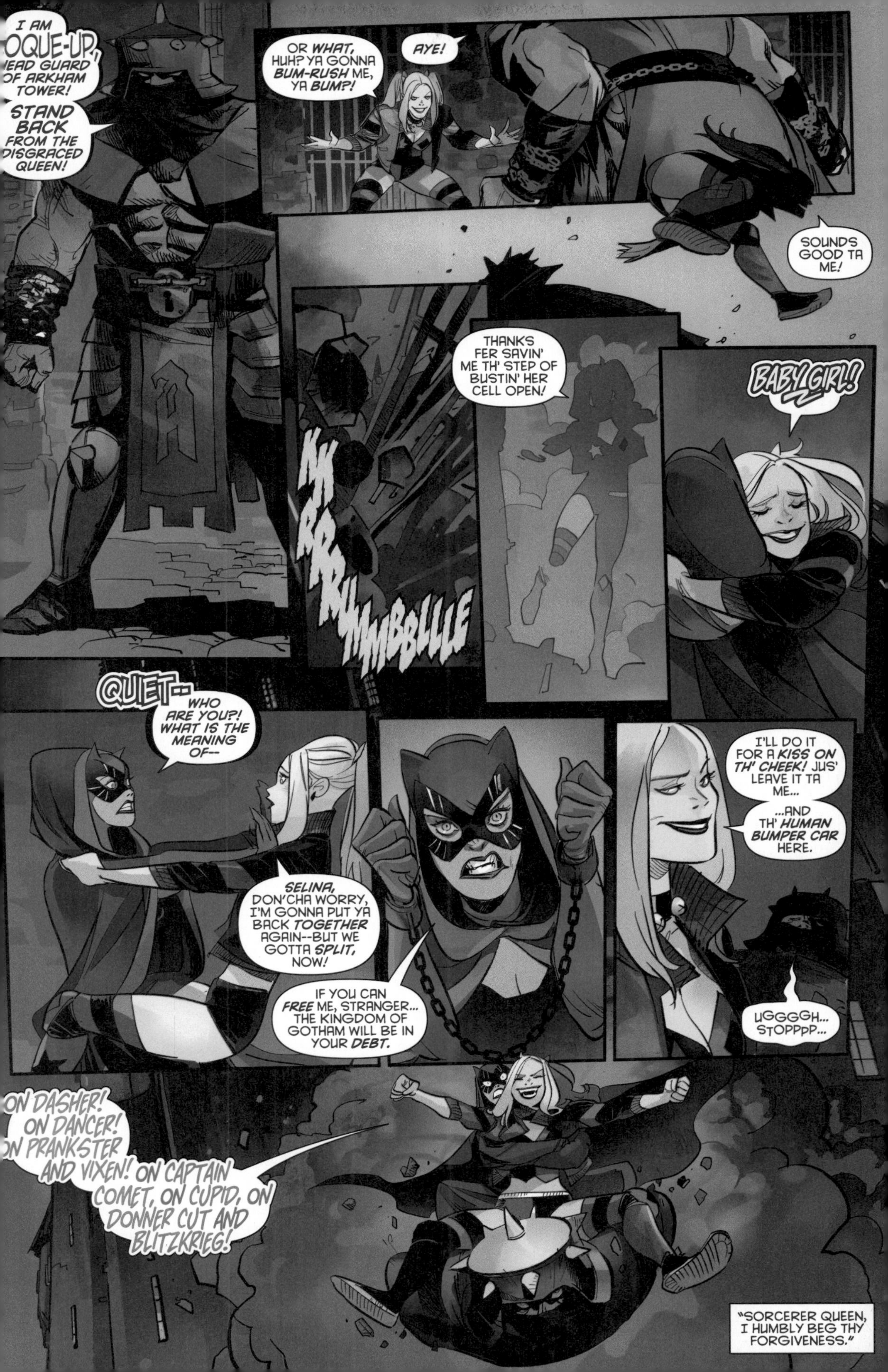
I AM OQUE-UP, HEAD GUARD OF ARKHAM TOWER!
STAND BACK FROM THE DISGRACED QUEEN!
OR WHAT, HUH? YA GONNA BUM-RUSH ME, YA BUM?!
AYE!
SOUNDS GOOD TA ME!
KKRRRUMMBBLLLE
THANKS FER SAVIN' ME TH' STEP OF BUSTIN' HER CELL OPEN!
BABY GIRL!
QUIET--
WHO ARE YOU?! WHAT IS THE MEANING OF--
SELINA, DON'CHA WORRY, I'M GONNA PUT YA BACK TOGETHER AGAIN--BUT WE GOTTA SPLIT, NOW!
IF YOU CAN FREE ME, STRANGER... THE KINGDOM OF GOTHAM WILL BE IN YOUR DEBT.
I'LL DO IT FOR A KISS ON TH' CHEEK! JUS' LEAVE IT TA ME...
...AND TH' HUMAN BUMPER CAR HERE.
UGGGGH... STOPPPP...
ON DASHER! ON DANCER! ON PRANKSTER AND VIXEN! ON CAPTAIN COMET, ON CUPID, ON DONNER CUT AND BLITZKRIEG!
"SORCERER QUEEN, I HUMBLY BEG THY FORGIVENESS."

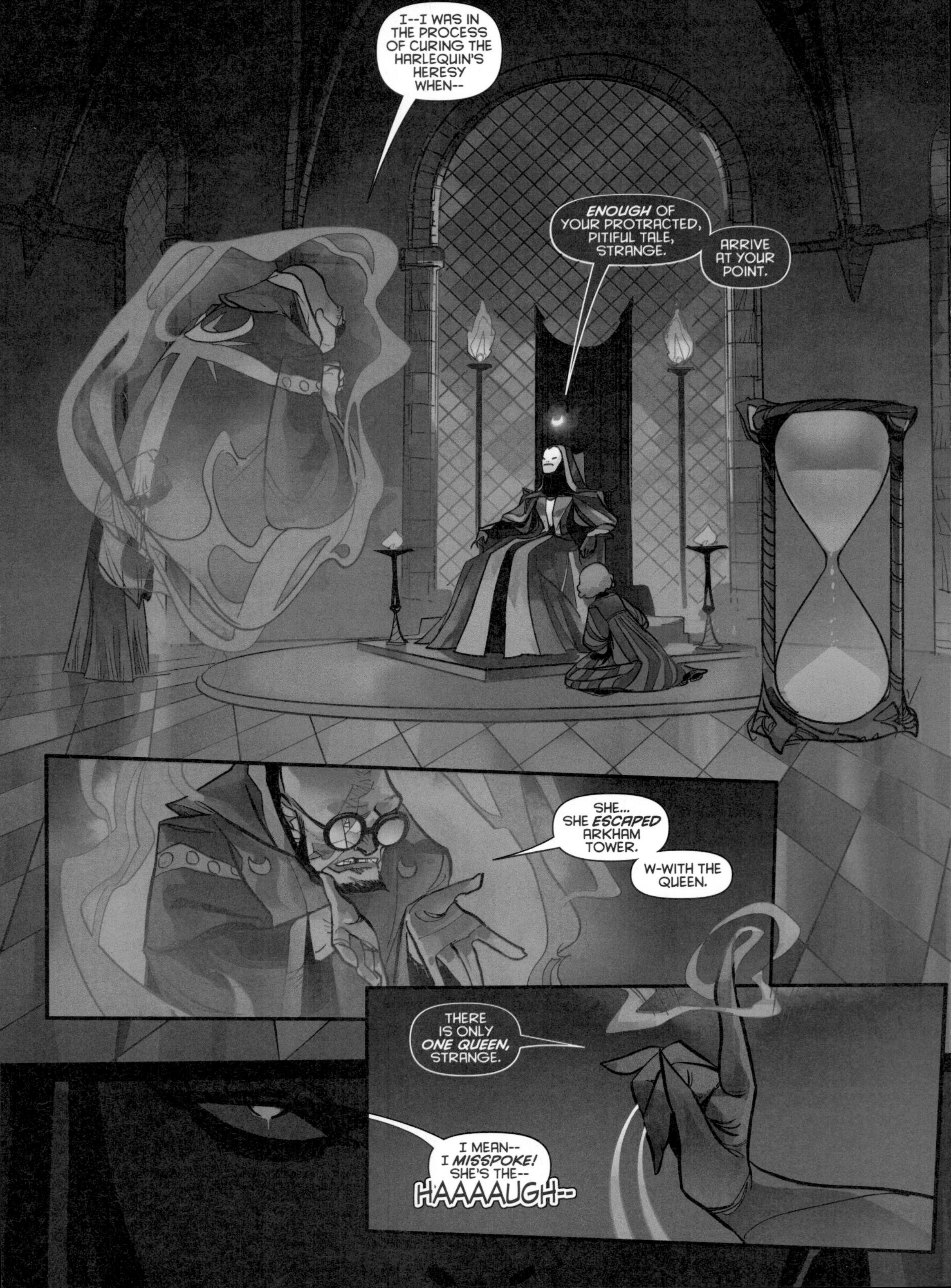
I--I WAS IN THE PROCESS OF CURING THE HARLEQUIN'S HERESY WHEN--
ENOUGH OF YOUR PROTRACTED, PITIFUL TALE, STRANGE.
ARRIVE AT YOUR POINT.
SHE... SHE *ESCAPED* ARKHAM TOWER.
W-WITH THE QUEEN.
THERE IS ONLY *ONE QUEEN,* STRANGE.
I MEAN-- I *MISSPOKE!* SHE'S THE--
HAAAAUGH--

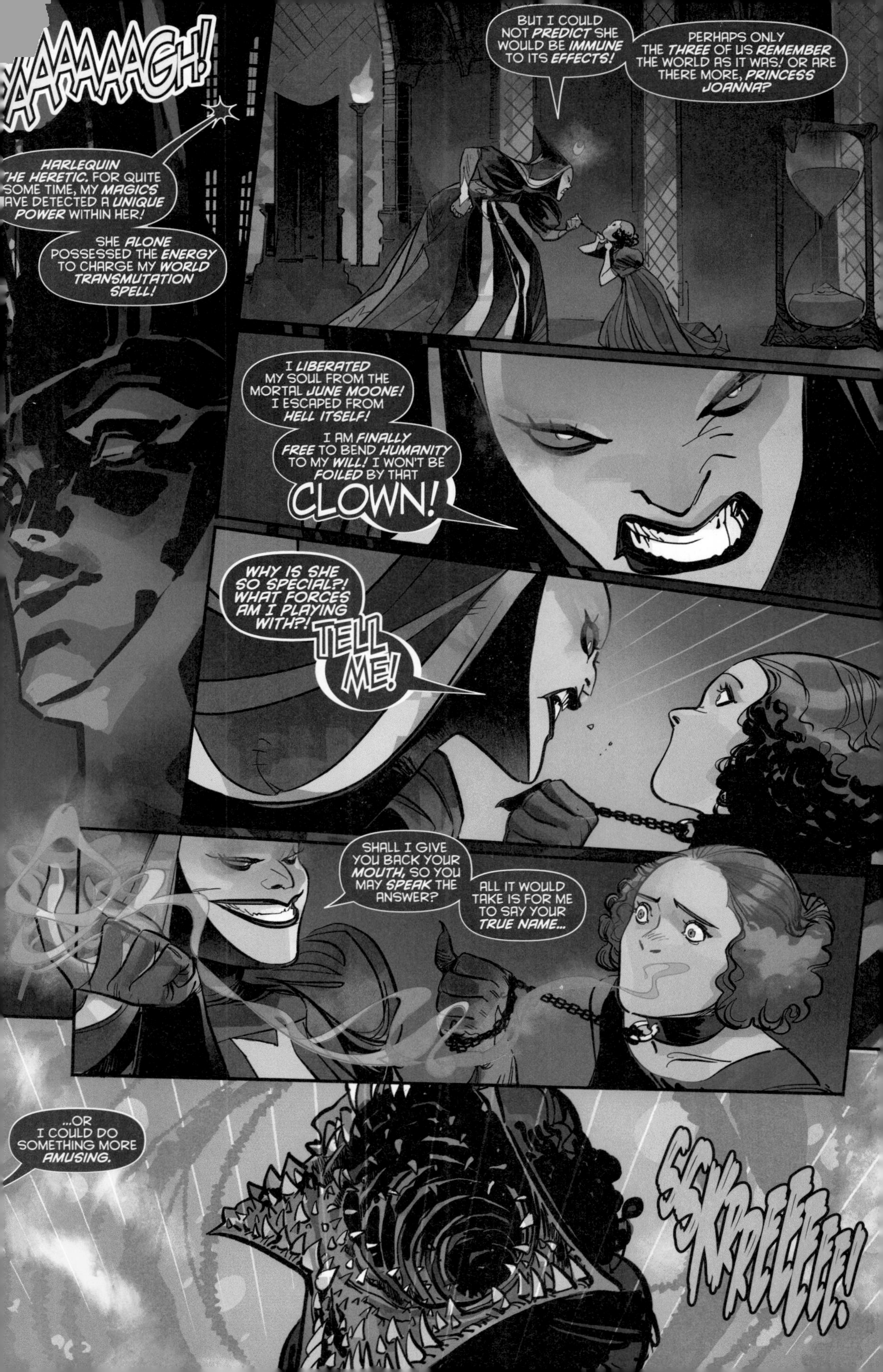
AAAAAAGH!
HARLEQUIN THE HERETIC. FOR QUITE SOME TIME, MY MAGICS HAVE DETECTED A UNIQUE POWER WITHIN HER!
SHE ALONE POSSESSED THE ENERGY TO CHARGE MY WORLD TRANSMUTATION SPELL!
BUT I COULD NOT PREDICT SHE WOULD BE IMMUNE TO ITS EFFECTS!
PERHAPS ONLY THE THREE OF US REMEMBER THE WORLD AS IT WAS! OR ARE THERE MORE, PRINCESS JOANNA?
I LIBERATED MY SOUL FROM THE MORTAL JUNE MOONE! I ESCAPED FROM HELL ITSELF!
I AM FINALLY FREE TO BEND HUMANITY TO MY WILL! I WON'T BE FOILED BY THAT CLOWN!
WHY IS SHE SO SPECIAL?! WHAT FORCES AM I PLAYING WITH?! TELL ME!
SHALL I GIVE YOU BACK YOUR MOUTH, SO YOU MAY SPEAK THE ANSWER?
ALL IT WOULD TAKE IS FOR ME TO SAY YOUR TRUE NAME...
...OR I COULD DO SOMETHING MORE AMUSING.
SCKREEEEE!

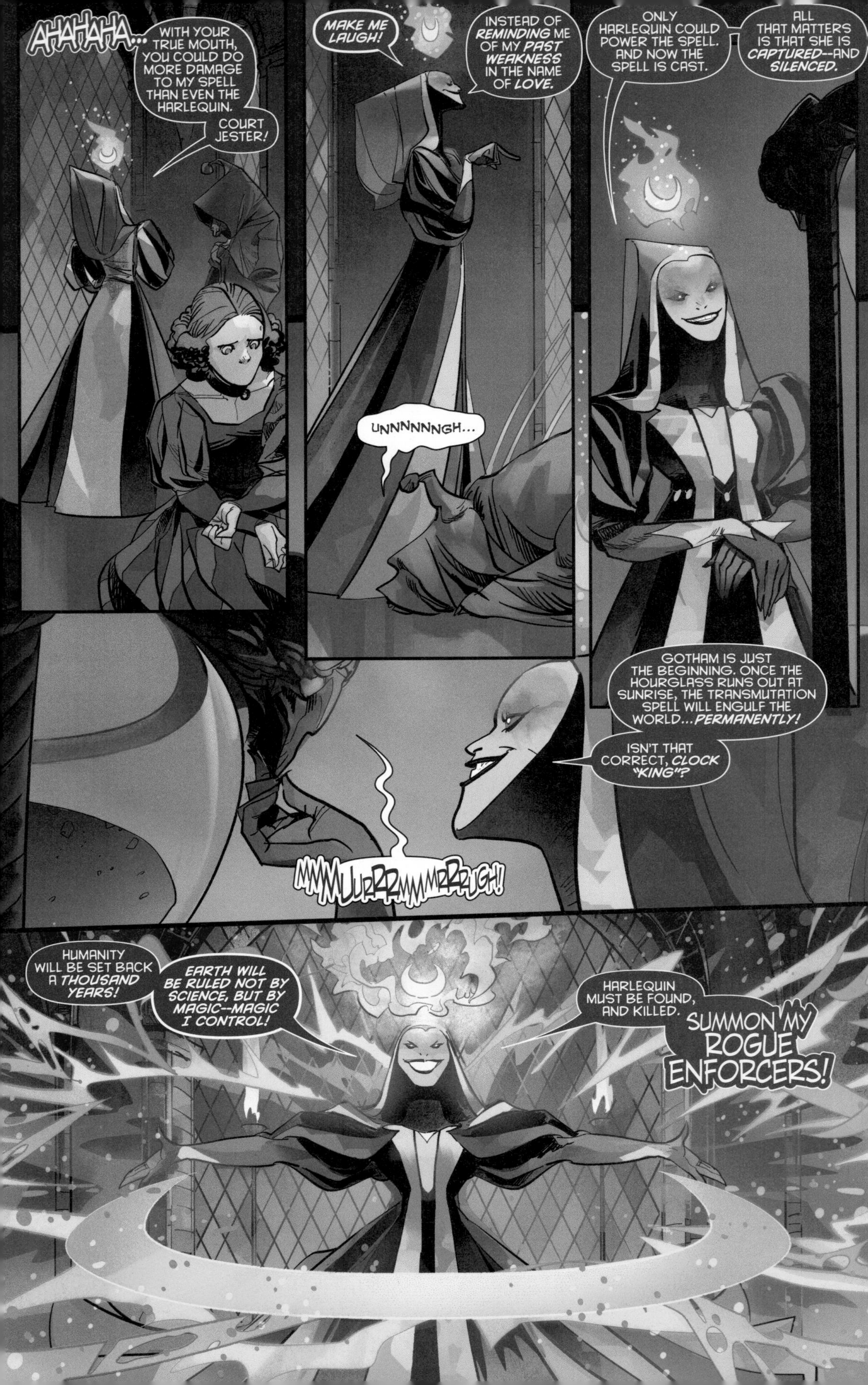
AHAHAHA...
WITH YOUR TRUE MOUTH, YOU COULD DO MORE DAMAGE TO MY SPELL THAN EVEN THE HARLEQUIN.
COURT JESTER!
MAKE ME LAUGH!
INSTEAD OF REMINDING ME OF MY PAST WEAKNESS IN THE NAME OF LOVE.
UNNNNNNGH...
ONLY HARLEQUIN COULD POWER THE SPELL. AND NOW THE SPELL IS CAST.
ALL THAT MATTERS IS THAT SHE IS CAPTURED--AND SILENCED.
GOTHAM IS JUST THE BEGINNING. ONCE THE HOURGLASS RUNS OUT AT SUNRISE, THE TRANSMUTATION SPELL WILL ENGULF THE WORLD...PERMANENTLY!
ISN'T THAT CORRECT, CLOCK "KING"?
MMMMURRRMMMRRRUGH!
HUMANITY WILL BE SET BACK A THOUSAND YEARS!
EARTH WILL BE RULED NOT BY SCIENCE, BUT BY MAGIC--MAGIC I CONTROL!
HARLEQUIN MUST BE FOUND, AND KILLED.
SUMMON MY ROGUE ENFORCERS!

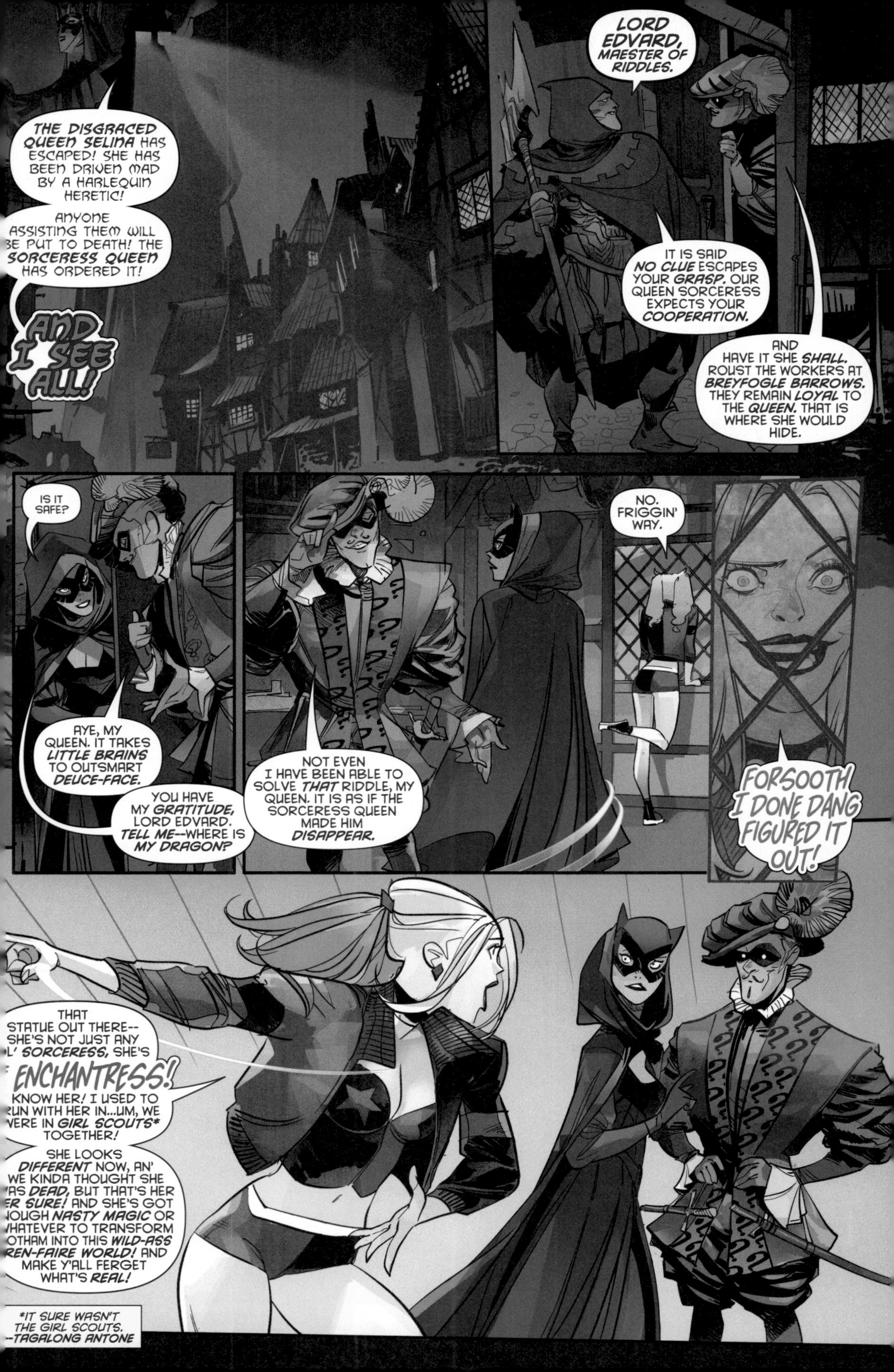
THE DISGRACED QUEEN SELINA HAS ESCAPED! SHE HAS BEEN DRIVEN MAD BY A HARLEQUIN HERETIC!
ANYONE ASSISTING THEM WILL BE PUT TO DEATH! THE SORCERESS QUEEN HAS ORDERED IT!
AND I SEE ALL!
LORD EDVARD, MAESTER OF RIDDLES.
IT IS SAID NO CLUE ESCAPES YOUR GRASP. OUR QUEEN SORCERESS EXPECTS YOUR COOPERATION.
AND HAVE IT SHE SHALL. ROUST THE WORKERS AT BREYFOGLE BARROWS. THEY REMAIN LOYAL TO THE QUEEN. THAT IS WHERE SHE WOULD HIDE.
IS IT SAFE?
AYE, MY QUEEN. IT TAKES LITTLE BRAINS TO OUTSMART DEUCE-FACE.
YOU HAVE MY GRATITUDE, LORD EDVARD. TELL ME--WHERE IS MY DRAGON?
NOT EVEN I HAVE BEEN ABLE TO SOLVE THAT RIDDLE, MY QUEEN. IT IS AS IF THE SORCERESS QUEEN MADE HIM DISAPPEAR.
NO. FRIGGIN' WAY.
FORSOOTH I DONE DANG FIGURED IT OUT!
THAT STATUE OUT THERE-- SHE'S NOT JUST ANY OL' SORCERESS, SHE'S ENCHANTRESS!
KNOW HER! I USED TO RUN WITH HER IN...UM, WE WERE IN GIRL SCOUTS* TOGETHER!
SHE LOOKS DIFFERENT NOW, AN' WE KINDA THOUGHT SHE WAS DEAD, BUT THAT'S HER FER SURE! AND SHE'S GOT ENOUGH NASTY MAGIC OR WHATEVER TO TRANSFORM GOTHAM INTO THIS WILD-ASS REN-FAIRE WORLD! AND MAKE Y'ALL FERGET WHAT'S REAL!
*IT SURE WASN'T THE GIRL SCOUTS. --TAGALONG ANTONE

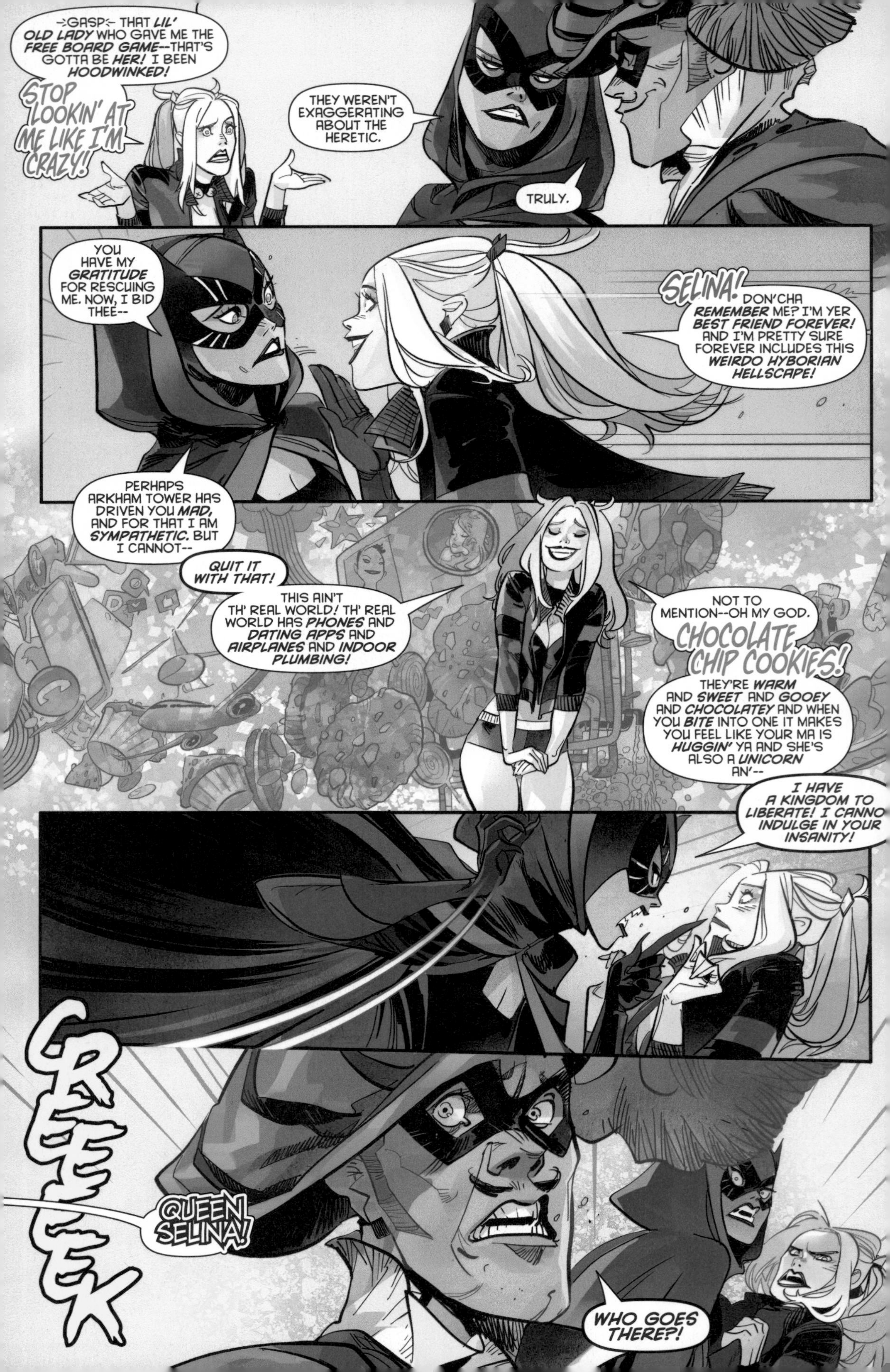

⇝GASP⇜ THAT LIL' OLD LADY WHO GAVE ME THE FREE BOARD GAME--THAT'S GOTTA BE HER! I BEEN HOODWINKED!
STOP LOOKIN' AT ME LIKE I'M CRAZY!
THEY WEREN'T EXAGGERATING ABOUT THE HERETIC.
TRULY.
YOU HAVE MY GRATITUDE FOR RESCUING ME. NOW, I BID THEE--
SELINA! DON'CHA REMEMBER ME? I'M YER BEST FRIEND FOREVER! AND I'M PRETTY SURE FOREVER INCLUDES THIS WEIRDO HYBORIAN HELLSCAPE!
PERHAPS ARKHAM TOWER HAS DRIVEN YOU MAD, AND FOR THAT I AM SYMPATHETIC. BUT I CANNOT--
QUIT IT WITH THAT!
THIS AIN'T TH' REAL WORLD! TH' REAL WORLD HAS PHONES AND DATING APPS AND AIRPLANES AND INDOOR PLUMBING!
NOT TO MENTION--OH MY GOD. CHOCOLATE CHIP COOKIES!
THEY'RE WARM AND SWEET AND GOOEY AND CHOCOLATEY AND WHEN YOU BITE INTO ONE IT MAKES YOU FEEL LIKE YOUR MA IS HUGGIN' YA AND SHE'S ALSO A UNICORN AN'--
I HAVE A KINGDOM TO LIBERATE! I CANNO INDULGE IN YOUR INSANITY!
CREEEK
QUEEN SELINA!
WHO GOES THERE?!

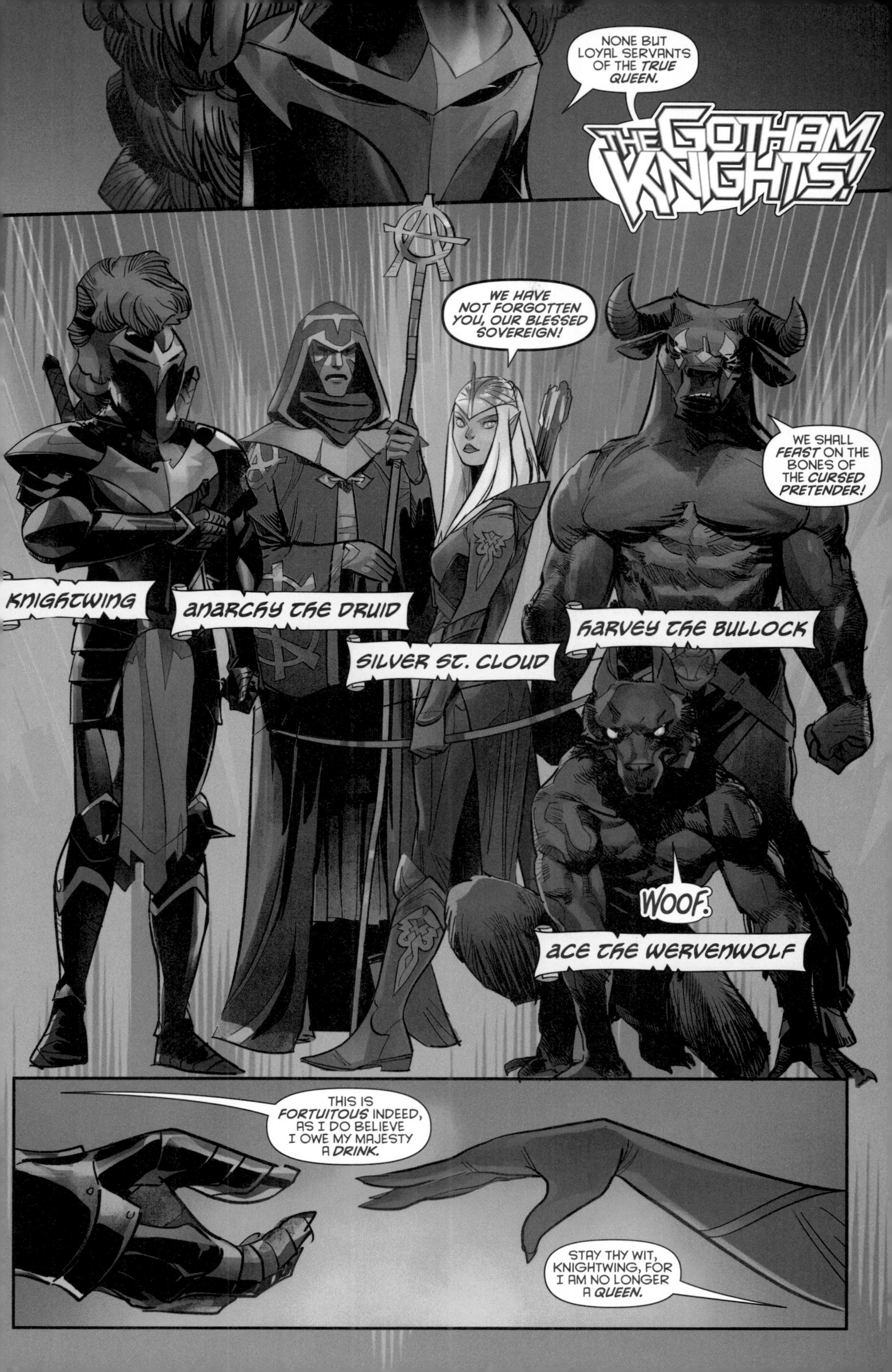
NONE BUT LOYAL SERVANTS OF THE TRUE QUEEN.
THE GOTHAM KNIGHTS!
WE HAVE NOT FORGOTTEN YOU, OUR BLESSED SOVEREIGN!
WE SHALL FEAST ON THE BONES OF THE CURSED PRETENDER!
KNIGHTWING
ANARCHY THE DRUID
SILVER ST. CLOUD
HARVEY THE BULLOCK
WOOF.
ACE THE WERVENWOLF
THIS IS FORTUITOUS INDEED, AS I DO BELIEVE I OWE MY MAJESTY A DRINK.
STAY THY WIT, KNIGHTWING, FOR I AM NO LONGER A QUEEN.

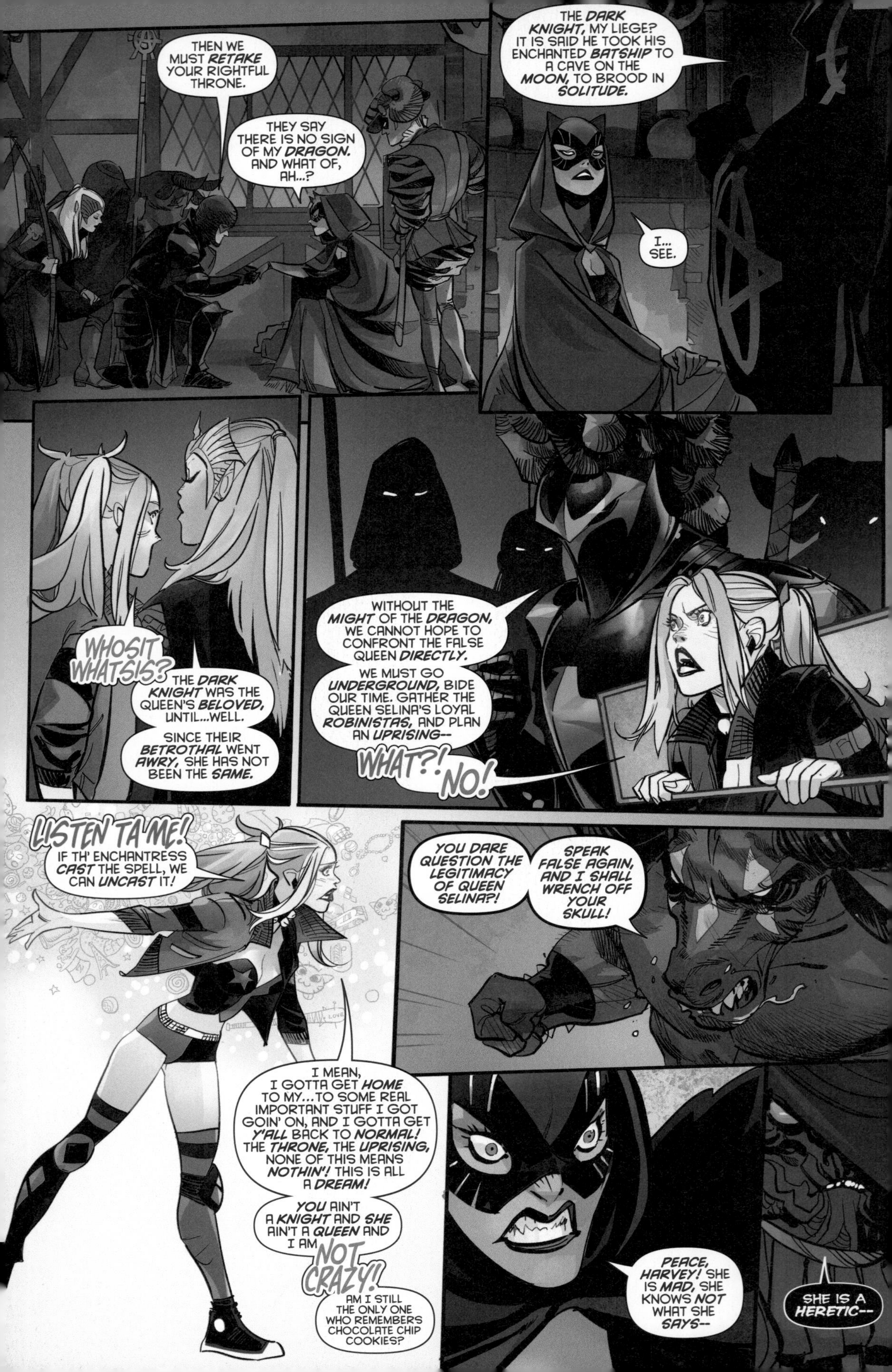

THEN WE MUST RETAKE YOUR RIGHTFUL THRONE.
THEY SAY THERE IS NO SIGN OF MY DRAGON. AND WHAT OF, AH...?
THE DARK KNIGHT, MY LIEGE? IT IS SAID HE TOOK HIS ENCHANTED BATSHIP TO A CAVE ON THE MOON, TO BROOD IN SOLITUDE.
I... SEE.
WHOSIT WHATSIS?
THE DARK KNIGHT WAS THE QUEEN'S BELOVED, UNTIL...WELL.
SINCE THEIR BETROTHAL WENT AWRY, SHE HAS NOT BEEN THE SAME.
WITHOUT THE MIGHT OF THE DRAGON, WE CANNOT HOPE TO CONFRONT THE FALSE QUEEN DIRECTLY.
WE MUST GO UNDERGROUND, BIDE OUR TIME. GATHER THE QUEEN SELINA'S LOYAL ROBINISTAS, AND PLAN AN UPRISING--
WHAT?! NO!
LISTEN TA ME!
IF TH' ENCHANTRESS CAST THE SPELL, WE CAN UNCAST IT!
YOU DARE QUESTION THE LEGITIMACY OF QUEEN SELINA?!
SPEAK FALSE AGAIN, AND I SHALL WRENCH OFF YOUR SKULL!
I MEAN, I GOTTA GET HOME TO MY...TO SOME REAL IMPORTANT STUFF I GOT GOIN' ON, AND I GOTTA GET Y'ALL BACK TO NORMAL! THE THRONE, THE UPRISING, NONE OF THIS MEANS NOTHIN'! THIS IS ALL A DREAM!
YOU AIN'T A KNIGHT AND SHE AIN'T A QUEEN AND I AM NOT CRAZY!
AM I STILL THE ONLY ONE WHO REMEMBERS CHOCOLATE CHIP COOKIES?
PEACE, HARVEY! SHE IS MAD, SHE KNOWS NOT WHAT SHE SAYS--
SHE IS A HERETIC--

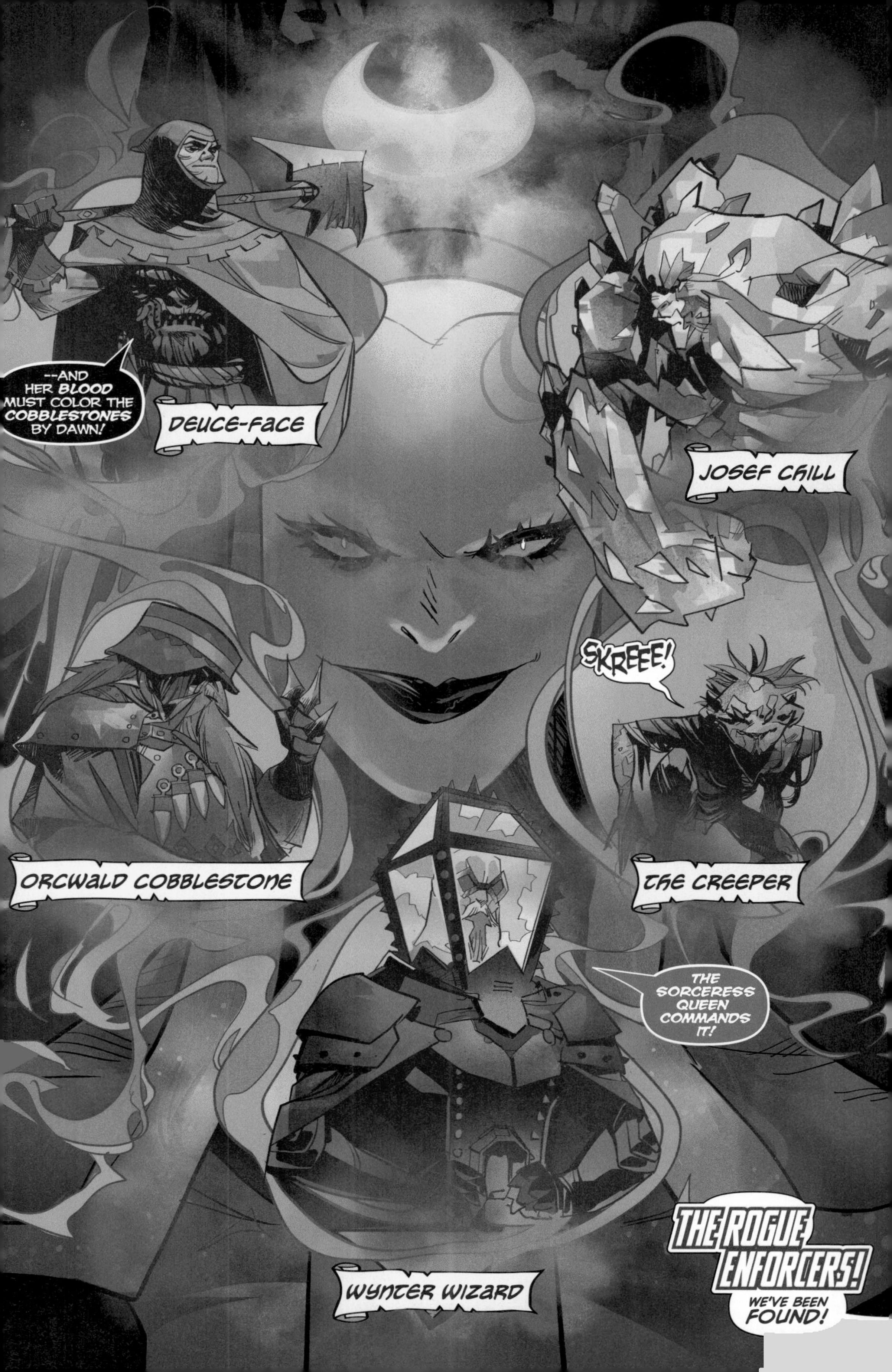
--AND HER BLOOD MUST COLOR THE COBBLESTONES BY DAWN!
DEUCE-FACE
JOSEF CHILL
SKREEE!
ORCWALD COBBLESTONE
THE CREEPER
THE SORCERESS QUEEN COMMANDS IT!
THE ROGUE ENFORCERS!
WE'VE BEEN FOUND!
WYNTER WIZARD

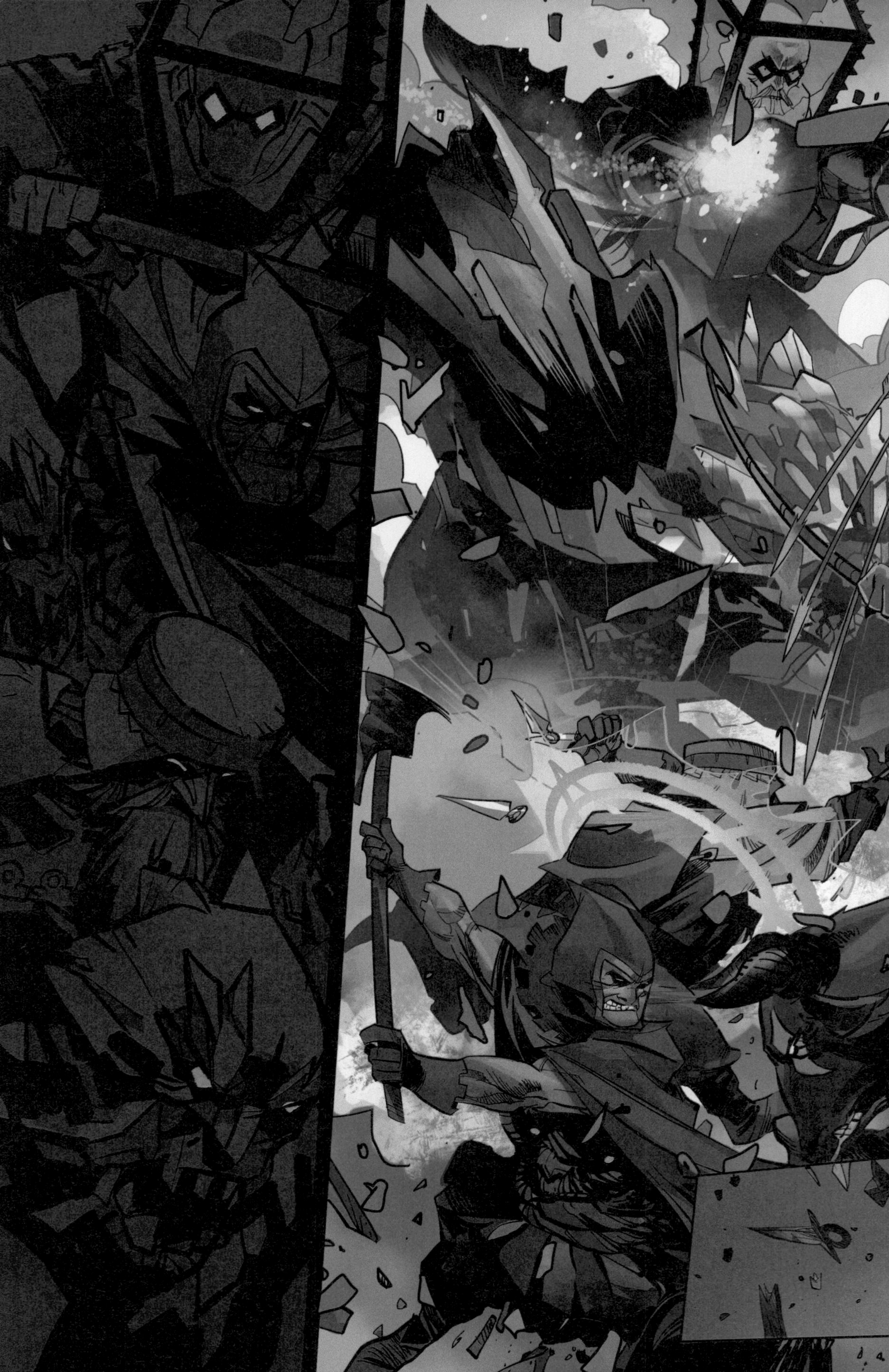

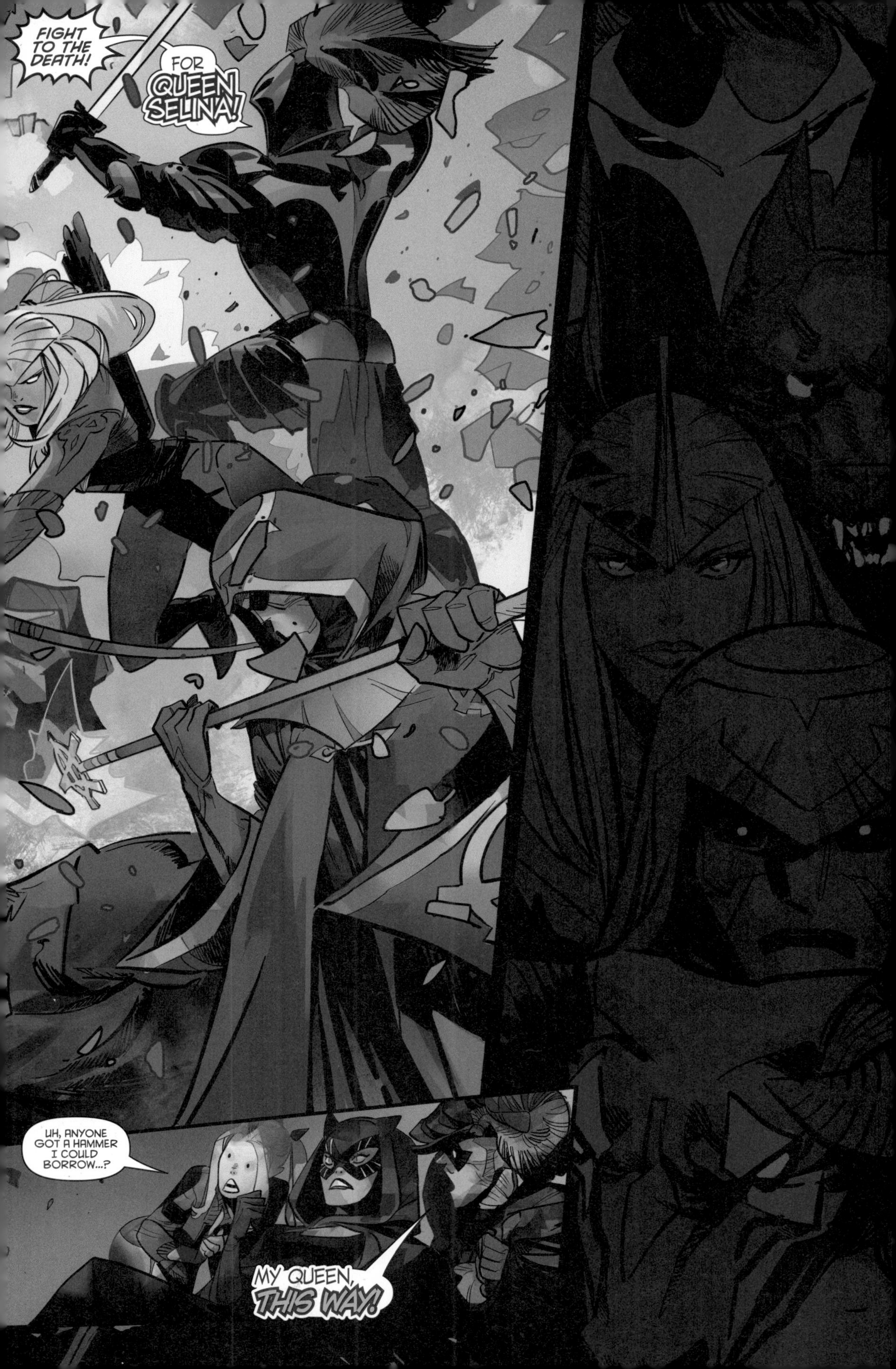
FIGHT TO THE DEATH!
FOR QUEEN SELINA!
UH, ANYONE GOT A HAMMER I COULD BORROW...?
MY QUEEN, THIS WAY!

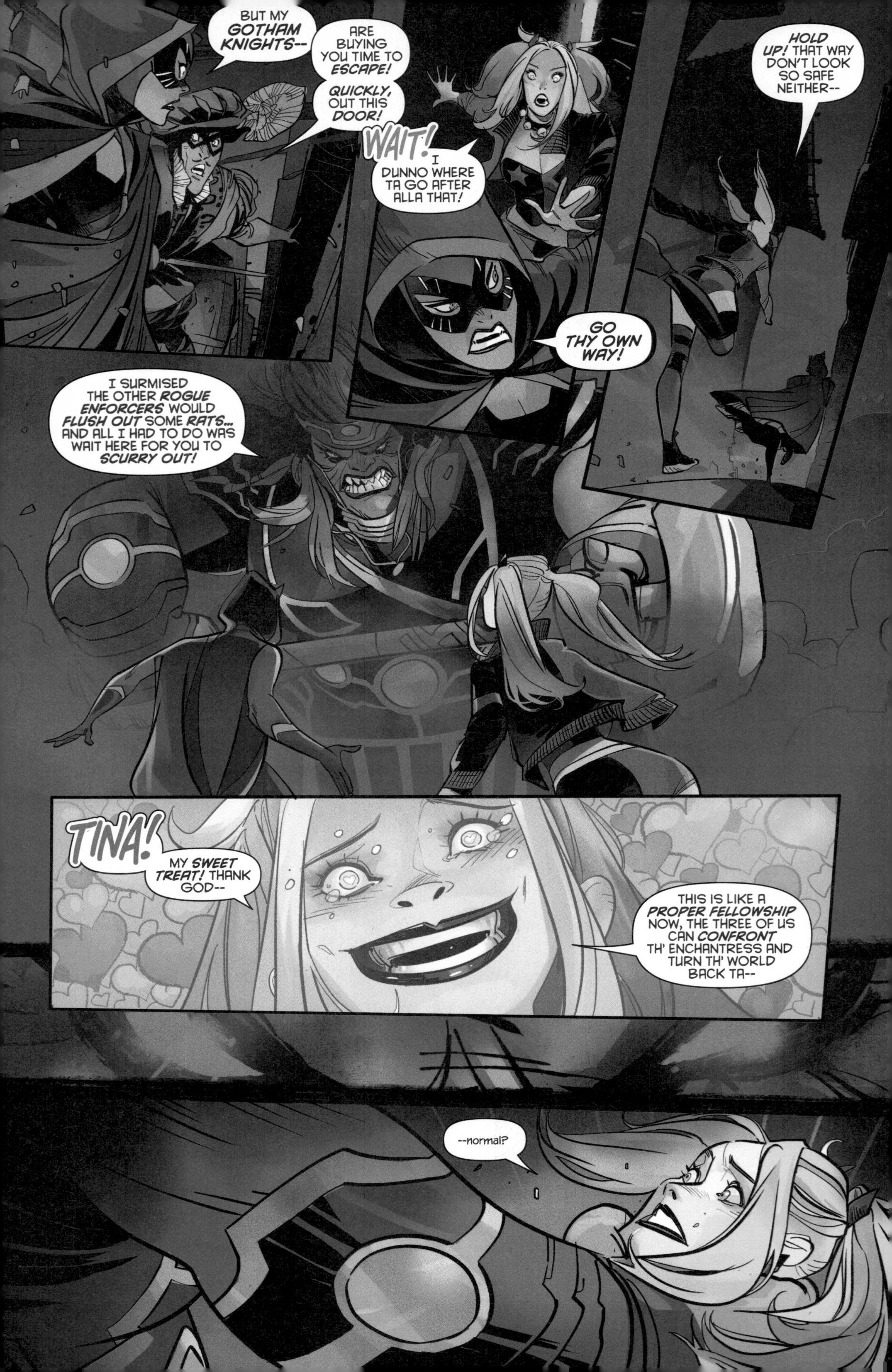
BUT MY GOTHAM KNIGHTS--
ARE BUYING YOU TIME TO ESCAPE!
QUICKLY, OUT THIS DOOR!
WAIT!
I DUNNO WHERE TA GO AFTER ALLA THAT!
GO THY OWN WAY!
HOLD UP! THAT WAY DON'T LOOK SO SAFE NEITHER--
I SURMISED THE OTHER ROGUE ENFORCERS WOULD FLUSH OUT SOME RATS... AND ALL I HAD TO DO WAS WAIT HERE FOR YOU TO SCURRY OUT!
TINA!
MY SWEET TREAT! THANK GOD--
THIS IS LIKE A PROPER FELLOWSHIP NOW, THE THREE OF US CAN CONFRONT TH' ENCHANTRESS AND TURN TH' WORLD BACK TA--
--normal?

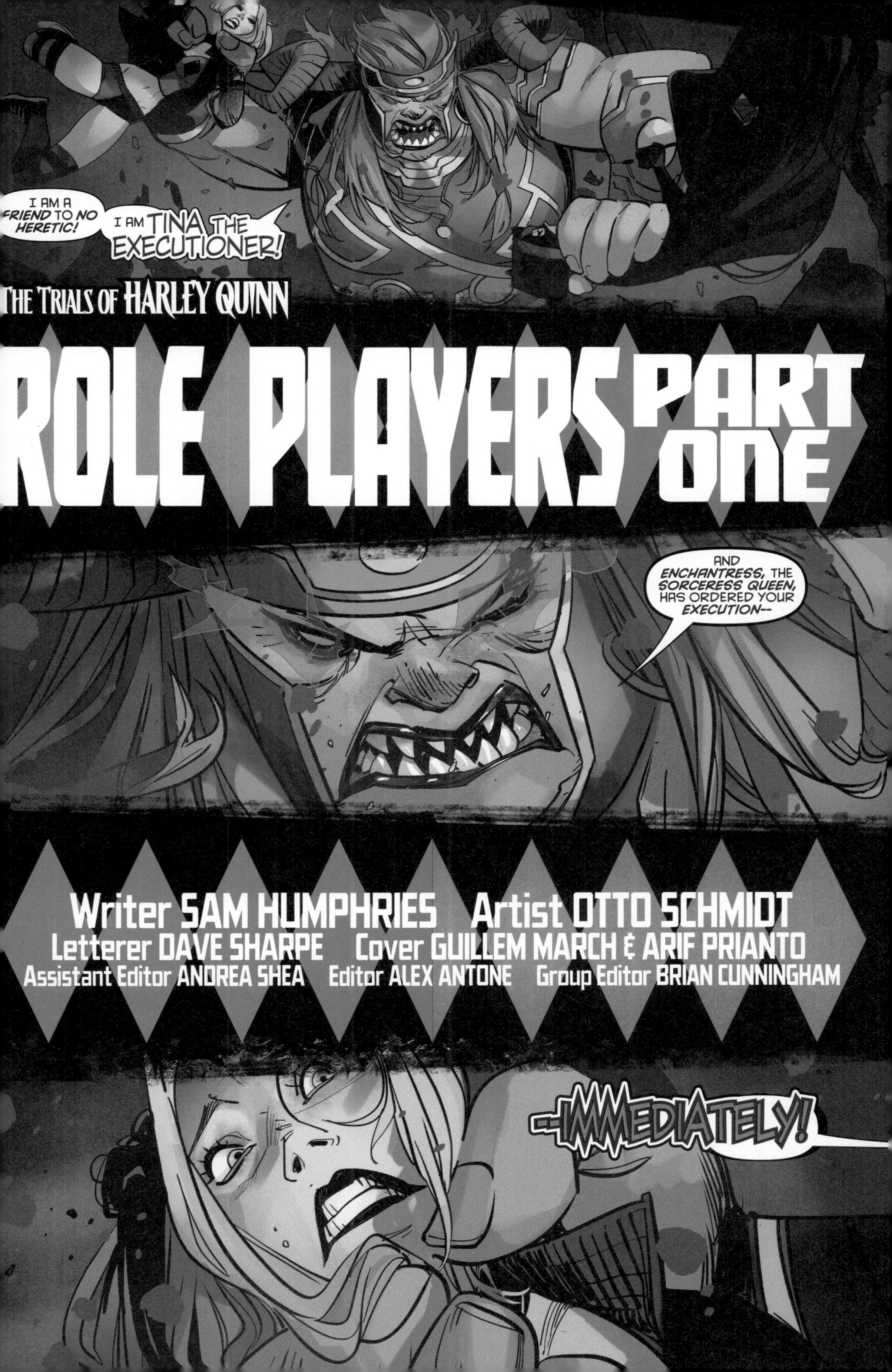
I AM A FRIEND TO NO HERETIC!
I AM TINA THE EXECUTIONER!
THE TRIALS OF HARLEY QUINN
ROLE PLAYERS PART ONE
AND ENCHANTRESS, THE SORCERESS QUEEN, HAS ORDERED YOUR EXECUTION--
--IMMEDIATELY!
Writer SAM HUMPHRIES Artist OTTO SCHMIDT
Letterer DAVE SHARPE Cover GUILLEM MARCH & ARIF PRIANTO
Assistant Editor ANDREA SHEA Editor ALEX ANTONE Group Editor BRIAN CUNNINGHAM

Woof!

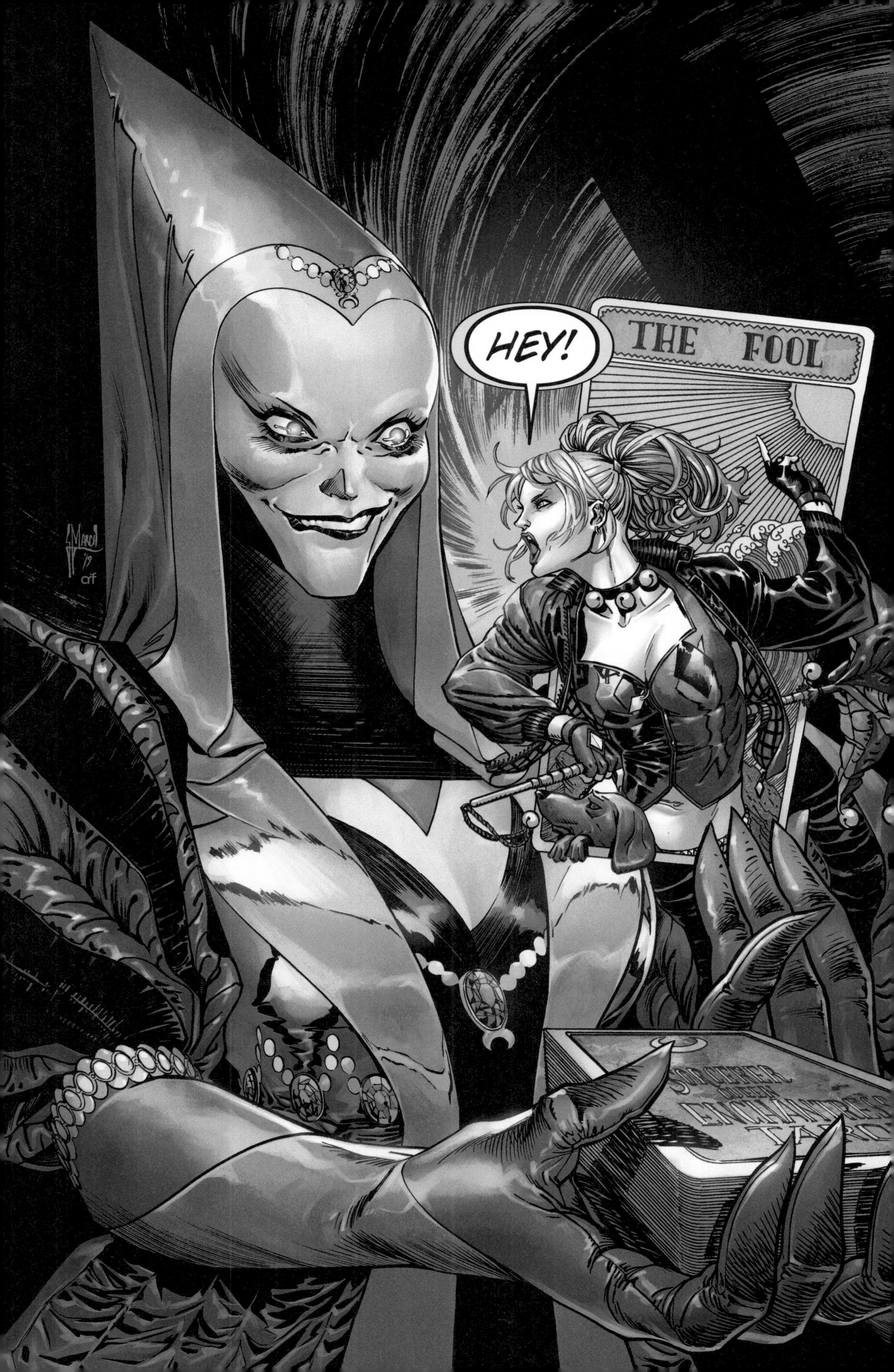
HEY!
THE FOOL
SORCERER

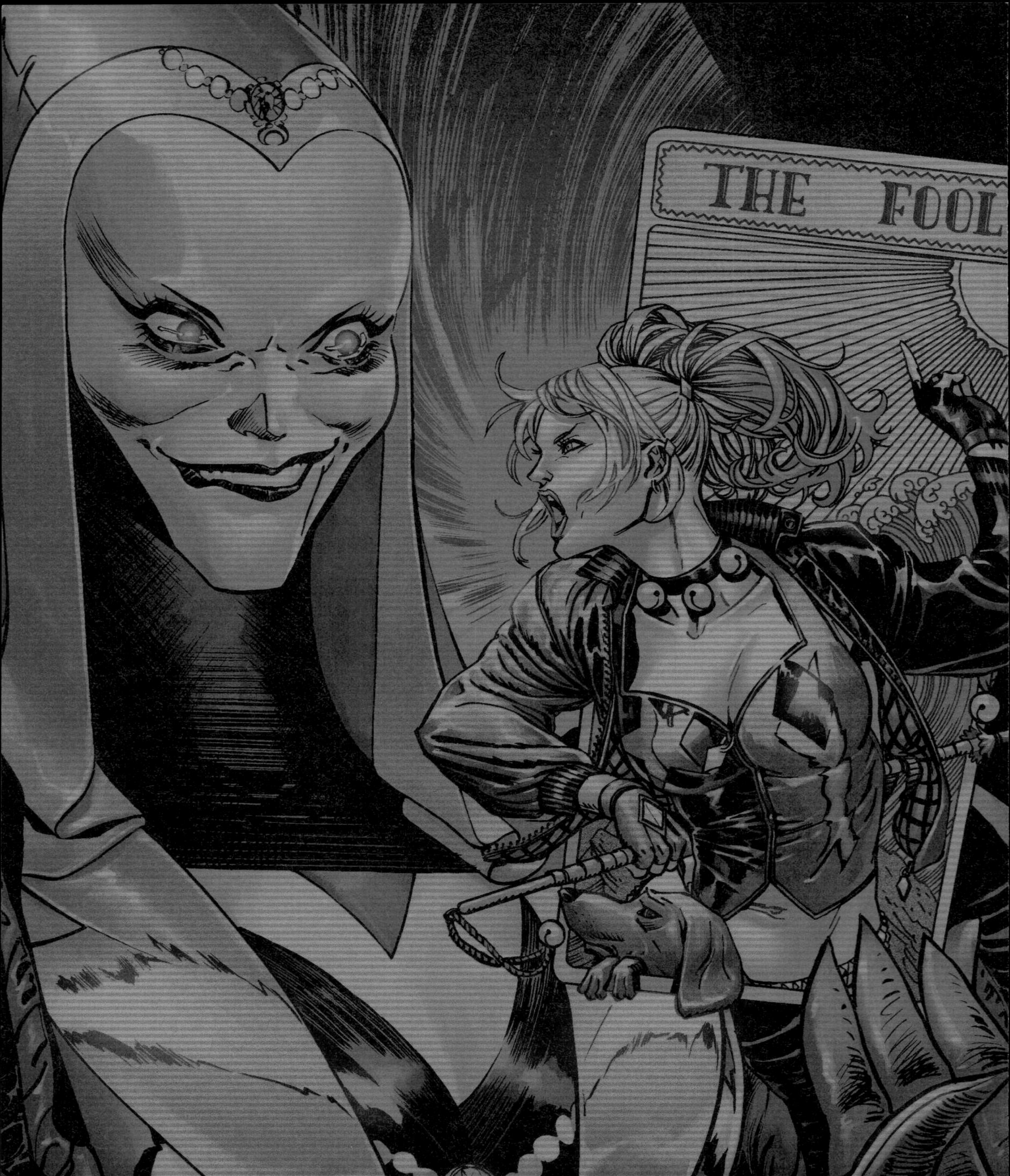
THE FOOL

HARLEY QUINN
#62

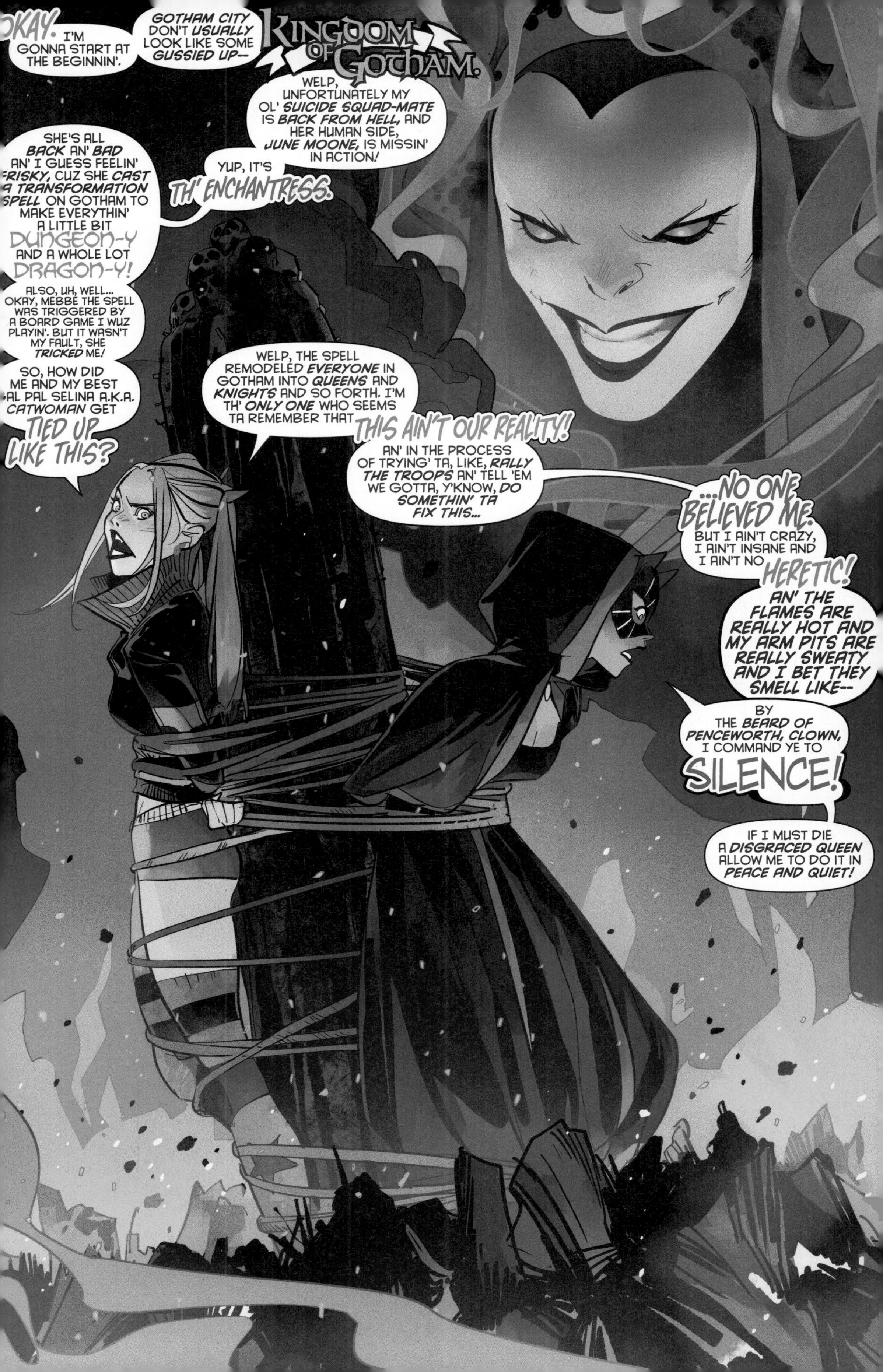
OKAY. I'M GONNA START AT THE BEGINNIN'.
GOTHAM CITY DON'T USUALLY LOOK LIKE SOME GUSSIED UP--
KINGDOM OF GOTHAM.
WELP, UNFORTUNATELY MY OL' SUICIDE SQUAD-MATE IS BACK FROM HELL, AND HER HUMAN SIDE, JUNE MOONE, IS MISSIN' IN ACTION!
YUP, IT'S TH' ENCHANTRESS.
SHE'S ALL BACK AN' BAD AN' I GUESS FEELIN' FRISKY, CUZ SHE CAST A TRANSFORMATION SPELL ON GOTHAM TO MAKE EVERYTHIN' A LITTLE BIT DUNGEON-Y AND A WHOLE LOT DRAGON-Y!
ALSO, UH, WELL... OKAY, MEBBE THE SPELL WAS TRIGGERED BY A BOARD GAME I WUZ PLAYIN'. BUT IT WASN'T MY FAULT, SHE TRICKED ME!
SO, HOW DID ME AND MY BEST GAL PAL SELINA A.K.A. CATWOMAN GET TIED UP LIKE THIS?
WELP, THE SPELL REMODELED EVERYONE IN GOTHAM INTO QUEENS AND KNIGHTS AND SO FORTH. I'M TH' ONLY ONE WHO SEEMS TA REMEMBER THAT THIS AIN'T OUR REALITY!
AN' IN THE PROCESS OF TRYING' TA, LIKE, RALLY THE TROOPS AN' TELL 'EM WE GOTTA, Y'KNOW, DO SOMETHIN' TA FIX THIS...
...NO ONE BELIEVED ME.
BUT I AIN'T CRAZY, I AIN'T INSANE AND I AIN'T NO HERETIC!
AN' THE FLAMES ARE REALLY HOT AND MY ARM PITS ARE REALLY SWEATY AND I BET THEY SMELL LIKE--
BY THE BEARD OF PENCEWORTH, CLOWN, I COMMAND YE TO SILENCE!
IF I MUST DIE A DISGRACED QUEEN ALLOW ME TO DO IT IN PEACE AND QUIET!

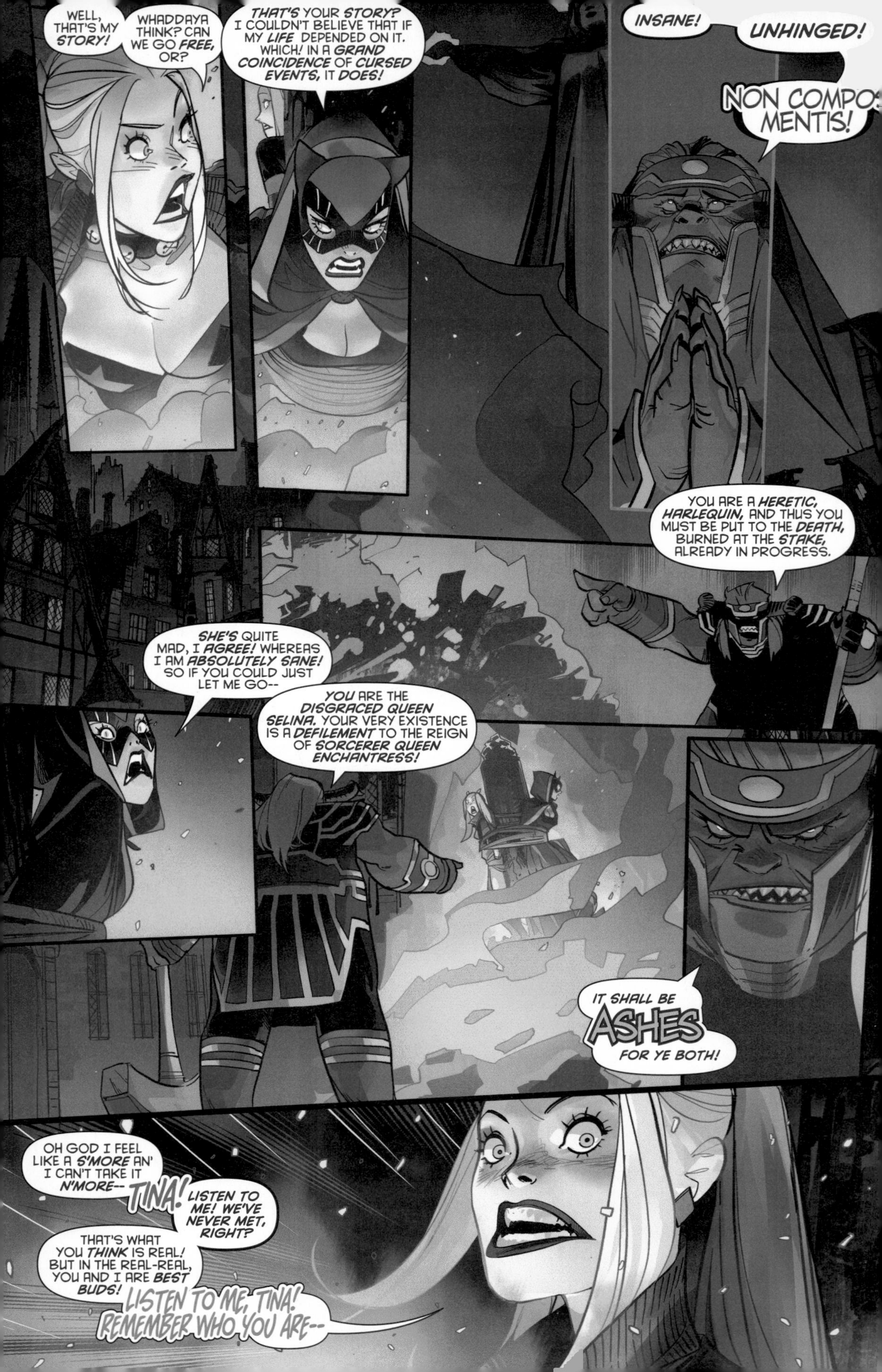
WELL, THAT'S MY STORY!
WHADDAYA THINK? CAN WE GO FREE, OR?
THAT'S YOUR STORY? I COULDN'T BELIEVE THAT IF MY LIFE DEPENDED ON IT. WHICH! IN A GRAND COINCIDENCE OF CURSED EVENTS, IT DOES!
INSANE!
UNHINGED!
NON COMPOS MENTIS!
YOU ARE A HERETIC, HARLEQUIN, AND THUS YOU MUST BE PUT TO THE DEATH, BURNED AT THE STAKE, ALREADY IN PROGRESS.
SHE'S QUITE MAD, I AGREE! WHEREAS I AM ABSOLUTELY SANE! SO IF YOU COULD JUST LET ME GO--
YOU ARE THE DISGRACED QUEEN SELINA. YOUR VERY EXISTENCE IS A DEFILEMENT TO THE REIGN OF SORCERER QUEEN ENCHANTRESS!
IT SHALL BE ASHES FOR YE BOTH!
OH GOD I FEEL LIKE A S'MORE AN' I CAN'T TAKE IT N'MORE--
TINA!
LISTEN TO ME! WE'VE NEVER MET, RIGHT?
THAT'S WHAT YOU THINK IS REAL! BUT IN THE REAL-REAL, YOU AND I ARE BEST BUDS!
LISTEN TO ME, TINA! REMEMBER WHO YOU ARE--

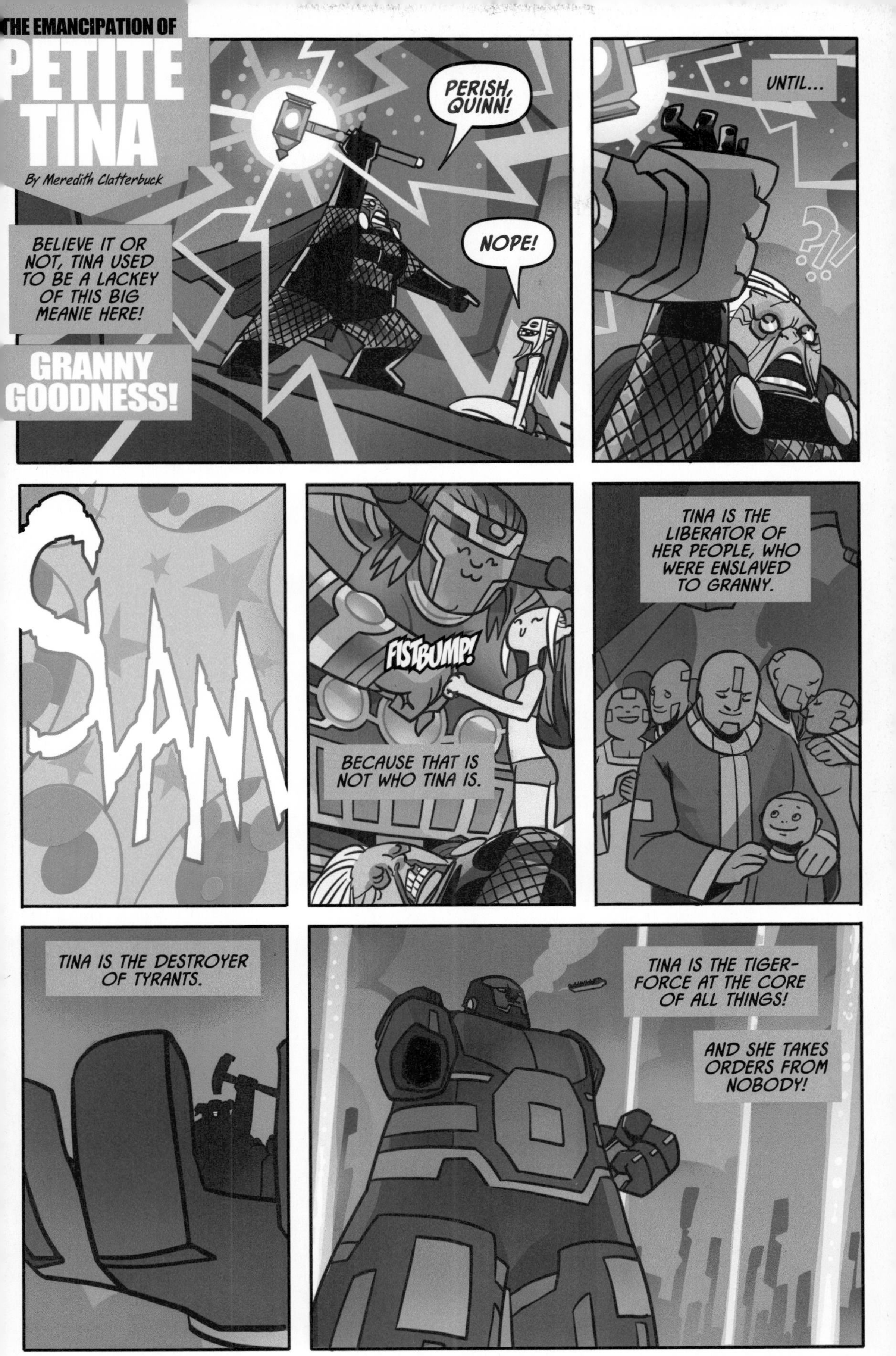
THE EMANCIPATION OF
PETITE TINA
By Meredith Clatterbuck
BELIEVE IT OR NOT, TINA USED TO BE A LACKEY OF THIS BIG MEANIE HERE!
GRANNY GOODNESS!
PERISH, QUINN!
NOPE!
UNTIL...
?!!
SLAM
FISTBUMP!
BECAUSE THAT IS NOT WHO TINA IS.
TINA IS THE LIBERATOR OF HER PEOPLE, WHO WERE ENSLAVED TO GRANNY.
TINA IS THE DESTROYER OF TYRANTS.
TINA IS THE TIGER-FORCE AT THE CORE OF ALL THINGS!
AND SHE TAKES ORDERS FROM NOBODY!

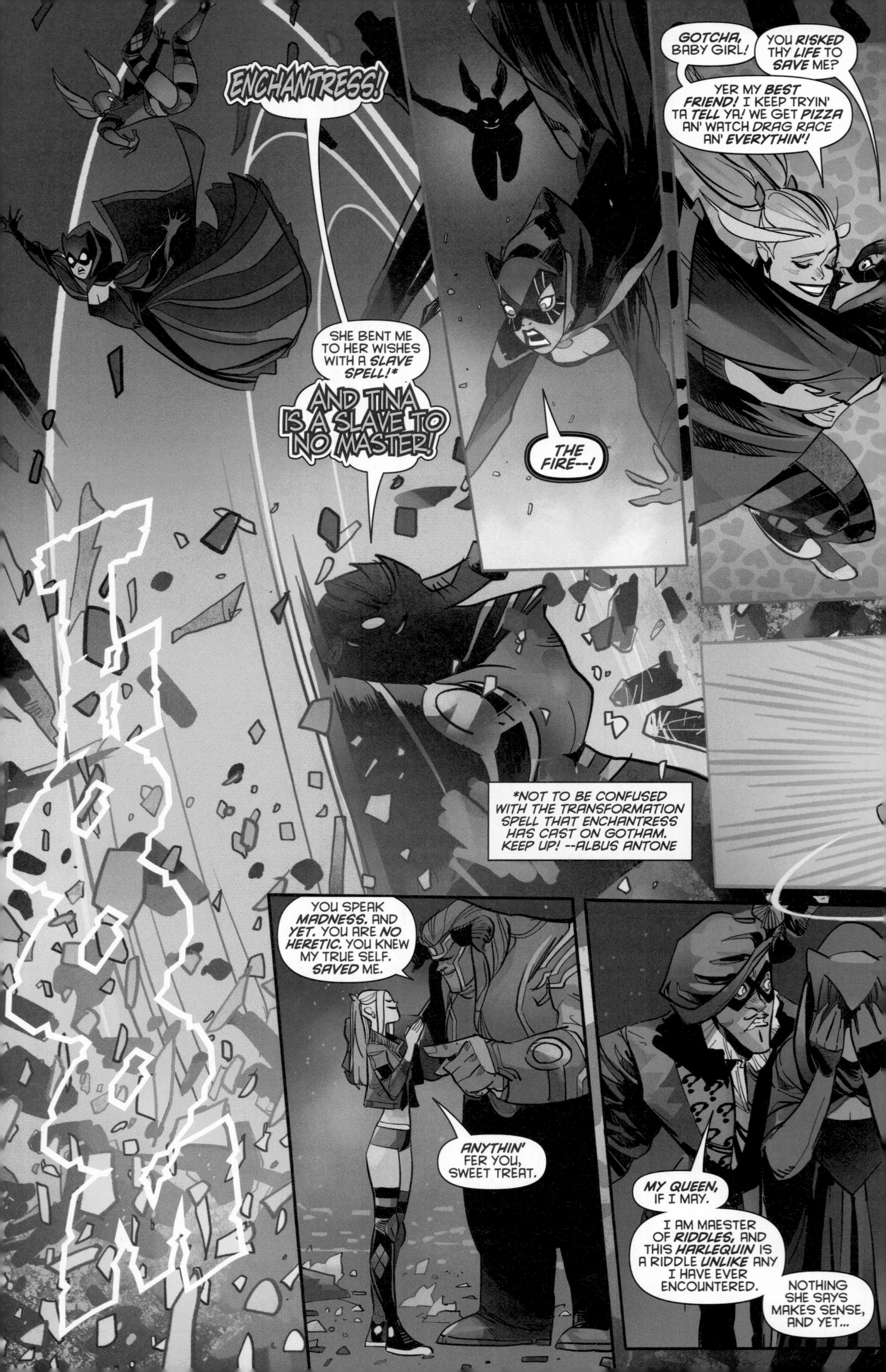
ENCHANTRESS!
SHE BENT ME TO HER WISHES WITH A SLAVE SPELL!*
AND TINA IS A SLAVE TO NO MASTER!
THE FIRE--!
GOTCHA, BABY GIRL!
YOU RISKED THY LIFE TO SAVE ME?
YER MY BEST FRIEND! I KEEP TRYIN' TA TELL YA! WE GET PIZZA AN' WATCH DRAG RACE AN' EVERYTHIN'!
*NOT TO BE CONFUSED WITH THE TRANSFORMATION SPELL THAT ENCHANTRESS HAS CAST ON GOTHAM. KEEP UP! --ALBUS ANTONE
YOU SPEAK MADNESS. AND YET. YOU ARE NO HERETIC. YOU KNEW MY TRUE SELF. SAVED ME.
ANYTHIN' FER YOU, SWEET TREAT.
MY QUEEN, IF I MAY.
I AM MAESTER OF RIDDLES, AND THIS HARLEQUIN IS A RIDDLE UNLIKE ANY I HAVE EVER ENCOUNTERED.
NOTHING SHE SAYS MAKES SENSE, AND YET...

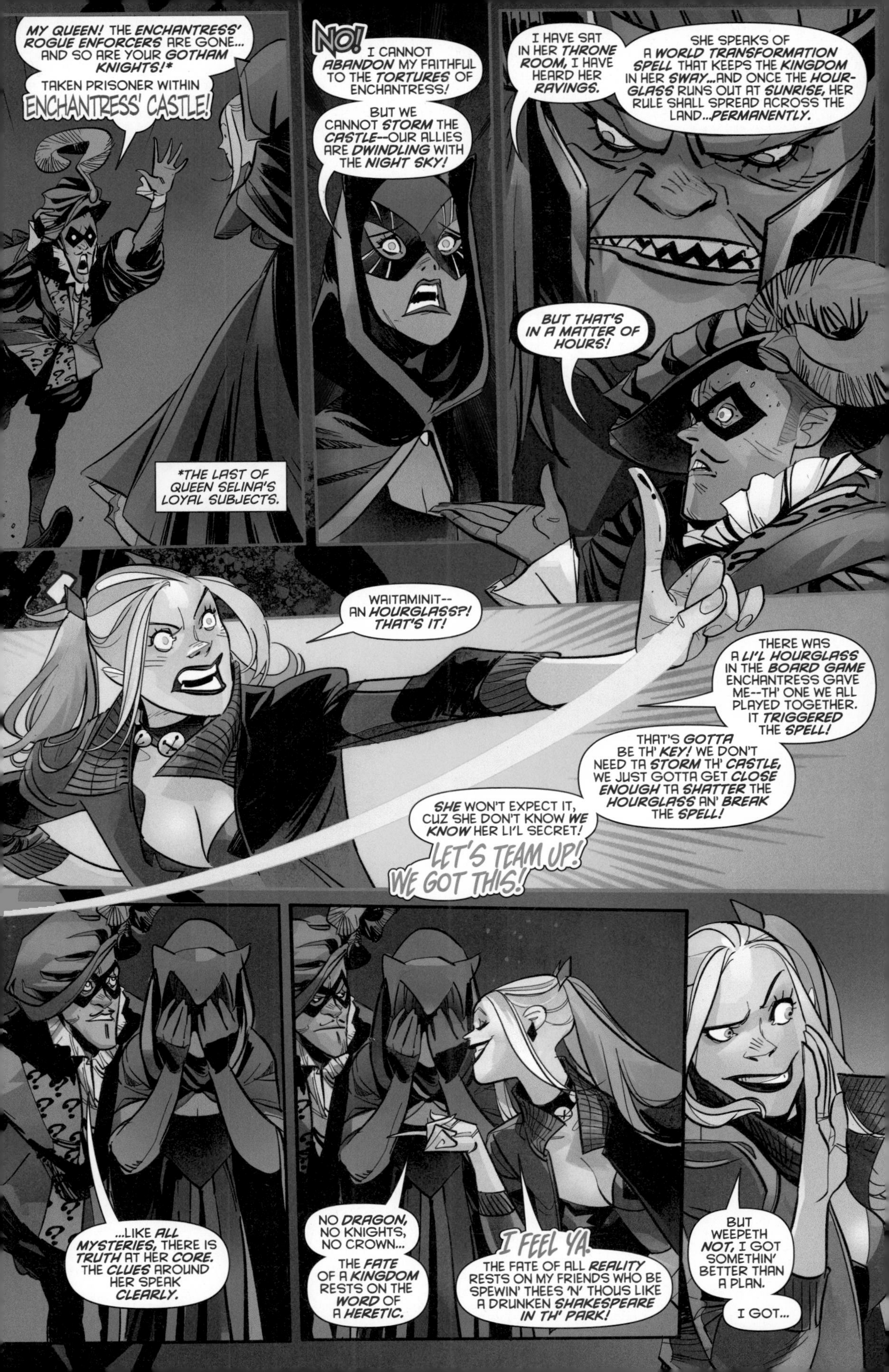
MY QUEEN! THE ENCHANTRESS' ROGUE ENFORCERS ARE GONE... AND SO ARE YOUR GOTHAM KNIGHTS!*
TAKEN PRISONER WITHIN
ENCHANTRESS' CASTLE!
*THE LAST OF QUEEN SELINA'S LOYAL SUBJECTS.
NO!
I CANNOT ABANDON MY FAITHFUL TO THE TORTURES OF ENCHANTRESS!
BUT WE CANNOT STORM THE CASTLE--OUR ALLIES ARE DWINDLING WITH THE NIGHT SKY!
I HAVE SAT IN HER THRONE ROOM, I HAVE HEARD HER RAVINGS.
SHE SPEAKS OF A WORLD TRANSFORMATION SPELL THAT KEEPS THE KINGDOM IN HER SWAY...AND ONCE THE HOURGLASS RUNS OUT AT SUNRISE, HER RULE SHALL SPREAD ACROSS THE LAND...PERMANENTLY.
BUT THAT'S IN A MATTER OF HOURS!
WAITAMINIT-- AN HOURGLASS?! THAT'S IT!
THERE WAS A LI'L HOURGLASS IN THE BOARD GAME ENCHANTRESS GAVE ME--TH' ONE WE ALL PLAYED TOGETHER. IT TRIGGERED THE SPELL!
THAT'S GOTTA BE TH' KEY! WE DON'T NEED TA STORM TH' CASTLE, WE JUST GOTTA GET CLOSE ENOUGH TA SHATTER THE HOURGLASS AN' BREAK THE SPELL!
SHE WON'T EXPECT IT, CUZ SHE DON'T KNOW WE KNOW HER LI'L SECRET!
LET'S TEAM UP!
WE GOT THIS!
...LIKE ALL MYSTERIES, THERE IS TRUTH AT HER CORE. THE CLUES AROUND HER SPEAK CLEARLY.
NO DRAGON, NO KNIGHTS, NO CROWN...
THE FATE OF A KINGDOM RESTS ON THE WORD OF A HERETIC.
I FEEL YA.
THE FATE OF ALL REALITY RESTS ON MY FRIENDS WHO BE SPEWIN' THEES 'N' THOUS LIKE A DRUNKEN SHAKESPEARE IN TH' PARK!
BUT WEEPETH NOT, I GOT SOMETHIN' BETTER THAN A PLAN.
I GOT...

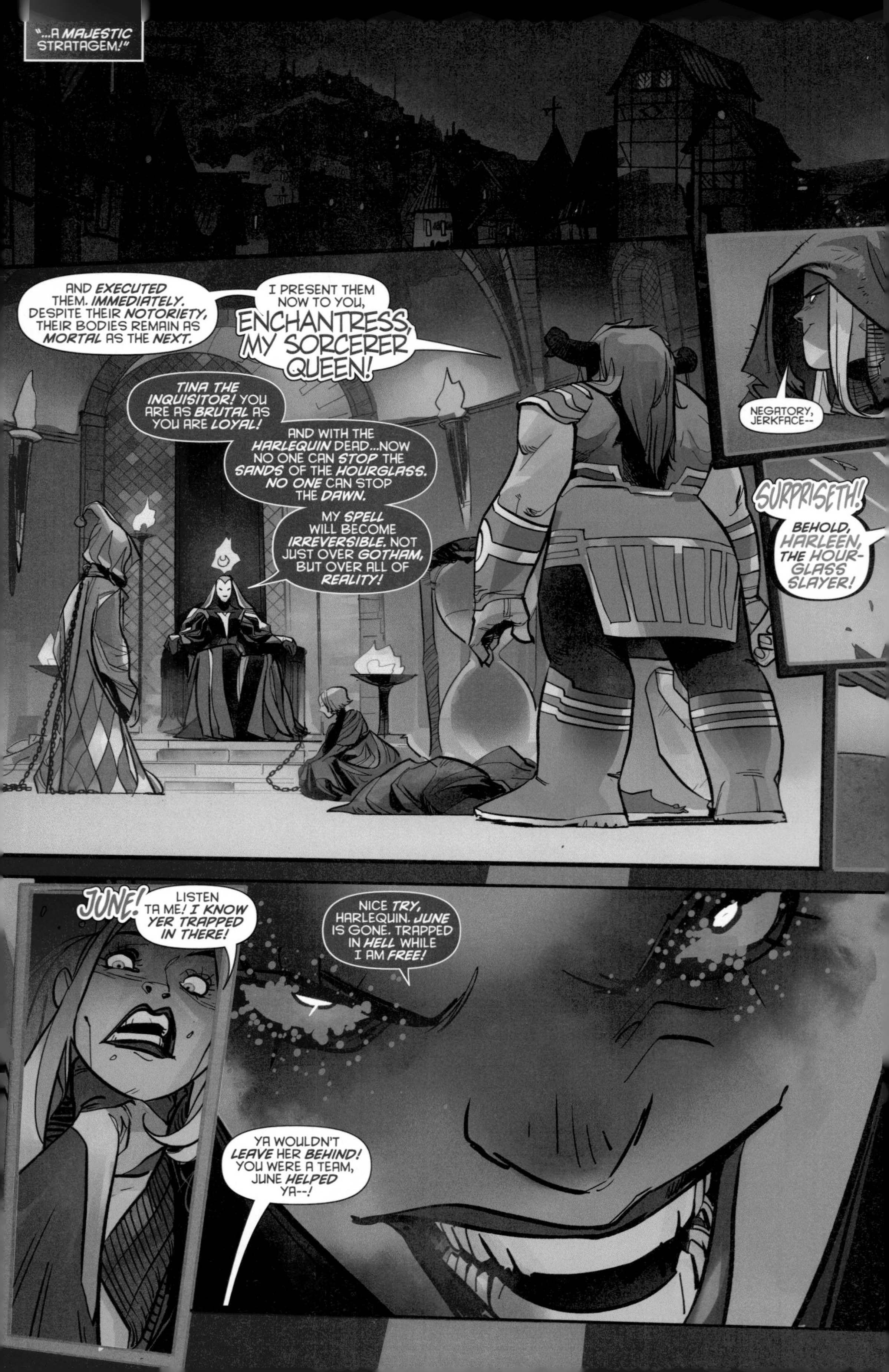
"...A MAJESTIC STRATAGEM!"
AND EXECUTED THEM. IMMEDIATELY. DESPITE THEIR NOTORIETY, THEIR BODIES REMAIN AS MORTAL AS THE NEXT.
I PRESENT THEM NOW TO YOU, ENCHANTRESS, MY SORCERER QUEEN!
TINA THE INQUISITOR! YOU ARE AS BRUTAL AS YOU ARE LOYAL!
AND WITH THE HARLEQUIN DEAD...NOW NO ONE CAN STOP THE SANDS OF THE HOURGLASS. NO ONE CAN STOP THE DAWN.
MY SPELL WILL BECOME IRREVERSIBLE. NOT JUST OVER GOTHAM, BUT OVER ALL OF REALITY!
NEGATORY, JERKFACE--
SURPRISETH!
BEHOLD, HARLEEN, THE HOURGLASS SLAYER!
JUNE!
LISTEN TA ME! I KNOW YER TRAPPED IN THERE!
NICE TRY, HARLEQUIN. JUNE IS GONE. TRAPPED IN HELL WHILE I AM FREE!
YA WOULDN'T LEAVE HER BEHIND! YOU WERE A TEAM, JUNE HELPED YA--!

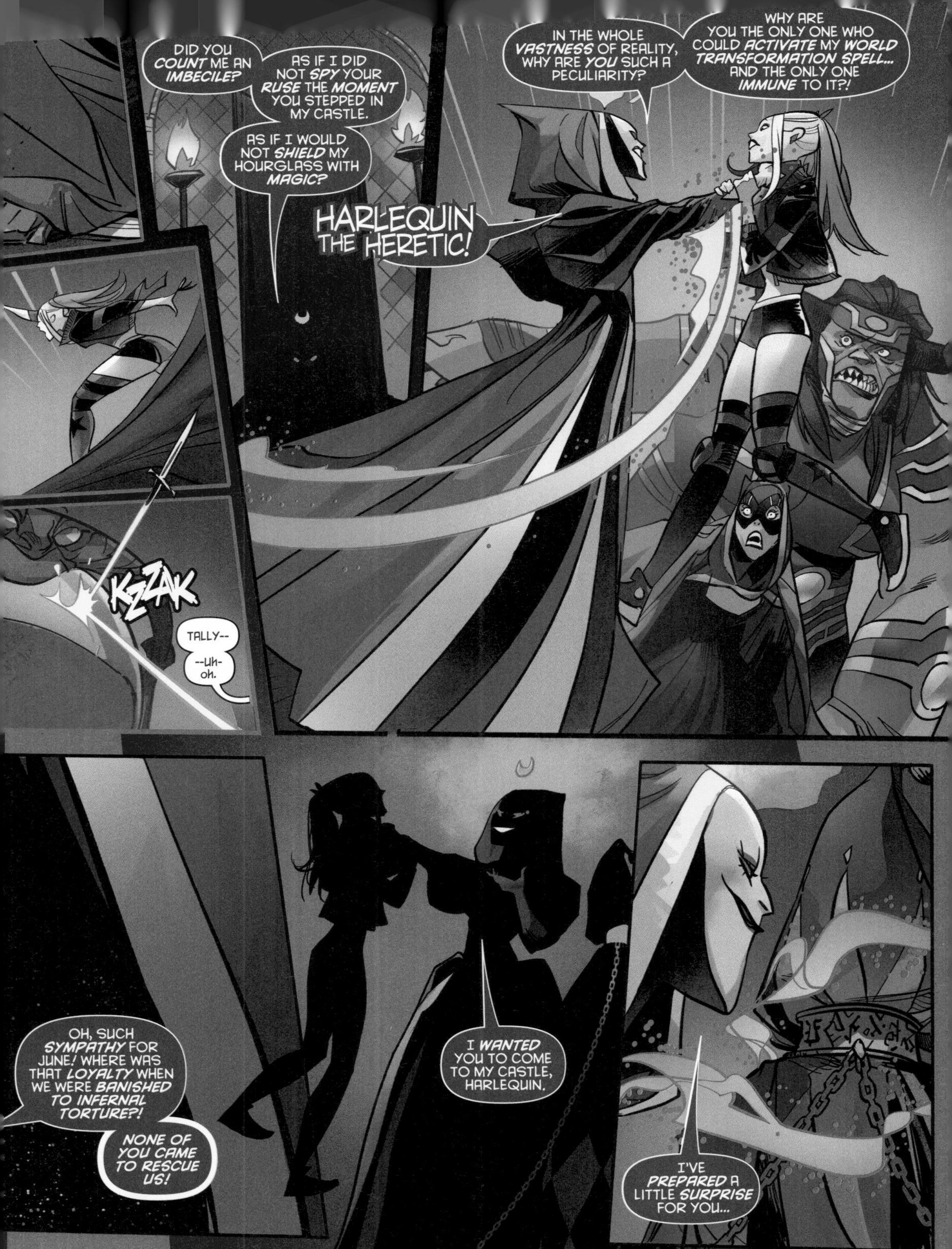

DID YOU COUNT ME AN IMBECILE?
AS IF I DID NOT SPY YOUR RUSE THE MOMENT YOU STEPPED IN MY CASTLE.
AS IF I WOULD NOT SHIELD MY HOURGLASS WITH MAGIC?
IN THE WHOLE VASTNESS OF REALITY, WHY ARE YOU SUCH A PECULIARITY?
WHY ARE YOU THE ONLY ONE WHO COULD ACTIVATE MY WORLD TRANSFORMATION SPELL... AND THE ONLY ONE IMMUNE TO IT?!
HARLEQUIN THE HERETIC!
KZZAK
TALLY--
--uh-oh.
OH, SUCH SYMPATHY FOR JUNE! WHERE WAS THAT LOYALTY WHEN WE WERE BANISHED TO INFERNAL TORTURE?!
NONE OF YOU CAME TO RESCUE US!
I WANTED YOU TO COME TO MY CASTLE, HARLEQUIN.
I'VE PREPARED A LITTLE SURPRISE FOR YOU...

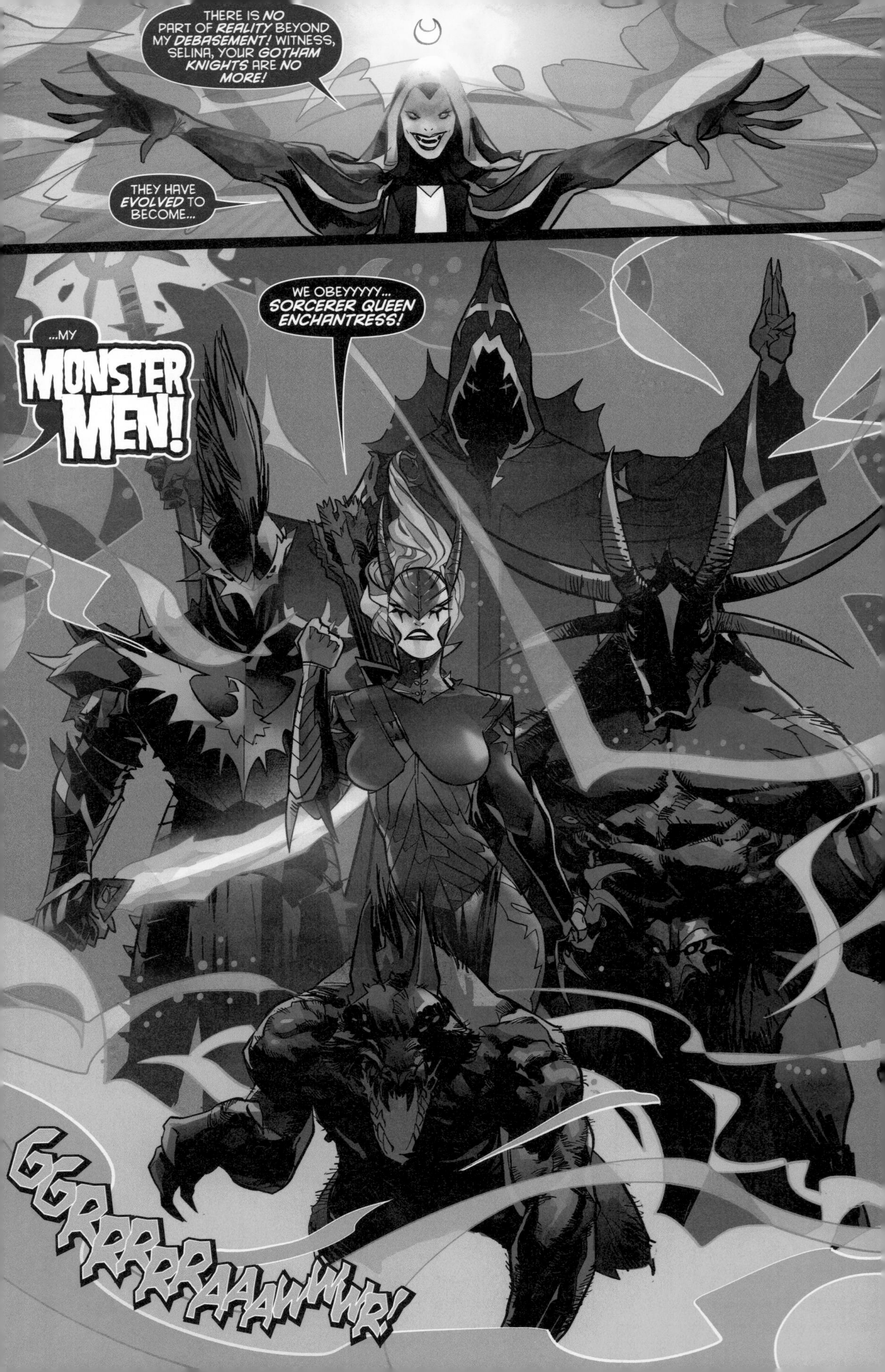
THERE IS *NO* PART OF *REALITY* BEYOND MY *DEBASEMENT!* WITNESS, SELINA, YOUR *GOTHAM KNIGHTS* ARE *NO MORE!*
THEY HAVE *EVOLVED* TO BECOME...
...MY MONSTER MEN!
WE OBEYYYYY... *SORCERER QUEEN ENCHANTRESS!*
GGRRRRRRAAAWWWR!

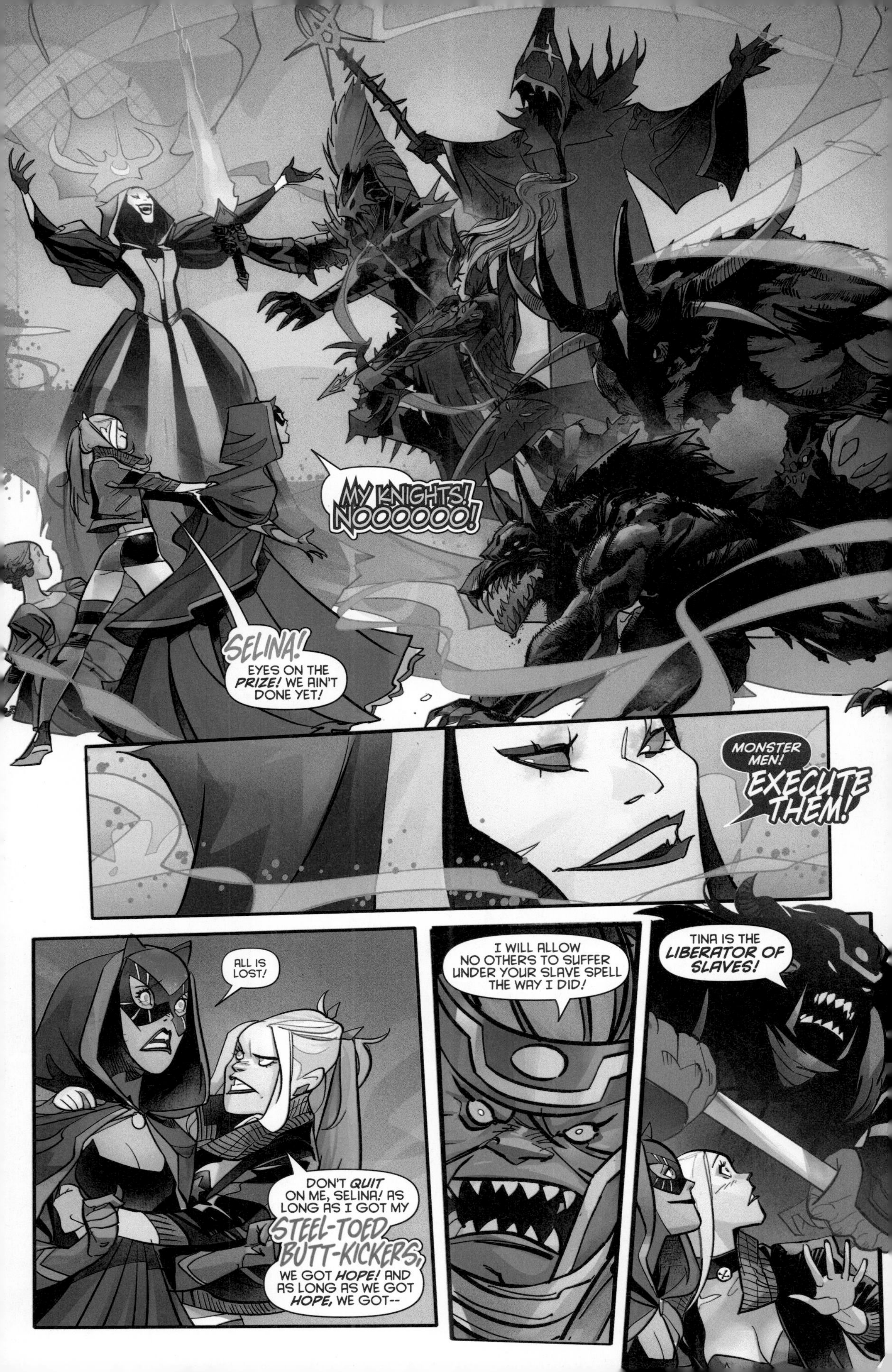
MY KNIGHTS! NOOOOOOO!
SELINA! EYES ON THE PRIZE! WE AIN'T DONE YET!
MONSTER MEN! EXECUTE THEM!
ALL IS LOST!
DON'T QUIT ON ME, SELINA! AS LONG AS I GOT MY STEEL-TOED BUTT-KICKERS, WE GOT HOPE! AND AS LONG AS WE GOT HOPE, WE GOT--
I WILL ALLOW NO OTHERS TO SUFFER UNDER YOUR SLAVE SPELL THE WAY I DID!
TINA IS THE LIBERATOR OF SLAVES!

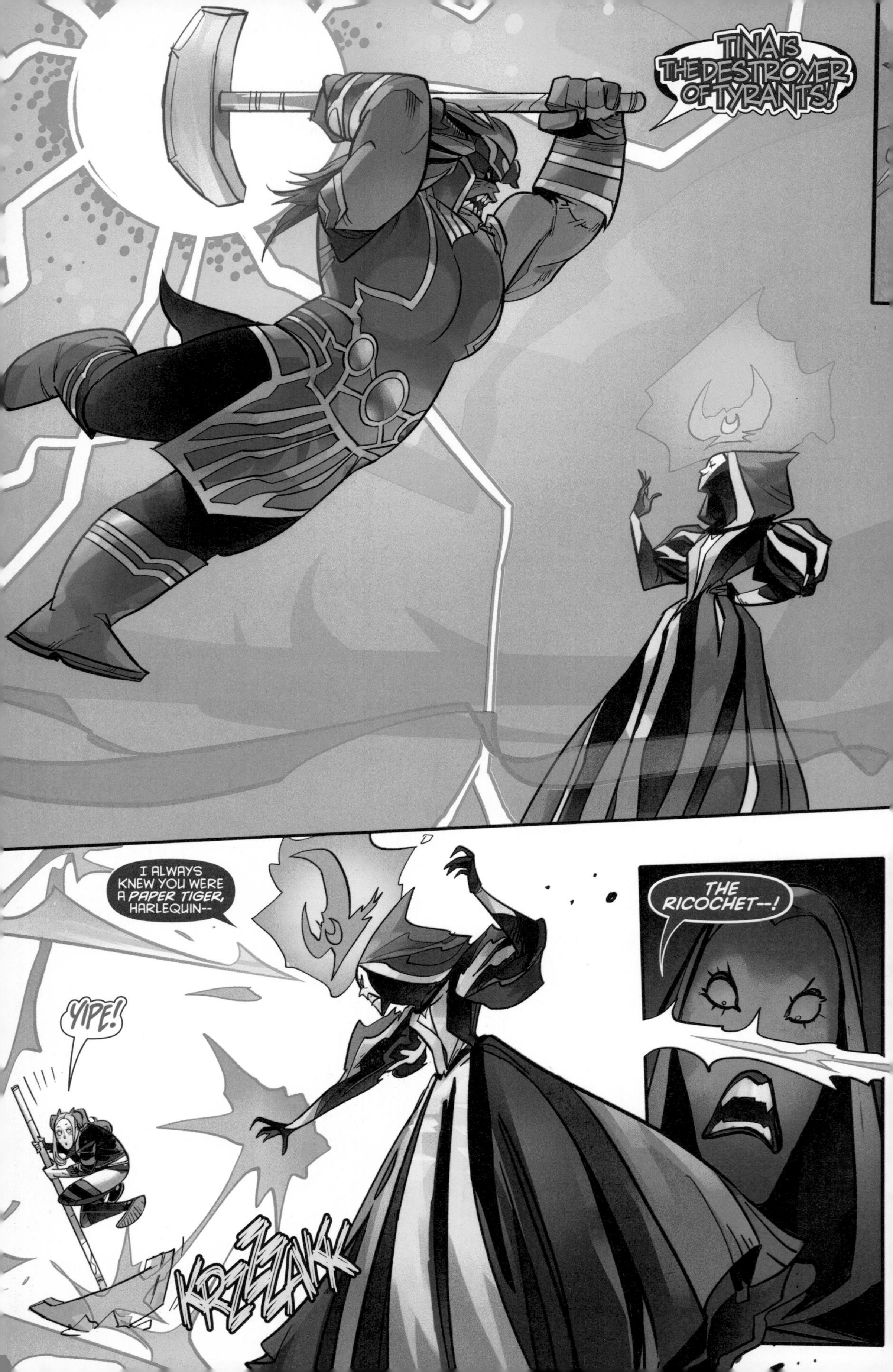
TINA IS THE DESTROYER OF TYRANTS!
I ALWAYS KNEW YOU WERE A *PAPER TIGER,* HARLEQUIN--
THE RICOCHET--!
YIPE!
KRZZZAKK

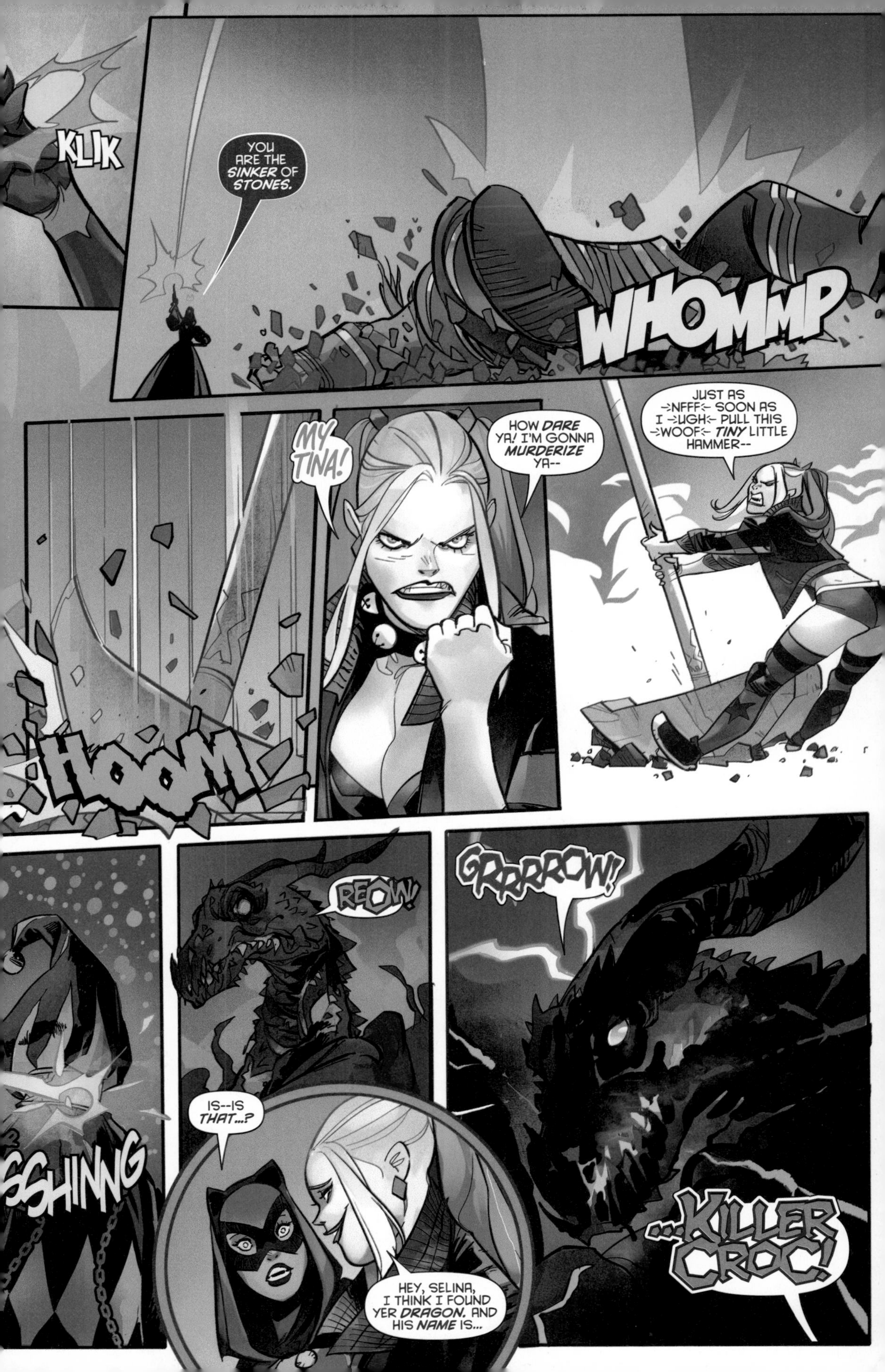

KLIK
YOU ARE THE SINKER OF STONES.
WHOMMP
HOOM
MY TINA!
HOW DARE YA! I'M GONNA MURDERIZE YA--
JUST AS ~NFFF~ SOON AS I ~UGH~ PULL THIS ~WOOF~ TINY LITTLE HAMMER--
SHINNG
REOW!
GRRRROW!
IS--IS THAT...?
HEY, SELINA, I THINK I FOUND YER DRAGON. AND HIS NAME IS...
...KILLER CROC!

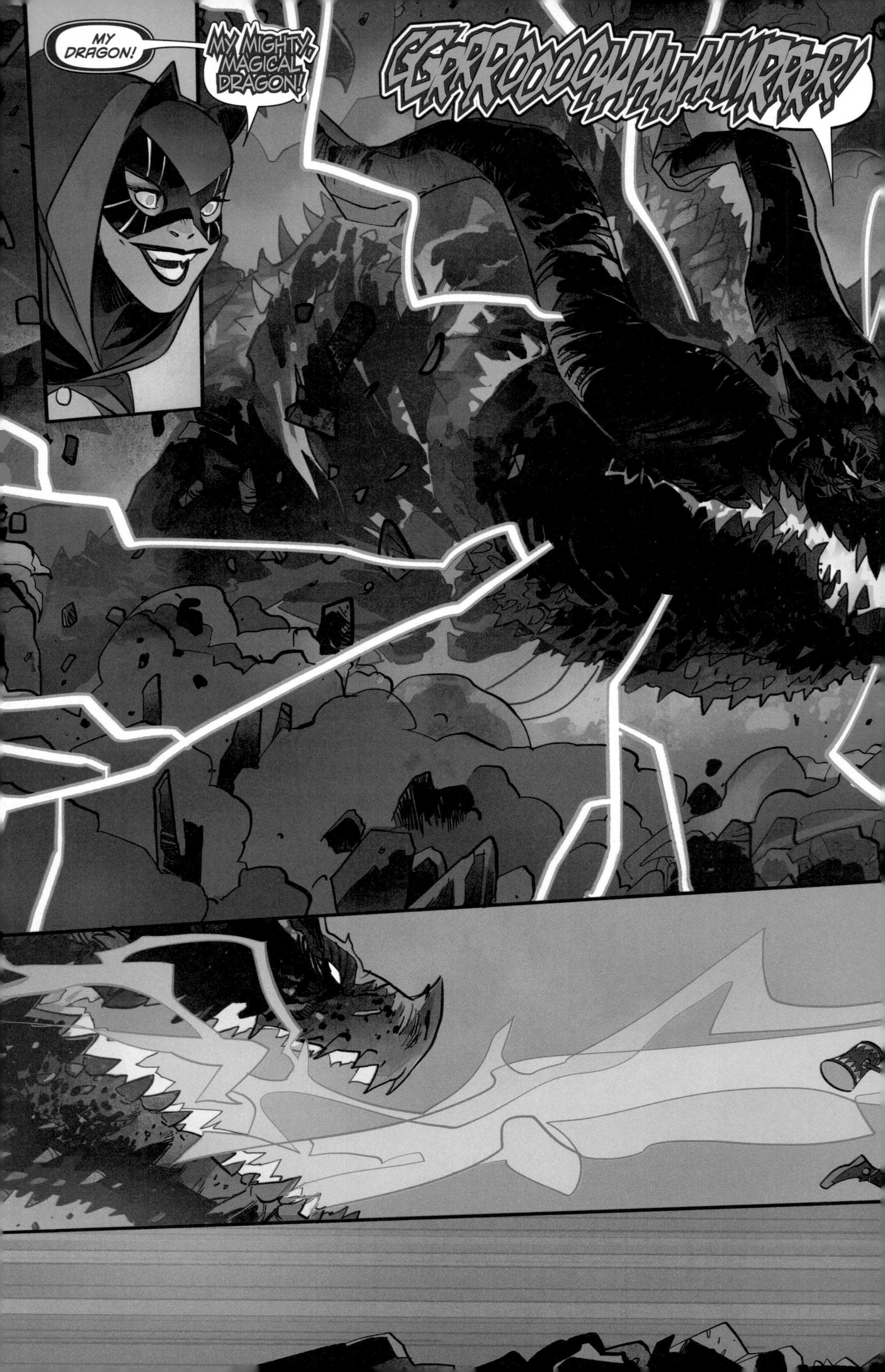
MY DRAGON!
MY MIGHTY, MAGICAL DRAGON!
GGRRROOOOOAAAAAAAWRRRR!

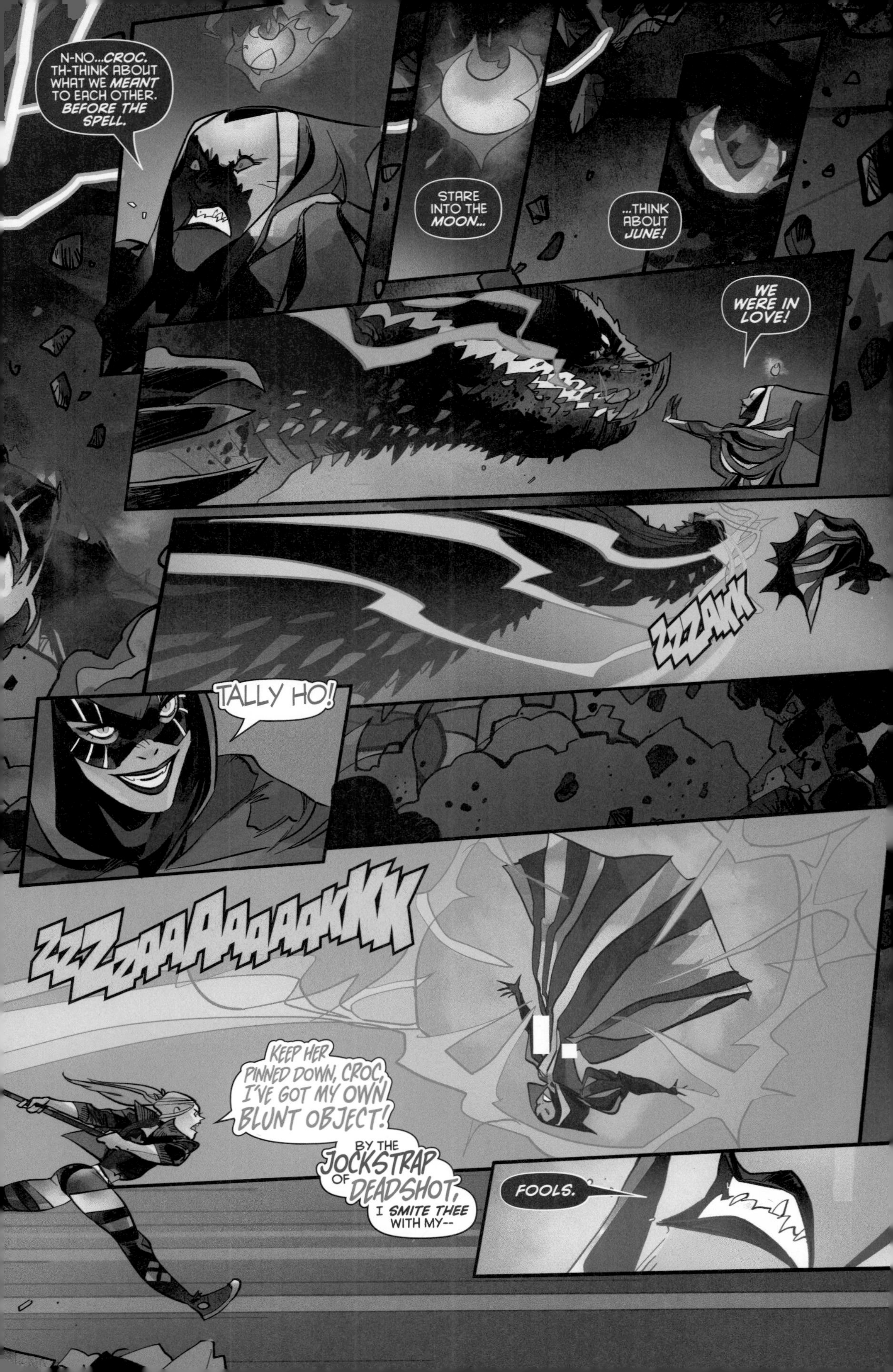
N-NO...CROC. TH-THINK ABOUT WHAT WE MEANT TO EACH OTHER. BEFORE THE SPELL.
STARE INTO THE MOON...
...THINK ABOUT JUNE!
WE WERE IN LOVE!
ZZZAKK
TALLY HO!
ZZZZAAAAAAAAKKKK
KEEP HER PINNED DOWN, CROC, I'VE GOT MY OWN BLUNT OBJECT!
BY THE JOCKSTRAP OF DEADSHOT, I SMITE THEE WITH MY--
FOOLS.

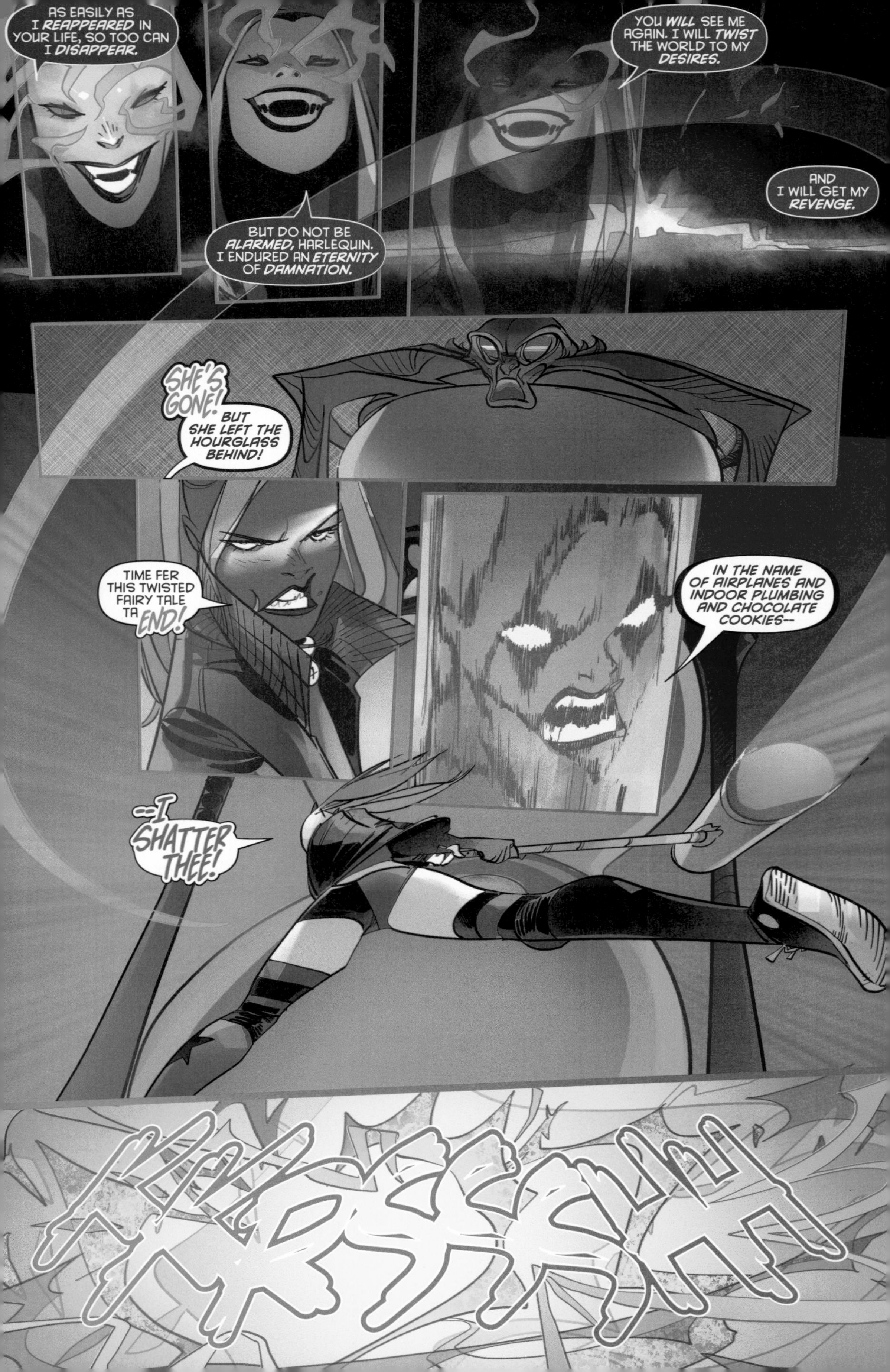
AS EASILY AS I REAPPEARED IN YOUR LIFE, SO TOO CAN I DISAPPEAR.
BUT DO NOT BE ALARMED, HARLEQUIN. I ENDURED AN ETERNITY OF DAMNATION.
YOU WILL SEE ME AGAIN. I WILL TWIST THE WORLD TO MY DESIRES.
AND I WILL GET MY REVENGE.
SHE'S GONE!
BUT SHE LEFT THE HOURGLASS BEHIND!
TIME FER THIS TWISTED FAIRY TALE TA END!
IN THE NAME OF AIRPLANES AND INDOOR PLUMBING AND CHOCOLATE COOKIES--
--I SHATTER THEE!
KKKRRRSSSHHH

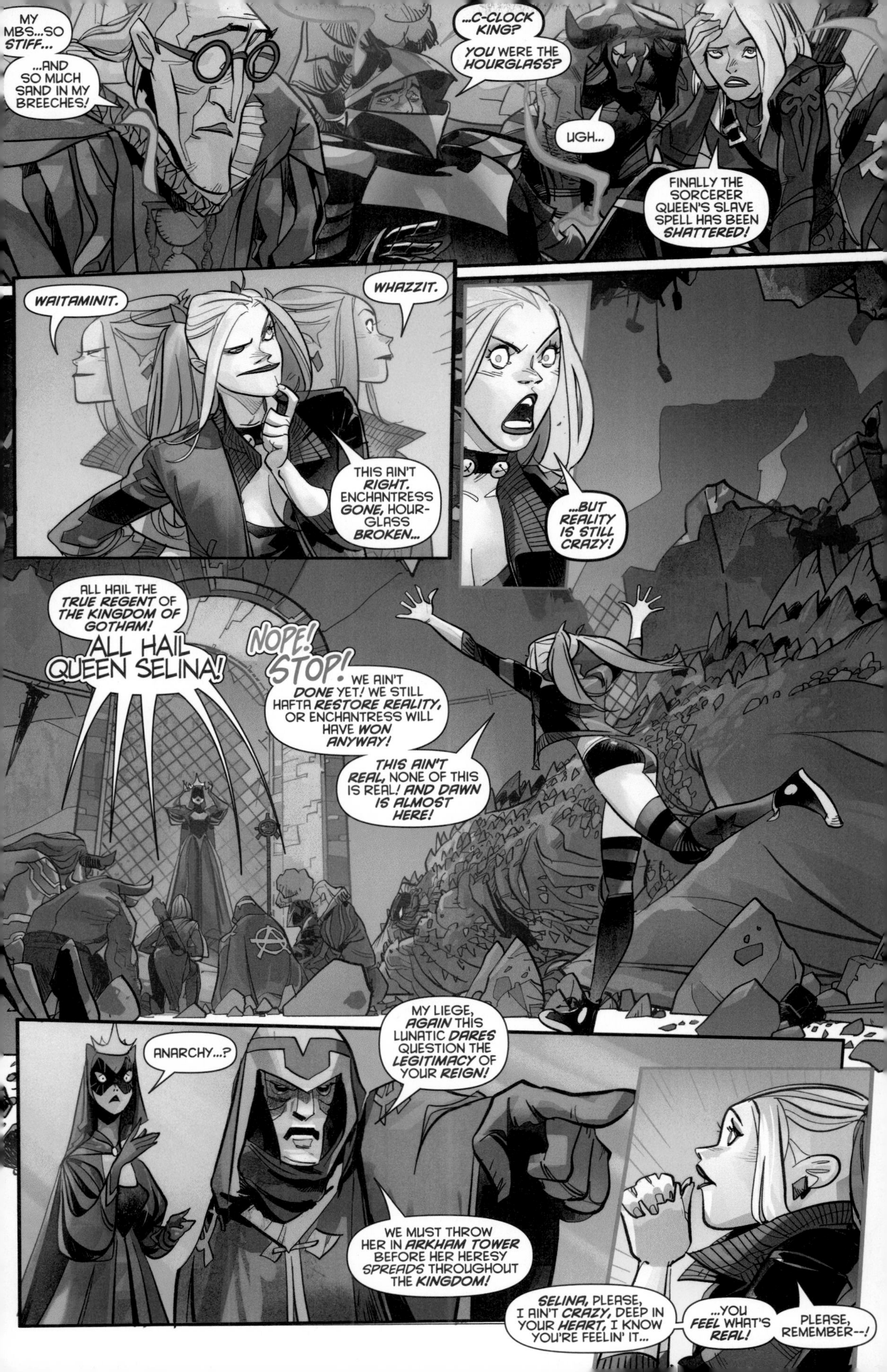
MY
MBS...SO
STIFF...
...AND
SO MUCH
SAND IN MY
BREECHES!
...C-CLOCK
KING?
YOU WERE THE
HOURGLASS?
UGH...
FINALLY THE
SORCERER
QUEEN'S SLAVE
SPELL HAS BEEN
SHATTERED!
WAITAMINIT.
WHAZZIT.
THIS AIN'T
RIGHT.
ENCHANTRESS
GONE, HOUR-
GLASS
BROKEN...
...BUT
REALITY
IS STILL
CRAZY!
ALL HAIL THE
TRUE REGENT OF
THE KINGDOM OF
GOTHAM!
ALL HAIL
QUEEN SELINA!
NOPE!
STOP!
WE AIN'T
DONE YET! WE STILL
HAFTA RESTORE REALITY,
OR ENCHANTRESS WILL
HAVE WON
ANYWAY!
THIS AIN'T
REAL, NONE OF THIS
IS REAL! AND DAWN
IS ALMOST
HERE!
ANARCHY...?
MY LIEGE,
AGAIN THIS
LUNATIC DARES
QUESTION THE
LEGITIMACY OF
YOUR REIGN!
WE MUST THROW
HER IN ARKHAM TOWER
BEFORE HER HERESY
SPREADS THROUGHOUT
THE KINGDOM!
SELINA, PLEASE,
I AIN'T CRAZY, DEEP IN
YOUR HEART, I KNOW
YOU'RE FEELIN' IT...
...YOU
FEEL WHAT'S
REAL!
PLEASE,
REMEMBER--!

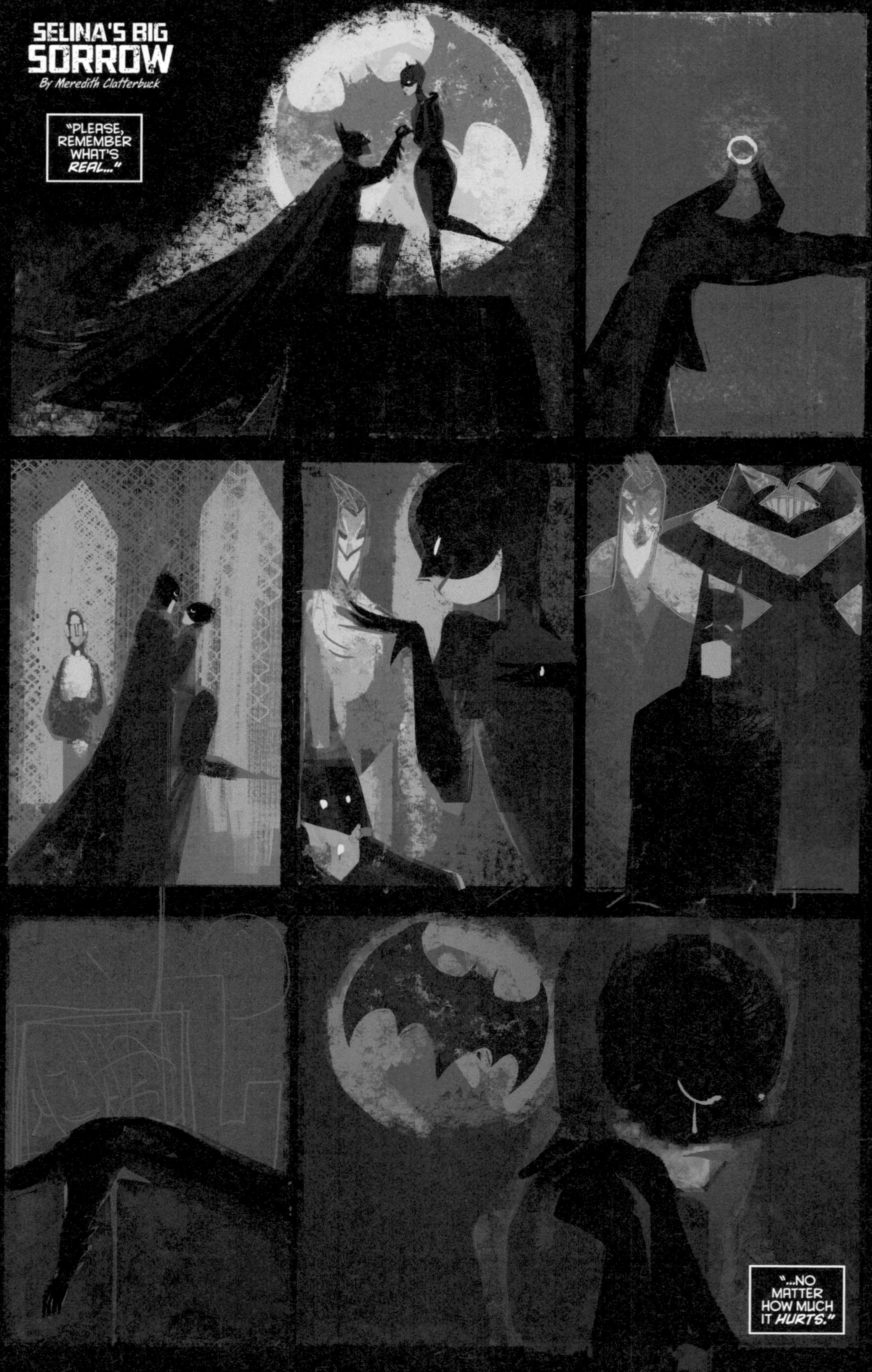
SELINA'S BIG SORROW
By Meredith Clatterbuck
"PLEASE, REMEMBER WHAT'S *REAL*..."
"...NO MATTER HOW MUCH IT *HURTS*."

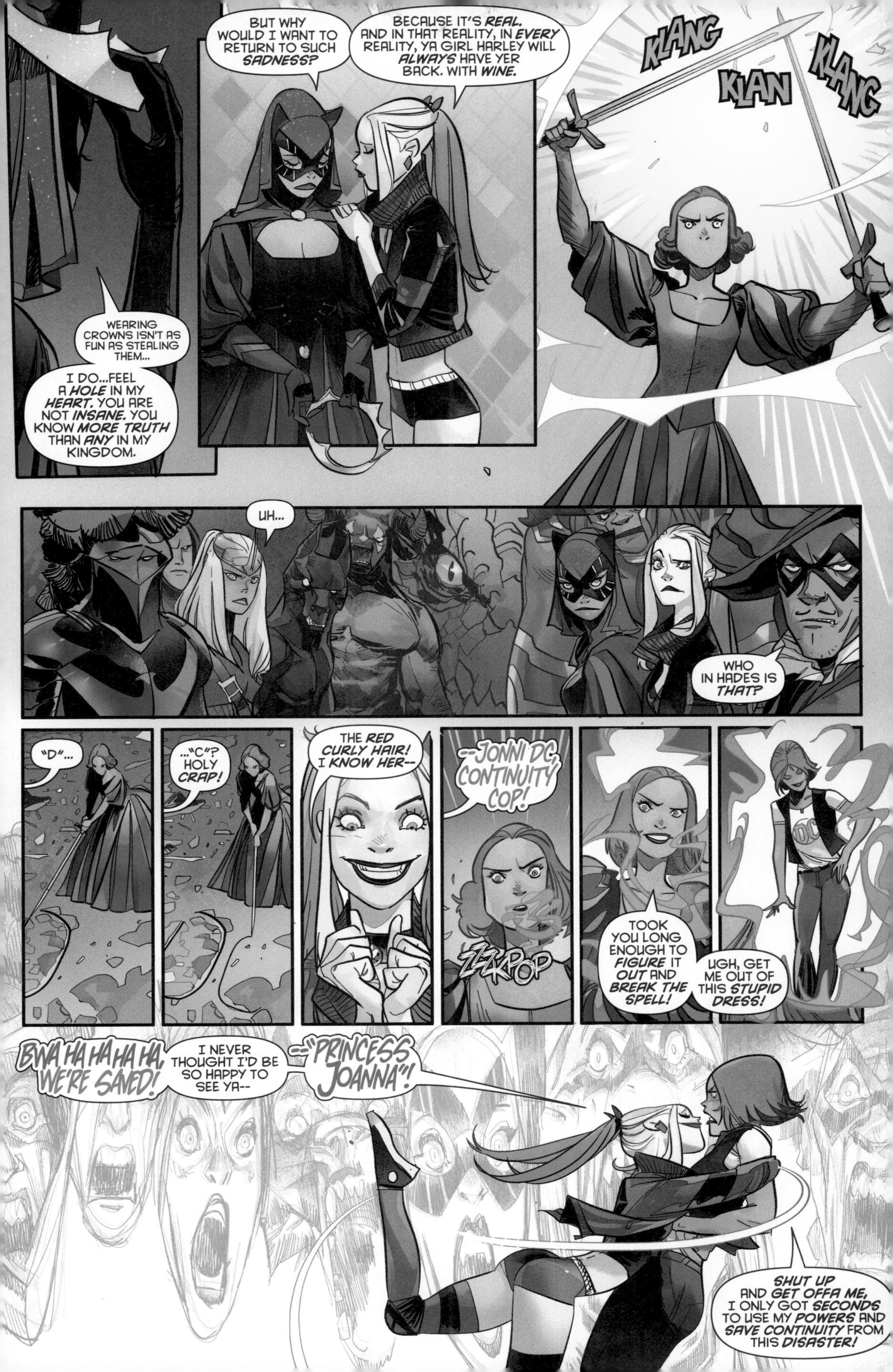

BUT WHY WOULD I WANT TO RETURN TO SUCH SADNESS?
BECAUSE IT'S REAL. AND IN THAT REALITY, IN EVERY REALITY, YA GIRL HARLEY WILL ALWAYS HAVE YER BACK. WITH WINE.
WEARING CROWNS ISN'T AS FUN AS STEALING THEM...
I DO...FEEL A HOLE IN MY HEART. YOU ARE NOT INSANE. YOU KNOW MORE TRUTH THAN ANY IN MY KINGDOM.
KLANG
KLAN
KLANG
UH...
WHO IN HADES IS THAT?
"D"...
..."C"? HOLY CRAP!
THE RED CURLY HAIR! I KNOW HER--
--JONNI DC, CONTINUITY COP!
ZZZKPOP
TOOK YOU LONG ENOUGH TO FIGURE IT OUT AND BREAK THE SPELL!
UGH, GET ME OUT OF THIS STUPID DRESS!
BWA HA HA HA HA, WE'RE SAVED!
I NEVER THOUGHT I'D BE SO HAPPY TO SEE YA--
--"PRINCESS JOANNA"!
SHUT UP AND GET OFFA ME, I ONLY GOT SECONDS TO USE MY POWERS AND SAVE CONTINUITY FROM THIS DISASTER!

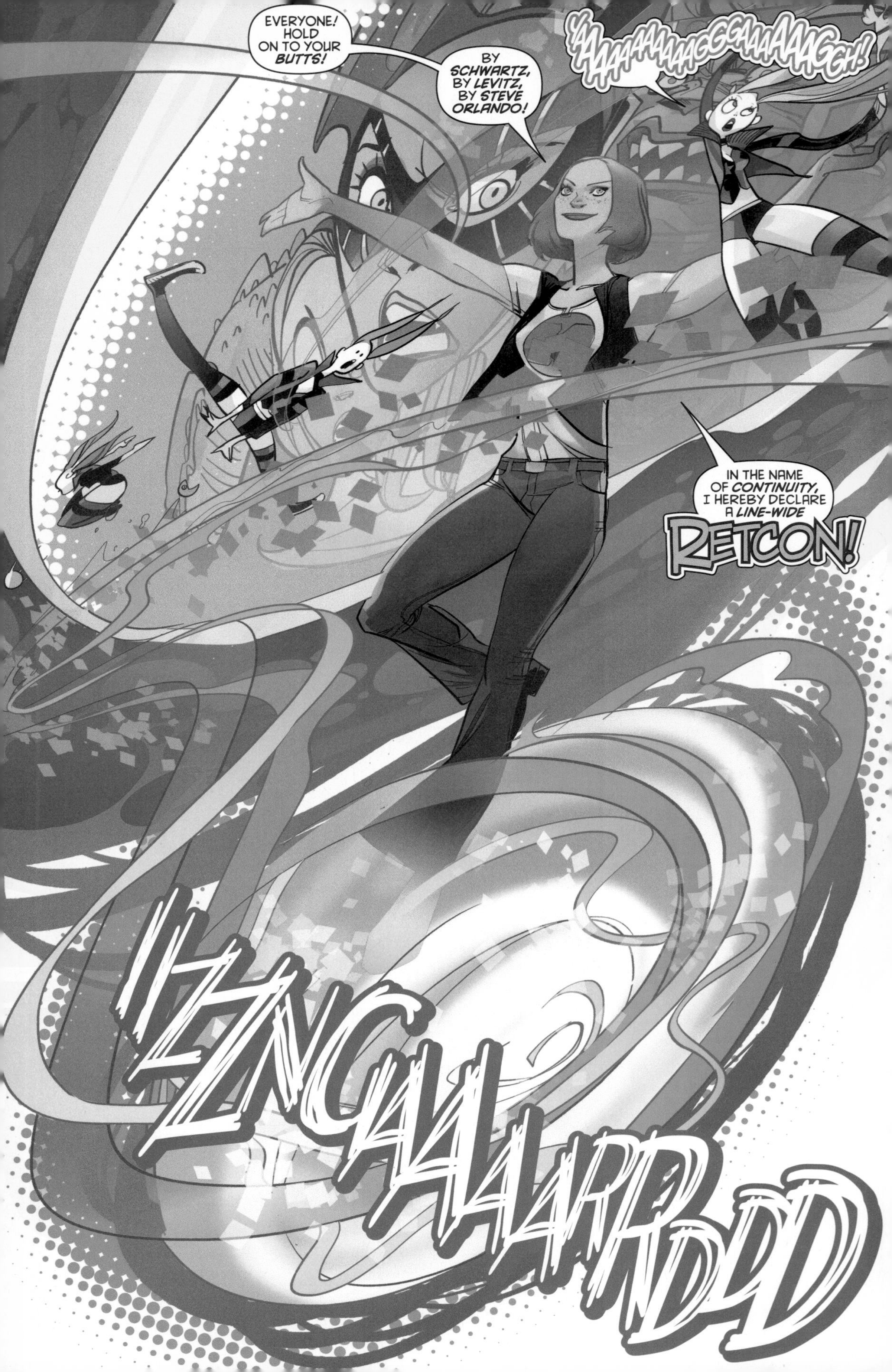
EVERYONE! HOLD ON TO YOUR BUTTS!
BY SCHWARTZ, BY LEVITZ, BY STEVE ORLANDO!
YAAAAAAAAAAGGAAAAAAGGH!
IN THE NAME OF CONTINUITY, I HEREBY DECLARE A LINE-WIDE
RETCON!

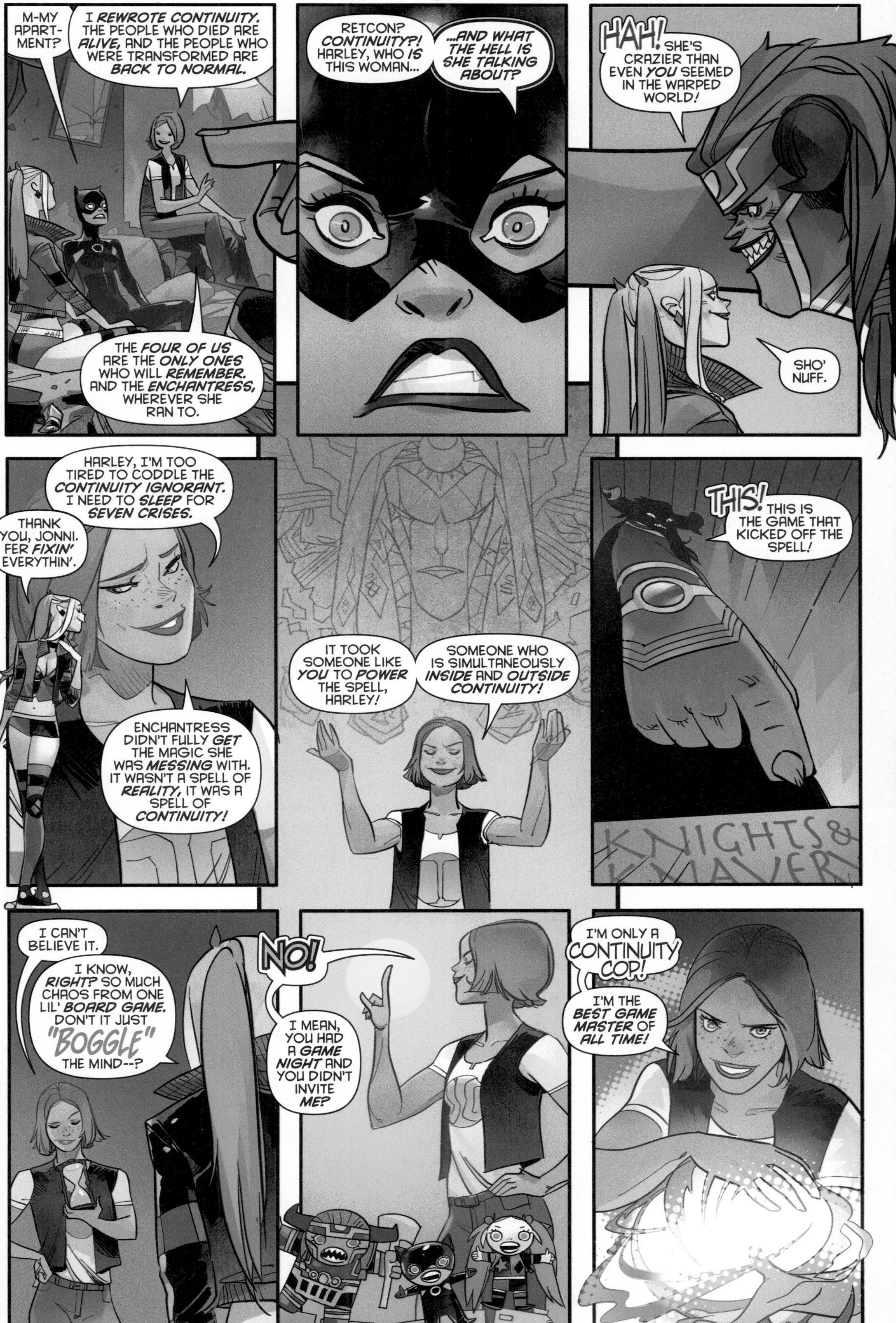
M-MY APART-MENT?
I REWROTE CONTINUITY. THE PEOPLE WHO DIED ARE ALIVE, AND THE PEOPLE WHO WERE TRANSFORMED ARE BACK TO NORMAL.
THE FOUR OF US ARE THE ONLY ONES WHO WILL REMEMBER. AND THE ENCHANTRESS, WHEREVER SHE RAN TO.
RETCON? CONTINUITY?! HARLEY, WHO IS THIS WOMAN...
...AND WHAT THE HELL IS SHE TALKING ABOUT?
HAH! SHE'S CRAZIER THAN EVEN YOU SEEMED IN THE WARPED WORLD!
SHO' NUFF.
HARLEY, I'M TOO TIRED TO CODDLE THE CONTINUITY IGNORANT. I NEED TO SLEEP FOR SEVEN CRISES.
THANK YOU, JONNI. FER FIXIN' EVERYTHIN'.
ENCHANTRESS DIDN'T FULLY GET THE MAGIC SHE WAS MESSING WITH. IT WASN'T A SPELL OF REALITY, IT WAS A SPELL OF CONTINUITY!
IT TOOK SOMEONE LIKE YOU TO POWER THE SPELL, HARLEY!
SOMEONE WHO IS SIMULTANEOUSLY INSIDE AND OUTSIDE CONTINUITY!
THIS! THIS IS THE GAME THAT KICKED OFF THE SPELL!
KNIGHTS & KNAVERY
I CAN'T BELIEVE IT.
I KNOW, RIGHT? SO MUCH CHAOS FROM ONE LIL' BOARD GAME. DON'T IT JUST "BOGGLE" THE MIND--?
NO!
I MEAN, YOU HAD A GAME NIGHT AND YOU DIDN'T INVITE ME?
I'M ONLY A CONTINUITY COP!
I'M THE BEST GAME MASTER OF ALL TIME!

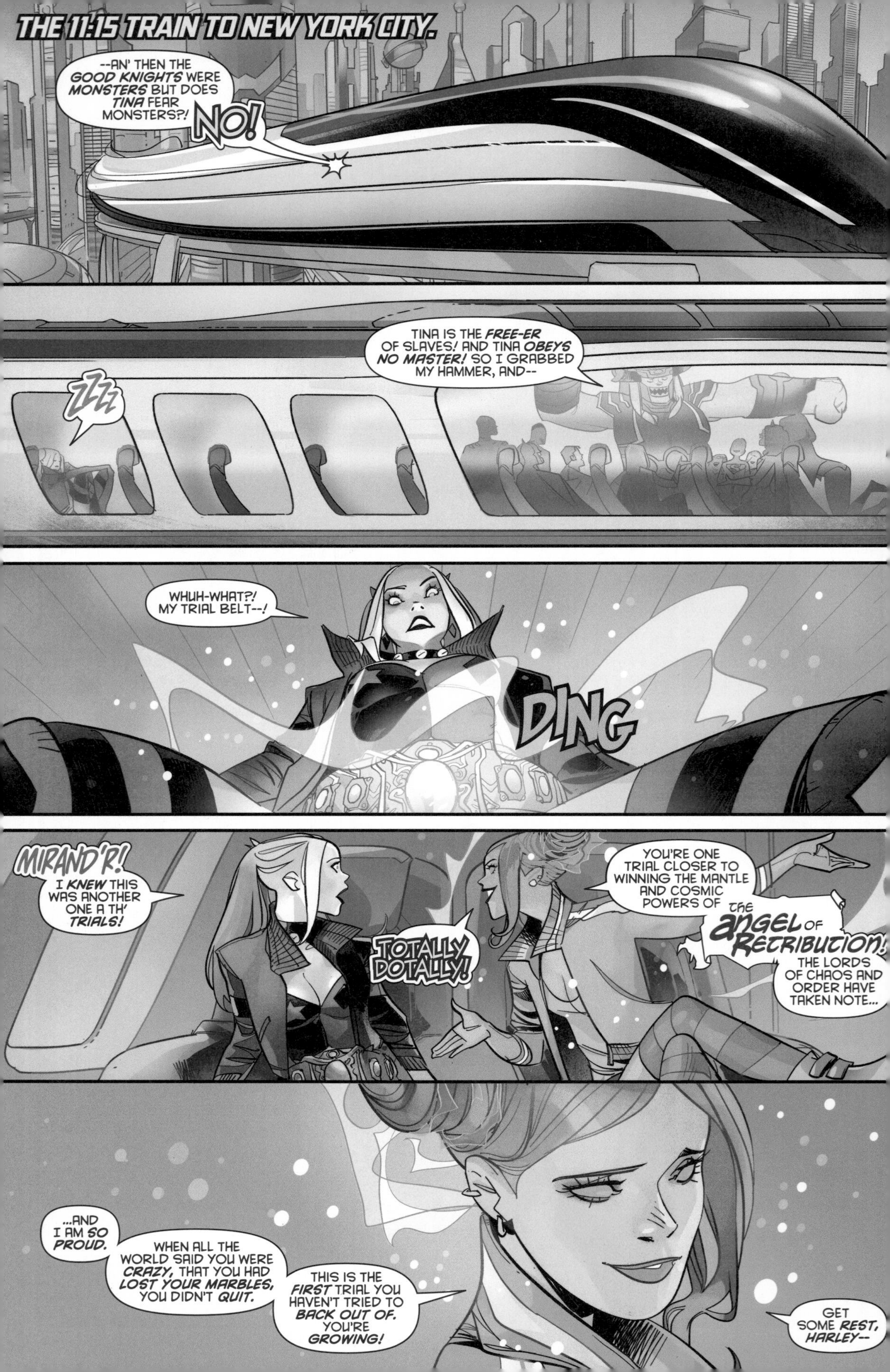
THE 11:15 TRAIN TO NEW YORK CITY.
--AN' THEN THE GOOD KNIGHTS WERE MONSTERS BUT DOES TINA FEAR MONSTERS?! NO!
TINA IS THE FREE-ER OF SLAVES! AND TINA OBEYS NO MASTER! SO I GRABBED MY HAMMER, AND--
ZZZZ
WHUH-WHAT?! MY TRIAL BELT--!
DING
MIRAND'R! I KNEW THIS WAS ANOTHER ONE A TH' TRIALS!
TOTALLY DOTALLY!
YOU'RE ONE TRIAL CLOSER TO WINNING THE MANTLE AND COSMIC POWERS OF THE ANGEL OF RETRIBUTION!
THE LORDS OF CHAOS AND ORDER HAVE TAKEN NOTE...
...AND I AM SO PROUD.
WHEN ALL THE WORLD SAID YOU WERE CRAZY, THAT YOU HAD LOST YOUR MARBLES, YOU DIDN'T QUIT.
THIS IS THE FIRST TRIAL YOU HAVEN'T TRIED TO BACK OUT OF. YOU'RE GROWING!
GET SOME REST, HARLEY--

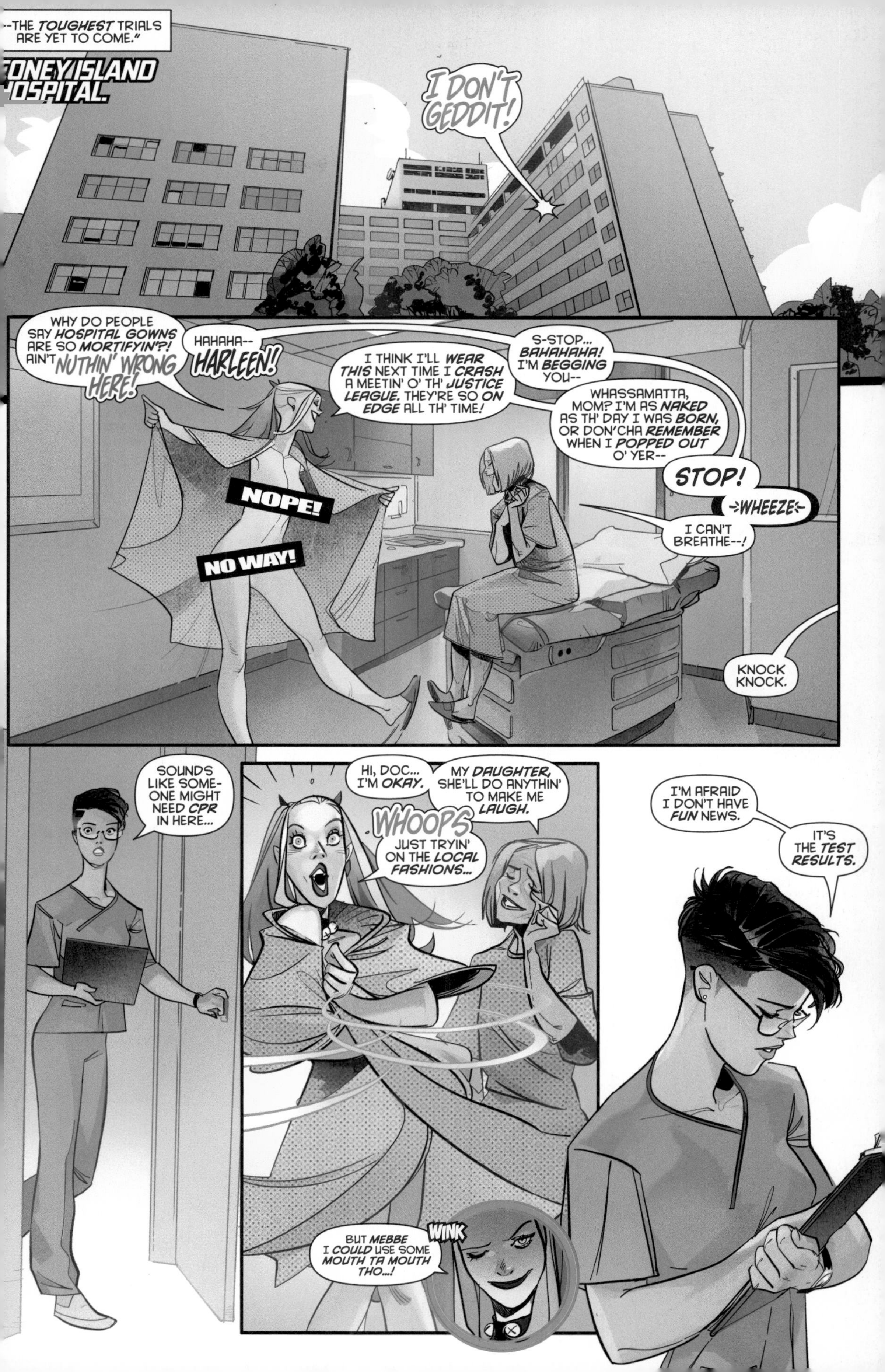
--THE TOUGHEST TRIALS ARE YET TO COME."
CONEY ISLAND HOSPITAL.
I DON'T GEDDIT!
WHY DO PEOPLE SAY HOSPITAL GOWNS ARE SO MORTIFYIN'?! AIN'T NUTHIN' WRONG HERE!
HAHAHA-- HARLEEN!
I THINK I'LL WEAR THIS NEXT TIME I CRASH A MEETIN' O' TH' JUSTICE LEAGUE. THEY'RE SO ON EDGE ALL TH' TIME!
S-STOP... BAHAHAHA! I'M BEGGING YOU--
WHASSAMATTA, MOM? I'M AS NAKED AS TH' DAY I WAS BORN, OR DON'CHA REMEMBER WHEN I POPPED OUT O' YER--
STOP!
-WHEEZE-
I CAN'T BREATHE--!
NOPE!
NO WAY!
KNOCK KNOCK.
SOUNDS LIKE SOME-ONE MIGHT NEED CPR IN HERE...
HI, DOC... I'M OKAY.
MY DAUGHTER, SHE'LL DO ANYTHIN' TO MAKE ME LAUGH.
WHOOPS
JUST TRYIN' ON THE LOCAL FASHIONS...
WINK
BUT MEBBE I COULD USE SOME MOUTH TA MOUTH THO...!
I'M AFRAID I DON'T HAVE FUN NEWS.
IT'S THE TEST RESULTS.

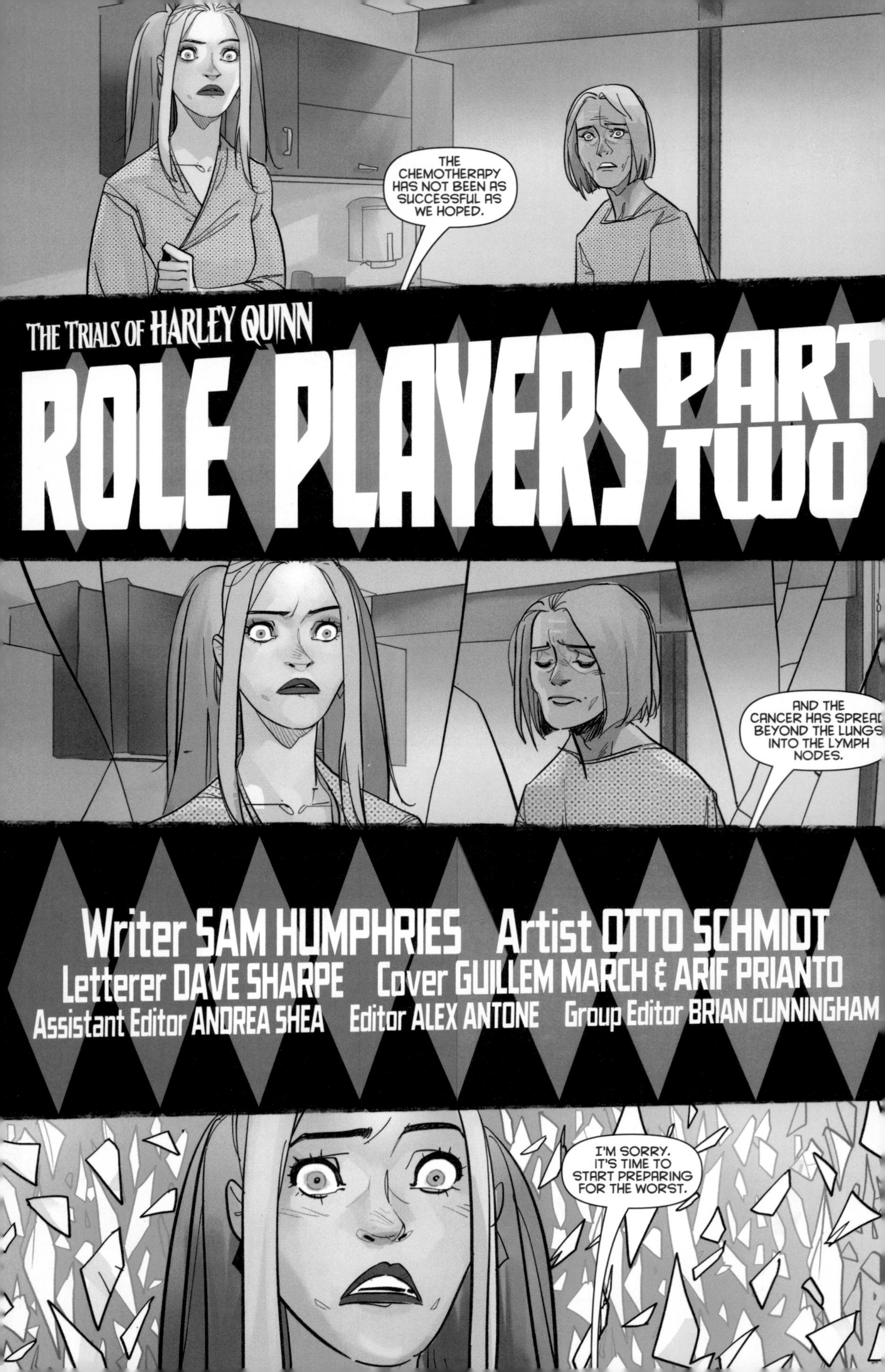
THE CHEMOTHERAPY HAS NOT BEEN AS SUCCESSFUL AS WE HOPED.
THE TRIALS OF HARLEY QUINN
ROLE PLAYERS PART TWO
AND THE CANCER HAS SPREAD BEYOND THE LUNGS INTO THE LYMPH NODES.
Writer SAM HUMPHRIES Artist OTTO SCHMIDT
Letterer DAVE SHARPE Cover GUILLEM MARCH & ARIF PRIANTO
Assistant Editor ANDREA SHEA Editor ALEX ANTONE Group Editor BRIAN CUNNINGHAM
I'M SORRY. IT'S TIME TO START PREPARING FOR THE WORST.

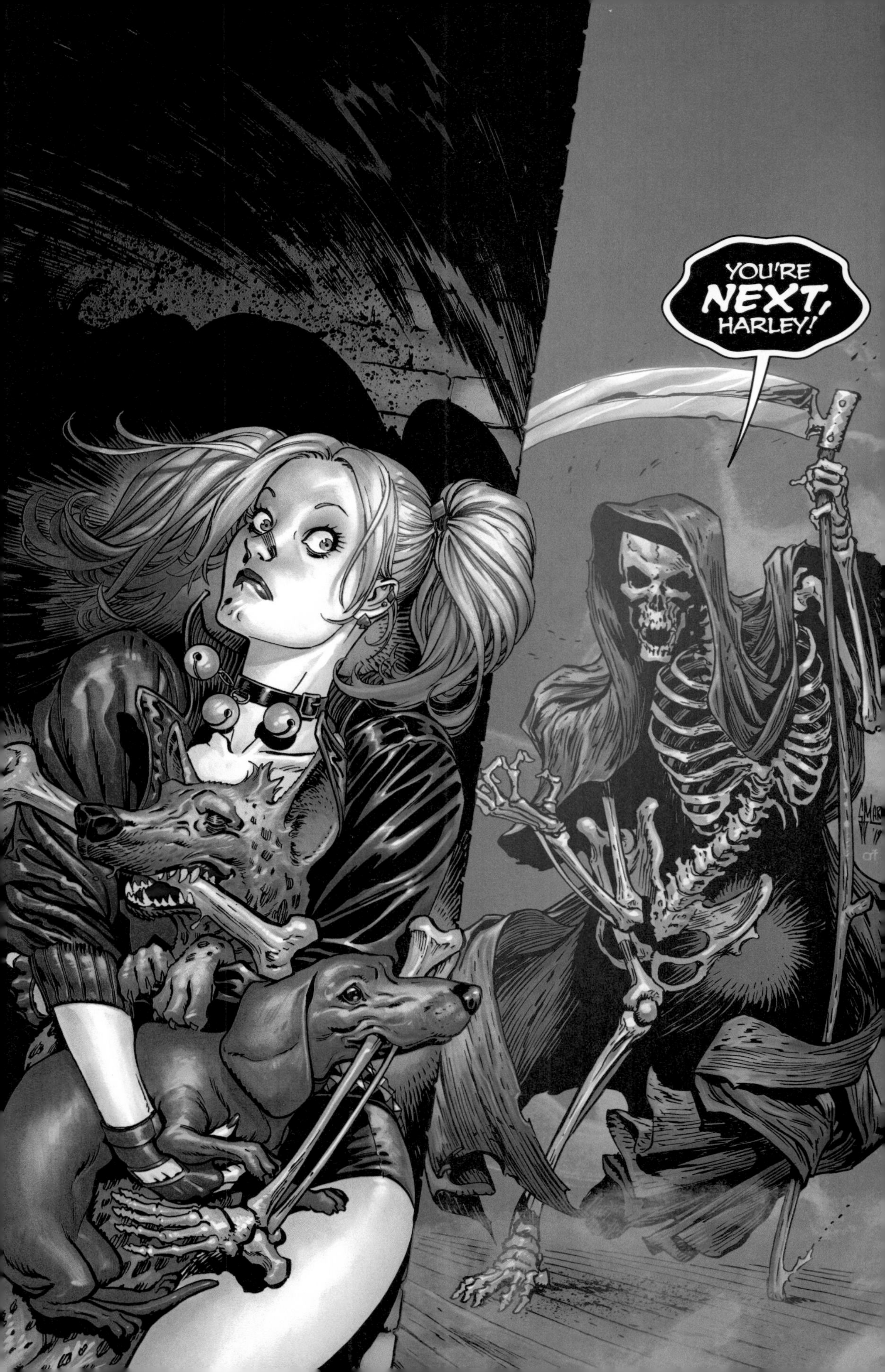
YOU'RE NEXT, HARLEY!

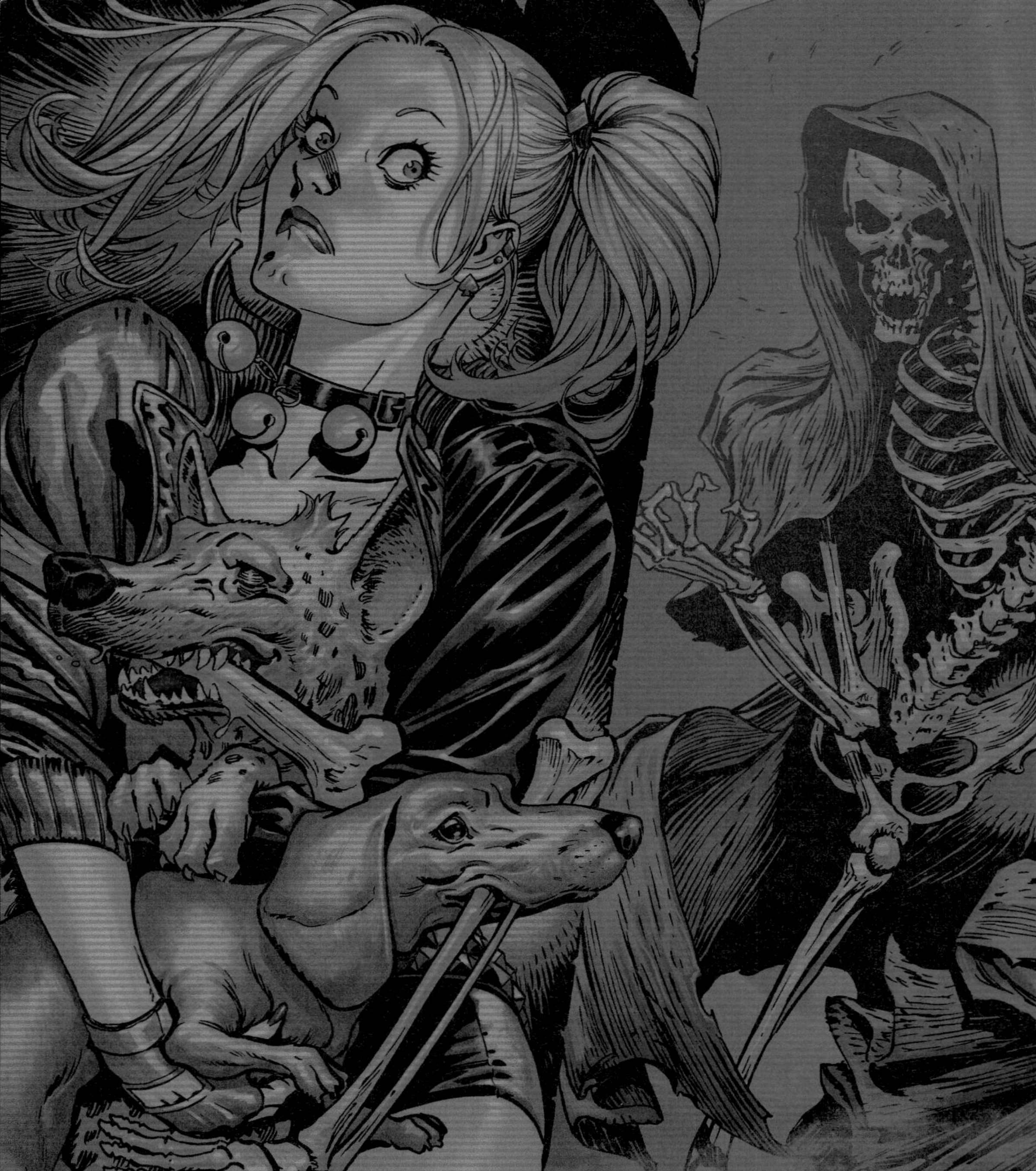

HARLEY QUINN
#63

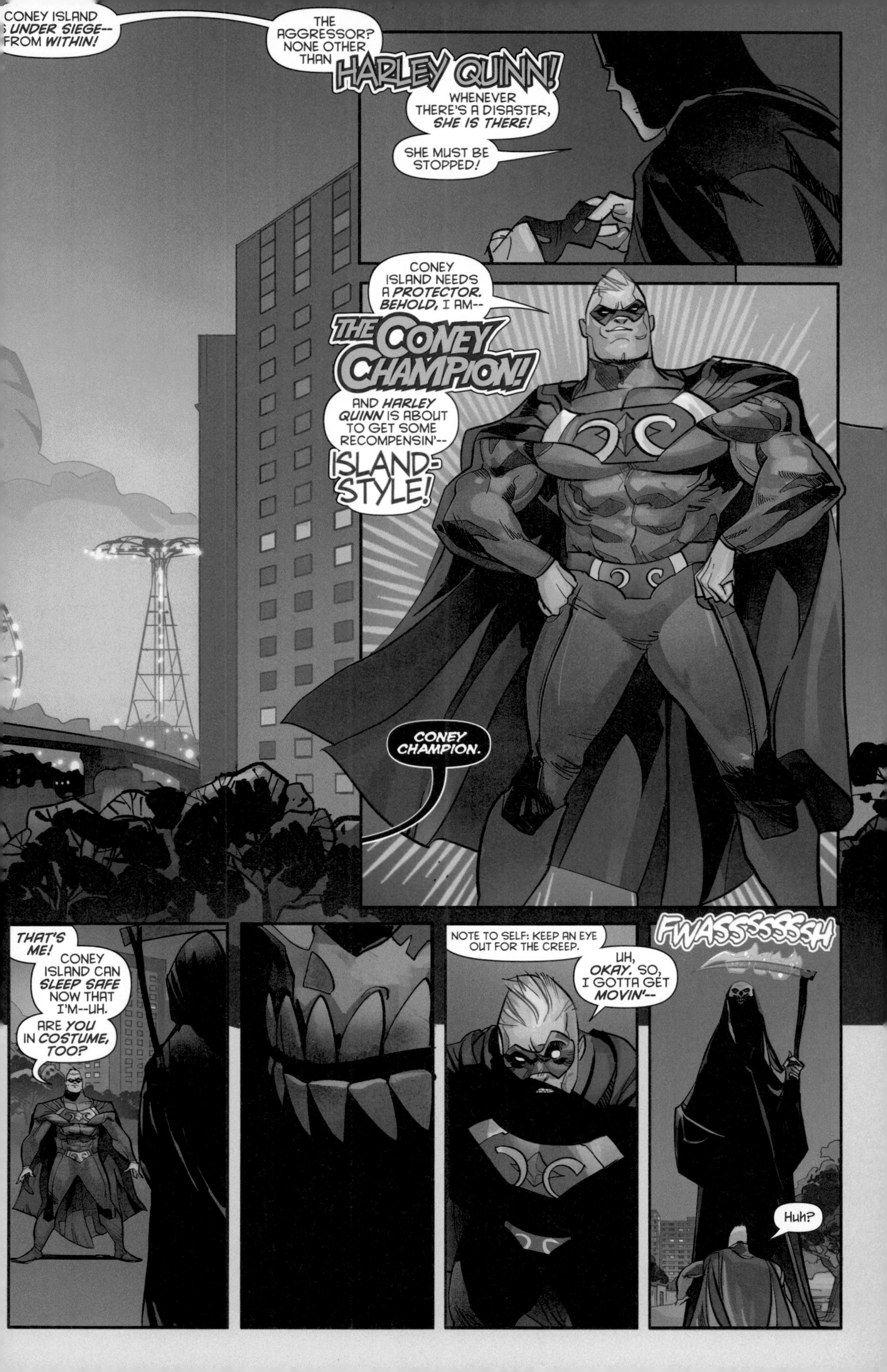

CONEY ISLAND IS UNDER SIEGE-- FROM WITHIN!
THE AGGRESSOR? NONE OTHER THAN HARLEY QUINN!
WHENEVER THERE'S A DISASTER, SHE IS THERE!
SHE MUST BE STOPPED!
CONEY ISLAND NEEDS A PROTECTOR. BEHOLD, I AM-- THE CONEY CHAMPION!
AND HARLEY QUINN IS ABOUT TO GET SOME RECOMPENSIN'-- ISLAND-STYLE!
CONEY CHAMPION.
THAT'S ME!
CONEY ISLAND CAN SLEEP SAFE NOW THAT I'M--UH.
ARE YOU IN COSTUME, TOO?
NOTE TO SELF: KEEP AN EYE OUT FOR THE CREEP.
UH, OKAY. SO, I GOTTA GET MOVIN'--
FWASSSSSSSH
Huh?

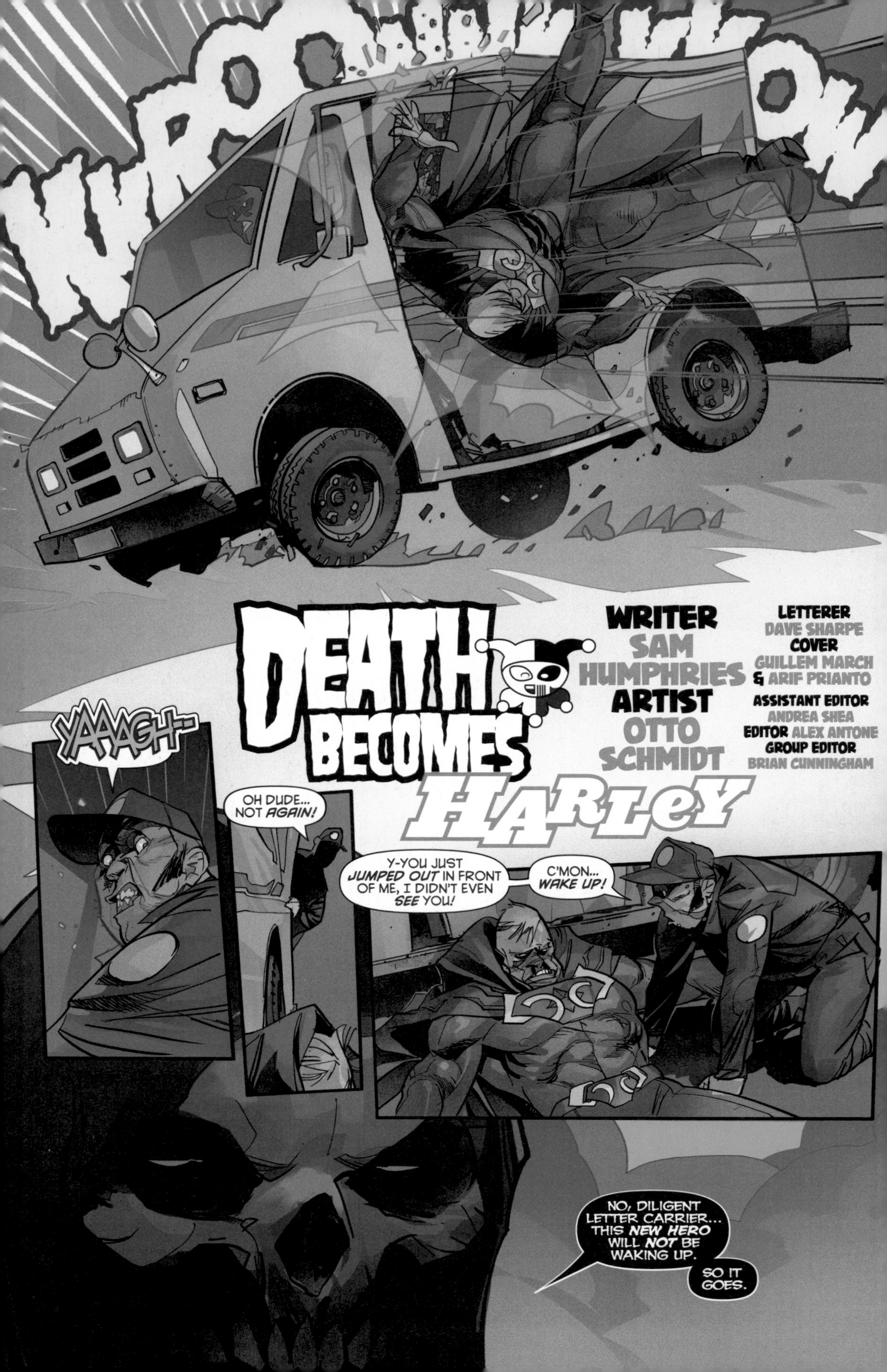
WHROOMMMMMM
DEATH BECOMES HARLEY
WRITER SAM HUMPHRIES
ARTIST OTTO SCHMIDT
LETTERER DAVE SHARPE
COVER GUILLEM MARCH & ARIF PRIANTO
ASSISTANT EDITOR ANDREA SHEA
EDITOR ALEX ANTONE
GROUP EDITOR BRIAN CUNNINGHAM
YAAAGH--
OH DUDE... NOT AGAIN!
Y-YOU JUST JUMPED OUT IN FRONT OF ME, I DIDN'T EVEN SEE YOU!
C'MON... WAKE UP!
NO, DILIGENT LETTER CARRIER... THIS NEW HERO WILL NOT BE WAKING UP.
SO IT GOES.

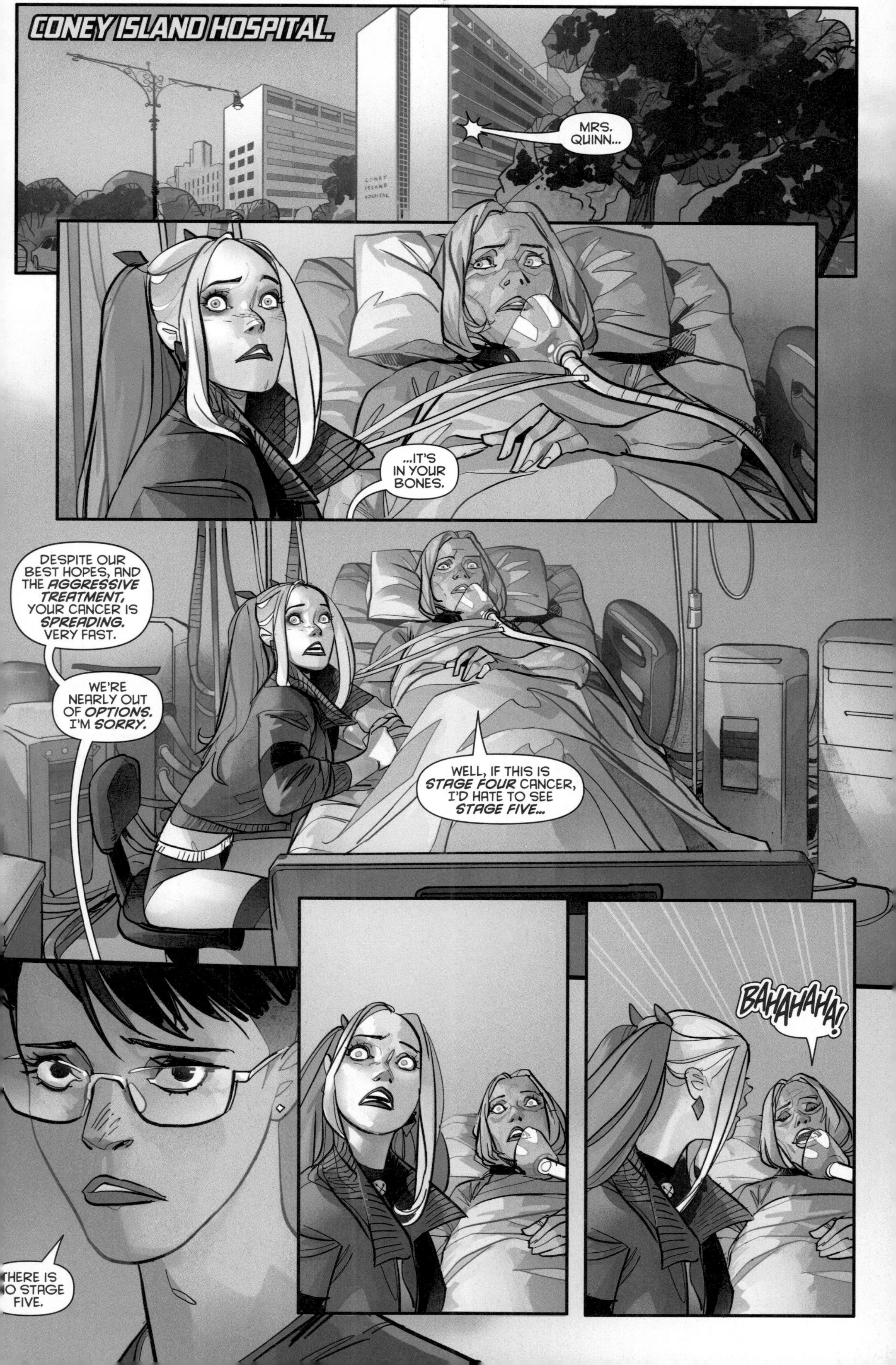
CONEY ISLAND HOSPITAL.
CONEY ISLAND HOSPITAL
MRS. QUINN...
...IT'S IN YOUR BONES.
DESPITE OUR BEST HOPES, AND THE AGGRESSIVE TREATMENT, YOUR CANCER IS SPREADING. VERY FAST.
WE'RE NEARLY OUT OF OPTIONS. I'M SORRY.
WELL, IF THIS IS STAGE FOUR CANCER, I'D HATE TO SEE STAGE FIVE...
THERE IS
O STAGE
FIVE.
BAHAHAHA!

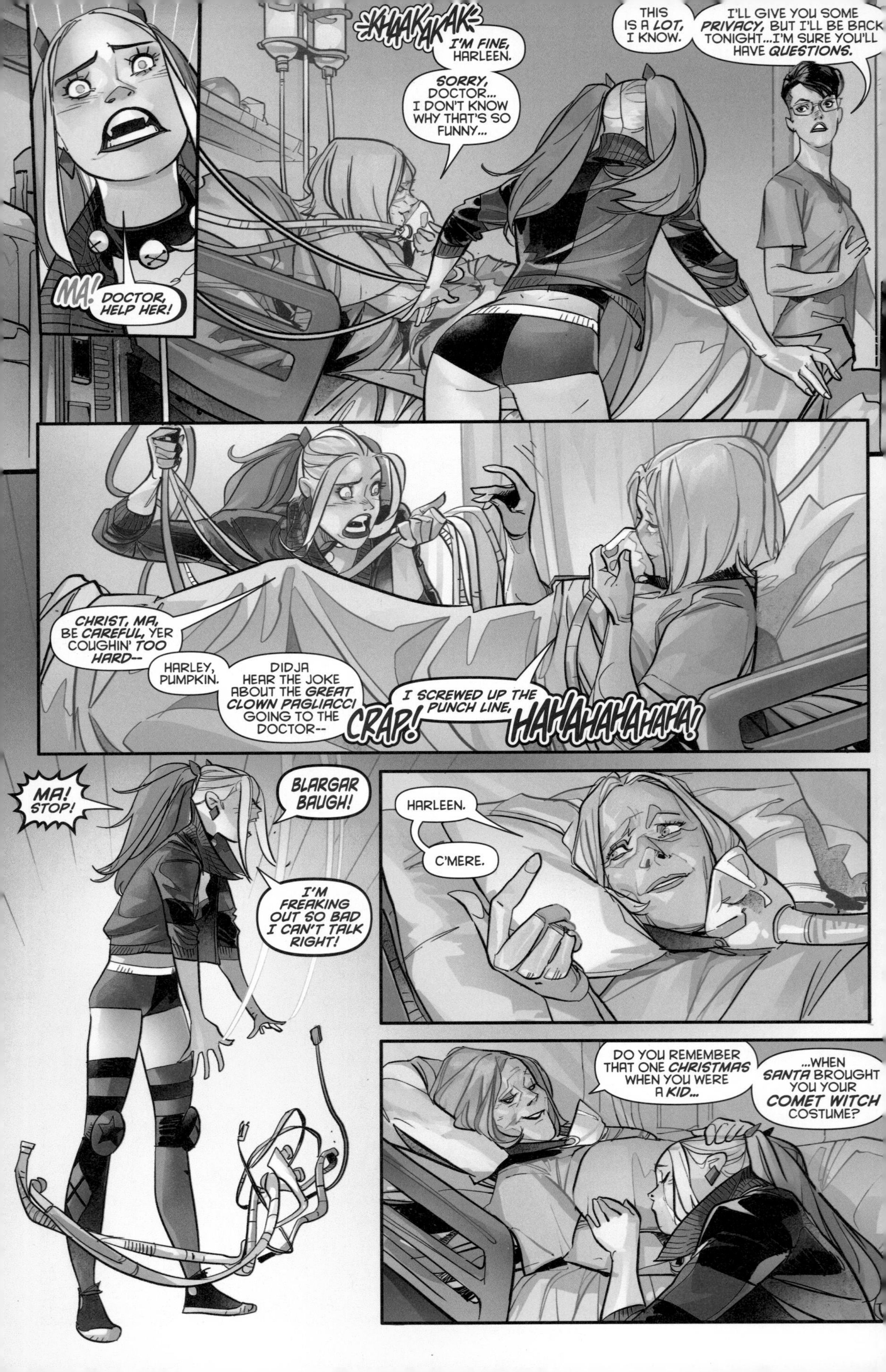
MA! DOCTOR, HELP HER!
KHAAKAKAK
I'M FINE, HARLEEN.
SORRY, DOCTOR... I DON'T KNOW WHY THAT'S SO FUNNY...
THIS IS A LOT, I KNOW.
I'LL GIVE YOU SOME PRIVACY, BUT I'LL BE BACK TONIGHT...I'M SURE YOU'LL HAVE QUESTIONS.
CHRIST, MA, BE CAREFUL, YER COUGHIN' TOO HARD--
HARLEY, PUMPKIN.
DIDJA HEAR THE JOKE ABOUT THE GREAT CLOWN PAGLIACCI GOING TO THE DOCTOR--
CRAP!
I SCREWED UP THE PUNCH LINE,
HAHAHAHAHAHAHA!
MA! STOP!
BLARGAR BAUGH!
I'M FREAKING OUT SO BAD I CAN'T TALK RIGHT!
HARLEEN.
C'MERE.
DO YOU REMEMBER THAT ONE CHRISTMAS WHEN YOU WERE A KID...
...WHEN SANTA BROUGHT YOU YOUR COMET WITCH COSTUME?

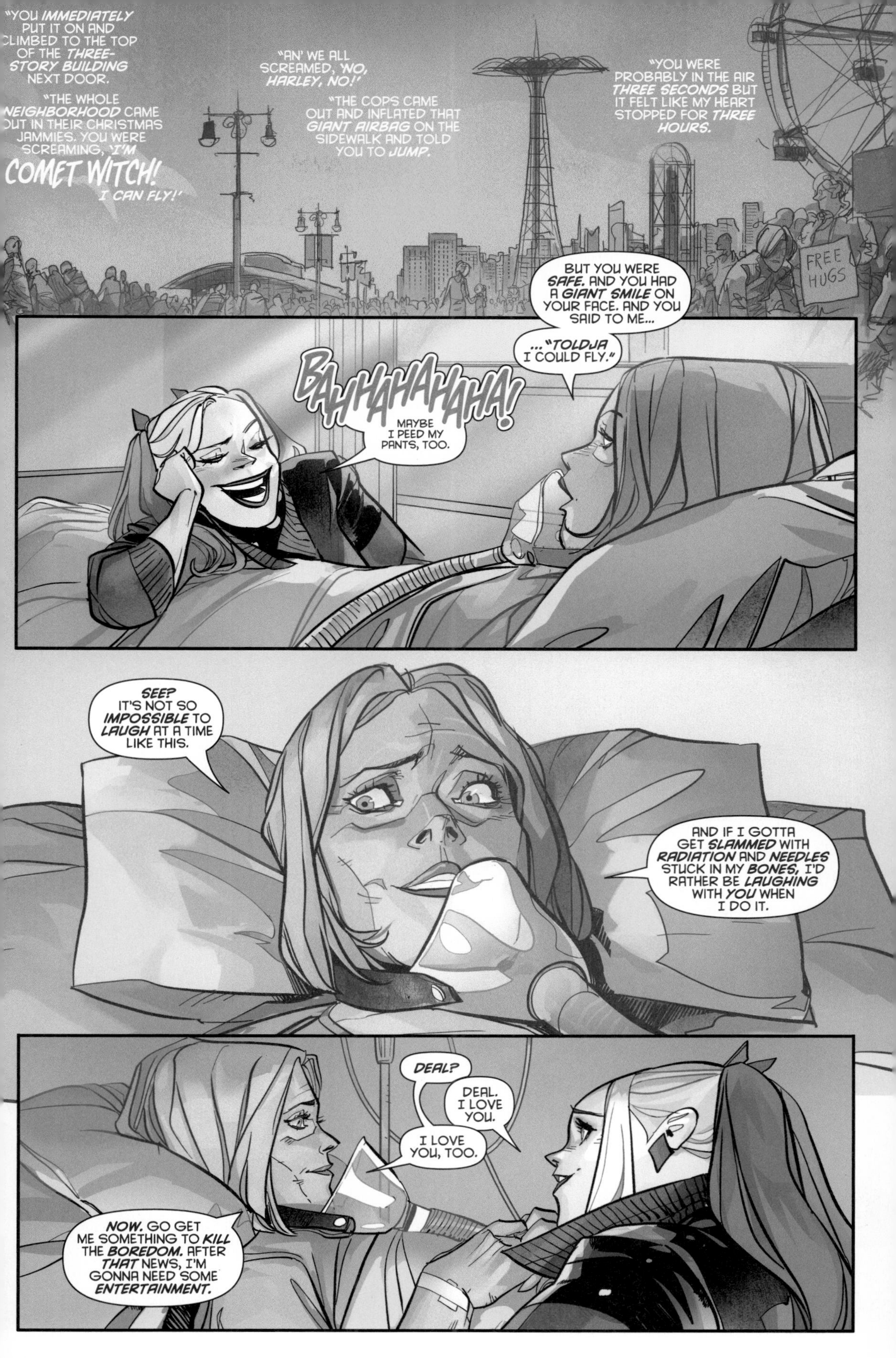
"YOU IMMEDIATELY PUT IT ON AND CLIMBED TO THE TOP OF THE THREE-STORY BUILDING NEXT DOOR.
"THE WHOLE NEIGHBORHOOD CAME OUT IN THEIR CHRISTMAS JAMMIES. YOU WERE SCREAMING, 'I'M COMET WITCH! I CAN FLY!'
"AN' WE ALL SCREAMED, 'NO, HARLEY, NO!'
"THE COPS CAME OUT AND INFLATED THAT GIANT AIRBAG ON THE SIDEWALK AND TOLD YOU TO JUMP.
"YOU WERE PROBABLY IN THE AIR THREE SECONDS BUT IT FELT LIKE MY HEART STOPPED FOR THREE HOURS.
FREE HUGS
BUT YOU WERE SAFE. AND YOU HAD A GIANT SMILE ON YOUR FACE. AND YOU SAID TO ME...
..."TOLDJA I COULD FLY."
BAHHAHAHAHA!
MAYBE I PEED MY PANTS, TOO.
SEE? IT'S NOT SO IMPOSSIBLE TO LAUGH AT A TIME LIKE THIS.
AND IF I GOTTA GET SLAMMED WITH RADIATION AND NEEDLES STUCK IN MY BONES, I'D RATHER BE LAUGHING WITH YOU WHEN I DO IT.
DEAL?
DEAL. I LOVE YOU.
I LOVE YOU, TOO.
NOW. GO GET ME SOMETHING TO KILL THE BOREDOM. AFTER THAT NEWS, I'M GONNA NEED SOME ENTERTAINMENT.

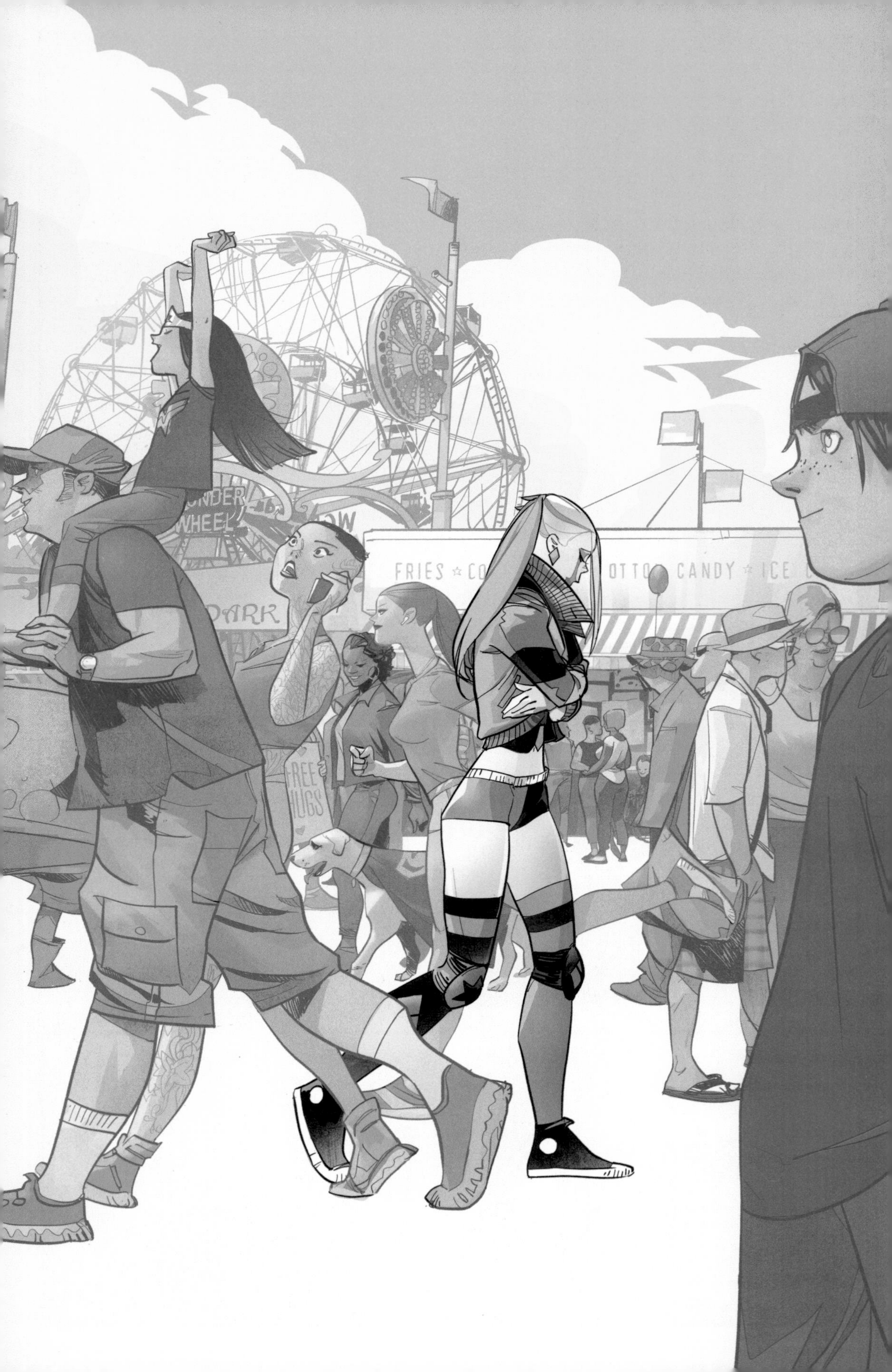
ONDER
WHEEL
FRIES ☆ CO
OTTO CANDY ☆ ICE
DARK
FREE HUGS

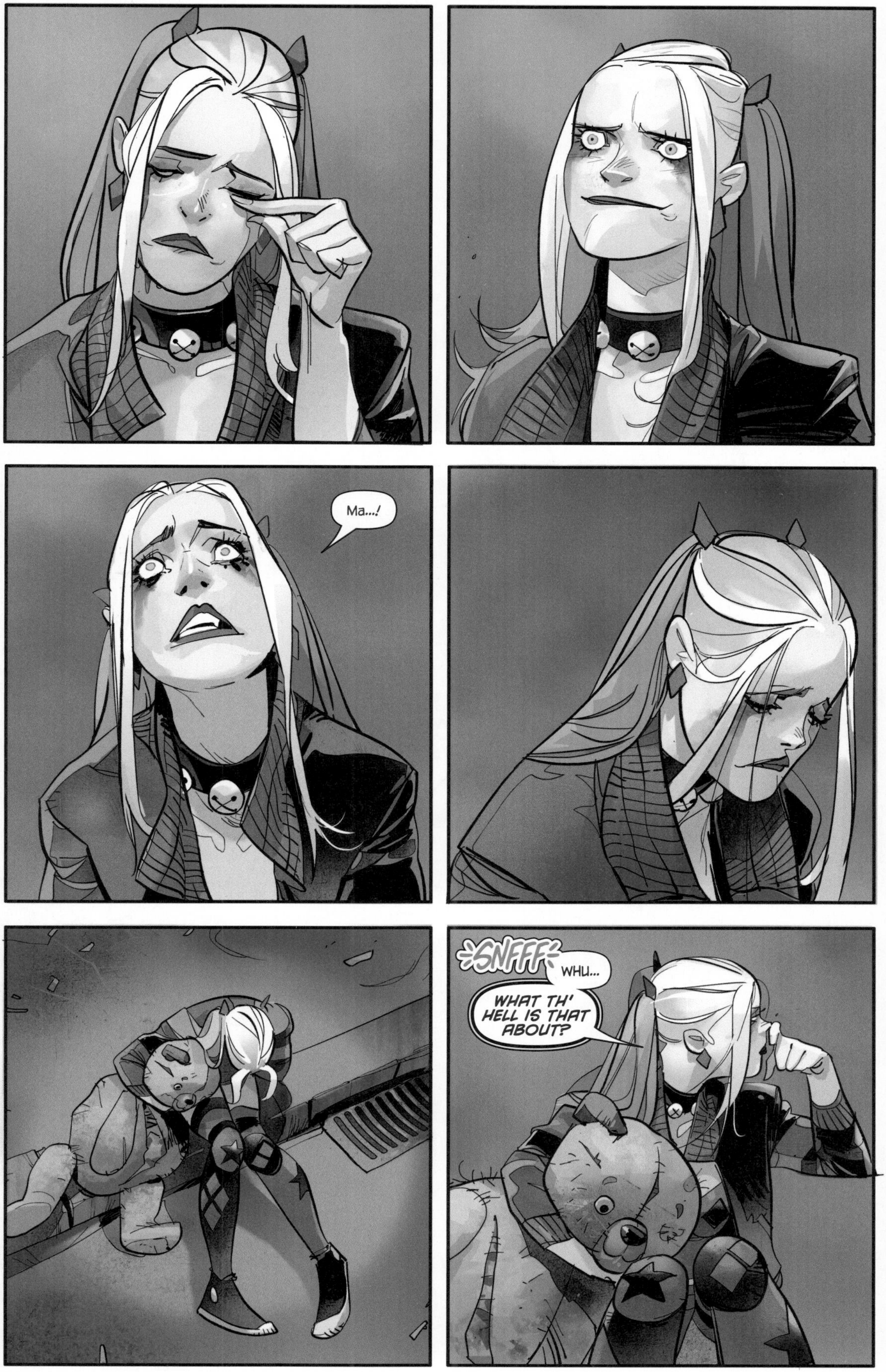

Ma...!
SNFFF
WHU...
WHAT TH' HELL IS THAT ABOUT?

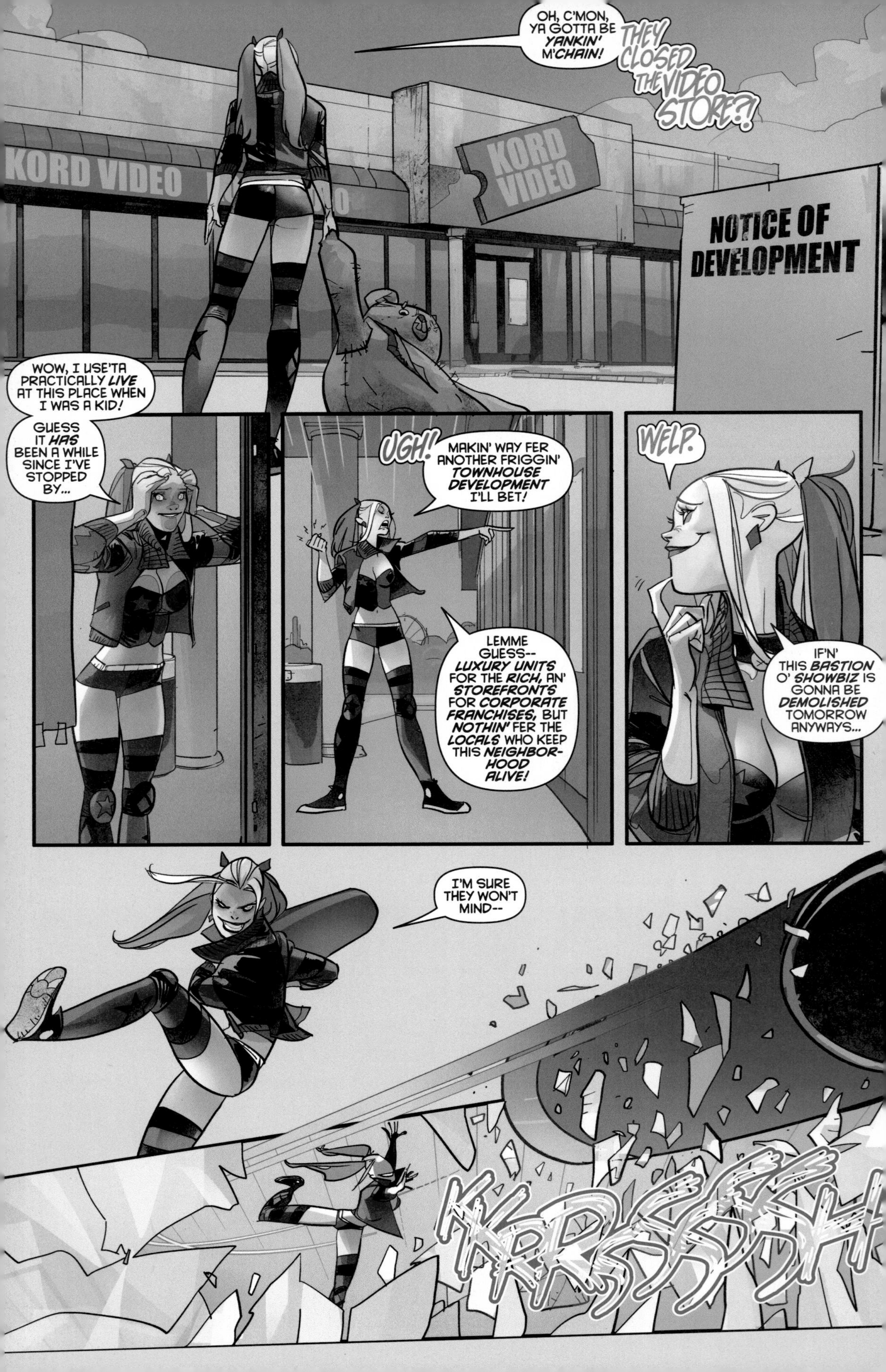
OH, C'MON, YA GOTTA BE YANKIN' M'CHAIN!
THEY CLOSED THE VIDEO STORE?!
KORD VIDEO
KORD VIDEO
NOTICE OF DEVELOPMENT
WOW, I USE'TA PRACTICALLY LIVE AT THIS PLACE WHEN I WAS A KID!
GUESS IT HAS BEEN A WHILE SINCE I'VE STOPPED BY...
UGH!
MAKIN' WAY FER ANOTHER FRIGGIN' TOWNHOUSE DEVELOPMENT I'LL BET!
LEMME GUESS-- LUXURY UNITS FOR THE RICH, AN' STOREFRONTS FOR CORPORATE FRANCHISES, BUT NOTHIN' FER THE LOCALS WHO KEEP THIS NEIGHBOR-HOOD ALIVE!
WELP.
IF'N' THIS BASTION O' SHOWBIZ IS GONNA BE DEMOLISHED TOMORROW ANYWAYS...
I'M SURE THEY WON'T MIND--
KRRSSSSH

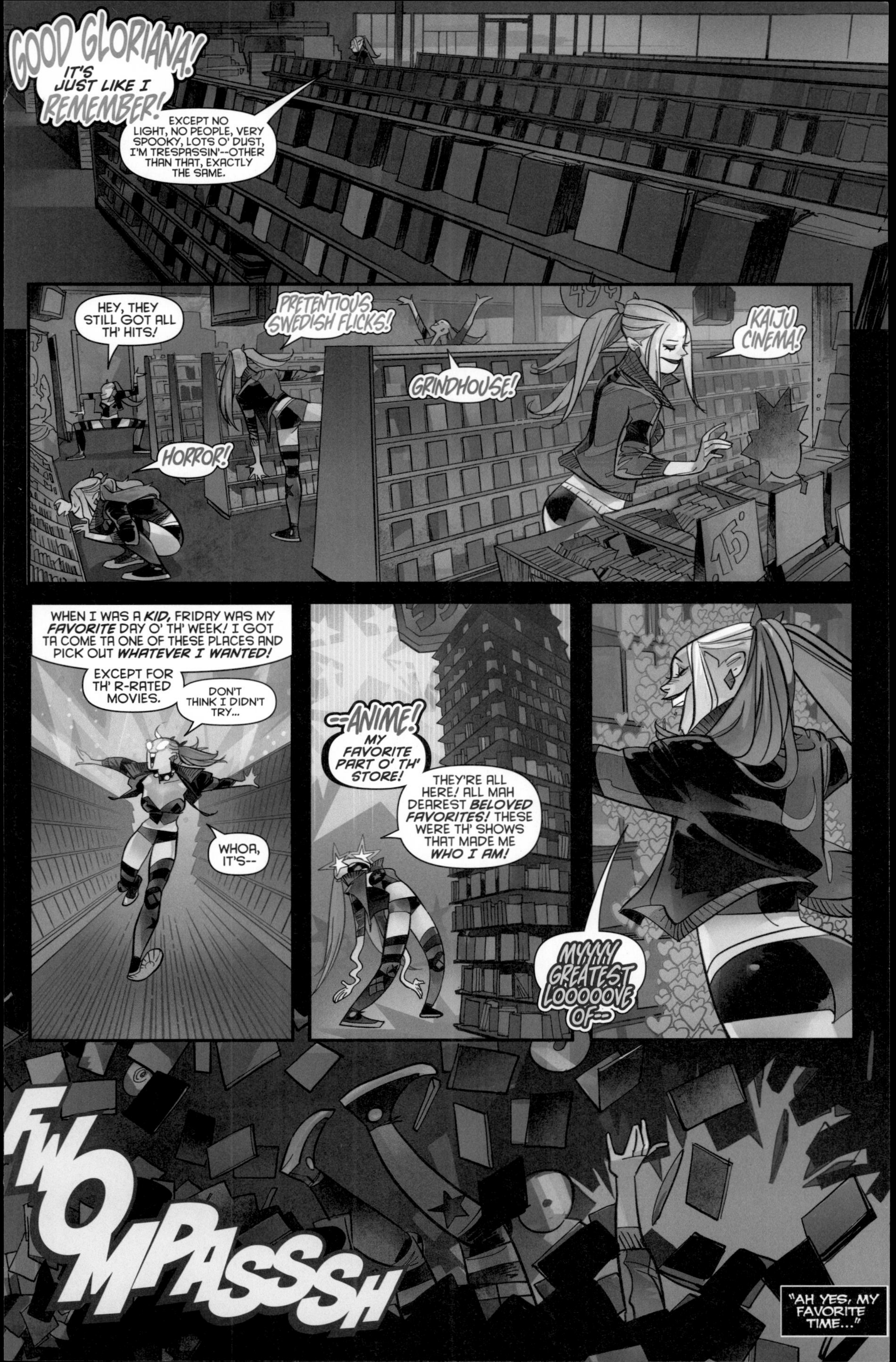
GOOD GLORIANA! IT'S JUST LIKE I REMEMBER!
EXCEPT NO LIGHT, NO PEOPLE, VERY SPOOKY, LOTS O' DUST, I'M TRESPASSIN'--OTHER THAN THAT, EXACTLY THE SAME.
HEY, THEY STILL GOT ALL TH' HITS!
HORROR!
PRETENTIOUS SWEDISH FLICKS!
GRINDHOUSE!
KAIJU CINEMA!
WHEN I WAS A KID, FRIDAY WAS MY FAVORITE DAY O' TH' WEEK! I GOT TA COME TA ONE OF THESE PLACES AND PICK OUT WHATEVER I WANTED!
EXCEPT FOR TH' R-RATED MOVIES.
DON'T THINK I DIDN'T TRY...
WHOA, IT'S--
--ANIME! MY FAVORITE PART O' TH' STORE!
THEY'RE ALL HERE! ALL MAH DEAREST BELOVED FAVORITES! THESE WERE TH' SHOWS THAT MADE ME WHO I AM!
MYYYY GREATEST LOOOOOVE OF--
FWOMPASSSH
"AH YES, MY FAVORITE TIME..."

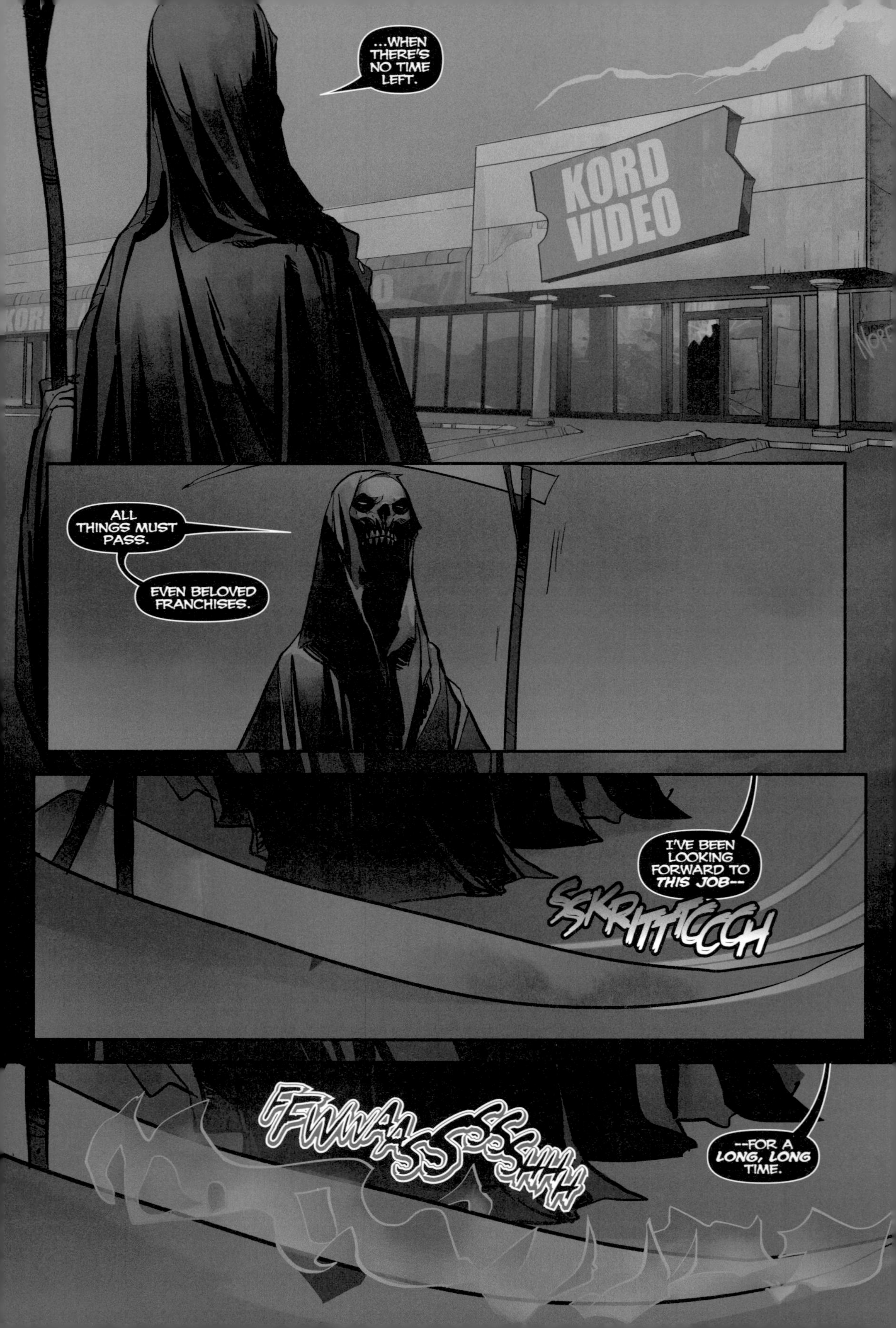
...WHEN THERE'S NO TIME LEFT.
KORD VIDEO
ALL THINGS MUST PASS.
EVEN BELOVED FRANCHISES.
I'VE BEEN LOOKING FORWARD TO *THIS JOB*--
SSKRITTTCCCH
FFWWASSSSHHH
--FOR A **LONG, LONG** TIME.

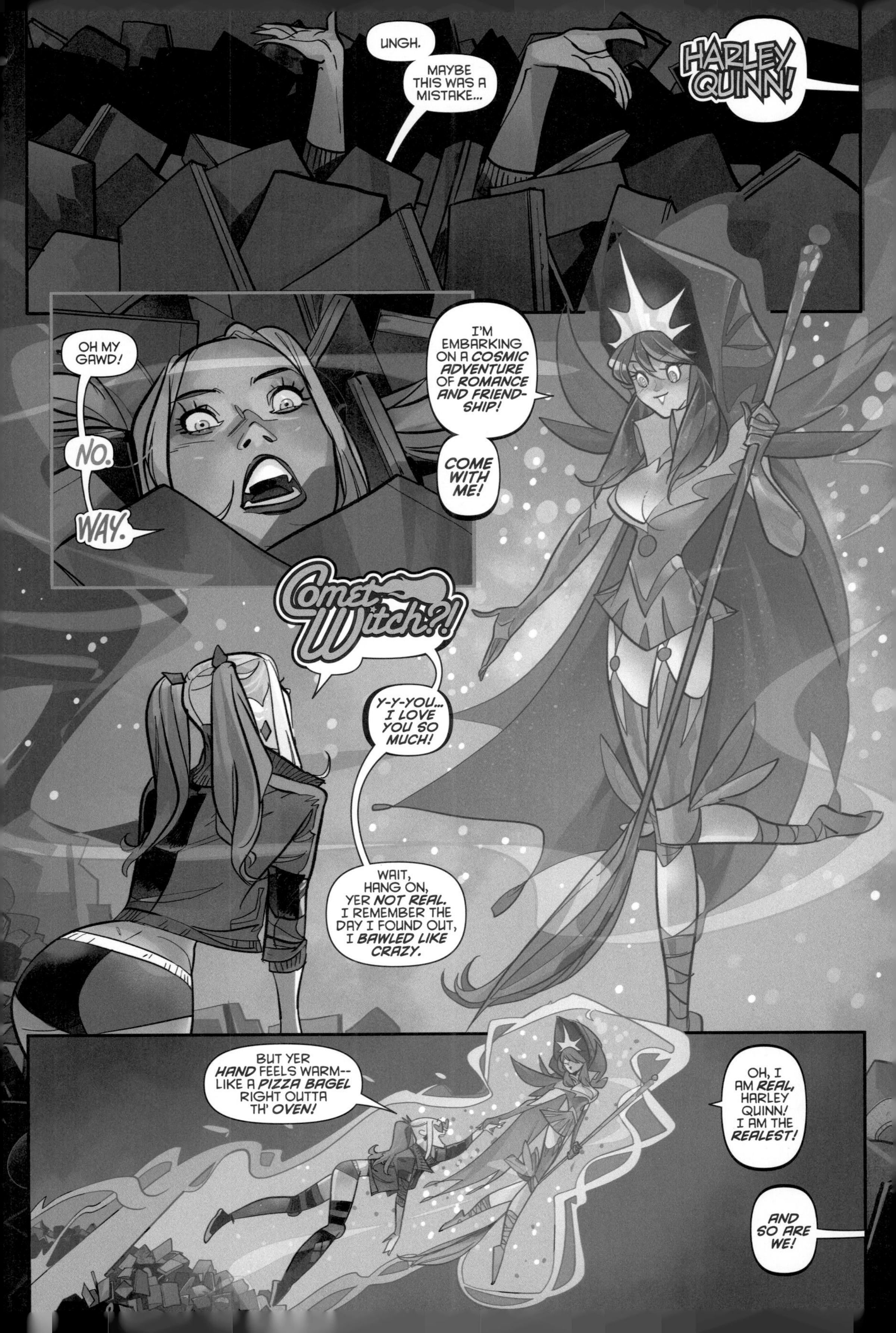
UNGH.
MAYBE THIS WAS A MISTAKE...
HARLEY QUINN!
OH MY GAWD!
NO.
WAY.
I'M EMBARKING ON A COSMIC ADVENTURE OF ROMANCE AND FRIEND-SHIP!
COME WITH ME!
Comet Witch?!
Y-Y-YOU... I LOVE YOU SO MUCH!
WAIT, HANG ON, YER NOT REAL. I REMEMBER THE DAY I FOUND OUT, I BAWLED LIKE CRAZY.
BUT YER HAND FEELS WARM-- LIKE A PIZZA BAGEL RIGHT OUTTA TH' OVEN!
OH, I AM REAL, HARLEY QUINN! I AM THE REALEST!
AND SO ARE WE!

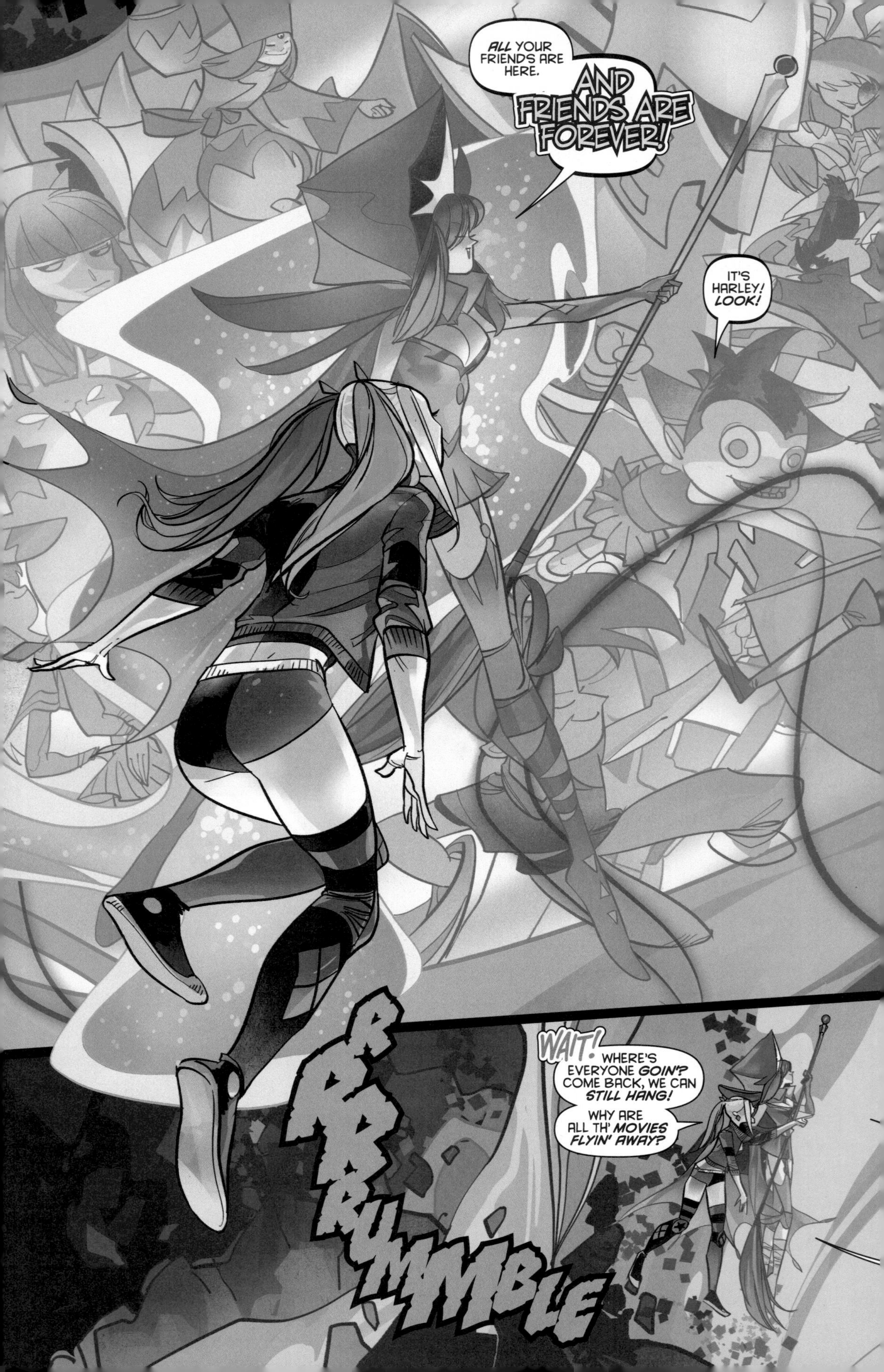
ALL YOUR FRIENDS ARE HERE.
AND FRIENDS ARE FOREVER!
IT'S HARLEY! LOOK!
WAIT! WHERE'S EVERYONE GOIN'? COME BACK, WE CAN STILL HANG!
WHY ARE ALL TH' MOVIES FLYIN' AWAY?
RRRRUMMMBLE

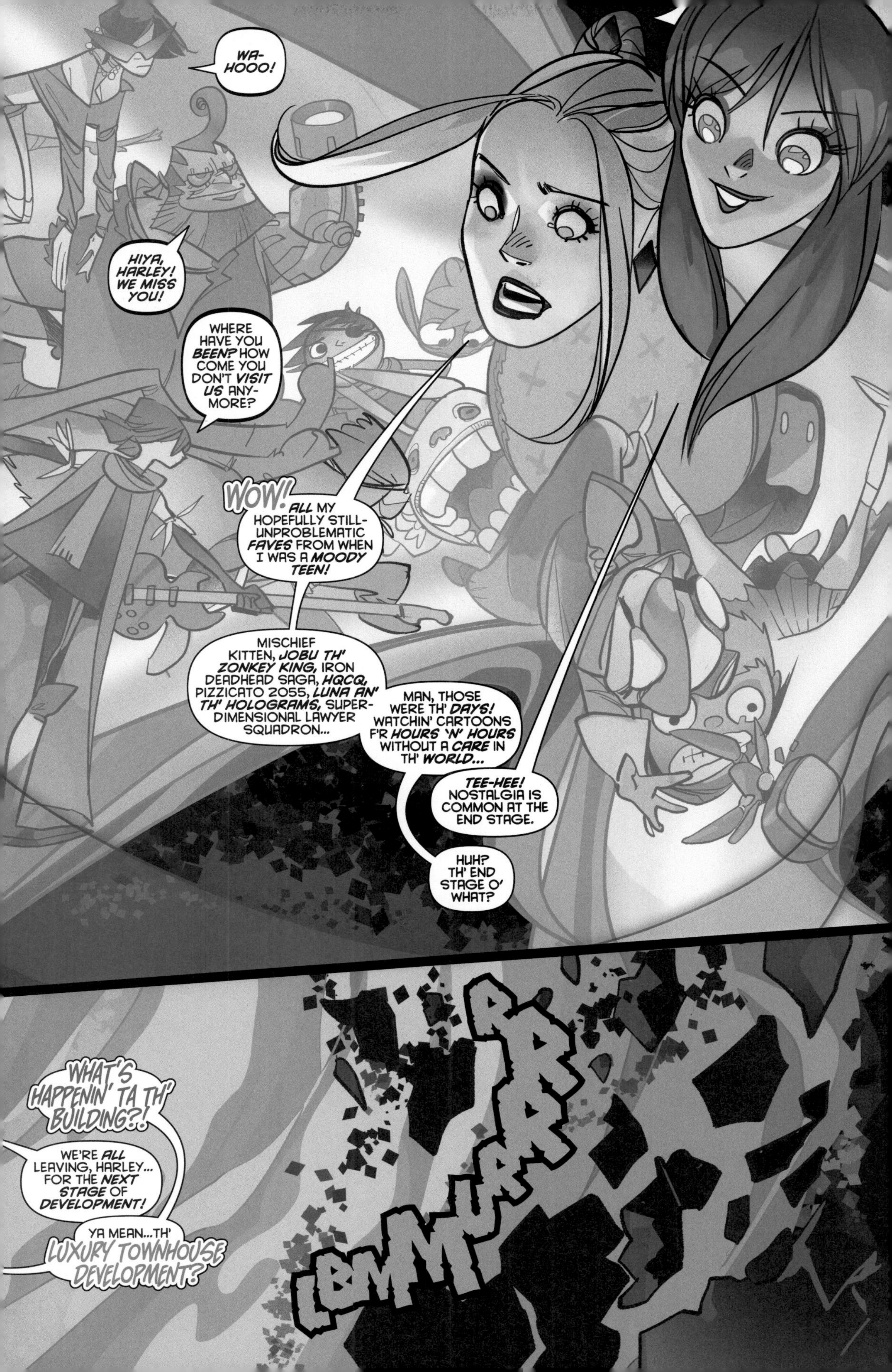

WA-HOOO!
HIYA, HARLEY! WE MISS YOU!
WHERE HAVE YOU BEEN? HOW COME YOU DON'T VISIT US ANYMORE?
WOW! ALL MY HOPEFULLY STILL-UNPROBLEMATIC FAVES FROM WHEN I WAS A MOODY TEEN!
MISCHIEF KITTEN, JOBU TH' ZONKEY KING, IRON DEADHEAD SAGA, HQCQ, PIZZICATO 2055, LUNA AN' TH' HOLOGRAMS, SUPER-DIMENSIONAL LAWYER SQUADRON...
MAN, THOSE WERE TH' DAYS! WATCHIN' CARTOONS F'R HOURS 'N' HOURS WITHOUT A CARE IN TH' WORLD...
TEE-HEE! NOSTALGIA IS COMMON AT THE END STAGE.
HUH? TH' END STAGE O' WHAT?
BMMMRRR
WHAT'S HAPPENIN' TA TH' BUILDING?!
WE'RE ALL LEAVING, HARLEY... FOR THE NEXT STAGE OF DEVELOPMENT!
YA MEAN...TH' LUXURY TOWNHOUSE DEVELOPMENT?

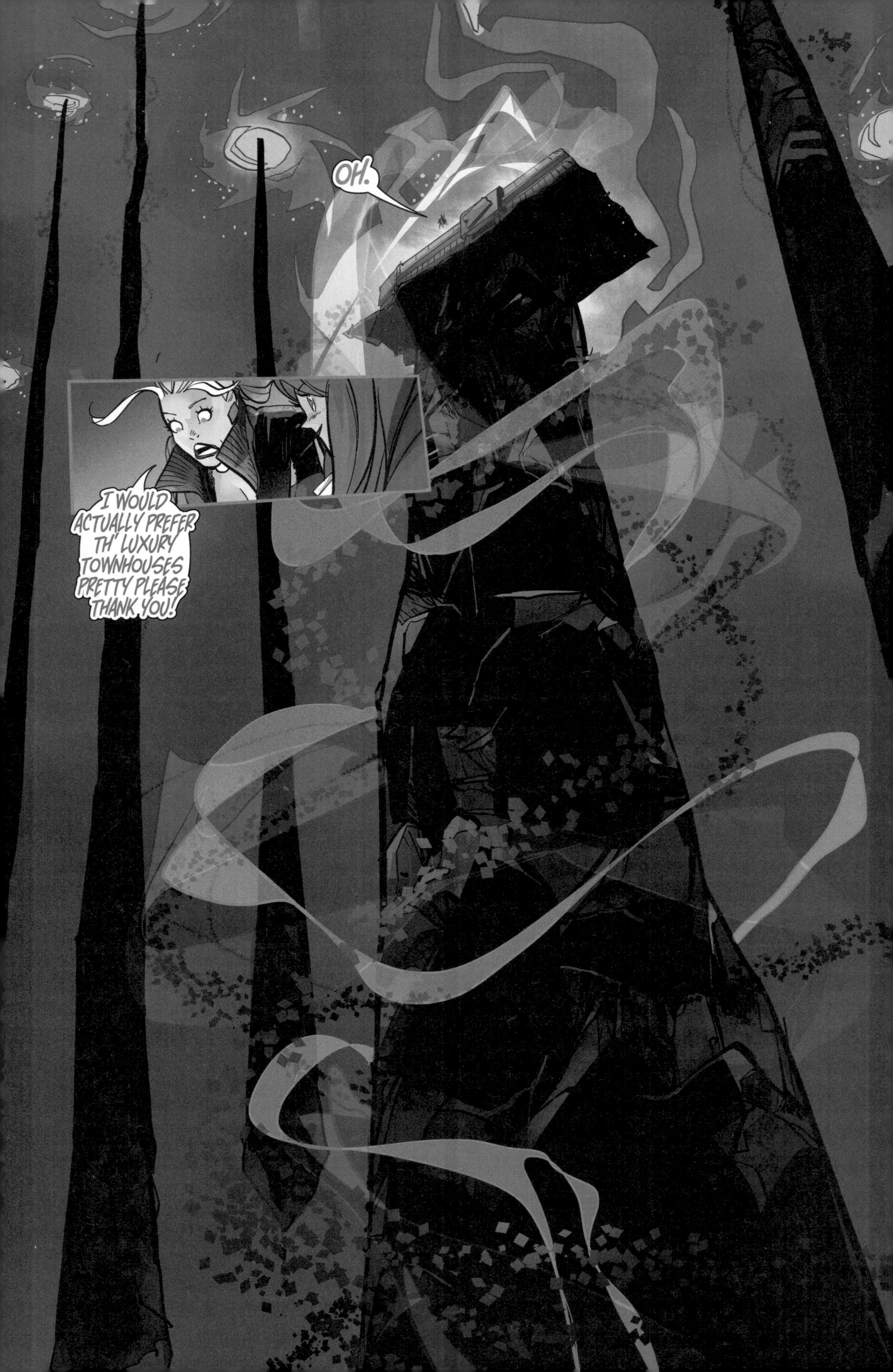
OH.
I WOULD ACTUALLY PREFER TH' LUXURY TOWNHOUSES PRETTY PLEASE THANK YOU!

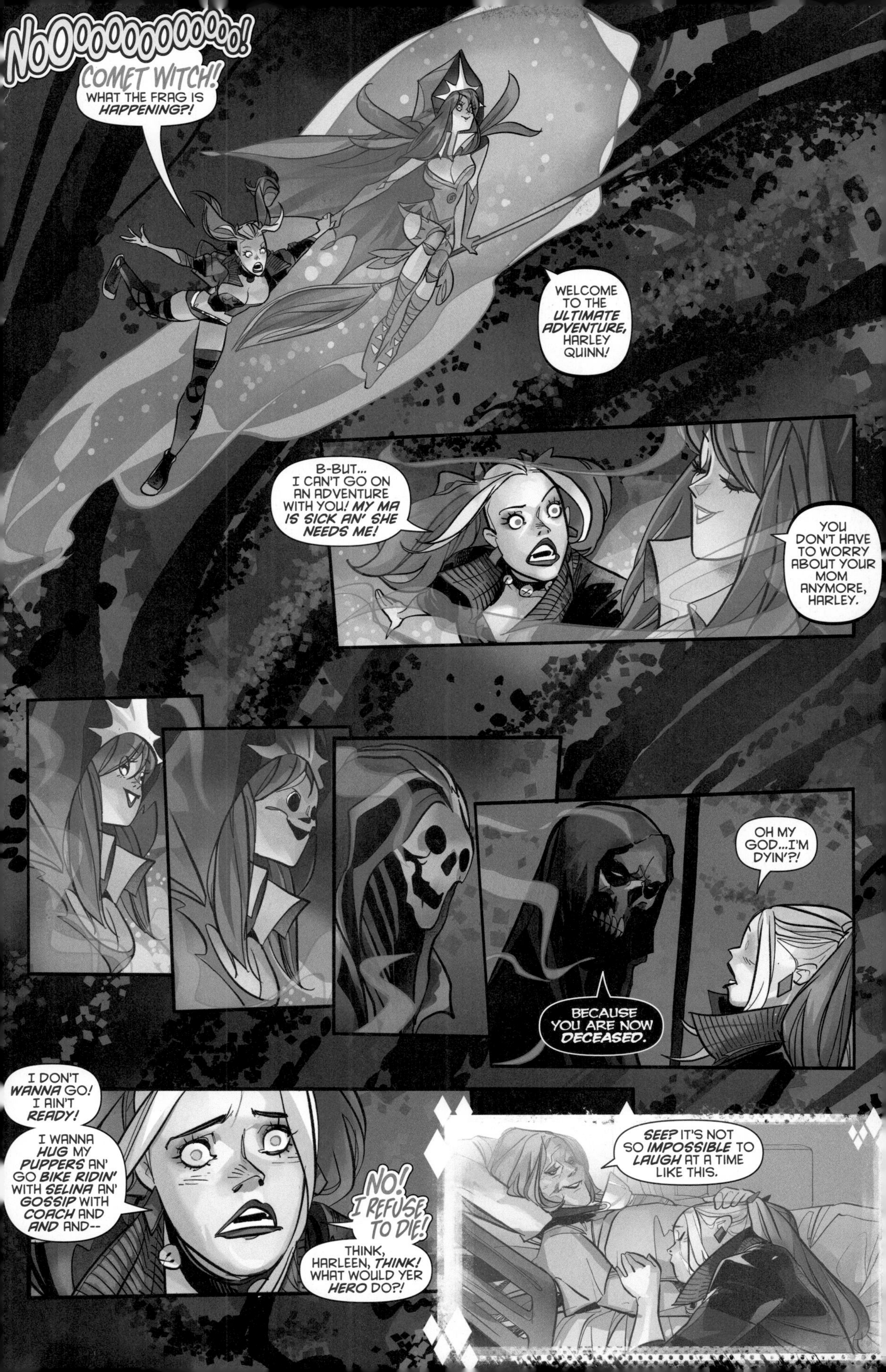
NoOoooooooooooo!
COMET WITCH! WHAT THE FRAG IS HAPPENING?!
WELCOME TO THE ULTIMATE ADVENTURE, HARLEY QUINN!
B-BUT... I CAN'T GO ON AN ADVENTURE WITH YOU! MY MA IS SICK AN' SHE NEEDS ME!
YOU DON'T HAVE TO WORRY ABOUT YOUR MOM ANYMORE, HARLEY.
BECAUSE YOU ARE NOW DECEASED.
OH MY GOD...I'M DYIN'?!
I DON'T WANNA GO! I AIN'T READY!
I WANNA HUG MY PUPPERS AN' GO BIKE RIDIN' WITH SELINA AN' GOSSIP WITH COACH AND AND AND--
NO! I REFUSE TO DIE!
THINK, HARLEEN, THINK! WHAT WOULD YER HERO DO?!
SEE? IT'S NOT SO IMPOSSIBLE TO LAUGH AT A TIME LIKE THIS.

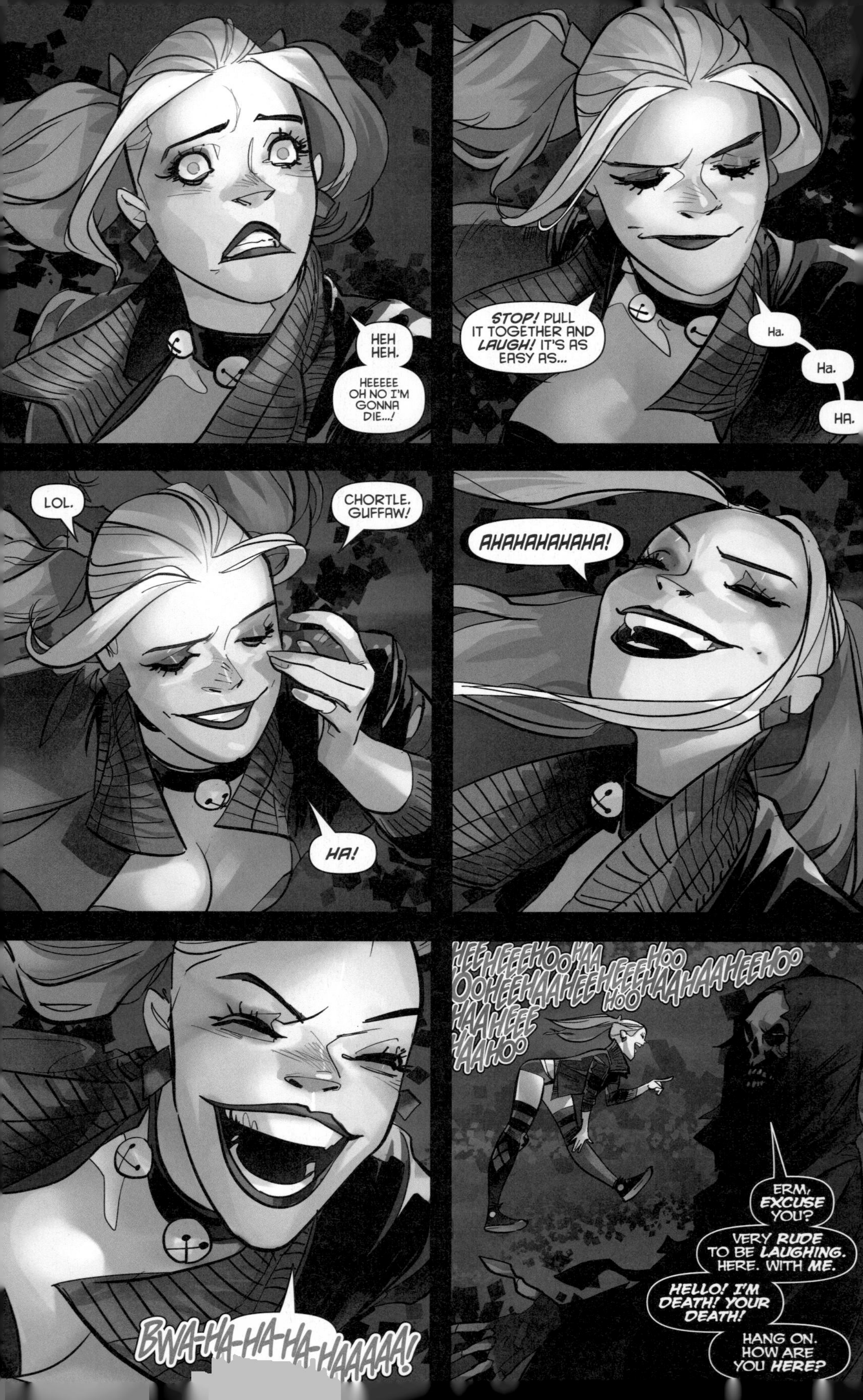
HEH HEH.
HEEEEE OH NO I'M GONNA DIE...!
STOP! PULL IT TOGETHER AND LAUGH! IT'S AS EASY AS...
Ha.
Ha.
HA.
LOL.
CHORTLE. GUFFAW!
HA!
AHAHAHAHAHA!
BWA-HA-HA-HA-HAAAAA!
HEEHEEEEHOoHAA OoHEEHAAHEEHEEEHoo HooHAAHAAHEEHOo HAAHEEE HAAHOo
ERM, EXCUSE YOU?
VERY RUDE TO BE LAUGHING. HERE. WITH ME.
HELLO! I'M DEATH! YOUR DEATH!
HANG ON. HOW ARE YOU HERE?

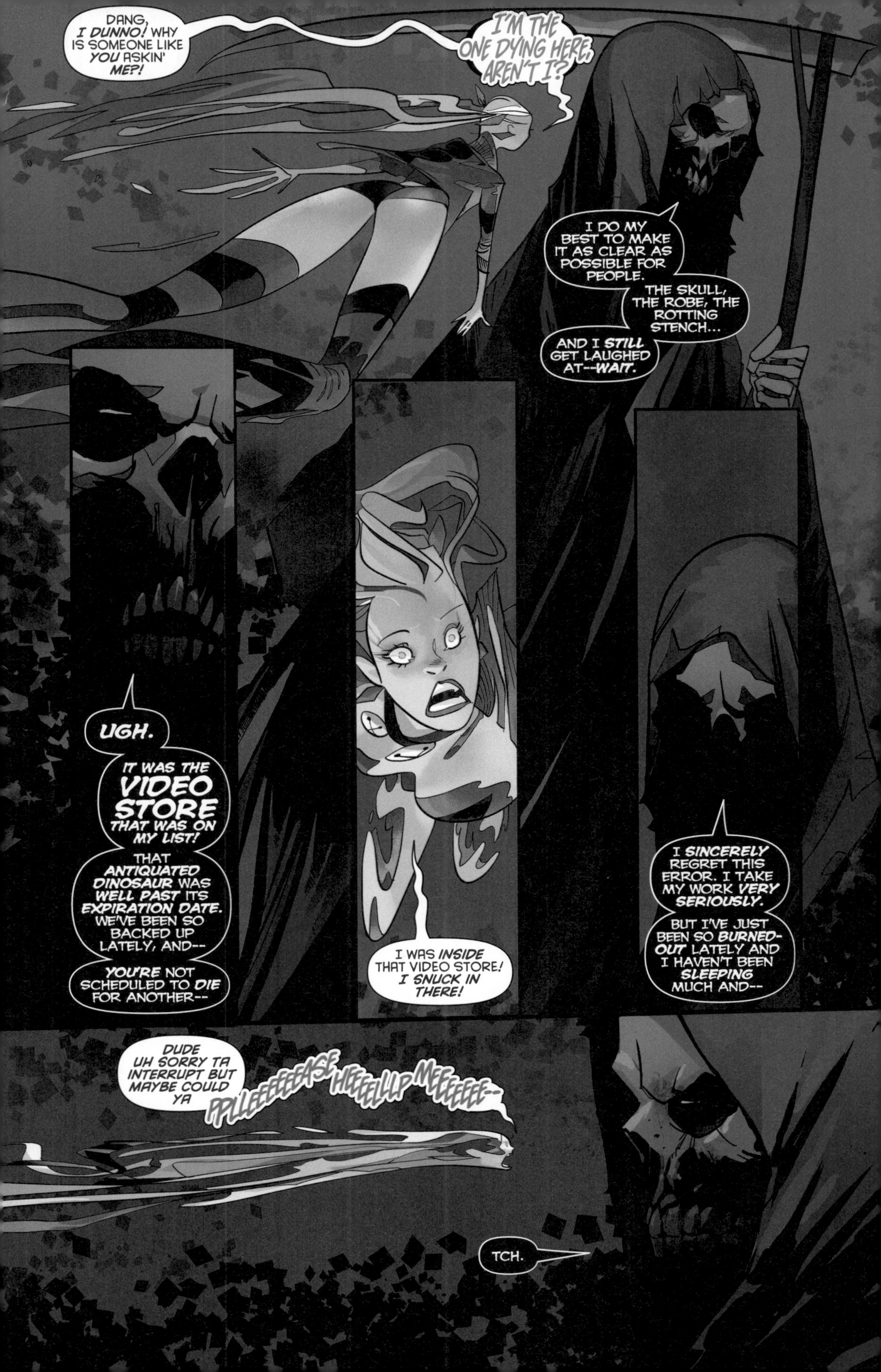
DANG, I DUNNO! WHY IS SOMEONE LIKE YOU ASKIN' ME?!
I'M THE ONE DYING HERE, AREN'T I?
I DO MY BEST TO MAKE IT AS CLEAR AS POSSIBLE FOR PEOPLE.
THE SKULL, THE ROBE, THE ROTTING STENCH...
AND I STILL GET LAUGHED AT--WAIT.
UGH.
IT WAS THE VIDEO STORE THAT WAS ON MY LIST!
THAT ANTIQUATED DINOSAUR WAS WELL PAST ITS EXPIRATION DATE. WE'VE BEEN SO BACKED UP LATELY, AND--
YOU'RE NOT SCHEDULED TO DIE FOR ANOTHER--
I WAS INSIDE THAT VIDEO STORE! I SNUCK IN THERE!
I SINCERELY REGRET THIS ERROR. I TAKE MY WORK VERY SERIOUSLY.
BUT I'VE JUST BEEN SO BURNED-OUT LATELY AND I HAVEN'T BEEN SLEEPING MUCH AND--
DUDE UH SORRY TA INTERRUPT BUT MAYBE COULD YA
PPLLEEEEEEEASE HEEEELLLP MEEEEEEE--
TCH.

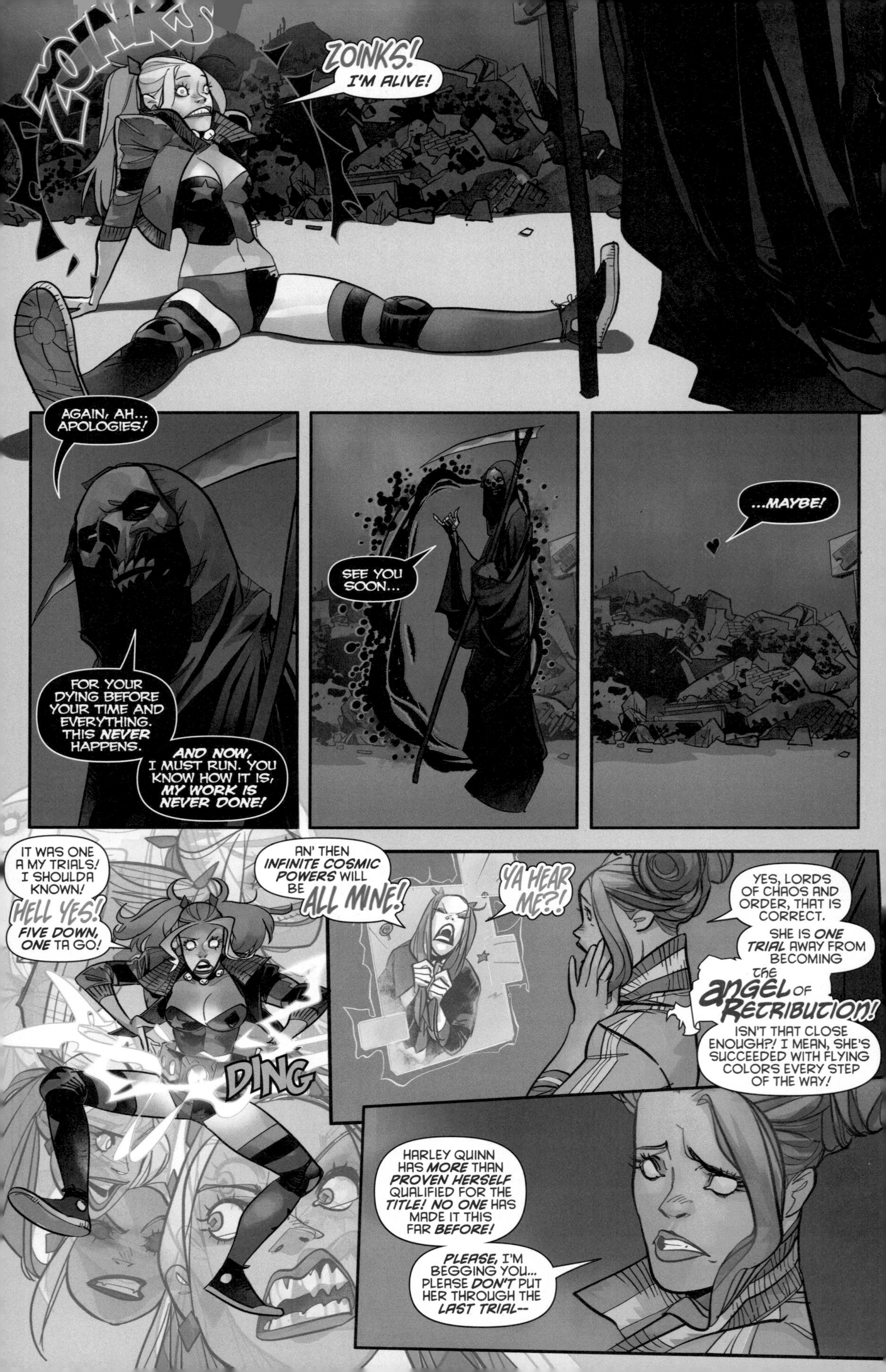
ZOINKS
ZOINKS! I'M ALIVE!
AGAIN, AH... APOLOGIES!
FOR YOUR DYING BEFORE YOUR TIME AND EVERYTHING. THIS NEVER HAPPENS.
AND NOW, I MUST RUN. YOU KNOW HOW IT IS, MY WORK IS NEVER DONE!
SEE YOU SOON...
...MAYBE!
IT WAS ONE A MY TRIALS! I SHOULDA KNOWN!
HELL YES! FIVE DOWN, ONE TA GO!
AN' THEN INFINITE COSMIC POWERS WILL BE ALL MINE!
YA HEAR ME?!
DING
YES, LORDS OF CHAOS AND ORDER, THAT IS CORRECT.
SHE IS ONE TRIAL AWAY FROM BECOMING THE ANGEL OF RETRIBUTION!
ISN'T THAT CLOSE ENOUGH?! I MEAN, SHE'S SUCCEEDED WITH FLYING COLORS EVERY STEP OF THE WAY!
HARLEY QUINN HAS MORE THAN PROVEN HERSELF QUALIFIED FOR THE TITLE! NO ONE HAS MADE IT THIS FAR BEFORE!
PLEASE, I'M BEGGING YOU... PLEASE DON'T PUT HER THROUGH THE LAST TRIAL--

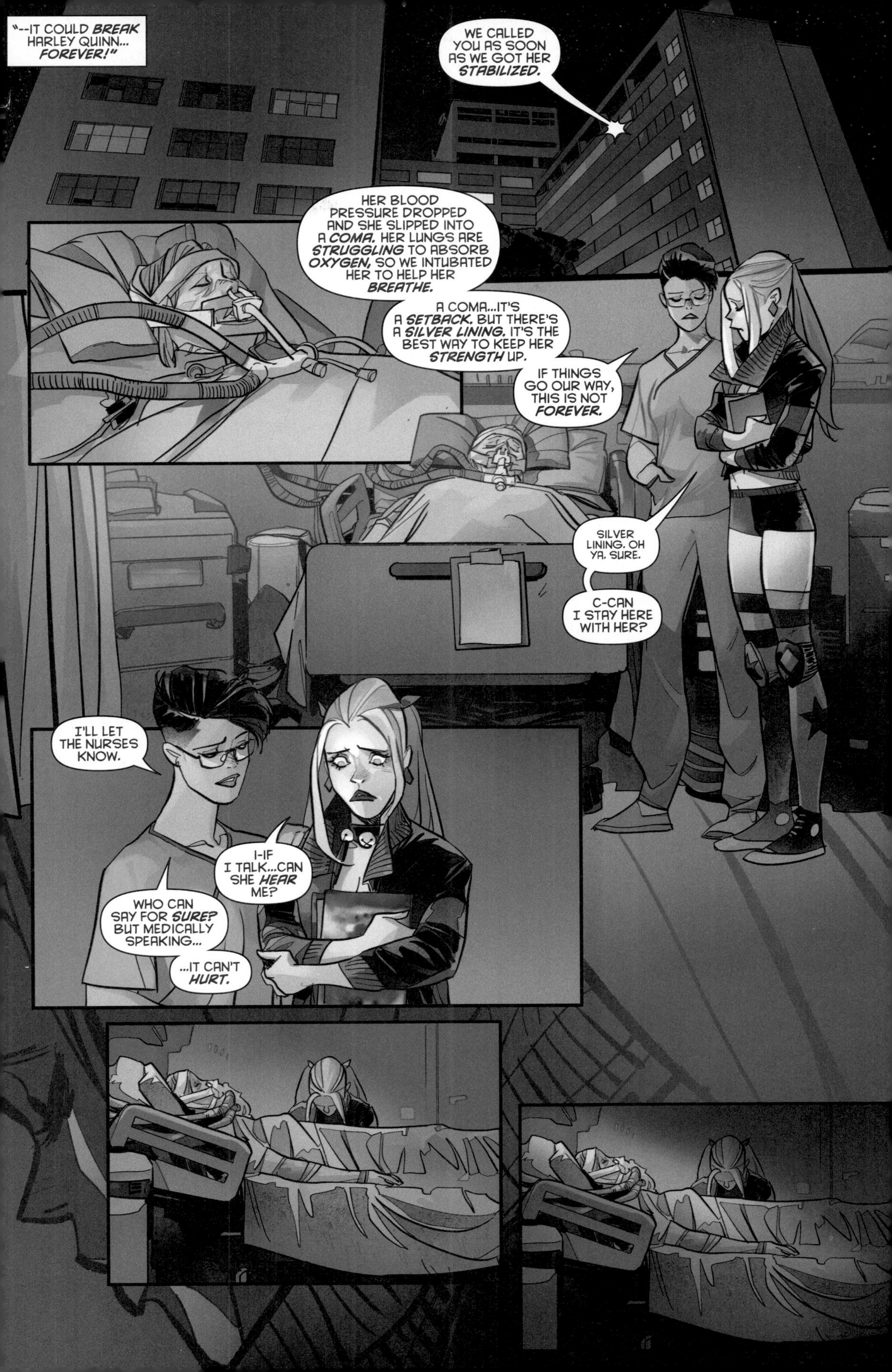
"--IT COULD BREAK HARLEY QUINN... FOREVER!"
WE CALLED YOU AS SOON AS WE GOT HER STABILIZED.
HER BLOOD PRESSURE DROPPED AND SHE SLIPPED INTO A COMA. HER LUNGS ARE STRUGGLING TO ABSORB OXYGEN, SO WE INTUBATED HER TO HELP HER BREATHE.
A COMA...IT'S A SETBACK. BUT THERE'S A SILVER LINING. IT'S THE BEST WAY TO KEEP HER STRENGTH UP.
IF THINGS GO OUR WAY, THIS IS NOT FOREVER.
SILVER LINING. OH YA. SURE.
C-CAN I STAY HERE WITH HER?
I'LL LET THE NURSES KNOW.
I-IF I TALK...CAN SHE HEAR ME?
WHO CAN SAY FOR SURE? BUT MEDICALLY SPEAKING...
...IT CAN'T HURT.

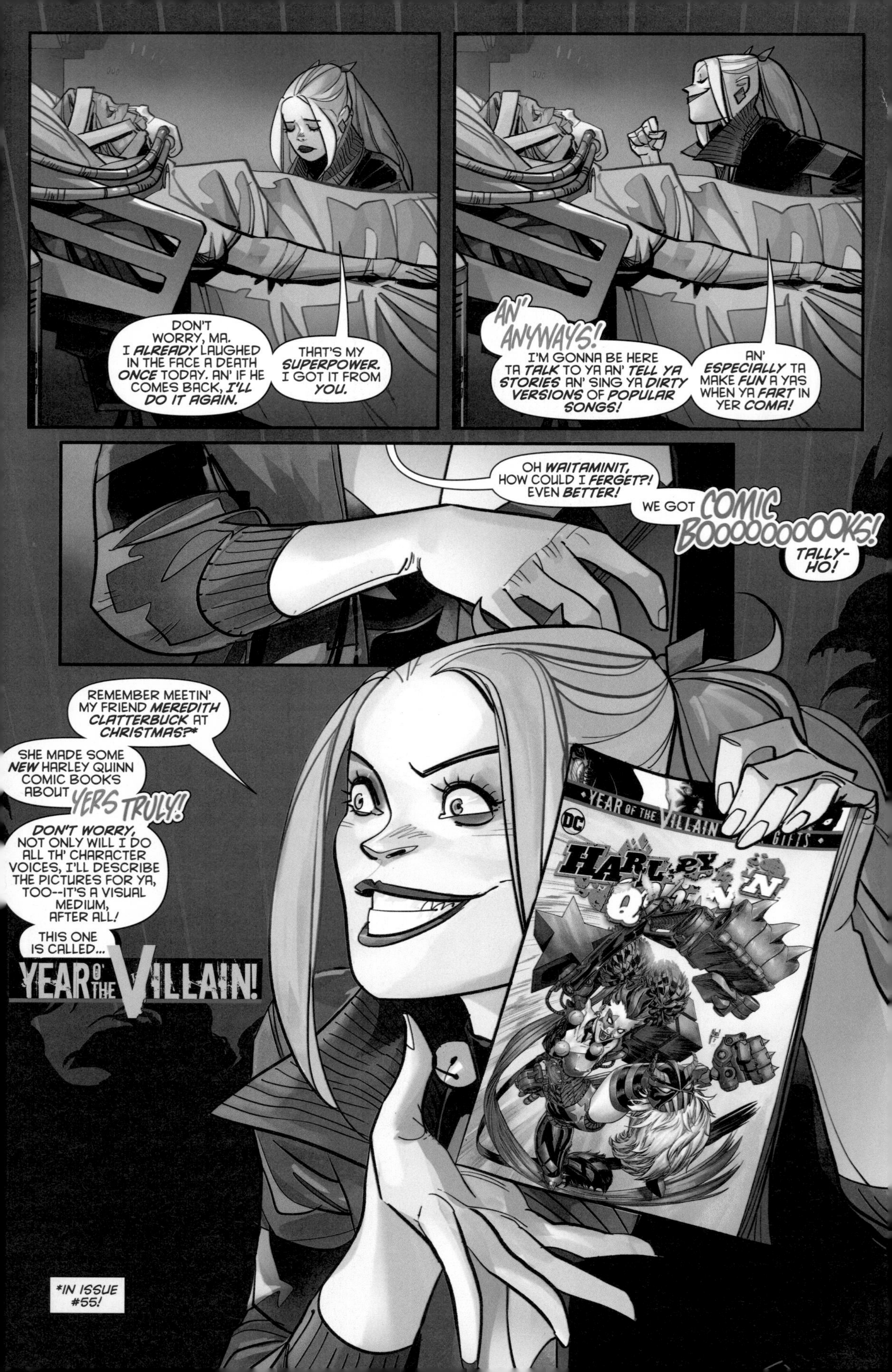
DON'T WORRY, MA. I ALREADY LAUGHED IN THE FACE A DEATH ONCE TODAY. AN' IF HE COMES BACK, I'LL DO IT AGAIN.
THAT'S MY SUPERPOWER. I GOT IT FROM YOU.
AN' ANYWAYS!
I'M GONNA BE HERE TA TALK TO YA AN' TELL YA STORIES AN' SING YA DIRTY VERSIONS OF POPULAR SONGS!
AN' ESPECIALLY TA MAKE FUN A YAS WHEN YA FART IN YER COMA!
OH WAITAMINIT, HOW COULD I FERGET?! EVEN BETTER!
WE GOT COMIC BOOOOOOOOOOKS!
TALLY-HO!
REMEMBER MEETIN' MY FRIEND MEREDITH CLATTERBUCK AT CHRISTMAS?*
SHE MADE SOME NEW HARLEY QUINN COMIC BOOKS ABOUT YERS TRULY!
DON'T WORRY, NOT ONLY WILL I DO ALL TH' CHARACTER VOICES, I'LL DESCRIBE THE PICTURES FOR YA, TOO--IT'S A VISUAL MEDIUM, AFTER ALL!
THIS ONE IS CALLED...
YEAR O' THE VILLAIN!
YEAR OF THE VILLAIN
DC
HARLEY QUINN
*IN ISSUE #55!

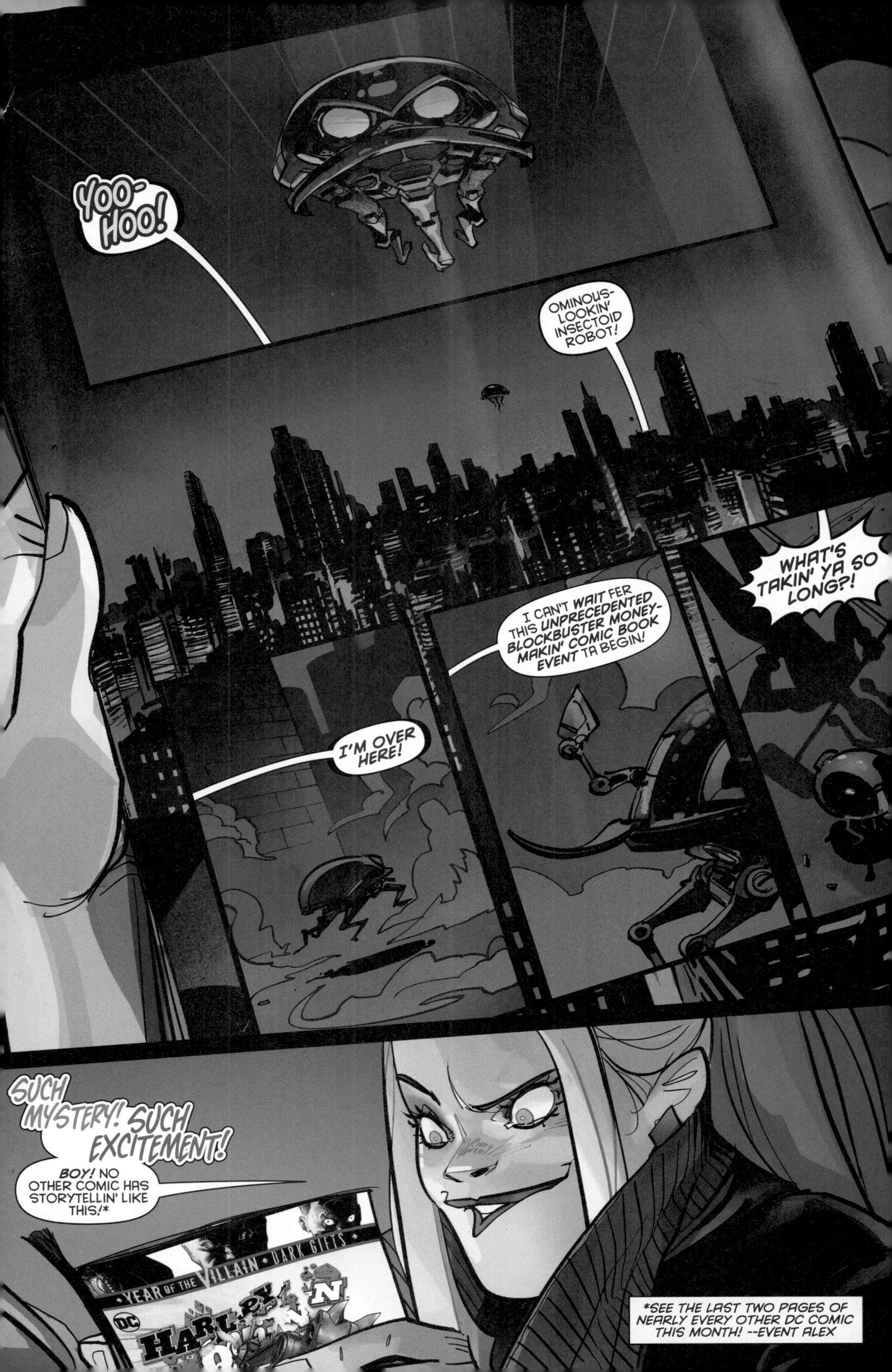
YOO-HOO!
OMINOUS-LOOKIN' INSECTOID ROBOT!
I CAN'T WAIT FER THIS UNPRECEDENTED BLOCKBUSTER MONEY-MAKIN' COMIC BOOK EVENT TA BEGIN!
WHAT'S TAKIN' YA SO LONG?!
I'M OVER HERE!
SUCH MYSTERY! SUCH EXCITEMENT!
BOY! NO OTHER COMIC HAS STORYTELLIN' LIKE THIS!*
YEAR OF THE VILLAIN · DARK GIFTS
*SEE THE LAST TWO PAGES OF NEARLY EVERY OTHER DC COMIC THIS MONTH! --EVENT ALEX

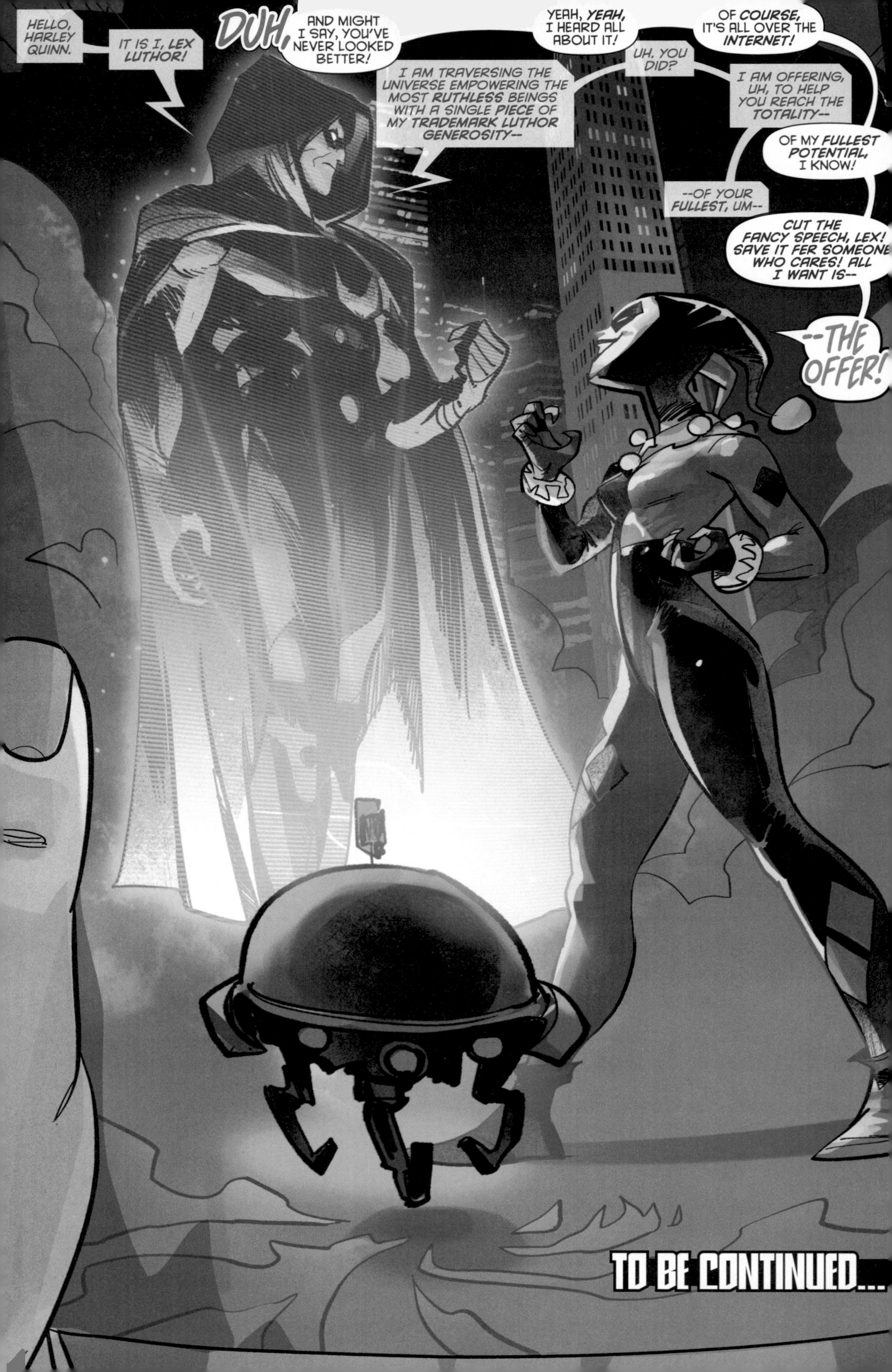
HELLO, HARLEY QUINN.
IT IS I, LEX LUTHOR!
DUH,
AND MIGHT I SAY, YOU'VE NEVER LOOKED BETTER!
I AM TRAVERSING THE UNIVERSE EMPOWERING THE MOST RUTHLESS BEINGS WITH A SINGLE PIECE OF MY TRADEMARK LUTHOR GENEROSITY--
YEAH, YEAH, I HEARD ALL ABOUT IT!
UH. YOU DID?
OF COURSE, IT'S ALL OVER THE INTERNET!
I AM OFFERING, UH, TO HELP YOU REACH THE TOTALITY--
OF MY FULLEST POTENTIAL, I KNOW!
--OF YOUR FULLEST, UM--
CUT THE FANCY SPEECH, LEX! SAVE IT FER SOMEONE WHO CARES! ALL I WANT IS--
--THE OFFER!
TO BE CONTINUED...

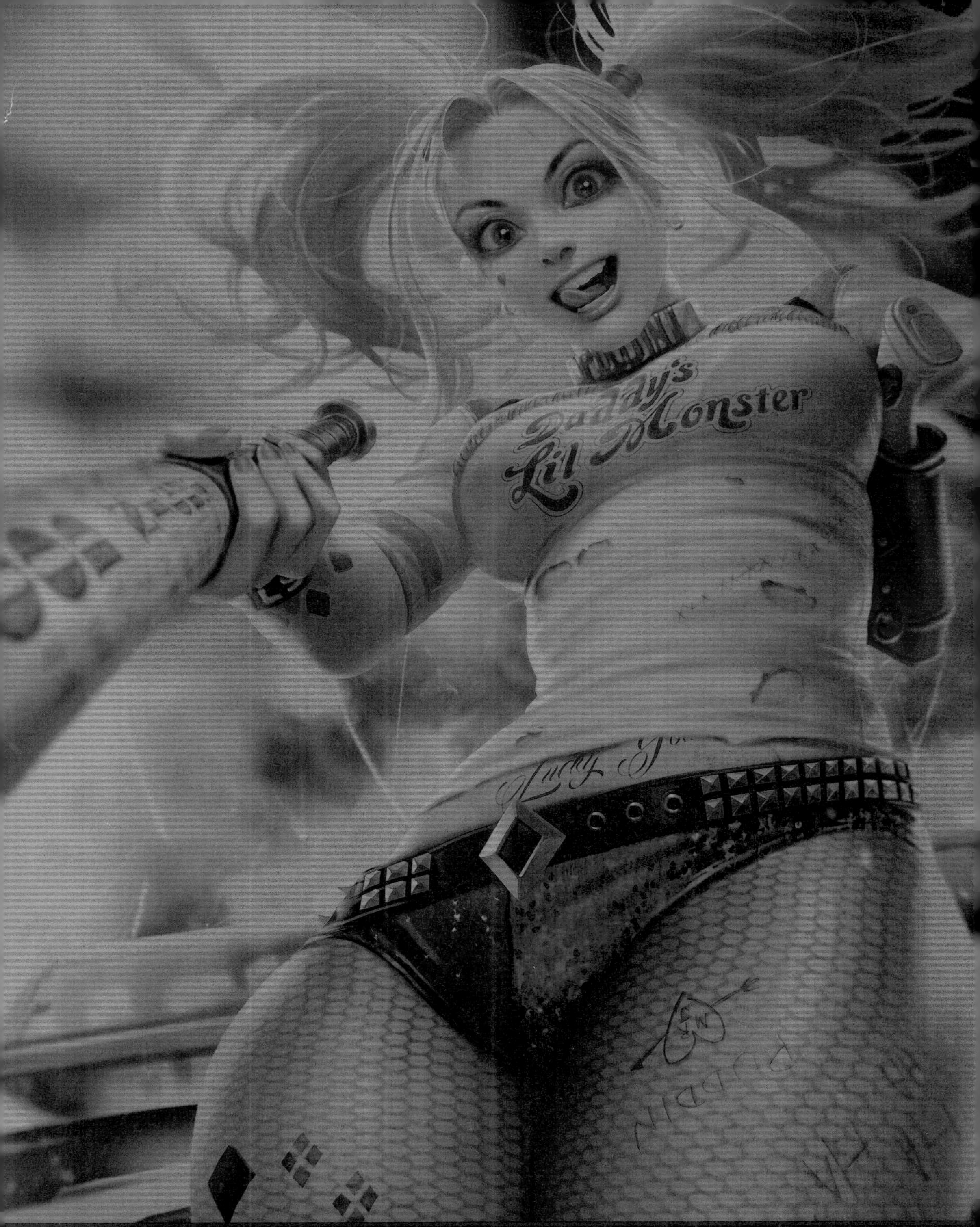
Daddy's Lil Monster

VARIANT COVER GALLERY

HARLEY QUINN #55 variant cover
by FRANK CHO and SABINE RICH

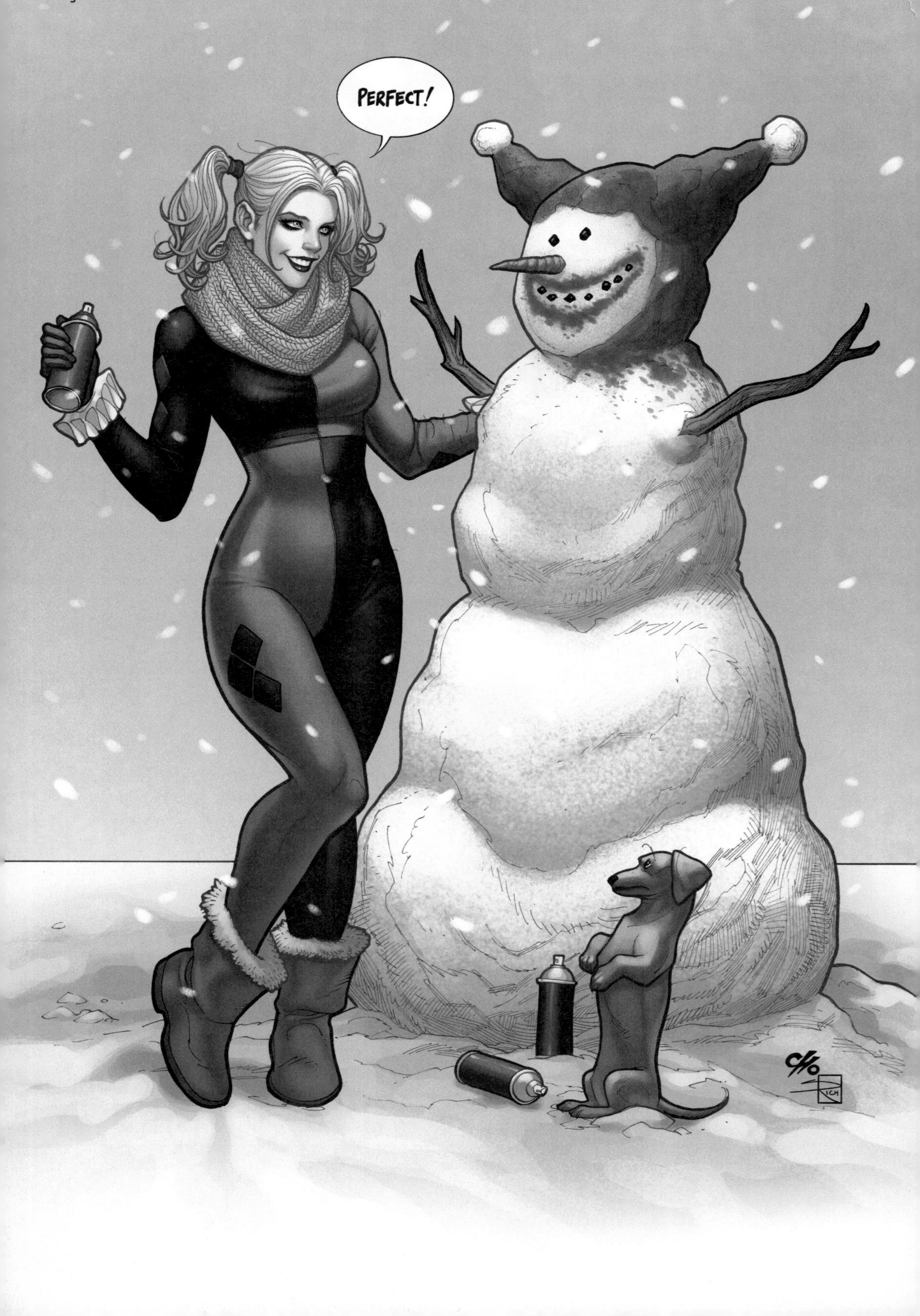
PERFECT!

HARLEY QUINN #57 variant cover
by JULIAN TOTINO TEDESCO

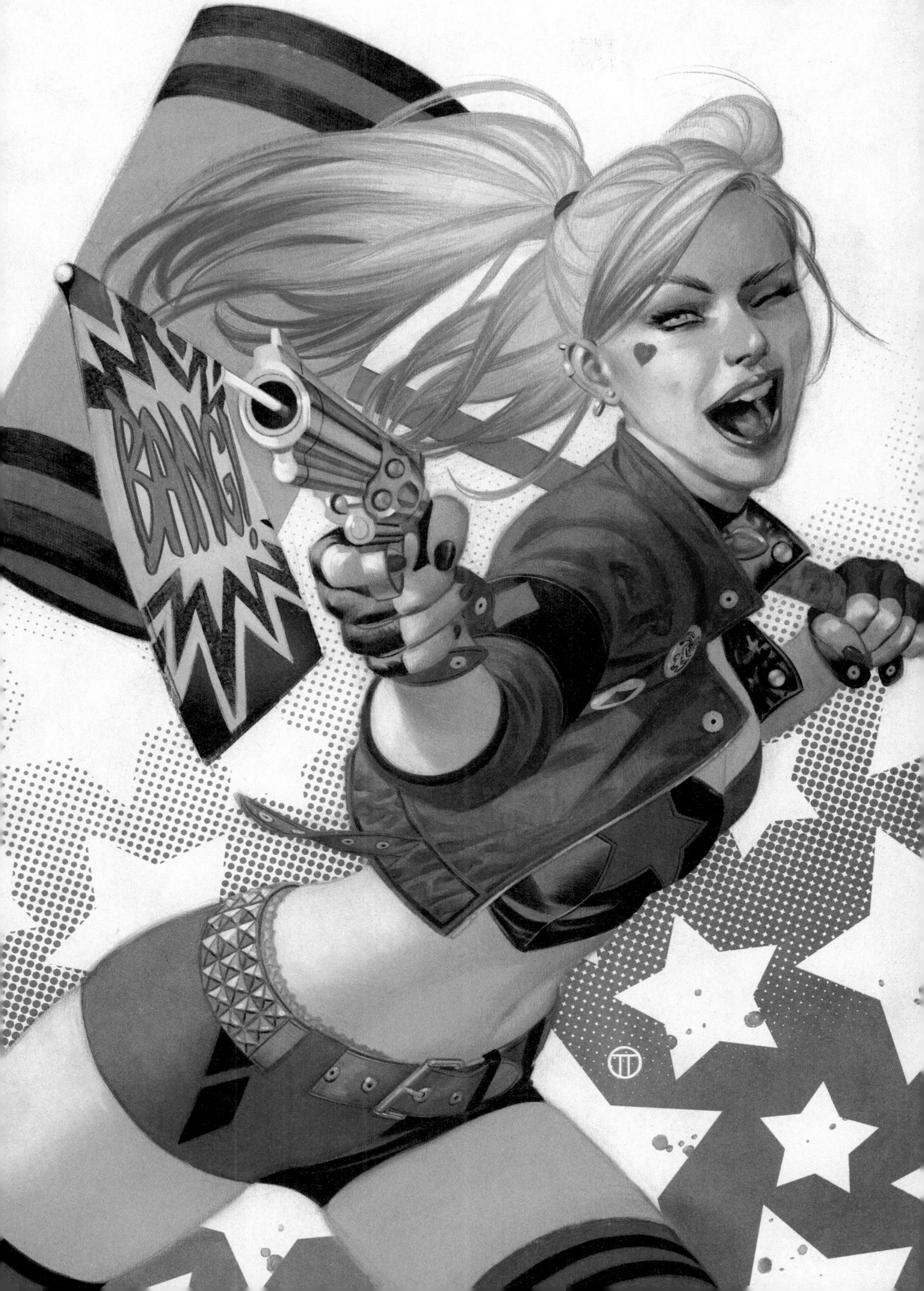
BANG!

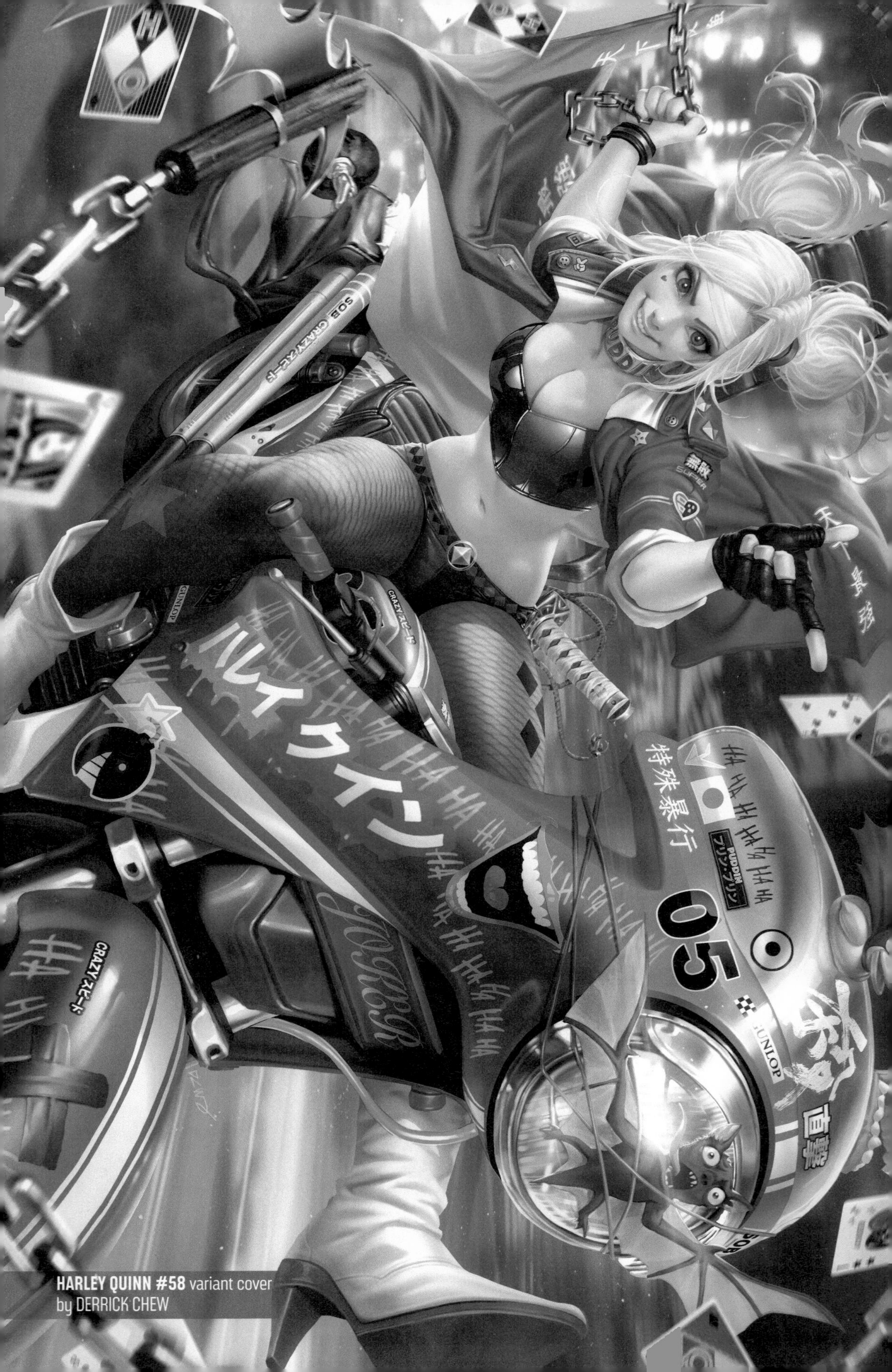
特殊暴行
PUDDIN
05
DUNLOP
CRAZYスピード
SOB

HARLEY QUINN #58 variant cover
by DERRICK CHEW

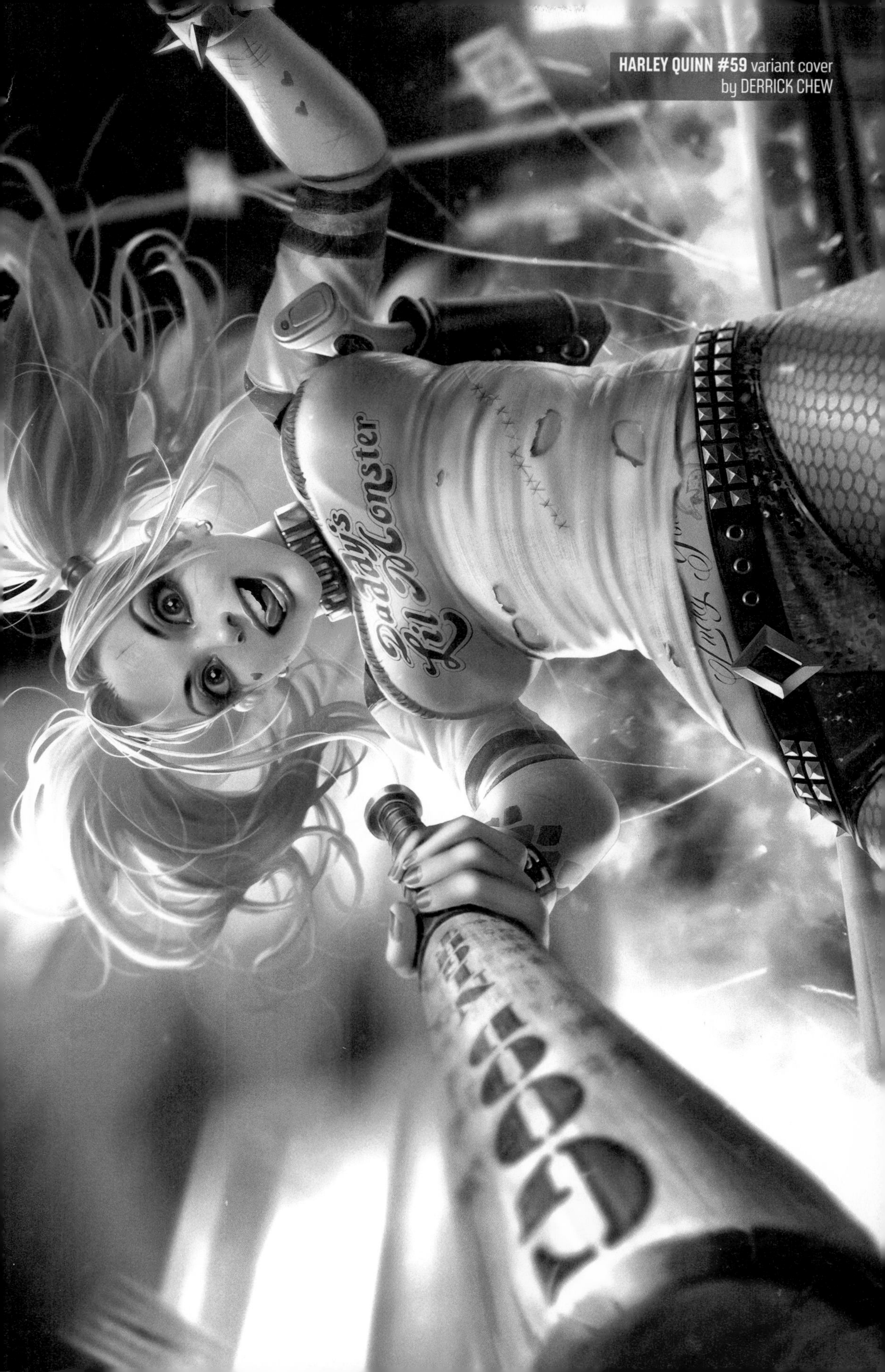
Daddy's Lil Monster

HARLEY QUINN #59 variant cover
by DERRICK CHEW

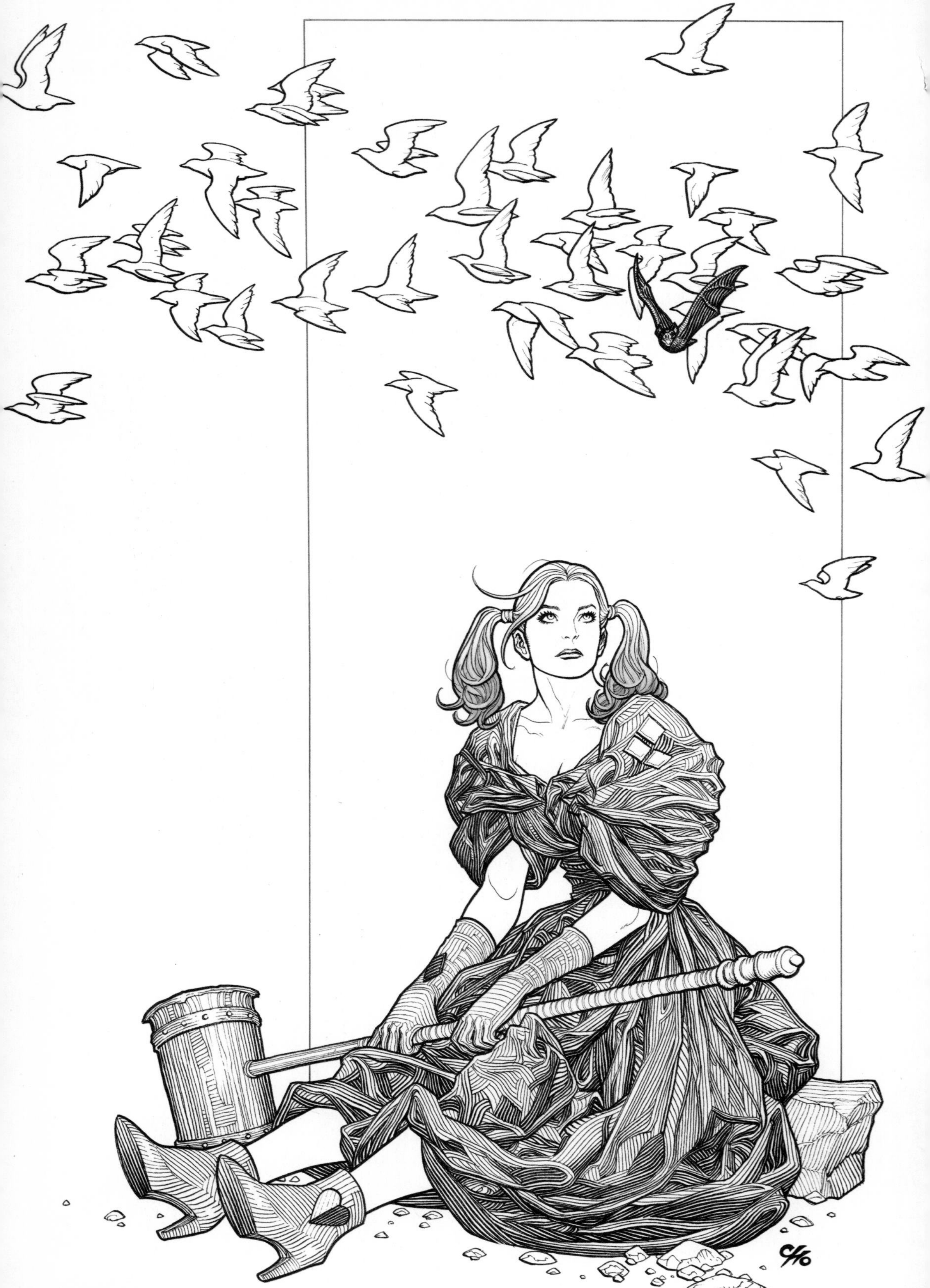
CHO

HARLEY QUINN #60 variant cover
by FRANK CHO

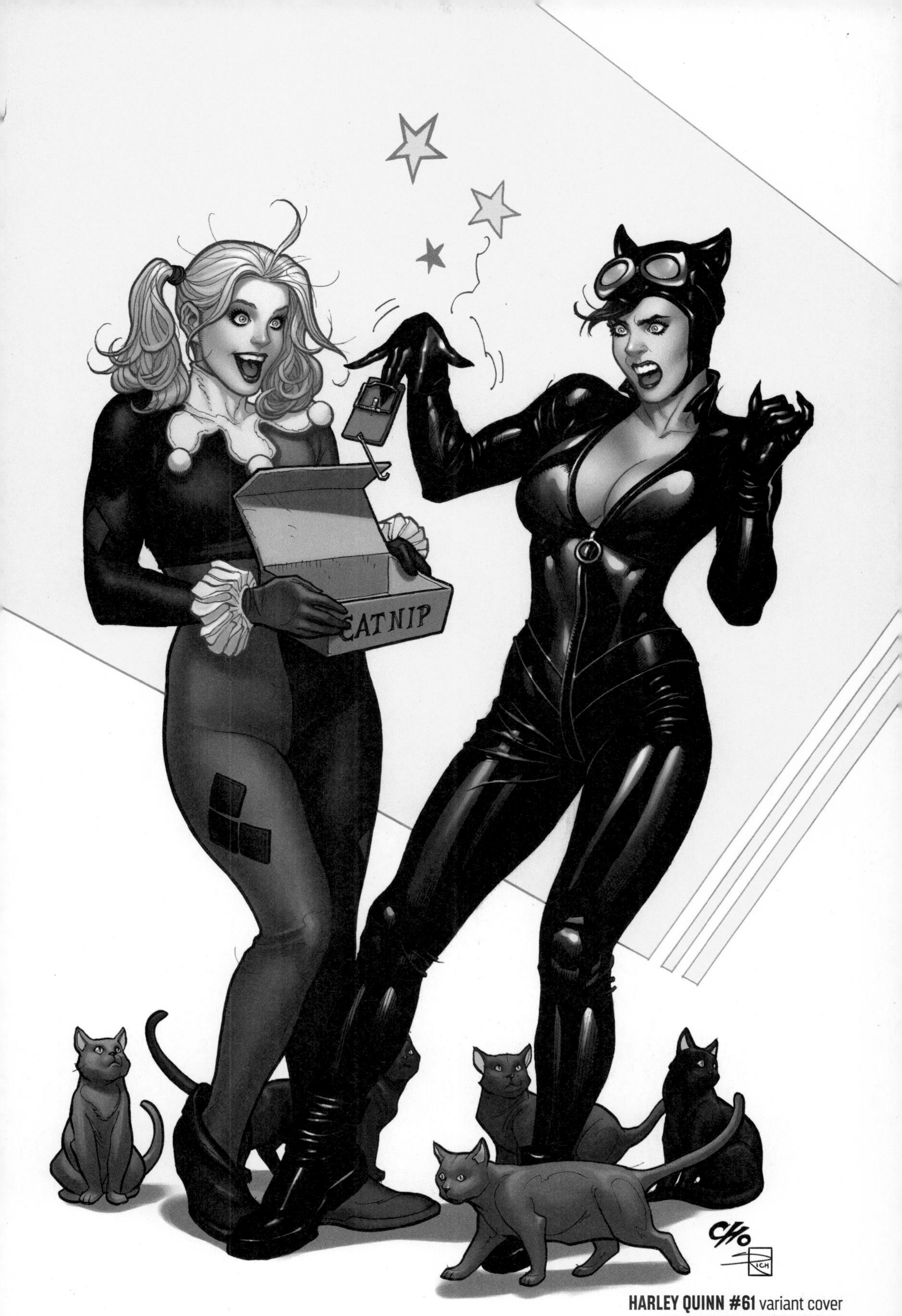
CATNIP
CHO
RICH

HARLEY QUINN #61 variant cover
by FRANK CHO and SABINE RICH

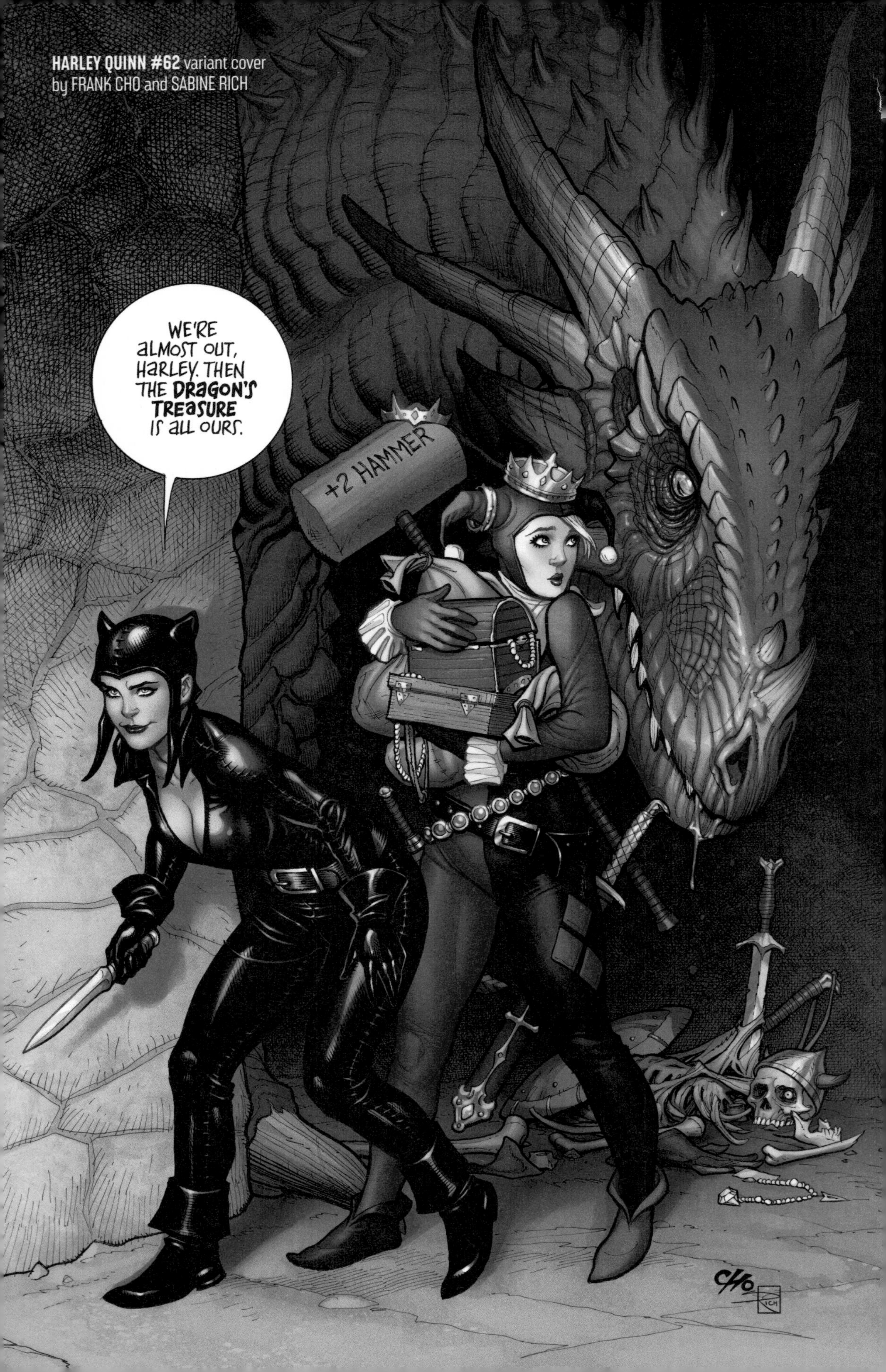
WE'RE ALMOST OUT, HARLEY. THEN THE DRAGON'S TREASURE IS ALL OURS.
+2 HAMMER
CHO
RICH

HARLEY QUINN #62 variant cover
by FRANK CHO and SABINE RICH

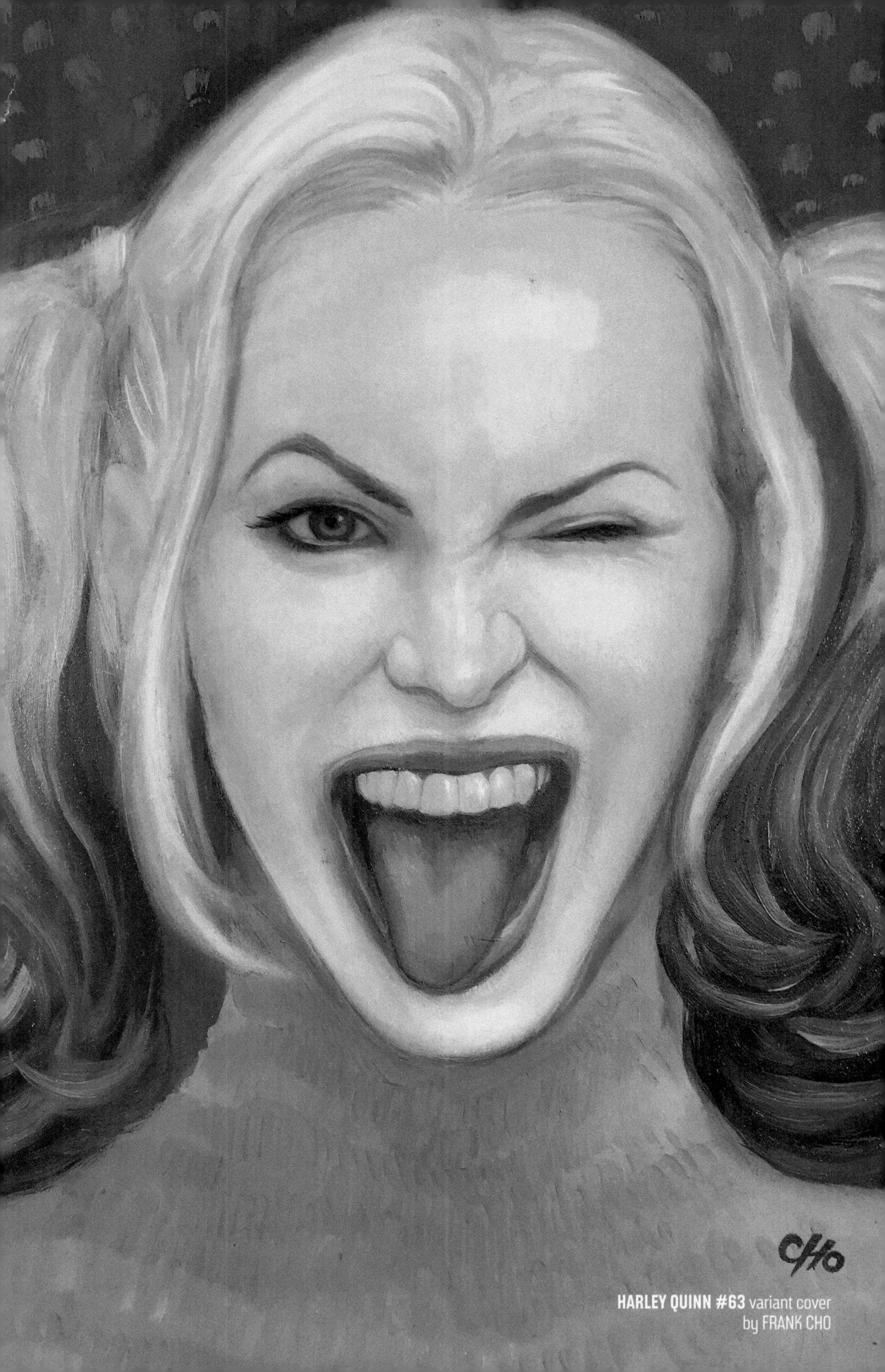
CHO

HARLEY QUINN #63 variant cover
by FRANK CHO

"A pretty irresistible hook..."
– THE ONION A.V. CLUB

DC
"A CLEVERLY WRITTEN, OUTSTANDING READ FROM BEGINNING TO END." — USA TODAY
THE NEW 52!
SUICIDE SQUAD
VOLUME 1 KICKED IN THE TEETH
ADAM GLASS FEDERICO DALLOCCHIO CLAYTON HENRY

SUICIDE SQUAD

VOL. 1: KICKED IN THE TEETH

ADAM GLASS with
FEDERICO DALLOCCHIO

DC
THE NEW 52!
SUICIDE SQUAD
"A CLEVERLY WRITTEN, OUTSTANDING READ FROM BEGINNING TO END." — USA TODAY
VOLUME 2 BASILISK RISING
ADAM GLASS FERNANDO DAGNINO

**SUICIDE SQUAD
VOL. 2: BASILISK RISING**

DC
THE NEW 52!
SUICIDE SQUAD
"A CLEVERLY WRITTEN, OUTSTANDING READ FROM BEGINNING TO END." — USA TODAY
VOLUME 3 DEATH IS FOR SUCKERS
DEADSHOT
ADAM GLASS HENRIK JONSSON SANDU FLOREA

**SUICIDE SQUAD
VOL. 3: DEATH IS FOR SUCKERS**

READ THE ENTIRE EPIC!

SUICIDE SQUAD VOL. 4:
DISCIPLINE AND PUNISH

SUICIDE SQUAD VOL. 5:
WALLED IN

"A cleverly written, outstanding read from beginning to end."
– USA TODAY

Get more DC graphic novels wherever comics and books are sold!

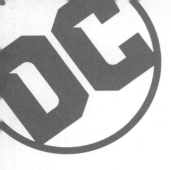

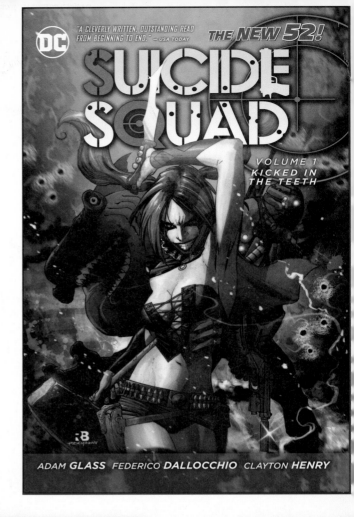

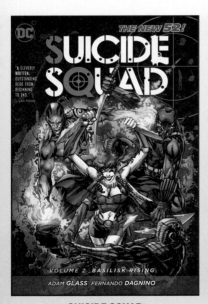

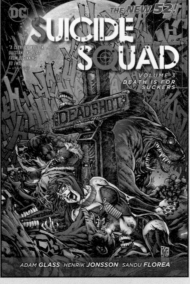

"Chaotic and unabashedly fun."
– IGN

HARLEY QUINN

VOL. 1: HOT IN THE CITY
AMANDA CONNER
with JIMMY PALMIOTTI
& CHAD HARDIN

**HARLEY QUINN
VOL. 2: POWER OUTAGE**

**HARLEY QUINN
VOL. 3: KISS KISS BANG STAB**

READ THE ENTIRE EPIC!

HARLEY QUINN VOL. 4:
A CALL TO ARMS

HARLEY QUINN VOL. 5:
THE JOKER'S LAST LAUGH

"I'm enjoying this a great deal;
it's silly, it's funny, it's irreverent."
– COMIC BOOK RESOURCES

"A smart concept, snappy one-liners and a great twist to match a tag-team of talented artists."
–NEWSARAMA

"Every bit as chaotic and unabashedly fun as one would expect."
–IGN

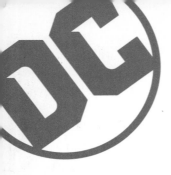

HARLEY QUINN

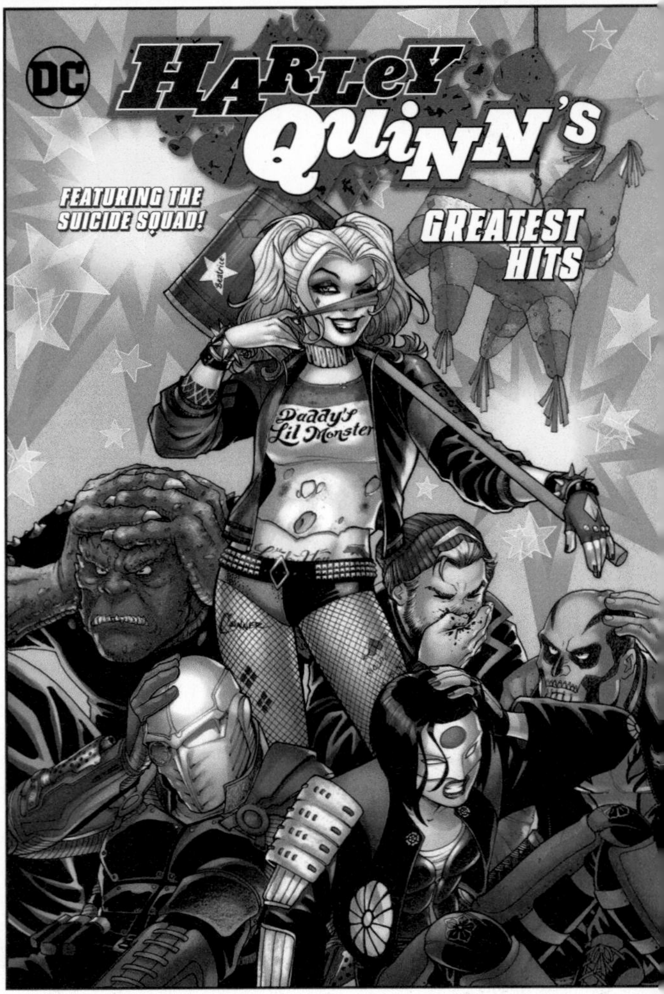
HARLEY QUINN'S
FEATURING THE SUICIDE SQUAD!
GREATEST HITS
Daddy's Lil Monster

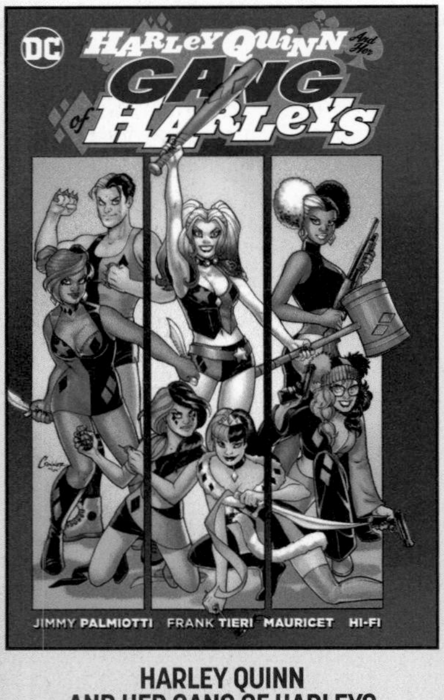
HARLEY QUINN And Her GANG of HARLEYS
JIMMY PALMIOTTI FRANK TIERI MAURICET HI-FI

HARLEY QUINN
AND HER GANG OF HARLEYS

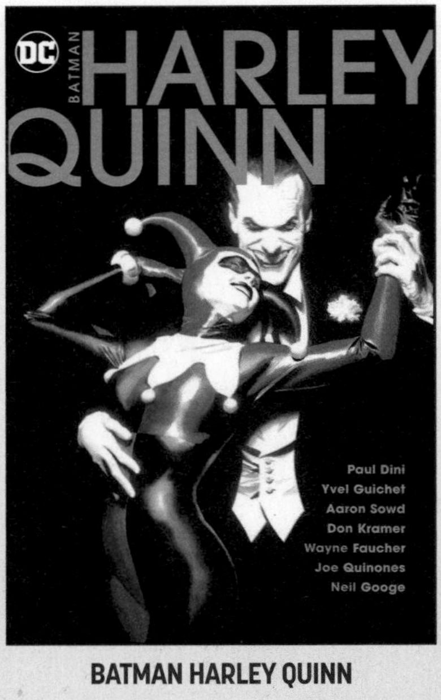
BATMAN
HARLEY QUINN
Paul Dini
Yvel Guichet
Aaron Sowd
Don Kramer
Wayne Faucher
Joe Quinones
Neil Googe

BATMAN HARLEY QUINN

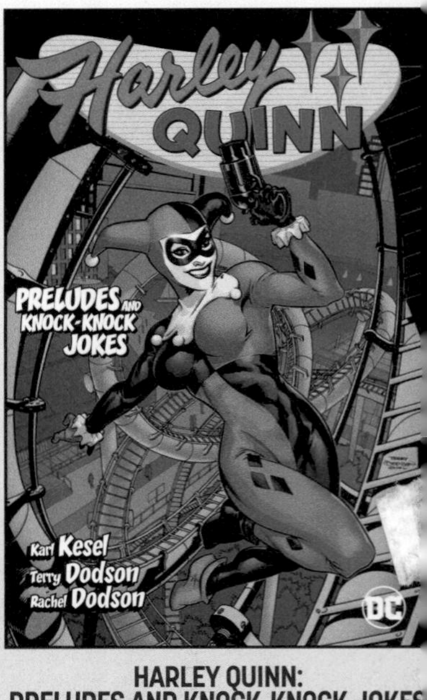
Harley QUINN
PRELUDES AND KNOCK-KNOCK JOKES
Karl Kesel
Terry Dodson
Rachel Dodson

HARLEY QUINN:
PRELUDES AND KNOCK-KNOCK JOKES

Get more DC graphic novels wherever comics and books are sold!